Distributed Processing in the CICS Environment

A Guide to MRO/ISC

Distributed Processing in the CICS Environment

A Guide to MRO/ISC

Arlene J. Wipfler

Intertext Publications
McGraw-Hill Book Company

New York St. Louis San Francisco Auckland Bogotá
Hamburg London Madrid Mexico Milan Montreal
New Delhi Panama Paris São Paulo
Singapore Sidney Tokyo Toronto

Library of Congress Catalog Card Number 89-83753

10 9 8 7 6 5 4 3 2 1

ISBN 0-07-071136-4

Intertext Publications/Multiscience Press, Inc.
One Lincoln Plaza
New York, NY 10023

McGraw-Hill Book Company
1221 Avenue of the Americas
New York, NY 10020

Composed in Ventura Publisher by Context, Inc.

To the memory of my parents:
Moe and Mary Epstein

Contents

Preface

Online systems have developed and grown dramatically over the past decade. It is not at all uncommon for a single large company or financial institution to have numerous online CICS systems. Users of online systems have also grown more sophisticated and demand access to information that is distributed throughout various online regions and databases. CICS Intercommunication provides the facilities so that remote resource access is easily accomplished. Using Intercommunication resources of any connected online region are available to CICS application programs. In most cases, the programmer need not even be aware of the fact that a file or data queue is remote. Resource access includes read, write, and update capability. Furthermore, where applicable, CICS provides coordination of distributed updates via SYNCPOINT and backout processing. Effectively, this links together distributed online systems so that resources can be made available regardless of where the resource is located. This multi-system environment greatly expands data processing functionality. A good understanding of CICS Intercommunication is therefore important for all technicians, system designers, and application programmers who are engaged in the design, implementation, and support of CICS systems.

CICS Intercommunication is important in yet another way. This facility provides a flexible platform for building distributed environments involving non–system level products. As intelligent work stations replace dumb terminals, CICS Intercommunication provides the facilities needed to interface with these work stations and take advantage of their processing capabilities. To this end, CICS application programs can communicate with programs running in intelligent work stations. File or database information can be downloaded by a mainframe program, edited and displayed by a work station program, updated by a user, validated by a workstation program and, when update is complete, uploaded back to the mainframe for database update. In this endeavor many application controls are required to ensure the integrity of data. However, having the ability to exploit the processing potential of intelligent work stations is an exciting capability, especially since this enables a company or organization to optimize the use of data communication circuits and thereby lower network costs.

HOW THIS BOOK CAME INTO BEING

This book has grown out of my experience as a CICS technician and teacher. During the last few years I have developed a firm conviction that the future of CICS and online programming is based upon the ability to provide distributed information and processing capabilities to end users through the facilities offered within Intercommunication. To that end I have become engrossed in this aspect of CICS programming. Since I believe that the future of online programming is tied largely to Intercommunication, I felt that a general purpose textbook on this topic would be useful to many individuals involved in data processing. I was also encouraged by Jay Ranade to undertake this task, and he is a wonderfully persuasive and inspiring individual.

WHO THIS BOOK IS WRITTEN FOR

This book is intended for CICS technicians, application designers, and programmers. It was my goal in writing this text to provide under one cover a comprehensive examination of Intercommunication facilities that would be useful to systems programmers and applications people as well. I have therefore endeavored to cover all aspects of CICS Intercommunication in a very thorough manner. To this end, there may be more systems programming information provided than the typical application programmer needs to know or more application-oriented information than a systems programmer requires. I personally have always believed that it is better to know more than less, and I have always found that seemingly extraneous knowledge has proved invaluable when there were bugs or other problems. Also, the reader is at liberty to skim those portions of the book that are not pertinent to his/her interests.

A COMMENT REGARDING STYLE

As an aid to the reader, I have used italics to emphasize important terms and used bold text to mark important definitions or conclusions.

As much as possible I have tried to write this book in a conversational style much as if I were conversing with someone. It is my wish as an author that you find this book easy to read and understand.

WHAT IS COVERED IN THIS BOOK

Chapters 1 and 2 provide a fairly in-depth introduction to CICS Intercommunication. The facilities available are discussed, as are the systems programming requirements and design considerations. Thus these chapters provide an overview of the more in-depth discussion that follows in the succeeding chapters. Chapter 3 is a summary of IBM's Systems Network Architecture, which provides the reader with enough background in SNA to understand some of the more intricate aspects of CICS Intercommunication. Chapter 4 deals with CICS Installation Requirements for Using Intercommunication and the Link Definitions that are required to interconnect systems. Chapter 5 completes the discussion of general resource definitions. Chapter 6 discusses Transaction Routing; how it works, required resource definitions, and application programming considerations are presented. Function Shipping is covered in depth in Chapter 7. Chapter 8 provides an in-depth discussion of Asynchronous Processing. Chapters 9 through 15 provide detailed information about Distributed Transaction Processing. There are four chapters on the LU-TYPE 6.2, or Advanced Program-to-Program Communication (APPC).

1

Introduction to CICS Intercommunication

1.1 INTERCOMMUNICATION DEFINED

CICS Intercommunication enables CICS to communicate with other CICS and non-CICS systems/programs. **The purpose of Intercommunication is to make it possible for CICS to engage in distributed processing.** As such, resources available in one CICS system can be made available for use by end users of any interconnected system. Thus an application program running in one CICS can access and update files or queues in other systems. However, shared resources can include entities other than files or queues. Before we begin to discuss sharable resources or mechanisms for utilizing CICS Intercommunication, we should briefly define two major types of Intercommunication.

1.2 TYPES OF INTERCOMMUNICATION

There are two main types of CICS Intercommunication. Multi-Region Operation is the first kind, and InterSystem Communication is the other. These two varieties of Intercommunication describe the manner in which the systems are connected. Multi-Region Operation (MRO) always takes place between two CICS regions that are within the same host computer. InterSystem Communication (ISC) takes place between CICS systems or CICS and non-CICS systems/programs that are connected via a communications network. The communications network must be built upon IBM's Systems Network Architecture, or SNA. Systems Network Architecture is discussed in detail in a subsequent chapter, where the implications and significance of using an SNA network will be explained. It is sufficient at this point to merely note that there is a dependence upon the presence of an SNA network to utilize InterSystem Communication.

1.2.1 Multi-Region Operation (MRO)

Multi-Region Operation is a CICS-specific mechanism that can be used to allow two CICS systems executing in different regions or partitions of the same host computer to communicate with each other. Figure 1-1 illustrates a sample MRO configuration. CICS1 and CICS2 are both executing within the same host computer, and the bidirectional arrow indicates that they are communicating with each other. The connection or link between CICS1 and CICS2 is directly between the two interconnected regions. In other words, there is no intervening network software between them. InterRegion Supervisor calls (SVCs) can be utilized between the two systems, or MVS cross-memory services can also be used. The key point here is to note that the communication is directly between the CICS systems.

One might inquire as to what is gained by having two CICS systems in the same mainframe communicate with each other. After all, couldn't they just be combined in a single region and therefore not require CICS Multi-Region operation? The answer to this question is

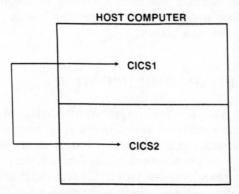

Figure 1-1 Multi-Region Operation. CICS1 and CICS2 are directly connected.

YES! The use of Multi-Region Operation provides solutions to problems that might be encountered if the CICS systems were, in fact, combined. Such problems include but are not limited to isolating an unreliable application from more reliable ones; obtaining relief from virtual storage constraints; providing separate areas or departments with autonomous CICS regions for scheduling, maintenance, or other purposes; segregating process-bound functions into a separate region for performance reasons; or enabling production files to be accessed from a test CICS region. **Thus the use of Multi-Region Operation is oriented to resolving operational difficulties in having a single all-encompassing CICS region.** The use of Multi-Region Operation does involve additional system overhead, but the compensation is that the operating environment is improved.

1.2.2   InterSystem Communication (ISC)

CICS InterSystem Communication enables CICS to communicate with CICS or non-CICS systems/programs. Thus InterSystem Communication, unlike Multi-Region Operation, is not a CICS-specific facility. With MRO, CICS can communicate solely with other CICS systems. Using ISC, CICS can communicate with any connected system/program supporting Systems Network Architecture's LUTYPE 6 protocols. (LUTYPE 6 protocols are explained in the subsequent chapter on SNA. At this point in our discussion it is sufficient to note that intercommunication requires LUTYPE 6 compatability.)

Figure 1-2 is an example of one possible configuration for InterSystem Communication. Note that CICS3 and CICS4 are both in the same host. However, in this diagram the link between the interconnected systems is not direct. Rather, as illustrated in the figure, communication between these systems passes through Advanced Communication Function/Virtual Telecommunication Access Method (ACF/VTAM). ACF/VTAM is an SNA access method which supports, among other things, direct application-to-application communication within the same host. The diagram illustrates a sample exchange in which CICS3 issues a request to CICS4 and CICS4 responds. At point 1 the request passes from CICS3 to ACF/VTAM. At point 2 ACF/VTAM passes the request to CICS4. CICS4 processes the request and returns a response at point 3. This response is directed to ACF/VTAM, which at point 4 delivers the response to CICS3.

Figure 1-3 is another possible implementation of InterSystem Communication. CICS5 and CICS6 are executing on different machines. Each host has ACF/VTAM as its SNA access method. The

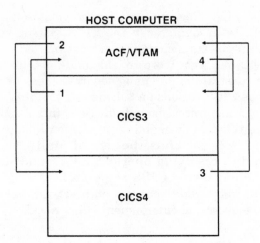

Figure 1-2 One possible configuration of CICS Intersystem Communication.

processors are directly attached utilizing a channel-to-channel adapter. This is another configuration supported by ACF/VTAM. In this illustration there is an exchange between the two CICS systems. At point 1 CICS5 issues a request for CICS6. This request passes to ACF/VTAM, which in turn passes the request to the ACF/VTAM in the other host at point 2. At point 3 the request is given to CICS6, which processes the request and creates an output response. The response is passed to the SNA access method at point 4 and conveyed to the originating host access method at point 5. The response is given to CICS5 at point 6.

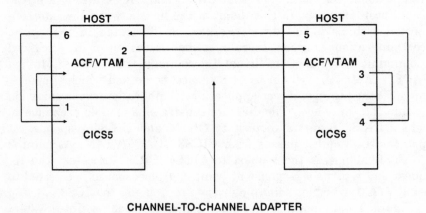

Figure 1-3 Another possible ISC configuration.

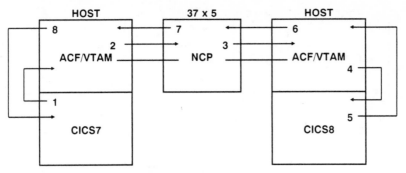

Figure 1-4 Another possible configuration for CICS ISC.

Figure 1-4 is a variation of Figure 1-3. In this figure the two hosts are at the same site but are not channel-attached. Rather, a communication front end processor is utilized to connect the hosts. The box labeled 37X5 represents this communication front end because the 3705, 3725, etc. are model numbers for IBM's communication front end processor line. Inside the 37X5 box are the letters NCP, which stand for Network Control Program. The NCP is generated by the systems programmer on site and loaded into the communications front end. The 37X5 with this installation generated NCP serves as a dedicated computer which handles the details of the communication process. In this way, the SNA access method offloads some of the network management work onto the front end processor. The 37X5 is channel attached to both local hosts and is part of the pathway for the request from CICS7 to CICS8. The numbers in the illustration depict the flow of data between the interconnected CICS systems. At point 1 CICS7 issues a request for CICS8. This request goes to ACF/VTAM in the same host. At point 2, ACF/VTAM passes the request to the NCP, which forwards the message to ACF/VTAM in the other host at point 3. At point 4 the request is directed to CICS8. After the response is created, CICS8 gives it to ACF/VTAM at point 5. At point 6 the message is passed to the NCP, and at point 7 the response is sent to ACF/VTAM in the originating host. At point 8 the message is forwarded to CICS7, and the request and response flows are complete.

Figure 1-5 illustrates yet another possible connection between two CICS systems. In this case CICS9 and CICS10 exist in separate and remote hosts. Each host contains an SNA access method, and each host has a local channel attached communications front-end processor. The 37X5 communication processors are connected via a remote communication link, which provides physical connectivity between

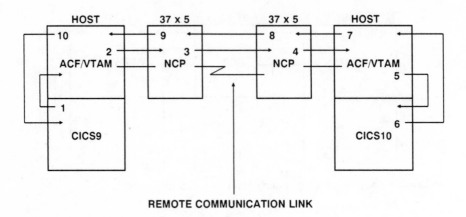

REMOTE COMMUNICATION LINK

Figure 1-5 Yet another possible ISC configuration.

the two hosts. The numbers 1 through 10 illustrate the sequence of data flow during an exchange between CICS9 and CICS10.

The location of an interconnected system and the physical configuration between systems are transparent to CICS. **InterSystem Communication is the same to CICS and our application programs utilizing Intercommunication services regardless of the actual configuration utilized.** In our diagrams we represented only CICS-to-CICS examples, but remember that using ISC permits CICS to communicate with CICS and non-CICS systems/programs.

1.2.3   MRO/ISC Summary

Multi-Region Operation is a CICS-specific function which enables CICS to communicate with another CICS system executing in the same mainframe. MRO is a direct CICS-to-CICS link with no intervening communication software such as ACF/VTAM or the Network Control Program (NCP). InterSystem Communication, on the other hand, involves exchanges between systems connected via an SNA network. In other words, there is always SNA software providing the communication pathway between the communicating systems. InterSystem Communication is possible between CICS and any software product which supports an appropriate flavor of SNA's LUTYPE 6 protocols.

1.3   FUNCTIONS OF INTERCOMMUNICATION

Utilizing either Multi-Region Operation or InterSystem Communication, there are four types of functions that are supported. There are, in some cases, distinctions between the way MRO or ISC actually process internally, and there are also instances where there are limitations that apply to one flavor of Intercommunication or the other. However, we will not address either of these issues at this point. In later chapters we will cover the differences and restrictions, but for now we will stress the concepts and functional capabilities of Intercommunication. The four types of functions that are supported include *Transaction Routing, Function Shipping, Asynchronous Processing* and *Distributed Transaction Processing*.

1.3.1   Transaction Routing

Transaction Routing permits a CICS system to route a transaction defined to it as remote to another CICS system. In the remote system the transaction is processed and a response is created. The response is then sent back to the originating CICS system. Using Transaction Routing, end users at CICS terminals are unaware of whether or not a requested TRANSID is serviced by the CICS system to which they are connected or by another CICS system. Thus CICS can handle transactions that are defined to it as either "local" or "remote." Local transactions are those which the local CICS is prepared to support. This means that the application program which processes the transaction is contained within the local CICS system. CICS services local transactions in the normal way: A task is begun to execute in the program named in association with the transaction. As a result of the task processing a response is created and the response is displayed on the user's terminal.

The definition of a "remote" transaction names a SYSID or system identifier of another CICS system to which the transaction is to be sent for processing. If a CICS terminal operator enters a request for a transaction that is defined as remote, CICS routes the transaction request to the named system. In the named remote system the routed transaction is defined as a "local" transaction and an application task is initiated to execute in the appropriate application program. When the output response is complete, the "remote" CICS system routes the response back to the "local" CICS. The "local" CICS then displays the response upon the terminal.

In the case of MRO, Transaction Routing gives several CICS systems a common face. For example, if there is a need to break a large CICS system into several smaller ones, Transaction Routing makes this "break-up" transparent to terminal users. Consider a CICS system with severe virtual storage constraints. System performance may be adversely affected by frequent "Short-on-Storage" or SOS occurrences. If tuning attempts are unsuccessful in alleviating the situation because the system is, indeed, storage-constrained, it may be necessary to break the single region into two or more individual regions. Without MRO Transaction Routing, end users would have to know which CICS region supports the various transactions that they perform. Furthermore, if terminal operators use transactions that are supported in different CICS regions, the operators would have to know which regions support which transactions. During normal day-to-day processing such terminal operators would have to log on to the correct CICS region, and unfortunately if they desired to perform a transaction serviced by another region, they would have to log off from one system and log on to another. Using Transaction Routing the problem is resolved in a user-friendly manner. End users log on to a CICS region, and their local CICS services all transactions requested. Local transactions are processed within the local region as usual and remote transactions are routed by CICS. Thus, even though the end user in fact utilizes services of two or more CICS systems, these separate regions present a uniform appearance. Figure 1-6 illustrates this use of Transaction Routing. Terminals 1

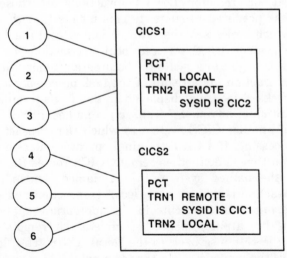

Figure 1-6 Users connected to either CICS1 or CICS2 can perform "TRN1" or "TRN2."

through 3 are connected to CICS1. These users may request TRN1 or
TRN2. If TRN2 is requested, CICS1 uses Transaction Routing and
automatically sends the request to CICS2. The converse is true of
users at terminals 4 through 6 who are connected to CICS2.

In an ISC environment Transaction Routing could be used to make
infrequently used transactions available to end users without requiring duplicate copies of application programs in separate CICS systems. Thus, keeping track of separate copies of application programs
and ensuring that programs are at a uniform maintenance level
would be unnecessary. Because ISC takes place over an SNA Network Transaction routing would not be desirable for use with heavily
utilized transactions. Routing transactions over a network will affect
response time and this has to be considered.

1.3.2   Function Shipping

**Function Shipping makes CICS resources available for ap-
plication program access regardless of whether or not the
resource is contained in the same CICS region as the application program.** Resources that are pertinent to Function Shipping
include Files, Temporary Storage Queues, Transient Data Queues,
and Transactions. Function shipping of a Transaction Initiation request via the START command is considered to be a special case of
Function Shipping referred to as Asynchronous Processing.
Asynchronous Processing is addressed in the next section, and we
will therefore limit our discussion at this point to Function Shipping
of file and queue access requests.

Function Shipping of file requests permits an application program
read and update access to files in interconnected systems. The application program need not be aware of the fact that an accessed file
is owned by another CICS system as long as the file is defined as
"remote" in the local CICS File Control Table (FCT). In this case, a
standard CICS access command such as READ, WRITE, or DELETE
is coded in the program. CICS determines from the local File Control
Table definition that the file is remote and Function Ships the request to the appropriate system named in the file's FCT entry. In the
remote file-owning system, the access request is executed. The result
of command execution is a response code and, if applicable, a data
record. Such results are returned to the requesting CICS system
which utilizes the information to satisfy the command issued by the
application program. Figure 1-7 illustrates Function Shipping of a
file access request. Two CICS systems are depicted as being con-

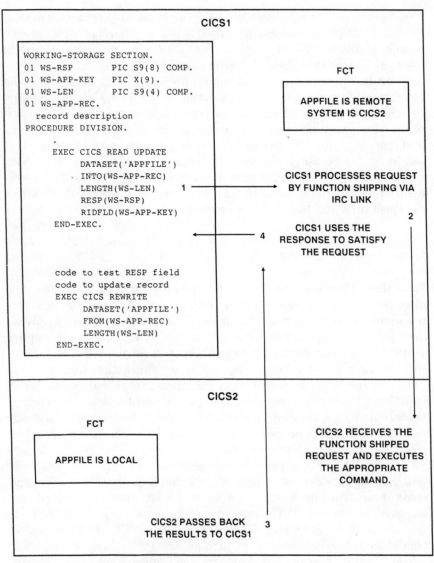

Figure 1-7 Function Shipping example.

nected by an intercommunication link. Note that CICS1 contains the
application program with the access request. The File Control Table
in CICS1 contains an entry for the "APPFILE" and defines the file as
remote and names CICS2 as the file owning region. The READ command in the application program in CICS1 causes the local CICS1
system to Function Ship the access request to CICS2. In CICS2 the

"APPFILE" is likewise defined in the File Control Table. However, in CICS2 the file is defined as a local data set. CICS2 receives the request Function Shipped by CICS1 and executes the appropriate command. The results of command execution are then returned to CICS1. If all goes well, CICS1 gets back a good return code and a data record. CICS1 uses this information to satisfy the application program access request. The data record is then updated by the program, and again Function Shipping takes place for the REWRITE command.

All CICS file commands can be used for access to remote files. Command coding is identical for local or remote files if such files are defined in the FCT. If a remote file is not defined in the local File Control Table, then the access command can utilize a *SYSID* option. The SYSID option provides the file-owning SYStem ID. When SYSID is included in a file command, the local CICS system does not examine the FCT. Rather, CICS automatically Function Ships the access request. In this latter case, CICS does not know the key size for a VSAM keyed file, and the command should include the KEYLENGTH option to specify the key size. Figure 1-8 illustrates the use of the SYSID and KEYLENGTH options. Note that CICS1 does not check its local File Control Table because the SYSID option is included in the READ command. CICS1 automatically uses Function Shipping to the system named with the SYSID option.

The major advantage of having remote files defined in the FCT is that application programmers are less aware of the location of resources. **When the FCT entry is included, command coding is identical to a command for local access.** However, whether or not the SYSID option is used, the application programmer should be aware of the fact that the resource being accessed is not locally owned. The reason for this is because there are errors/unusual conditions that can occur specifically in an Intercommunication environment. The application program should deal with these conditions *in addition* to the normal unusual conditions that can result from the command being executed.

Temporary Storage queues can be written, updated, read or deleted in remote systems. Normal CICS Temporary Storage commands are used for this access. The fact that Function Shipping is to be used can be indicated by including the SYSID option along with other options of the appropriate command, or the queue can be named as a remote queue in the Temporary Storage Table (TST).

Lastly, Transient Data destinations or queues can be accessed via Function Shipping. The normal CICS Transient Data commands are used to access remote queues. Both Intrapartition and

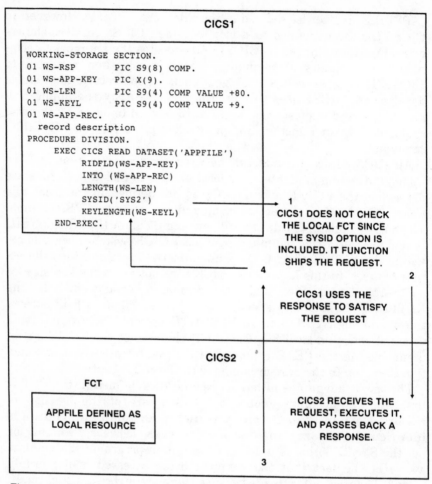

Figure 1-8 Function Shipping example using the SYSID option.

Extrapartition Transient Data queues can be targets of Function Shipping. You will recall that Intrapartition Transient Data queues can be utilized for Automatic Transaction Initiation (ATI). Such queue definitions in the Destination Control Table (DCT) include a trigger level or record count and a TRANSID which is to be initiated when the trigger level is reached. The TRANSID named in a queue's DCT entry must be owned by or local to the same system that owns the queue. Thus, an Intrapartition queue cannot be used to automatically initiate a transaction in a remote CICS system. In addition to the trigger level and TRANSID, an intrapartition queue's DCT entry can name a terminal that is required for transaction processing. Unlike the TRANSID, the terminal named in a queue's entry need not be local to the queue-owning CICS system. If a terminal is defined as remote, CICS will perform Transaction Routing to acquire the terminal in the terminal owning region. As with the other facilities discussed above, Transient Data queues can be defined as remote in the Destination Control Table (DCT), or the SYSID option can be included in application program access commands.

In an environment utilizing CICS Intercommunication, Function Shipping makes file or queue sharing a simple matter. This can be particularly useful if a VSAM file must be accessed from two or more regions. If Function Shipping is not used for file sharing and update access is required by multiple regions, VSAM file SHAREOPTIONS have to be set so that multiple users (CICS Regions) are allowed update access. However, file integrity cannot be guaranteed with such SHAREOPTIONS. Also, recovery/restart planning, if there is a CICS abend, becomes needlessly complex.

When utilizing Multi-Region Operation, one CICS region could function as a "file-server." The "file-serving" CICS could contain definitions for all files used by connected application regions. Function Shipping would allow file sharing, but the file would only be open to the "file-server." This eliminates SHAREOPTION and disposition issues and also insulates the files from application region abends. Recovery/restart only becomes an issue if the "file-server" abends, and if there are no application functions in the file region, the likelihood of this happening is dramatically decreased. Figure 1-9 illustrates the use of MRO Function Shipping to allow two CICS application processing regions to share files. In this diagram CICS3 is depicted as a file server. It is not necessary to have a separate file-serving CICS region, as the files could be defined as local resources in either of the application regions, or file ownership could be split between the regions. **The primary advantage of having a file-serving CICS region is that the files are then isolated from both application processing regions.** An abend in one of the application processing regions does not result in some or all of the files being unavailable to the other application processing region. An emergency restart of files is not necessary unless the file serving region abends due to a hardware or system software failure. Restarting of a failed application region is therefore simplified.

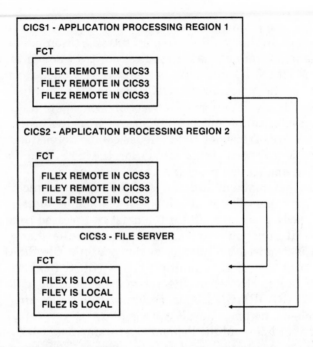

Figure 1-9 Function Shipping is used between CICS1 or CICS2 and the file serving CICS3. Thus application programs running in either CICS1 or CICS2 can share access to files managed by CIS3.

1.3.3   Asynchronous Processing

Asynchronous Processing enables an application program to start one or more asynchronous tasks in connected CICS regions. Such tasks are considered asynchronous because there is *no CICS synchronization* between them. In other words, CICS does not see a relationship between work done by asynchronous tasks. In contrast, CICS sees a relationship between work done across separate CICS systems when Function Shipping is utilized. Figure 1-10 illustrates this synchronization. In CICS1, task number 122 requires update access to a remote file owned by CICS2. CICS1 Function Ships the request and in CICS2 a record is added to the file. Subsequently, task 122 in CICS1 abends. CICS1 sends a notification of the abend to CICS2, and the modification to the protected FILEA is backed out. Backout is performed because there is CICS synchronization between the work done in the separate systems. This synchronization is completely lacking between asynchronous tasks and, therefore, **Asyn-**

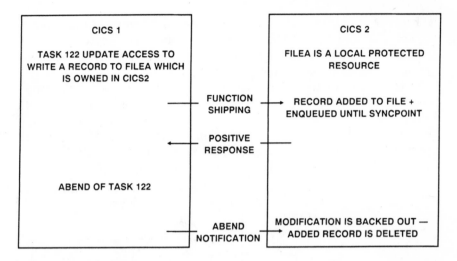

Figure 1-10 For function shipping there is synchronization between work done in separate CICS systems.

chronous Processing is not intended for use where local and remote protected resources are to be modified.

Asynchronous Processing can be implemented in two ways: use of the Interval Control START command or the Terminal Control SEND command with the LAST option.

START Command — A Special Case of Function Shipping The Interval Control START command can be used to initiate a task in a connected CICS system. In this case, the START command is Function Shipped to the other system. In the remote system, the START command is executed and a return code is passed back to the local CICS. Based upon the INTERVAL or TIME requested in the START command, the task is initiated. If the STARTed task abends in the remote CICS region, there is no notification sent back to the local CICS or the STARTing application task within the local CICS. This is because the STARTing and STARTed tasks are considered to be asynchronous from CICS's perspective.

The START command can be used to pass data to the STARTed task. There are four data options included in the START command. There is a free-form application-dependent area that is named with the FROM option and the LENGTH option defines the size of this free-form data area. There is an RTRANSID option that names a 4-byte field that ostensibly can be used to contain a TRANSID, an

RTERMID option that also names a 4-byte field which could contain a TERMID, and a QUEUE option that names an 8-byte field that can be used to pass a queue name. The manner in which these data-defining fields are used is not significant to CICS.

Figure 1-11 illustrates the use of the START command to implement Asynchronous Processing. A terminal user connected to CICS1 initiates a transaction that displays a menu that can be used to define search criteria for a search of a remote data base. After the user enters the information requested on the menu screen, CICS1 initi-

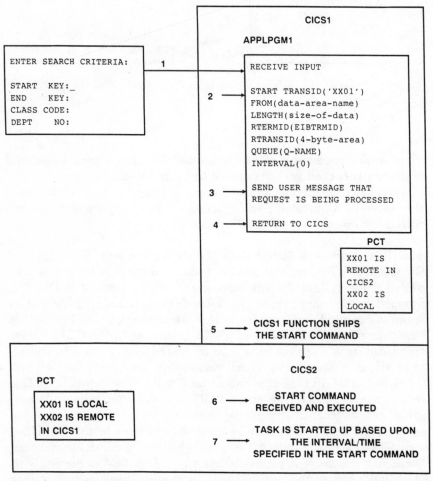

Figure 1-11 The START command can be used to initiate an asynchronous task in another CICS system.

ates a task to execute in APPLPGM1. This task receives and validates the entered data. When the search criteria pass validation, APPLPGM1 is to initiate a search of a remote data file owned by CICS2. Function Shipping could be used, but it would be necessary to initiate a browse of a remote file and then READNEXT so that all records from the start key through the end key could be retrieved and examined. Based upon the keyrange specified by the terminal operator, there could well be a very large number of records to be retrieved. Function Shipping has several disadvantages as a solution for this application. First, network traffic would probably be increased because all records within the keyrange would be retrieved from the remote system so that APPLPGM1 could examine them and determine which ones satisfy the other search criteria. Second, while this searching is going on and requests and responses are being shipped between the systems, *a human being is sitting at a terminal that is locked* because it is attached to a task in CICS1. Suppose that the user does not require a "realtime" response (not that Function Shipping would provide one in this case). APPLPGM1 could utilize Asynchronous Processing as depicted in Figure 1-11. The START command of APPLPGM1 is Function Shipped by CICS1. In CICS2 the shipped START command is executed and an asynchronous task is started as a result. CICS sees no relationship between the task executing in APPLPGM1 and the task initiated in the CICS2 region, but from the application perspective there most certainly is one. We know that the application program executing in CICS2 was written specifically to search the file in question and save all records that meet the search criteria. After APPLPGM1 has executed the START command, it sends a message to the user confirming that the search is being conducted and terminates. While the task in CICS2 is searching, the user in CICS1 can go on and do other functions at his/her terminal. However, we still need to get the selected records back from the CICS2 region.

Figure 1-12 illustrates a method for doing this. In CICS2, APPLPGM2 is named as the program to execute for the TRANSID "XX01" requested in the Function Shipped START command of Figure 1-11. APPLPGM2 contains a RETRIEVE command to obtain passed data. The INTO option names a data area that is coordinated between APPLPGM1 and APPLPGM2 so that the search criteria can be passed to APPLPGM2. The RTERMID option names a 4-byte field containing the original terminal operator's TERMID in CICS1. The RTRANSID option names a TRANSID that is remote to CICS2 and local to CICS1. The QUEUE option passes the name of a Temporary Storage queue that is local to CICS1. APPLPGM2 searches the ap-

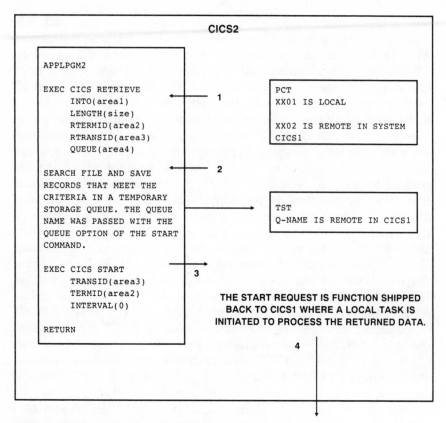

Figure 1-12 Remotely STARTed Asynchronous task.

propriate file. Any records that are found matching the search criteria are written to a Temporary Storage queue whose name was passed via the QUEUE option of the START command. CICS2 Function Ships the Temporary Storage WRITEQ TS commands to CICS1. The actual queue is, therefore, built in CICS1. When the file search is complete, APPLPGM2 issues a START command for the TRANSID passed via the RTRANSID option of the START command naming as a TERMINAL the terminal name passed with the RTERMID option. Then APPLPGM2 RETURNs control to CICS. The START request of APPLPGM2 is Function Shipped to CICS1. CICS1 executes the START command and a task is initiated to execute in an application program that schedules the display of data retrieved from CICS2.

In summary, our sample application involves the processing of three application programs executing in two different CICS systems. CICS itself does not perceive a relationship between the three separate tasks that perform this function. However, from our perspective the three programs must be coordinated with regard to data exchanged between them and the functions that they perform. In this example there was no updating to be done. Nor was there a requirement for a realtime response on behalf of the terminal operator. Because of these conditions, Asynchronous Processing is effective in this application.

SEND with LAST Option   Asynchronous Processing can also be implemented using the SEND command with the LAST option. Figure 1-13 contains some sample code utilizing the SEND LAST. For the sake of continuity we are using the same application as that described above for the START command. The comment in the beginning of the PROCEDURE DIVISION indicates that prior to the SEND command it is necessary to execute an ALLOCATE command. This command will be discussed in a later chapter. For now it is sufficient to understand that the ALLOCATE command requests that CICS provide an alternate network facility for a task. Having an alternate facility allows a task to SEND data to a network resource other than its principal facility. A task's principal facility is the network resource that caused the task to be initiated.

In our example, an operator entered search criteria into a terminal screen and pressed the enter key. As a result of this input, CICS initiated our task. Therefore, the operator's terminal is our task's principal facility. By default all output sent by a task goes to its principal facility. However, our task needs to SEND LAST to another CICS system and therefore requires an alternate facility. As a result of the ALLOCATE command CICS returns an ID that must be used in any SEND command directed to the task's alternate facility. This ID can name a SESSION or conversation with the other system. At this point it is not possible to distinguish between a SESSION or conversation because we would become entangled in detailed topics that are discussed in subsequent chapters. For our purposes we will use a SESSION whose ID is saved in the data field named "SESS-ID."

Note that the TRANSID to be initiated in the remote system is placed in the first 4 bytes of the data that is sent. This tells the remote CICS system which transaction to initiate. The remaining data fields in the "PASS-DATA" area include the search arguments, a 4-byte field named TRN2, and an 8-byte area called Q-NAME. The

```
WORKING-STORAGE SECTION.
01  SESS-ID                 PIC X(4).
01  PASS-DATA.
    04  TRN                 PIC X(4).
    04  DLM                 PIC X.
    04  PASS-START-KEY      PIC X(9).
    04  PASS-END-KEY        PIC X(9).
    04  PASS-CLASS-CD       PIC X(5).
    04  PASS-DPT-NO         PIC XXX.
    04  TRN2                PIC X(4).
    04  Q-NAME.
        06  QTRM            PIC X(4).
        06  QTRN            PIC X(4).
01  DATA-OBTAINED-FROM-TRMNL.
    04  START-KEY           PIC X(9).
    04  END-KEY             PIC X(9).
    04  CLASS-CD            PIC X(5).
    04  DPT-NO              PIC XXX.


PROCEDURE DIVISION.
*   MISSING ALLOCATE COMMAND WHICH IS USED TO OBTAIN
*   USE OF A SESSION WITH A REMOTE SYSTEM.  THE
*   SESSION IS LOANED TO THE TASK AS AN ALTERNATE
*   I.E. ADDITIONAL NETWORK RESOURCE.  CICS
*   RETURNS A SESSION ID SUBSEQUENT TO THE
*   ALLOCATE COMMAND.  THIS SESSION ID IS IN
*   EIBRSRCE WHEN CONTROL IS RETURNED TO THE TASK.

    MOVE EIBRSRCE           TO SESS-ID.
    MOVE 'XX01'             TO TRN.
    MOVE SPACES             TO DLM.
    MOVE START-KEY          TO PASS-START-KEY.
    MOVE END-KEY            TO PASS-END-KEY.
    MOVE CLASS-CD           TO PASS-CLASS-CD.
    MOVE DPT-NO             TO PASS-DPT-NO.
    MOVE 'XX02'             TO TRN2.
    MOVE EIBTRMID           TO QTRM.
    MOVE 'XX02'             TO QTRN.
    EXEC CICS SEND FROM(PASS-DATA) LENGTH(43)
         LAST    SESSION(SESS-ID) END-EXEC.

*   LAST OPTION OF SEND COMMAND TELLS CICS TO END
*   THIS TASK'S USE OF THE SESSION.
```

Figure 1-13 Asynchronous processing example using SEND...LAST.

LAST option included in the SEND command in Figure 1-13 indicates that this is the last output for the named SESSION. The task cannot use the SESSION for subsequent SEND/RECEIVE requests. This effectively disconnects the pathway between the SEND LAST task and the other system. The connection between the CICS systems remains in place but is not available to this task. The only thing that the SEND LAST task can do with the SESSION is to free it. In the remote CICS system "XX01" is used to initiate a task. The task performs a RECEIVE to obtain the data sent and does its processing. This includes saving selected records in a Temporary Storage queue whose name was passed in the Q-NAME field. When processing is complete, this task must initiate a transaction in the originating CICS system. However, since the task was initiated by a SEND LAST, the SESSION used for the SEND LAST transmission is not available to it. The task can obtain another SESSION to the originating system and do a SEND LAST over the newly acquired SESSION. The SEND data area begins with the TRANSID passed in the "TRN2" field and includes the name of the queue containing selected records. In this way, a task is started in the originating CICS system. This third task is not attached to the original terminal so it schedules the terminal's use. The TERMID is available as a component of the queue name. Interval Control START or some other application-specific mechanism can be used to schedule a task to display the search data.

Unlike the use of the START command discussed above, Asynchronous Processing utilizing the SEND LAST command is not a type of Function Shipping. **With Function Shipping a CICS function (i.e., command request) is shipped to another system wherein the command is executed. The data named in the SEND LAST command is sent to another system, not the command itself.**

Using SEND with the LAST option in our example required the inclusion of a SESSION option that named a connection to a remote system. In InterSystem Communication **the SESSION option is not universally applicable** to all intersystem connections. For an intersystem connection that does not support use of the SESSION option, the application program would have to be coded with different command options. If the type of connection changed, the program would require maintenance. The START command, on the other hand, can be used on all intersystem connections and does not require that the application programmer even know the type of connection between the CICS systems.

1.3.4 Distributed Transaction Processing

Distributed Transaction Processing permits synchronized application task processing across CICS systems/regions. With Asynchronous Processing there is no CICS synchronization between the asynchronous tasks. With Distributed Transaction Processing, CICS views the separate tasks as one distributed function or transaction. For recovery or backout purposes, it is as if CICS views the separate tasks engaged in Distributed Transaction Processing as if they were one Logical Unit of Work (LUW). Figure 1-14 illustrates this point. In CICS1 task number 125 is engaged in Distributed Transaction Processing with a task in CICS2. At this point we don't know how the distributed transaction was initiated but merely that it is going on. At point 3 the task in CICS1 sends information to its partner, indicating that an update is required. This is accomplished by the SEND command. At point 4 the task in CICS2 RECEIVEs this data and updates a local file that is defined as a protected

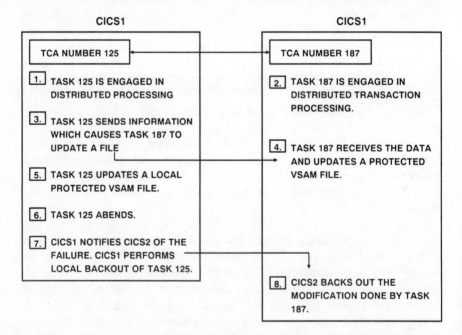

Figure 1-14 Distributed Transaction Processing. This is an example of the task synchronization involved in CICS Distributed Transaction Processing. Effectively, the work done by tasks 127 and 187 comprise one unit of work, which is either successful or requires coordinated backout.

resource within CICS2. At point 5 the task in CICS1 updates a local
VSAM file that is likewise defined as a protected resource. Through
the work of this distributed transaction we have now updated two
protected files owned by two connected CICS systems. At point 6 the
task in CICS1 abends. At point 7 CICS1 notifies CICS2 of the task
failure. Both CICS systems perceive a synchronized relationship between the tasks executing in their respective environments so that
the tasks represent a recoverable unit of work. Since task 125 has
failed, it is necessary for its work to be backed out. It is also necessary for CICS2 to back out the work done by task 187. **Because
Distributed Transaction Processing involves synchronization
between tasks in separate systems/regions, it is suitable for
use in applications that require distributed database updates.**
However, Distributed Transaction Processing connotes more than
mere distributed updating capability.

   If our application merely required that a remote file be updated,
we could have used CICS Function Shipping. With Function Shipping, CICS also recognizes a synchronized relationship between the
modifications to protected resources done in multiple systems/
regions. Figure 1-15 illustrates the synchronization inherent in Function Shipping. Note that when the task in CICS1 fails, the remote
system is notified and backout of the Function Shipped request is
performed. From the perspective of the application developer, the use
of Distributed Transaction Processing is more complex than Function
Shipping. With Function Shipping we only have to write the application program that will execute in CICS1. Using Distributed Transaction Processing, it is necessary to develop an additional application
program to execute in CICS2. This second program could, however,
be coded to do more than just receive data and perform an update.
Suppose, for example, that it were necessary to search additional
files to determine if the update is indeed feasible. In this case we
merely send one transmission of data and the program in CICS2 can
perform all of the validity checking and determine if the update is to
proceed. The program in CICS2 then notifies its partner of whether
or not the update has been accomplished, and the program in CICS1
can proceed accordingly. Thus, in a single SEND/RECEIVE sequence, we manage to validate and potentially update.

   Another example of an application suited to Distributed Transaction Processing is if multiple updates in a remote system/region are
mandated. If Function Shipping were utilized, each update would involve cross region/system communication. With distributed programs
the data for all updates could be sent and acted upon in one transmission. Thus, the overall processing time for the distributed func-

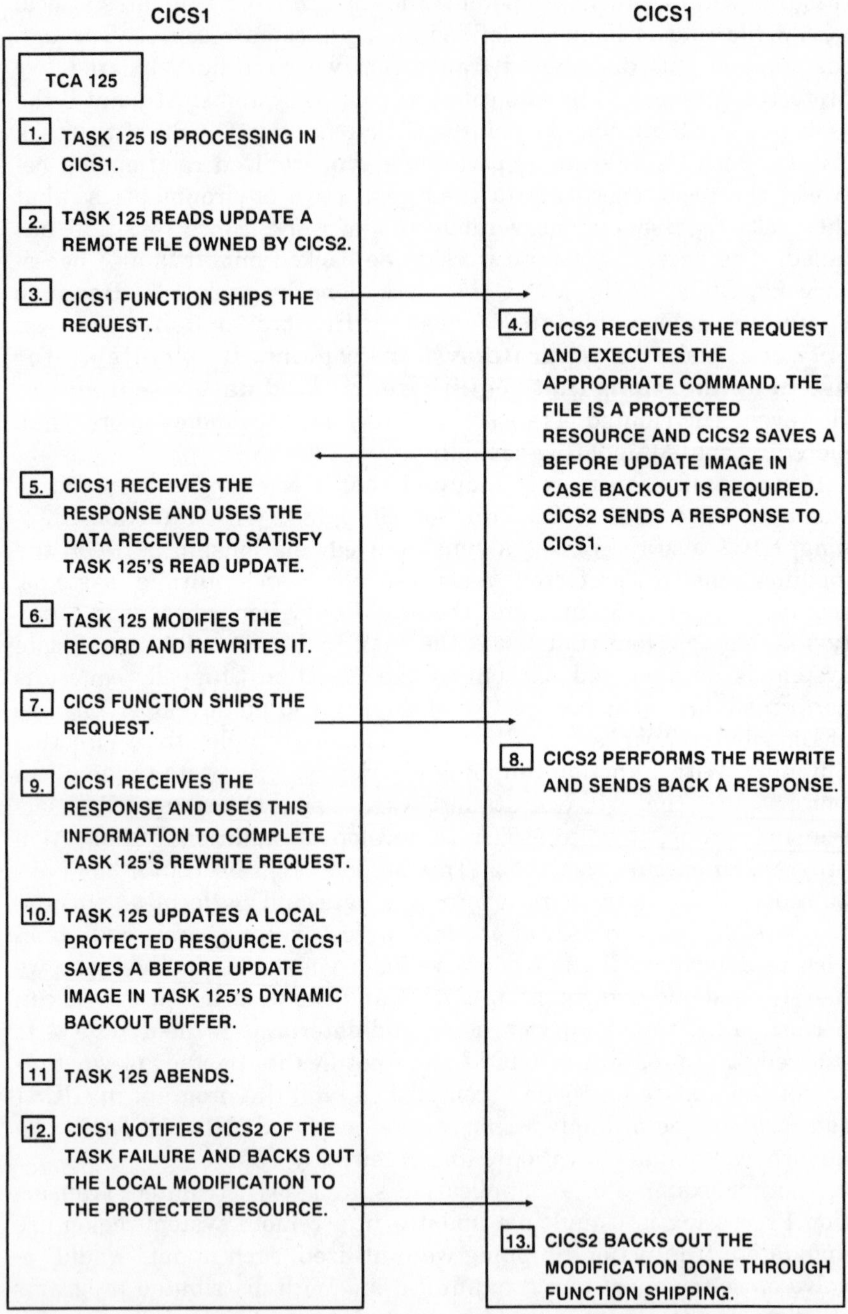

CICS1   CICS1

TCA 125

1. TASK 125 IS PROCESSING IN
CICS1.

2. TASK 125 READS UPDATE A
REMOTE FILE OWNED BY CICS2.

3. CICS1 FUNCTION SHIPS THE
REQUEST.

4. CICS2 RECEIVES THE REQUEST
AND EXECUTES THE
APPROPRIATE COMMAND. THE
FILE IS A PROTECTED
RESOURCE AND CICS2 SAVES A
BEFORE UPDATE IMAGE IN
5. CICS1 RECEIVES THE
RESPONSE AND USES THE
DATA RECEIVED TO SATISFY
TASK 125'S READ UPDATE.
CASE BACKOUT IS REQUIRED.
CICS2 SENDS A RESPONSE TO
CICS1.

6. TASK 125 MODIFIES THE
RECORD AND REWRITES IT.

7. CICS FUNCTION SHIPS THE
REQUEST.

8. CICS2 PERFORMS THE REWRITE
AND SENDS BACK A RESPONSE.

9. CICS1 RECEIVES THE
RESPONSE AND USES THIS
INFORMATION TO COMPLETE
TASK 125'S REWRITE REQUEST.

10. TASK 125 UPDATES A LOCAL
PROTECTED RESOURCE. CICS1
SAVES A BEFORE UPDATE
IMAGE IN TASK 125'S DYNAMIC
BACKOUT BUFFER.

11 TASK 125 ABENDS.

12. CICS1 NOTIFIES CICS2 OF THE
TASK FAILURE AND BACKS OUT
THE LOCAL MODIFICATION TO
THE PROTECTED RESOURCE.

13. CICS2 BACKS OUT THE
MODIFICATION DONE THROUGH
FUNCTION SHIPPING.

Figure 1-15 In Function Shipping CICS coordinates across systems to ensure
resource integrity of protected resources.

tion would be optimized. The time it takes for data to traverse a network is considerably greater than the time needed for CPU processing of a transaction. Therefore, distributed functions are best designed if the transmission of data between regions/systems is kept to a minimum. Distributed Transaction Processing enables the application developer to design and implement applications with a minimum of data transmission. This translates into better response time for the end user at a CICS terminal.

1.4 SUMMARY

CICS Intercommunication provides for the interconnection of separate CICS regions/systems. Multi-Region Operation allows multiple CICS regions in a single host processor to communicate directly with each other to make resources available to end users regardless of whether or not the resource is owned by the user's CICS region. **Multi-Region operation is oriented toward solving operational problems that preclude having a single large CICS region. InterSystem Communication is more general in that it enables CICS to communicate with CICS or non-CICS software products.** ISC requires a System Network Architecture (SNA) network as the pathway between connected systems. These two types of Intercommunication describe the connection between the communicating systems.

In both MRO and ISC environments there are four major functions that can be accomplished. Transaction Routing permits "remote" transactions to be directed to other systems for actual processing. Function Shipping enables CICS to ship command requests for remote resources to other systems for actual execution. Asynchronous Processing allows a CICS task to initiate a remote transaction which performs application dependent work. Using Asynchronous Processing, CICS does not perceive a relationship between the separate tasks, and therefore this facility is not appropriate for coordinated updating of resources. Distributed Transaction Processing, in contrast, does provide cross-system task coordination. Utilizing Distributed Transaction Processing, it is possible to break an application function into separate tasks in divergent CICS systems. The processing of these separate tasks is viewed by the respective CICS systems as a single unit of work for backout recovery purposes. Distributed Transaction Processing thus permits the development of distributed applications across connected CICS systems.

REVIEW EXERCISES

Provide a short answer to each question.

1. What is the purpose of CICS Intercommunication?
2. What are the two main types of CICS Intercommunication?
3. How do the two main types of Intercommunication differ?
4. Multi-Region Operation (MRO) allows CICS regions executing in the same host to communicate. The separate regions could be combined as one large CICS. What would be the benefit of using MRO?
5. Using InterSystem Communication, a CICS system can communicate with other CICS systems or non-CICS software. What dependencies or restrictions apply?
6. What does ACF/VTAM stand for, and what is it?
7. CICS Intercommunication can be utilized to implement four types of functions. Identify and give a brief description of each type.
8. Define the term local resource.
9. What is a remote resource?
10. Some CICS commands can include a SYSID option. What is the purpose of this option?
11. When using the SYSID option in file access commands, what other option might be required and why?
12. What is the major advantage of having remote resources defined in the appropriate CICS resource table?
13. A CICS task can initiate an asynchronous remote task. There are two ways of doing this. Give a brief description of each.
14. What is a principal facility? What is an alternate facility?
15. What does the LAST option of the SEND command tell CICS?
16. Both Asynchronous Processing and Distributed Transaction Processing allow a CICS task to initiate a task in a connected system. What is the major difference between these two functions of CICS Intercommunication?

ANSWERS TO REVIEW EXERCISES

Provide a short answer to each question.

1. *What is the purpose of CICS Intercommunication?*

   The purpose of CICS Intercommunication is to enable CICS to engage in distributed processing.

2. *What are the two main types of CICS Intercommunication?*

   Multi-Region Operation or MRO and InterSystem Communication or ISC.

3. *How do the two main types of Intercommunication differ?*

   MRO directly connects two CICS regions in the same host. Regions connected via MRO converse directly with each other using Interregion SVCs or MVS Cross Memory Services. ISC connects CICS to other CICS or non CICS systems/programs. The pathway between the connected systems is through an SNA network. In ISC the connected systems can reside in the same host or in different hosts.

4. *Multi-Region Operation (MRO) allows CICS regions executing in the same host to communicate. The separate regions could be combined as one large CICS. What would be the benefit of using MRO?*

   The benefit of using MRO is that we are able to solve operational problems that derive from having one large CICS. Such solutions could include improving system virtual storage constraints, offloading process-bound functions to a low-priority region to insulate interactive functions from the more CPU-intensive ones, or isolating an unreliable application into a separate environment.

5. *Using InterSystem Communication, a CICS system can communicate with other CICS systems or non-CICS software. What dependencies or restrictions apply?*

ISC is dependent upon a connection through an SNA network. Any interconnected software must support the SNA LUTYPE 6 protocols.

6. *What does ACF/VTAM stand for, and what is it?*

Advanced Communication Function/Virtual Telecommunication Access Method. ACF/VTAM is an SNA access method, meaning it is used in SNA networks to provide network access for application regions such as CICS.

7. *CICS Intercommunication can be utilized to implement four types of functions. Identify and give a brief description of each type.*

Transaction Routing — permits CICS to route transactions to other systems for actual processing.

Function Shipping — enables CICS to ship resource access requests to other systems so that both local and remote resources can be made available to applications running under CICS.

Asynchronous Processing — allows a CICS application task to initiate a task in a remote system. From a conceptual point of view the processing of these separate tasks may be part of a single application function, but CICS does not see any relationship between the separate tasks.

Distributed Transaction Processing — also allows a CICS task to initiate a remote task. However, in this instance, CICS does see the two separate tasks as pieces of a coordinated function. For this reason, backout recovery is provided for all protected resources modified across the connected tasks.

8. *Define the term local resource.*

A local resource is one that resides in a local CICS system. If an application task is executing under CICS1, CICS1 is the local system and any resources owned by CICS1 are local resources.

9. *What is a remote resource?*

A remote resource is one that resides in a system other than the local CICS. Both local and remote resources can be defined in CICS resource definition tables such as the File Control Table, Temporary Storage Table, Destination Control Table or Program Control Table.

10. *Some CICS commands can include a SYSID option. What is the purpose of this option?*

The inclusion of the SYSID option in file, temporary storage, and transient data access commands as well as the START command allows a program to access remote resources that are not defined in the local CICS system tables. The connection to the system defined with the SYSID option must, of course, be defined to the local CICS.

11. *When using the SYSID option in file access commands, what other option might be required and why?*

For access to VSAM keyed files the KEYLENGTH option must be used because CICS does not know the size of the key field which, of course, must be shipped with the file access request.

12. *What is the major advantage of having remote resources defined in the appropriate CICS resource table?*

The major advantage of having remote resources defined in the local resource tables is that application programmers code commands in an identical fashion as they do to access local resources. In either case, programs accessing remote resources will normally have to deal with unusual conditions specific to Intercommunication in addition to the conditions associated with the access command being executed.

13. *A CICS task can initiate an asynchronous remote task. There are two ways of doing this. Give a brief description of each.*

The Interval Control START command can be used to initiate a remote transaction and pass data to it. The START request is Function Shipped to the appropriate system wherein it is executed. The execution of the START request in the remote system leads to the initiation of a remote task based upon START expiration time.

The Terminal Control SEND with the LAST option can also be used to initiate a remote asynchronous task. The task using SEND LAST must already have or acquire a connection to the remote system. In ISC there are different types of intersystem connections and the application coding is type dependent.

14. *What is a principal facility? What is an alternate facility?*

A task's principal facility is the facility that caused the task's initiation. If, for example, a terminal operator enters a TRANSID and presses the ENTER key. The input from the terminal causes CICS to initiate a task. The terminal in question is the task's principal facility. Unless specifically indicated, a task's terminal control output is directed to its principal facility.

An alternate facility is a network resource acquired by a task in addition to its principal facility. Once a task acquires an alternate facility, it can direct Terminal Control output to the alternate facility.

15. *What does the LAST option of the SEND command tell CICS?*

The LAST option of the SEND command tells CICS that there is no more data to be sent or received over a connection. A task using SEND LAST over an intersystem connection cannot use the connection again. The only thing that the task can do is free the connection.

16. *Both Asynchronous Processing and Distributed Transaction Processing allow a CICS task to initiate a task in a connected system. What is the major difference between these two functions of CICS Intercommunication?*

There is no relationship between asynchronous tasks from CICS's perspective. In Distributed Transaction Processing the cross-system tasks are synchronized so that CICS perceives the separate tasks as one recoverable unit of work. For applications involving distributed resource updates, Asynchronous Processing should not be utilized.

2

DTP and System Requirements — A Closer View

2.1 DISTRIBUTED TRANSACTION PROCESSING — A CLOSER VIEW

In the previous chapter we defined Distributed Transaction Processing as a function of CICS Intercommunication that permits multiple tasks in divergent CICS regions to communicate with each other in order to perform a coordinated application transaction. However, we did not explain how the distributed tasks are initiated, how they become connected in a synchronized conversation, what mechanisms are available in CICS for coordinating the processing between them, why this coordination is necessary or how they can exchange application data and status information. In this chapter we will address these important aspects of Distributed Transaction Processing.

2.2 INITIATION OF A DISTRIBUTED TRANSACTION

The distributed transaction is initiated through a regular transaction initiation mechanism in CICS. Most typically this is accomplished by a terminal operator entering a TRANSID or selecting a choice from a menu screen on a CICS terminal. However, transactions can also be initiated through Interval Control START requests or as a result of reaching a trigger level or data threshold in an Intrapartition Transient Data queue. A distributed transaction is begun through one of these mechanisms. Figure 2-1 illustrates the initiation of a distributed transaction. An end user at a terminal connected to CICS1 enters a TRANSID and presses the ENTER key. As a result of this terminal input, CICS1 initiates task number 159 to execute in the program TRNPGM1.

Our application, however, involves more than just the execution of TRNPGM1. In addition, the program TRNPGM2 in CICS2 must execute, and there must be a coordinated conversation between the tasks processing in these two separate systems. More specifically, TRNPGM1 must acquire the use of a connection or Intercommunication link to CICS2 and initiate a task in CICS2. In the previous chapter we defined a task's Principal Facility as the facility that caused the task to be initiated. The operator's terminal in CICS1 is the principal facility of task 159. TRNPGM1, however, requires the use of a connection to CICS2 or an *alternate facility*.

Figure 2-1 illustrates that there is an existing Intercommunication link between the CICS systems. CICS1 and CICS2 are already connected to each other, and this connection can be viewed as a resource of the respective CICS systems. **TRNPGM1 utilizes an ALLO-**

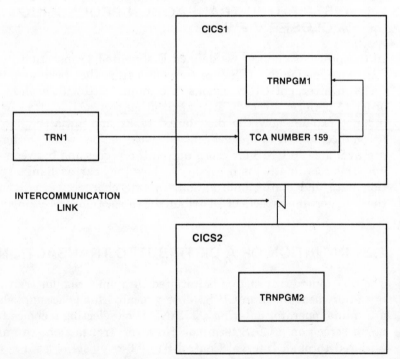

Figure 2-1 The initiation of a distributed transaction.

CATE command to request use of a connection to CICS2. Figure 2-2 illustrates the status of the distributed transaction subsequent to the use of the ALLOCATE command. Note that task 159 has use of an access path to CICS2 as an alternate facility.

Task 159 must now request the initiation of a remote process or task in CICS2. Unlike using the START command or SEND with the LAST option, in this case we require an ongoing connection between the two tasks. Task 159 will need to use its alternate facility to engage in a dialog or conversation with the remote task. The remote task must be connected to the other end of the Intercommunication Link that serves as task 159's alternate facility. There are several different mechanisms that can be utilized to initiate the remote process or task. The one selected depends upon the type of Intercommunication Link between the systems. The systems could be connected via an InterRegion Communication Link (IRC Link) if Multi-Region Operation is in use, if InterSystem Communication connects the systems, the link is an LUTYPE6. To make matters slightly more complex there are two flavors of LUTYPE 6: LUTYPE 6.1 and LUTYPE 6.2.

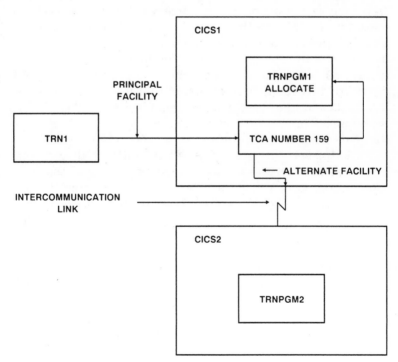

Figure 2-2   The distributed transaction subsequent to the execution of an ALLOCATE command.

Depending upon the type and flavor of the connection, one or more task initiation mechanisms can be chosen. At this point it is not necessary or even desirable to jump into the details of what choices and implications are involved with the different link types. This will all be explained in subsequent chapters. For now, it is sufficient to understand that specific commands and coding syntax are somewhat dependent upon the type of Intercommunication connection between the systems. This is mentioned so that the example can be seen in perspective as one way in which Distributed Transaction Processing can be accomplished. In our example we will use commands and syntax appropriate to an InterSystem LUTYPE 6.2 connection. A detailed scenario is given below solely to provide a model of Distributed Transaction Processing so that the reader can obtain a realistic view of this facility.

Returning to our example, Task 159 executes an ALLOCATE command naming the SYSID of CICS2. As a result of this command, CICS1 makes available the connection to CICS2 as an alternate facility for task 159. Task 159 will use the connection as a pathway for a conversation with a companion task in CICS2. When the conversation is complete, the resource will be released or freed from task 159. CICS1 will then be able to reuse the connection on behalf of other tasks. **During the processing of the ALLOCATE command, CICS1 assigns a CONVersation ID. This CONVID is returned subsequent to command execution in a field in the Execute Interface Block (EIBRSRCE).** Task 159 must save this CONVID and refer to it in all commands directing output to the conversation. If an output command does not name the CONVID, its target is the principal facility of task 159.

Task 159 now utilizes a CONNECT PROCESS command to connect a remote process or task at the other end of the InterSystem Connection. Task 159 is thus the initiator of the remote task and as such is called the *Front-End Transaction*. The task initiated in CICS2 is termed the *Back-End Transaction*. The Back-End Transaction is inititated as a result of information that is: 1) generated via the Front-End Transaction's execution of the CONNECT PROCESS command and 2) sent by CICS1 over the InterSystem Connection. Therefore, the principal facility of the remote task is the connection between the systems. Figure 2-3 illustrates the conversation at this point.

Figure 2-4 contains the format of the CONNECT PROCESS command. The CONVID option names the alternate facility over which the remote process is to be connected, and the PROCNAME option identifies the remote process. In CICS a process or task is initiated

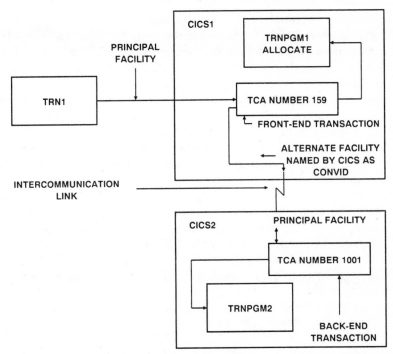

Figure 2-3 Distributed Transaction subsequent to execution of the CONNECT PROCESS command.

via a TRANSID, and therefore PROCNAME specifies the TRANSID to be initiated in the remote system. The size of the process name or TRANSID is defined by the PROCLENGTH option. Typically, a CICS TRANSID is 4 bytes in length. The degree of synchronization required for the conversation is specified by the SYNCLEVEL option. If, for example, the distributed transaction involves updates to protected resources across CICS systems, it would be desirable to have the highest level of synchronization that includes full

```
EXEC CICS CONNECT PROCESS
    CONVID(field-name)
    PROCNAME(process-name)
    PROCLENGTH(size-of-process-name)
    SYNCLEVEL(value of 0, 1, or 2)
    PIPLIST(name-of-pips)
    PIPLENGTH(pip-size)
```

Figure 2-4 Format of Connect Process Command.

SYNCPOINT capability. If, on the other hand, no updates are to be done, a lower level of synchronization can be selected. The PIPLIST option allows a Front-End Transaction to pass initialization information. CICS itself does not use PIP data, but other remote systems might well. If Process Initialization Parameter (PIP) data is included, its length is defined with the PIPLENGTH parameter. PIP data is optional and need not be sent. If included, Process Initialization Parameter data is application dependent. In the case of CICS, PIP data is not used for system purposes, and the application designer is free to use this type of information in any manner suited to the application.

Figure 2-5 is a sample of the coding in TRNPGM1 that we have discussed thus far. Note that subsequent to the ALLOCATE command, EIBRSRCE is saved in a field CONVID. The CONNECT PROCESS command utilizes the CONVID option to name the "conversation" to which its execution is applicable. The TRANSID to be initiated in CICS2 is provided in the command as "TRN2" and its

```
WORKING-STORAGE SECTION.
01  CONV-ID                    PIC X(4).
01  PIP-DATA.
    04  LEN1                   PIC S9(4) COMP VALUE +13.
    04  FILLER                 PIC S9(4) COMP VALUE 0.
    04  SKEY1                  PIC X(9).
    04  LEN2                   PIC S9(4) COMP VALUE +13.
    04  FILLER                 PIC S9(4) COMP VALUE 0.
    04  EKEY2                  PIC X(9).


PROCEDURE DIVISION.
        .
        .
        .

    EXEC CICS ALLOCATE SYSID('SYS1') END-EXEC.

    MOVE EIBRSRCE TO CONV-ID.

    EXEC CICS CONNECT PROCESS CONVID(CONV-ID)
            PROCNAME('TRN2')
            PROCLENGTH(4)
            SYNCLEVEL(2)
            PIPLIST(PIP-DATA)
            PIPLENGTH(26)
    END-EXEC.
        .
        .
        .
```

Figure 2-5 TRNPGM1 sample code.

length is defined as 4 bytes. The SYNCLEVEL requested is 2, which is the maximum synchronization level and means that full CICS SYNCPOINTing is to be utilized. TRNPGM1 is passing PIP data to TRNPGM2. This data is contained in the 01-Level data structure named PIP-DATA and is 26 bytes in length.

The Back-End Transaction is now initiated in CICS2. However, it needs to obtain the data passed as Process Initialization Parameters. Also, this task may seek to obtain other information about the "conversation." This can be accomplished through the use of the EXTRACT PROCESS command. Figure 2-6 illustrates the format of this command. The EXTRACT PROCESS options mirror those of the CONNECT PROCESS command discussed above. A sample of this command as it might be coded in TRNPGM2 is in Figure 2-7. After executing the EXTRACT PROCESS command, TRNPGM2 has obtained all of the information from the CONNECT PROCESS of TRNPGM1. The "conversation" is now initialized and the transactions are now ready to exchange information.

The flow of data between the conversing transactions will be such that one at a time is allowed to SEND data. The other must RECEIVE. This type of exchange is termed HALF-DUPLEX. It is duplex because they are both ultimately allowed to SEND data. But at any given time, only one of them (half of the conversation) is permitted to SEND. In other words, during the conversation one transaction is in the *SEND* state and the other is in the *RECEIVE* state. The EIBRECV field indicates a transaction's SEND/RECEIVE state. It is necessary that a transaction be in the SEND state in order to SEND. When the conversation is initialized, the Front-End Transaction is in the SEND state (EIBRECV set to Low-Values) and the Back-End Transaction is in the RECEIVE state (EIBRECV set to High-Values).

```
EXEC CICS EXTRACT PROCESS
     PROCNAME(32-byte-field)
     PROCLENGTH(2-byte-binary-field)
     CONVID(4-byte-field)
     SYNCLEVEL(2-byte-binary-field)
     PIPLIST(pointer/COBOL BLLCELL)
     PIPLENGTH(2-byte-binary-field)
```

Figure 2-6 Extract Process Command. The reason for the 32-byte field specified for the PROCNAME option is that CICS supports process names up to 32 bytes in length. CICS itself uses a 4-byte TRANSID. However, in support of other systems, it supports a larger process name.

```
WORKING-STORAGE SECTION.
01  DATA-FIELDS.
    04  TRN-ID        PIC X(32).
    04  TRN-LEN       PIC S9(4) COMP.
    04  CONV-ID       PIC X(4).
    04  SYNC-LEV      PIC S9(4) COMP.
    04  PIP-LEN       PIC S9(4) COMP.
    .
    .
    .
LINKAGE SECTION.
01  BLLS.
    04  FILLER        PIC S9(8) COMP.
    04  PIP-PTR       PIC S9(8) COMP.
01  PIP-DATA.
    04  P1-LEN        PIC S9(4) COMP.
    04  FILLER        PIC S9(4) COMP.
    04  PIP-KEY1      PIC X(9).
    04  P2-LEN        PIC S9(4) COMP.
    04  FILLER        PIC S9(4) COMP.
    04  PIP-KEY2      PIC X(9).

PROCEDURE DIVISION.
    .
    MOVE EIBTRMID  TO  CONV-ID.
    EXEC CICS EXTRACT PROCESS PROCNAME(TRN-ID)
        PROCLENGTH(TRN-LEN) CONVID(CONV-ID)
        SYNCLEVEL(SYNC-LEV)
        PIPLIST(PIP-PTR)
        PIPLENGTH(PIP-LEN)
    END-EXEC.
```

Figure 2-7a TRNPGM2 Extract Process Command — VS/COBOL.

2.3 CONDUCTING THE CONVERSATION

The Front-End Transaction can now use the Terminal Control SEND command to send data to the Back-End Transaction. The Back-End Transaction utilizes the RECEIVE command to obtain the data. At some point it is necessary for the Front-End Transaction to alter the SEND/RECEIVE state of the conversation. This enables the Back-End Transaction to SEND data. Alteration of the SEND/RECEIVE state can be accomplished by issuing a SEND command with the INVITE option. A SEND INVITE can be used whether or not data is included for transmission. The CONVERSE command also alters the SEND/RECEIVE State. It is up to the SEND state transaction to

```
WORKING-STORAGE SECTION.
01  DATA-FIELDS.
    04  TRN-ID          PIC X(32).
    04  TRN-LEN         PIC S9(4) COMP.
    04  CONV-ID         PIC X(4).
    04  SYNC-LEV        PIC S9(4) COMP.
    04  PIP-LEN         PIC S9(4) COMP.
    .
    .
    .
LINKAGE SECTION.
01  PIP-DATA.
    04  P1-LEN          PIC S9(4) COMP.
    04  FILLER          PIC S9(4) COMP.
    04  PIP-KEY1        PIC X(9).
    04  P2-LEN          PIC S9(4) COMP.
    04  FILLER          PIC S9(4) COMP.
    04  PIP-KEY2        PIC X(9).

PROCEDURE DIVISION.
    .
    MOVE EIBTRMID  TO  CONV-ID.
    EXEC CICS EXTRACT PROCESS PROCNAME(TRN-ID)
        PROCLENGTH(TRN-LEN) CONVID(CONV-ID)
        SYNCLEVEL(SYNC-LEV)
        PIPLIST(ADDRESS OF PIP-DATA)
        PIPLENGTH(PIP-LEN)
    END-EXEC.
```

Figure 2-7b TRNPGM2 Extract Process Command — COBOL II.

alter the SEND/RECEIVE state. However, for LUTYPE 6.2 connections it is possible for the RECEIVE state transaction to request to be placed into the SEND State. This can be accomplished by executing the ISSUE SIGNAL command. ISSUE SIGNAL results in the alteration of the SEND state transaction's EIB. The EIBSIG field is set on. If the SEND state transaction tests EIBSIG, it recognizes the request for a change of state.

2.4   COMMANDS FOR EXCHANGING STATUS INFORMATION

During the conversation between the distributed transactions, it may be necessary to exchange status information such as confirming correct processing or committing modifications to protected resources. Private confirmation can be exchanged by utilizing a SEND command with the CONFIRM option. This sets on a field in the conversation partner's EIB (EIBCONF) indicating that a status exchange is in process. Finding EIBCONF set on, a transaction can use the ISSUE CONFIRMATION to indicate a positive response. In addition to private confirmations, if the SYNCLEVEL is appropriate, conversing transactions can exchange CICS SYNCPOINTs and jointly commit protected resource updates. However, anticipated and unanticipated errors can ensue. It is therefore necessary for the transactions to have a way of indicating a negative response to confirmation. The SYNCPOINT ROLLBACK, ISSUE ERROR or ISSUE ABEND commands can be used for this purpose. The SYNCPOINT ROLLBACK initiates backout for an entire unit of work. The ISSUE ERROR and ISSUE ABEND commands set on a partner's EIB fields, which can be checked and acted upon. ISSUE ERROR merely sets on the EIB, whereas ISSUE ABEND aborts the conversation causing a TERMERR condition for the conversation partner. SYNCPOINT ROLLBACK, ISSUE ERROR, or ISSUE ABEND can be utilized regardless of SEND/RECEIVE state.

2.5   COORDINATING THE CONVERSATION

The distributed transaction represents a single coordinated application unit of work. As such, if all needed resources were local, it would be possible to perform the transaction in one application program. However, because of the location of resources, it is necessary to split processing into multiple programs executing in different regions. **The separate transactions are thus parts of a whole, and the programs should be jointly planned.** Will PIP data be used? If so, for what purpose? Is there a requirement for synchronization? If so, what SYNCLEVEL is required? When the transactions have been initiated, what processing is required of each of the conversing partners? How long will the Front-End Transaction remain in the SEND state? What data will be exchanged? Can the Back-End Transaction use an ISSUE SIGNAL command? If the EIB-SIG field indicates that a partner has used ISSUE SIGNAL, what is expected of the transaction receiving the SIGNAL? It is likewise necessary to choose and coordinate the commands used for confirmation. For example, if one transaction SENDs with the CONFIRM option, the other transaction should be checking the EIBCONF field to see if confirmation has indeed been requested. The responses to SEND CONFIRM should also be planned so that a conversation partner can check the EIB and determine the course of processing.

2.6   SUMMARY OF DISTRIBUTED TRANSACTION PROCESSING

Distributed Transaction Processing enables the application developer to implement transactions that require the coordinated processing of application programs executing in diverse CICS regions/systems. There are commands that are designated for such programs. Using the ALLOCATE command a task can request use of an alternate network facility. Having been allocated a facility for a conversation, a task can initiate a remote process. The remote process can obtain information about the conversation. Commands can be used to exchange data and status information. **The exact commands used and the syntax of some commands is dependent upon the type of connection between the systems in question, so it is necessary to know whether MRO, ISC LUTYPE 6.1, or LUTYPE 6.2 is in place.**

2.7   SAMPLE CASES OF CICS INTERCOMMUNICATION

Now that we have discussed the facilities available in CICS Intercommunication, it is important to examine some sample cases. In an actual environment where Intercommunication is utilized, we would normally find multiple kinds of Intercommunication implemented.

2.7.1   Transaction Routing and Function Shipping Combined

In Chapter 1 we indicated that Multi-Region Operation is oriented toward improving the operational environment by splitting a single CICS region into multiple connected regions. As a sample case let's consider a region in which there are application programs that routinely cause storage violations and other application errors that result in frequent CICS abends. All users of this CICS region are inconvenienced when the system crashes. Furthermore, system abends require that an emergency restart be performed and system outages can, therefore, be of fairly long duration. Furthermore, one of the applications within this region is critical. When this application is down, the company is in an emergency state, as it is not possible to conduct business.

Additionally, the EDP auditors have concluded that there is a serious problem in having storage violations in a region where updates are performed. They have wisely pointed out that CICS detects a misuse of storage as a violation only if a CICS storage area such as a storage chain is overlayed. However, an illegal use of storage that changed a customer's account balance would not be detected by CICS. One cannot assume that storage violators will affect only CICS areas. As a matter of fact, it is highly likely that non-CICS storage will also be corrupted. This means that our system is running at risk to data integrity.

It is obvious to all concerned that something has to be done to improve the situation. If time were of little consequence and there was no problem with data integrity, we could track down all of the application errors and fix the programs in question. However, we need an immediate solution to the problem and one that does not involve time-consuming application program maintenance. By migrating to an MRO environment as quickly as it can be implemented, we can overcome the major difficulties. There are, however, several steps. First, we must isolate the application programs that are causing system problems. Second, we must implement MRO. Third, we should attempt to find and resolve application errors. By converting to an MRO environment we can keep the applications operational and obtain the necessary time to debug the faulty programs.

Figure 2-8 illustrates the Multi-Region Operation environment. In this example we have carried MRO to its logical conclusion utilizing both Transaction Routing and Function Shipping. CICS1 is a terminal serving CICS. All terminals in the network are defined in this region's Terminal Control Table. The Program Control Table in CICS1 contains a definition of all transactions as being remote in either CICS2 or CICS3. CICS2 is reserved for the critical and stable applications. CICS3 is the outcast region in which faulty applications reside. This region should not contain programs that update files or databases because of the storage violators that are processing in this region. CICS4 executes as a file server. All of the files used by CICS2 and CICS3 are defined in the File Control Table in CICS4 as local files. The FCTs in CICS2 and CICS3 define remote files that reside in CICS4. A user connected to a terminal owned by CICS1 enters a TRANSID. CICS1 performs Transaction Routing to one of the application regions. As file access is required, the application regions perform function shipping to CICS4.

The conversion to MRO can be accomplished without modifying application programs. However, CICS table maintenance will be required. In our example, it will be necessary to define InterRegion Communication (IRC) Links between the communicating CICS systems. CICS1-to-CICS2, CICS2-to-CICS1, CICS1-to-CICS3, CICS3-to-

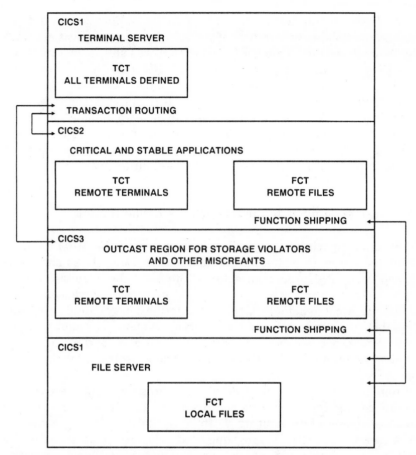

Figure 2-8 MRO using Transaction Routing and Function Shipping.

CICS1, CICS2-to-CICS4, CICS4-to-CICS2, CICS3-to-CICS4 and CICS4-to-CICS3. The IRC Links are defined in the respective Terminal Control Tables. A new Program Control Table (PCT) with remote transactions is required for CICS1. CICS2 and CICS3 each require a Program Control Table with local transaction definitions. The application regions also require separate Processing Program Tables (PPTs) with definitions of local programs. CICS2 and CICS3 each require File Control Tables in which files are defined as remote. In CICS4 the File Control Table contains the actual local definitions of files.

In this example, we utilized CICS Intercommunication to solve operational problems that needed to be handled in a timely fashion. We had an existing set of programs and there was no time to change them. However, in terms of planning new applications we have choices about how we can best use CICS Intercommunication. This section dealt with a single CICS region that was split using up MRO. In subsequent sections we address both MRO and ISC. The one distinction between MRO and ISC that must be borne in mind throughout is that the path between CICS systems connected via ISC is "longer," especially if that path involves a remote data communication network. Taking this into account along with any application requirements for a timely response is critical in choosing how to implement functions under Intercommunication.

2.7.2   Considerations in the Use of Transaction Routing

Transaction Routing is primarily oriented toward the MRO environment. Its use in InterSystem Communication connections should be limited to lightly used transactions. Suppose, for example, that a credit analyst online to a credit approval system has occasional need to look up a customer's history. The information required is readily available in a connected customer service system. Through transaction routing, a customer service inquiry could be performed in the remote system and the retrieved information displayed for the credit analyst.

From the vantage point of application programming there are no special coding considerations for programs that are executed as a result of Transaction Routing. Both conversational and pseudo-conversational transactions are supported. However, for transactions that interact with a video terminal, pseudo-conversational programming would be strongly recommended. Conversational programs in an Intercommunication environment would tie up resources in multiple CICS systems and would therefore be even less desirable than in a single-system environment.

BMS mapping facilities may be utilized as in a single system environment. BMS maps and the application programs that use them must reside in the same system since mapping is performed in the transaction owning region. BMS Paging may also be utilized. The creation of the logical message takes place in the transaction owning region. When the logical message is complete it is shipped to the terminal-owning region where the actual terminal paging is performed. Figure 2-9 lists the special considerations in the use of Transaction Routing.

```
*  NO SPECIAL CODING CONSIDERATIONS:

   BMS MAPPING AND PAGING ARE SUPPORTED

   PSEUDO-CONVERSATIONAL AND CONVERSATIONAL
   PROGRAMS ARE SUPPORTED ALTHOUGH
   PSEUDO-CONVERSATIONAL PROGRAMS ARE
   STRONGLY RECOMMENDED FOR VIDEO
   TERMINAL INTERACTION.

   ORIENTED TOWARD MRO ALTHOUGH TRANSACTION
   ROUTING CAN BE UTILIZED FOR LIGHTLY
   USED TRANSACTIONS IN AN ISC
   ENVIRONMENT (SUPPORTED ONLY ON LUTYPE6.2
   LINKS).
```

Figure 2-9 Transaction routing — special considerations.

2.7.3   Considerations in the Use of Function Shipping

In electing to use Function Shipping it is important to bear in mind that each access command requires a trip to and from the connected CICS system. The Function Shipped request is transmitted to the remote system and the response is sent back. For a READ UPDATE and REWRITE sequence, there would be four transmissions of data as illustrated in Figure 2-10.

However, Function Shipping requires very little in the way of specific application coding. Normal CICS access commands are used

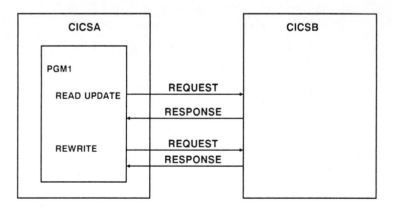

Figure 2-10 Transmissions between connected CICS systems in support of file update using function shipping.

as in a single CICS environment. However, it may be necessary to include the SYSID option for resources not locally defined. Application programs should also include a few more unusual condition tests for those conditions that are specific to the Intercommunication environment.

In terms of resource updates, CICS backout synchronization applies for cross-system Function Shipping. Function Shipping is, thus, best suited to applications in which there is limited access to remote resources. Heavy access such as numerous record updates or file browsing would be better designed using other types of Intercommunication. Figure 2-11 summarizes the key considerations in the use of Function Shipping.

As an example of the use of Function Shipping let's consider an inventory management system which provides terminal operators with the ability to look up inventory figures for particular stock numbers. Merchandise is actually stocked in two warehouses, and at each site there is an online system. In order to provide information regarding the total amount of merchandise in both locations, it is necessary to read local and remote inventory master files. Since a single file access is all that is required, Function Shipping is the most expedient way to implement this application.

```
*  FUNCTION SHIPPING IS EASY TO CODE.  NORMAL CICS
   COMMANDS ARE USED AS IN A SINGLE-SYSTEM
   ENVIRONMENT.

*  MAY NECESSITATE USE OF THE SYSID OPTION FOR NON-
   LOCALLY DEFINED RESOURCES.

*  WOULD NORMALLY INVOLVE EXTRA CONDITION HANDLING
   FOR UNUSUAL CONDITIONS PARTICULAR TO
   INTERCOMMUNICATION.

*  UPDATE SYNCHRONIZATION OF PROTECTED RESOURCES
   (I.E., SYNCPOINT OR BACKOUT) IS PROVIDED
   ACROSS SYSTEMS.

*  IF ACCESS IS LIMITED CAN PROVIDE A 'REALTIME'
   RESPONSE BUT REMEMBER THAT EACH COMMAND
   REQUIRES TWO TRANSMISSIONS.
```

Figure 2-11 Function Shipping — special considerations.

2.7.4   Considerations in the Use of Asynchronous Processing

Asynchronous Processing is indicated when an application can be implemented without the necessity of providing a realtime response. If a terminal operator is sitting and waiting for a response, then Asynchronous Processing should not be utilized. Additionally, because CICS does not provide coordination between asynchronous tasks, this facility is not appropriate where cross-system updates are to be performed. Use of Asynchronous Processing implies that there is application work to be performed in multiple regions and that an end user can wait for notification of the results of this work.

Application programs must be written to perform all of the processing involved. In the previous chapter there was an example of a file search function implemented using Asynchronous Processing. Using that example as a basis, we can conclude that there would be three application programs that would have to be coded. Figure 2-12 illustrates this function in slightly more detail than discussed in the previous chapter. Note that there are four application programs utilized. PGM1 interacts with the end user to obtain the search criteria. It then performs a START of a remote TRANSID and passes data in the START request. This data includes the search criteria requested by the user, the name of the user's terminal in CICS1, the name of a Temporary Storage Queue to be built in CICS1, and the name of a TRANSID to be started back in CICS1 when the search is complete. This TRANSID is associated with PGM3 in CICS1. As a result of the START request done by PGM1, a task is initiated in CICS2. This task executes in PGM2. PGM2 does a retrieve to obtain the passed data. It then performs the file browse and selects records that meet the search criteria. Such records are written to a Temporary Storage queue in CICS1. Having this task wait while records are Function Shipped to CICS1 is preferable to having a subsequent terminal interactive task in CICS1 read a remote queue. When the search is complete, PGM2 executes a START for the TRANSID passed to it from PGM1 naming the user's terminal in the TERMINAL option of the START command.

As a result a task is begun in CICS1. This task executes in PGM3 and is attached to the operator's terminal. However, it might not be desirable for this task to directly read the Temporary Storage queue and display the information on the terminal screen. The reason for this is that the terminal operator may be in the middle of a pseudo-conversational transaction. CICS perceives a terminal as being available for STARTing a task even if there is a waiting next TRANSID. An operator who has just keyed information into a data entry screen and is about to press ENTER may not appreciate the data entry screen disappearing and being replaced with new information. Therefore, it is necessary to plan the interface back to the terminal. This is dependent upon the nature of the application and the processing done by the terminal operator. For example, if the operator is performing a multi-screen data entry operation, it would normally be best to wait until the operator has completed the entire transaction. When the operator has completed data entry of a customer or an order and is about to go on to the next item, the time may be right to jump in with the display of returned records. On the other hand, it might be desirable to allow the operator to determine when the information should be displayed. Once the decision about how display scheduling is made, the remaining programs can be designed

Let's say that PGM3 sets a completion flag to indicate that there is information to be displayed and saves the name of the Temporary Storage queue containing the data. Again, there are choices about where the completion flag and queue name are saved. Three mechanisms come to mind, but these are by no means an exhaustive list. The Terminal Control Table User Area (TCTUA) can be used, or a memory table can be utilized with an entry in the table for each terminal requiring such scheduling. Last, a VSAM KSDS could be created. The file key could be the TERMinal IDentifier (TERMID).

If the terminal operator is going to determine when information is displayed by entering a TRANSID or choosing a menu option, then the operator should now be informed that the information is available. PGM3 can notify the operator of this fact by displaying a one-line message in a common message line area without disrupting the screen. The operator can continue with his/her work and at an appropriate time request the display of the returned records. This request would be serviced by PGM4 in Figure 2-12. PGM4 reads the TS queue and displays the returned records.

If, on the other hand, an application program is going to schedule the terminal display, then it is necessary to place the intelligence to test the completion flag in the appropriate program and have that program transfer control to the display program (PGM4 in Figure 2-12).

There is one last consideration in the use of Asynchronous Processing, and that involves the lack of coordination between asynchronous tasks from CICS's perspective. Suppose that a terminal operator enters a request and PGM1 runs and does its processing. PGM2 is initiated and abends without completing the queue or performing the START for the task to execute in PGM3. In this case PGM1 informed the operator that the request was being processed, but it is obvious

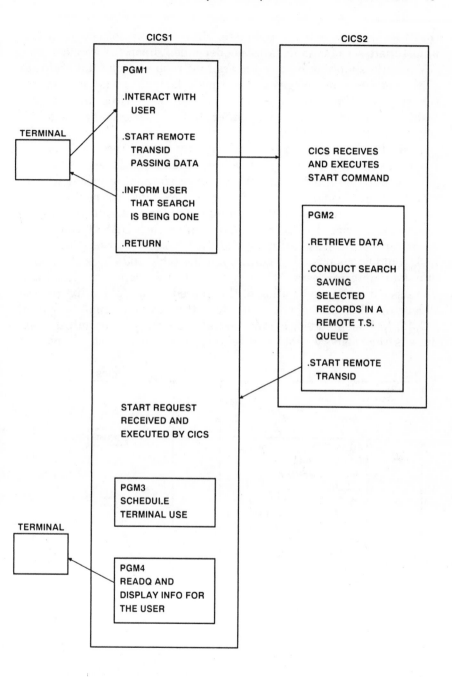

Figure 2-12 Sample application using Asynchronous Processing.

that the function will not complete. How we wish to deal with this unfortunate set of circumstances is dependent upon the application.

We could simply inform end users that requests may fail and that if a response is not received in a timely fashion, to merely reenter the request. However, requests may not be serviced in a timely fashion if the other system is suffering from performance degradation, or if the connection between the systems is temporarily disrupted. In this case, operators may ultimately receive duplicate responses for reentered requests and should be so advised.

We could also provide an application programming mechanism to monitor the servicing of requests. In our example we could, for instance, have a memory table with an entry for each outstanding request. PGM1 would update this table after each START command. At periodic intervals, utilizing the facilities of Interval Control, a task could be awakened to go through the table and check the status of outstanding requests. Those that are deemed "unsuccessful" could be reissued and an indication of this placed in the table. Figure 2-13 illustrates this implementation. Note that an additional program, PGM5, has been added. PGM5 is awakened every 15 minutes. It examines the memory table and reissues any requests that have not

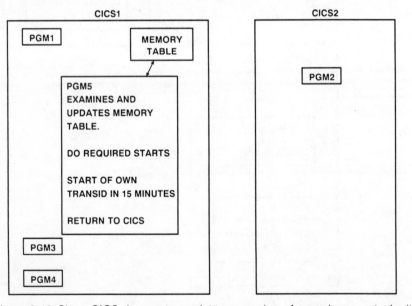

Figure 2-13 Since CICS does not correlate processing of asynchronous tasks it may be necessary in some applications to provide the intelligence to monitor successful completion of Asynchronous Processing based functions.

completed according to application specific criteria. After going through the table and performing any required START requests, PGM5 does a START for its own TRANSID for an interval of 15 minutes and then RETURNs to CICS.

PGM3 would, in addition to other processing, set a flag in the table indicating when a request has completed. When a request and all reissuances have completed, the table entry can be deleted. PGM3 would also need some mechanism for recognizing duplicate responses from reissued requests. To this end, each reissued request could carry a data field with a unique request number. The table information and unique request number could be utilized to recognize duplications of responses in PGM3. PGM3 would then be able to dispose of duplicate responses. If required, PGM5 could also cancel certain requests. For example, after reattempting a particular function a specified number of times, PGM5 could initiate a terminal-oriented task to inform the operator of the failure. The operator could then elect to make the request again at a later time. Figure 2-14 summarizes the considerations for use of Asynchronous Processing.

```
*   MUST WRITE ALL OF THE ASYNCHRONOUS PROCESSING
    PROGRAMS.

*   ERRORS IN THE REMOTE ASYNCHRONOUS TASK ARE NOT
    REPORTED BACK SO APPLICATION DESIGN MUST
    PROVIDE SOME KIND OF CHECKING  **  OR  **
    USER MUST BE INSTRUCTED TO REENTER REQUESTS
    THAT REMAIN OUTSTANDING FOR A GIVEN AMOUNT
    OF TIME.

*   NO      S Y N C H R O N I Z A T I O N

    .  NOT ORIENTED TO UPDATE FUNCTIONS

*   BECAUSE OF ITS ASYNCHRONOUS NATURE, ASYNCHRONOUS
    PROCESSING IS NOT ORIENTED TO A REALTIME
    RESPONSE.

*   INTERFACE BACK TO THE TERMINAL USER MUST BE
    COORDINATED BY APPLICATION PROGRAMS **  OR  **
    THE USER MUST BE TOLD TO CHECK ON THE RESULT
    PERIODICALLY.
```

Figure 2-14 Asynchronous Processing — special considerations.

2.7.5 Considerations in the Use of Distributed Transaction Processing

Distributed Transaction Processing is intended for applications in which processing must be split between interconnected systems. In some cases, it might prove more efficient to use Distributed Transaction Processing in place of Function Shipping. Consider an application in which several file updates are required. Function Shipping would necessitate more data transmissions to accomplish multiple updates than if all updates could be sent in one transmission of data between conversing transactions. **Fewer transmissions result in better response time for the distributed application.**

Let's consider an order entry application in which telephone operators enter customer orders for merchandise into CICS terminals. Inventory is kept in two warehouses in geographically distant cities. At each warehouse location there is a computer facility with a CICS system. Customers telephone in orders to one of the warehouse/computer sites. In some instances, particular stock items are kept in only one warehouse location and in other cases inventory items are stored in both warehouses. Therefore, part of processing an entered order is to determine on an item-by-item basis where the item is stocked and arrange for shipment according to originating warehouse. In other words, a single customer order may well be split internally into two orders, one to be shipped from warehouse number one and the other from warehouse number two.

In analyzing this application, it is first necessary to define all of the processes that have to be performed, including the files to be updated. To facilitate this process let's first consider the application as if we were operating in a single-system environment. This transaction encompasses the data entry of multiple screens of information. The first screen illustrated in Figure 2-15 requires the entry of a customer number, a purchase order number, and a requested shipment date. Subsequent to the entry of this information, a screen is

```
ORDER ENTRY TRANSACTION

ENTER THE FOLLOWING INFORMATION
CUSTOMER NUMBER: _
P.O. NUMBER:
SHIPMENT DATE:
```

Figure 2-15 Initial order entry screen.

```
ORDER NUMBER:     _____          DATE:  _____

CUSTOMER NUMBER:_____           P.O. NUMBER:  _____

       NAME:    _____
                _____


CUSTOMER ADDRESS:_____
                 _____
                 _____
                 _____



SHIP TO ADDRESS: _____
                 _____
                 _____
                 _____




SHIPMENT DATE:    _____         TOTAL DOLLAR AMOUNT:  _____

TERMS:  _____
```

Figure 2-16 Customer information screen.

displayed which contains information about the customer placing the order. Figure 2-16 depicts the customer information screen.

The system generates an order number and retrieves customer name and address information from a customer master file. Customer information can be altered by the terminal operator as appropriate. Subsequent to the correct entry of this information, the operator is presented with merchadise entry screens. Figure 2-17 illustrates the merchandise entry screen. The operator enters a stock number (SKU) and the ordered quantity for each item, and a single screen permits entry of up to 20 items. Orders that involve more than 20 items are accommodated by sending the merchandise entry screen multiple times. Product description, unit price, and extended price are supplied by the system utilizing information from an Inventory Master File.

PF key use allows a terminal operator to scroll back to prior screens to permit the correction of entered information. When the order is complete, the operator presses a PF key to indicate that the system is to process it. Figure 2-18 is a diagram of the programs that process this transaction. There is a control program which manages the routing and control functions between the screen handling

SKU	PRODUCT DESCRIPTION	ORDERED QUANTITY	UNIT PRICE	EXTENDED PRICE	OUT/S IND.
___	___	___	___	___	___
___	___	___	___	___	___
___	___	___	___	___	___
___	___	___	___	___	___
___	___	___	___	___	___
___	___	___	___	___	___
___	___	___	___	___	___
___	___	___	___	___	___
___	___	___	___	___	___
___	___	___	___	___	___
___	___	___	___	___	___
___	___	___	___	___	___
___	___	___	___	___	___
___	___	___	___	___	___
___	___	___	___	___	___

Figure 2-17 Merchandise entry screen.

programs. When the transaction is initiated, the control program processes first. It sends the screen depicted in Figure 2-15 and RETURNs to CICS with its own TRANSID. After the operator enters the required order/customer information, the control program verifies the customer number, allocates a commarea, supplies the date, and generates an order number. The Control Program then XCTLs to the Customer Information Handling Program. This module reads the Customer Master File and displays the customer and order information illustrated in Figure 2-16.

At this point in transaction processing, the TOTAL DOLLAR AMOUNT information is unknown and is therefore not shown. After displaying the screen, this program RETURNs to CICS with its own TRANSID. The operator is allowed to alter the P.O. NUMBER, SHIP TO ADDRESS, or SHIPMENT DATE. Subsequent to operator entry, the Customer Information Handling Program receives control and verifies any modified information. If information is incorrectly entered, an error message is sent and the operator is allowed to fix the data in error. After data has passed validation, the program saves the PF key information (EIBAID) and validated data in the commarea and XCTLs to the Control Program.

The Control Program then passes control to the Merchandise Processing Program. This module sends the screen illustrated in Fig-

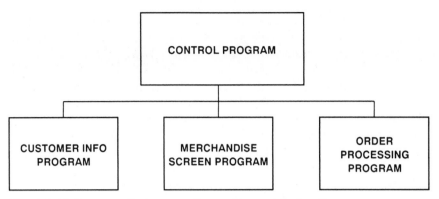

Figure 2-18 Programs that process the customer order function.

ure 2-17 and RETURNs with its own TRANSID. When reinvoked, subsequent to operator input, this module validates entered information. If an invalid SKU or QUANTITY is entered, the program displays an error message and RETURNs with its own TRANSID. When a Merchandise screen has been correctly entered, the information is saved in the commarea along with the contents of EIBAID, and control is passed back to the Control Program. The Control Program determines the next program to process by interrogating the saved PF key information in the commarea. When the operator presses "order complete" PF key, control is passed to the order processing program, which attempts to do the processing necessary to complete the order. This involves the final validation of all entered information, the calculation of the TOTAL DOLLAR AMOUNT information, and the updating of online files. Figure 2-19 contains an I/O diagram of this module.

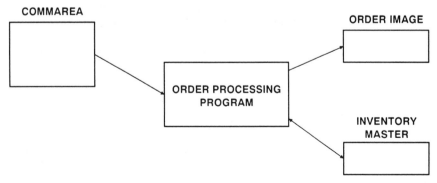

Figure 2-19 I/O diagram of the Order Processing Program.

The commarea data collected by the screen-handling modules is a primary source of Input. This module examines the Inventory Master File for each SKU ordered. If there is sufficient Quantity on Hand, then this field is decremented by the ORDERED QUANTITY, and a Reserved Inventory Field is updated to reflect the reservation of merchandise for the order. If the ORDERED QUANTITY is not available, then an Out-of-Stock Indicator is set on in the commarea. After all items have been processed, a record is written to the Order Image File and transaction processing is complete.

Having analyzed the application from a single-system perspective, we are now ready to deal with the processing of an order across CICS systems. It is apparent that during the data entry of an order, there is no necessity for interfacing with the remote system. It is only during the execution of the Order Processing Program that there is a need to obtain and update remote file information. It is conceivable that many or all of the items in a particular order are handled by the remote warehouse. In that case, it would be necessary to update the remote Inventory Master File multiple times and the Order Image File once.

We can immediately dismiss Asynchronous Processing as a means of implementing this application for two reasons. First, there is potentially cross-system updating, and we need CICS backout if there is a failure during transaction processing. Second, there is a human being awaiting a response indicating that order processing is complete. We don't have a means of obtaining a response back from an asynchronous task.

Function Shipping is a viable option from the vantage point of providing backout recovery. However, imagine for a moment a human being sitting at a terminal waiting while each Inventory Master update results in four cross-system transmissions (READ UPDATE request, Response, REWRITE request, and Response) as well as an addition of a record to the Order Image File. Clearly, the way to implement this function is to utilize Distributed Transaction Processing.

Figure 2-20 illustrates the processing done in the conversation partners. When the Order Processing Program determines that the commarea information is correct, it begins to process the order. This involves determining which inventory items are to be shipped from the remote site. The module constructs a record with information regarding all SKUs requiring remote processing. The ALLOCATE command is used to obtain a CONVID and use of a connection with the remote system. The CONNECT PROCESS command initiates the remote process and passes PIP data, which in this application

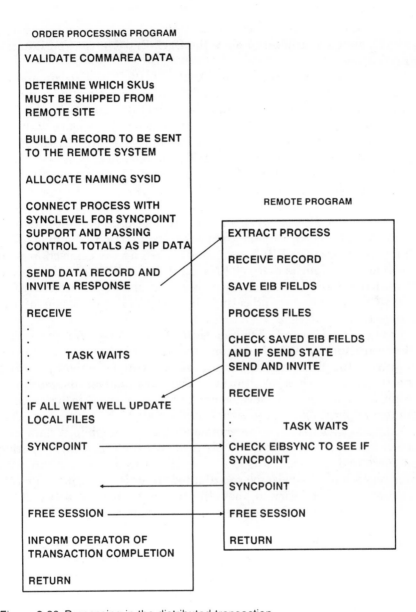

Figure 2-20 Processing in the distributed transaction.

contains control totals. The remote update record is sent, and the INVITE option is utilized to place the Back-End Transaction into the SEND State.

The remote process uses the EXTRACT PROCESS command to obtain the control totals passed as PIP data. This module then does a RECEIVE and performs the file processing. It then checks the EIB to ensure that it is in the SEND State and sends a response with the INVITE option to place its conversation partner in the SEND State. The Front-End Transaction RECEIVEs the response. If all went well in the remote system, local files are updated. Then this module performs a SYNCPOINT so that modifications to protected resources in both systems are committed. The Back-End Transaction is informed of its partner's SYNCPOINT via the EIB and proceeds with its own SYNCPOINT. Then, having completed its function, the Back-End Transaction uses the FREE command to free up the connection with the remote system and RETURNs control to CICS. The Front-End Transaction likewise FREEs the connection and sends a message to the terminal operator indicating the successful completion of the transaction.

Using Distributed Transaction Processing for the implementation of this function provides the synchronization required for cross-system updates as well as accomplishing the function with a minimum of data transmissions. However, in terms of application development, it is necessary to write coordinated application programs that perform all of the processing. This coordination means that the commands used to exchange data and status information must be planned between the conversation partners and, it goes without saying, that the processing and data exchanged must likewise be coordinated. In order to implement this function, it is necessary to know the type of connection between the systems in question. Our example is based upon an ISC LUTYPE 6.2 Connection.

The functionality of Distributed Transaction Processing provides great flexibility in the development of distributed applications. However, its use requires greater skill in terms of application development. With the other facilities of Intercommunication, application programmers need not code entire programs based upon an intersystem environment. Some command options may have to be included and additional unusual conditions should be dealt with, but by and large the skill level required is the know-how to write CICS programs. **Writing programs for Distributed Transaction Processing, on the other hand, requires knowledge of new commands and techniques beyond writing programs for a**

* APPLICATION PROGRAMS MUST BE WRITTEN TO DO ALL
  OF THE PROCESSING ACROSS SYSTEMS

* IT IS NECESSARY TO CODE SPECIFICALLY FOR THE
  TYPE OF CONNECTION BETWEEN THE SYSTEMS

  * IT IS A WAY OF OPTIMIZING CROSS-SYSTEM DATA
    TRANSMISSIONS FOR MULTIPLE FILE/RESOURCE
    UPDATES

  * CONNOTES CROSS-SYSTEM PROCESSING ASIDE FROM THE
    UPDATE OF A SINGLE RESOURCE

* PROVIDES APPLICATION DEVELOPER MUCH MORE CONTROL
  OVER THE APPLICATION FUNCTIONALITY

* PROVIDES SYNCHRONIZATION BETWEEN CONVERSING
  TRANSACTIONS -- BOTH BACKOUT AND SYNCPOINT
  PROCESSING IS COORDINATED BETWEEN THE
  SYSTEMS (AT THE APPROPRIATE SYNCLEVEL)

* APPLICATION PROGRAMS MUST BE DESIGNED TO CONVERSE
  WITH EACH OTHER BASED UPON APPLICATION DESIGNED
  PROTOCOLS

Figure 2-21 Special consideration for use of DTP.

single-system environment. Figure 2-21 lists special considerations in the use of Distributed Transaction Processing.

2.8   OVERVIEW OF SYSTEM REQUIREMENTS

In order to utilize any type of CICS Intercommunication, it is necessary to have available resources external to CICS and CICS table definitions. External resources include the hardware and software connections between the systems. CICS table definitions are required to define interconnected systems and, possibly, remote resources to be utilized.

2.8.1   General Requirements for Intercommunication

In the following chapters we will discuss some of the external resources beyond CICS that are needed in support of CICS InterSystem Communication. For now, suffice it to say that these things are required for there to be a connecting link between CICS systems in an

ISC environment. Although these objects exist outside of CICS, they obviously must be present. Within CICS the Terminal Control Table (TCT) contains a definition of interconnected systems. Each system's SYSIDNT or System ID is defined therein. The system definition is specific to the type of connection between particular systems. That is, MRO, LUTYPE 6.1, and LUTYPE 6.2 connections are defined uniquely and explicitly. **The TCT System definitions are always required for any type of Intercommunication.** Therefore, subsequent descriptions of table definitions particular to different functions of Intercommunication assume the presence of TCT System Definitions in all cases.

2.8.2   Table Entries for Transaction Routing

Transaction Routing requires that transactions be defined in both the terminal-owning and transaction-owning regions. The Program Control Table (PCT) is utilized to define both local and remote transactions. The terminal-owning region PCT must contain an entry for each remote transaction, and the transaction-owning region PCT must contain a local transaction definition. In addition, terminal definitions must be provided in the Terminal Control Table. In the terminal-owning region terminals are defined as local, and in the transaction-owning region terminals are defined as remote. **Thus, both regions in Transaction Routing require definitions of transactions and terminals.**

2.8.3   Table Entries for Resources Accessed Through Function Shipping

Resources accessed through Function Shipping require table definitions in the appropriate system tables. Files and Transient Data Queues require File Control Table and Destination Control Table entries, respectively, in the local resource-owning region. Temporary Storage Queues are defined in the local queue-owning region Temporary Storage Table, if such queues require security checking or are candidates for recovery. In addition to any local resource definition table entries, table entries may also be required in remote systems. If such remote table entries are not present, application programs utilizing Function Shipping services are required to include the SYSID option in resource access commands. The following sections provide a brief description of the information required in resource tables in remote sytems.

File Control Table — Remote Entries   In the File Control Table the systems programmer is able to provide a definition of remote files. The information specified includes the 1- to 8-character DDNAME used by application programs requesting access to the file. The ID of the remote file-owning system is also included, along with keylength and logical record size information. The remote file definition can optionally define a Resource Security Level for resource security checking, and a remote file name can be given. The remote file name, if included, provides an alternate name by which the file is known in the file-owning region. If a remote name is not specified, then the name of the file in the remote system is assumed to be the same as in the local system.

Temporary Storage Table — Remote Entries   The Temporary Storage Table can be utilized to define the queue names and system IDs of remote queues. As with remote FCT definitions, a remote queue name can also be specified if the queue is to have a different name in the queue-owning region.

Destination Control Table — Remote Entries   A DCT entry for a remote Transient Data Queue defines the DESTination ID or queue-name and the System ID of the queue-owning region. Optionally, a remote name, resource security level, and record size can be specified. If record length information is omitted from a queue's DCT entry, then application program commands accessing the remote queue must provide record size information.

Program Control Table — Remote Entries   Asynchronous   Processing utilizing the START command is considered to be a special case of Function Shipping. As such, remote TRANSIDs can be defined in the PCT. The System ID of the transaction-owning region is included along with other information in the PCT.

2.8.4   Local and Remote Table Entries for Distributed Transaction Processing

Aside from the SYSTEM definitions described above in the section dealing with the general requirements of Intercommunication, there are no remote table entries for Distributed Transaction Processing.

Of course, any transactions initiated in remote systems must be locally defined in the Program Control Table of the system in which the transaction is initiated.

2.8.5   Local and Remote Table Entries for Asynchronous Processing

Aside from the PCT definitions of remote transactions for Asynchronous Processing using the START Command as noted above and the SYSTEM definitions generally required there are no special definitions for Asynchronous Processing.

2.9   SUMMARY

We have now examined in some depth the different facilities available in CICS Intercommunication. We have also discussed the resources required to interconnect regions/systems and provided an overview of CICS table definitions. In subsequent chapters we will examine the internal CICS mechanisms that are used for each of the different facilities of Intercommunication. We will also address application programming issues in implementing distributed processing in CICS. However, before we proceed with these in-depth topics, it is advisable for us to digress and present some information on Systems Network Architecture, or SNA.

REVIEW EXERCISES

Mark each of the following True or False.

_____ 1.   When writing application programs that utilize Distributed Transaction Processing, it is necessary to know what type of connection exists between the systems in question.

_____ 2.   The ALLOCATE command permits a CICS transaction to request the use of an intersystem connection as an Alternate Facility.

_____ 3.   When a task completes its use of the intersystem connection, CICS terminates the connection.

_____ 4.   The mechanism by which a task initiates a remote process is somewhat specific to the type of connection between the systems.

___ 5. The CONNECT PROCESS command can be used over LUTYPE 6.2 connections. This command names the remote process (for CICS systems a TRANSID), can request a synchronization level for the conversation, and can name a PIPLIST. The PIPLIST names a data area with Process Initialization Parameter (PIP) data.

___ 6. Subsequent to the ALLOCATE command, CICS returns a CONVersation ID (CONVID) in the EIBRSRCE field. This value should be saved by the application program.

___ 7. PIP data is used by CICS and the systems programmer informs application programmers what values are required as PIP data.

___ 8. The CONVID value returned by CICS when a task's Alternate Facility is allocated must be referenced in any Terminal Control output commands directed to the Alternate Facility. Failure to provide the CONVID results in output being directed to a task's Principal Facility.

___ 9. During the processing of a distributed transaction, it is possible for both transactions to be sending data at the same time.

___ 10. In a distributed transaction conversation, one of the transactions is termed the Front-End Transaction and the other is called the Back-End Transaction. The one that initiates the remote process is the Back-End Transaction since transaction initiation is through an Alternate Facility or back-door type of resource.

Provide a short answer for each of the following.

1. What is the Front-End Transaction?
2. What is the Back-End Transaction?
3. What is meant by the term half-duplex as it pertains to the flow of data between distributed transactions?
4. When a distributed transaction is initiated, the Front-End and Back-End Transactions are in defined SEND/RECEIVE states. What is the status of the Front-End Transaction? The Back-End Transaction? How can the SEND/RECEIVE states be altered?
5. What is the ISSUE SIGNAL command? What does it cause to happen to the conversation partner's EIB? Cite one use for the ISSUE SIGNAL command.
6. What is the purpose of the INVITE option of the SEND command?

7. How does a transaction determine its SEND/RECEIVE state?
8. What is the purpose of the CONFIRM option of the SEND command? What does it do to the conversation partner's EIB?
9. What does the SYNCPOINT command cause to happen during a distributed transaction?
10. Why must programs that execute as parts of a distributed transaction be coordinated with each other?

ANSWERS TO REVIEW EXERCISE

Mark each of the following True or False.

1. **TRUE.** When writing application programs that utilize Distributed Transaction Processing, it is necessary to know what type of connection exists between the systems in question.
2. **TRUE.** The ALLOCATE command permits a CICS transaction to request the use of an intersystem connection as an Alternate Facility.
3. **FALSE.** When a task completes its use of the intersystem connection, CICS terminates the connection.
4. **TRUE.** The mechanism by which a task initiates a remote process is somewhat specific to the type of connection between the systems.
5. **TRUE.** The CONNECT PROCESS command can be used over LUTYPE 6.2 connections. This command names the remote process (for CICS systems a TRANSID), can request a synchronization level for the conversation, and can name a PIPLIST. The PIPLIST names a data area with Process Initialization Parameter (PIP) data.
6. **TRUE.** Subsequent to the ALLOCATE command, CICS returns a CONVersation ID (CONVID) in the EIBRSRCE field. This value should be saved by the application program.
7. **FALSE.** PIP data is used by CICS, and the systems programmer informs application programmers what values are required as PIP data.
8. **TRUE.** The CONVID value returned by CICS when a task's Alternate Facility is allocated must be referenced in any Terminal Control output commands directed to the Alternate Facility. Failure to provide the CONVID results in output being directed to a task's Principal Facility.

9. **FALSE.** During the processing of a distributed transaction, it is possible for both transactions to be sending data at the same time.

10. **FALSE.** In a distributed transaction conversation, one of the transactions is termed the Front-End Transaction and the other is called the Back-End Transaction. The one that initiates the remote process is the Back-End Transaction since transaction initiation is through an Alternate Facility or backdoor type of resource.

Provide a short answer for each of the following.

1. *What is the Front-End Transaction?*

The Front-End Transaction is the transaction that initiates the remote process. In order to do this the Front-End Transaction must acquire the use of a connection to a remote system. This is done with the ALLOCATE command naming the SYSID desired. CICS allocates a connection for the transaction's use and returns a CONVID in the EIBRSRCE field. This field value must be saved so that it can be referred to in any commands directed to the conversation.

The Front-End Transaction then initiates the remote process. For example, the CONNECT PROCESS command can be used for this purpose if the systems are connected via an LUTYPE 6.2 link.

2. *What is the Back-End Transaction?*

The Back-End Transaction is the transaction initiated by the Front-End Transaction. The Back-End Transaction resides in a system that is remote to the Front-End Transaction.

3. *What is meant by the term half-duplex as it pertains to the flow of data between distributed transactions?*

The term half-duplex in this context means that only one of the transactions can be SENDing data at a time. One of the transactions is in the SEND state and the other is in the RECEIVE state. Only a SEND state transaction can SEND.

4. *When a distributed transaction is initiated, the Front-End and Back-End Transactions are in defined SEND/RECEIVE states. What is the status of the Front-End Transaction? The Back-End Transaction? How can the SEND/RECEIVE states be altered?*

The Front-End Transaction is in the SEND state upon initiation of the distributed transaction. The Back-End Transaction is in the RECEIVE state. The SEND/RECEIVE states can be altered by the SEND state transaction. This is accomplished by including the INVITE option in a SEND command or issuing a CONVERSE command.

5. *What is the ISSUE SIGNAL command? What does it cause to happen to the conversation partner's EIB? Cite one use for the ISSUE SIGNAL command.*

The ISSUE SIGNAL command can be used to signal a conversation partner. This command turns on the EIBSIG field to indicate the signal. ISSUE SIGNAL can be used by a RECEIVE State transaction to request that its SEND state conversation partner reverse the SEND/RECEIVE status.

6. *What is the purpose of the INVITE option of the SEND command?*

The INVITE option of the SEND command is used to alter the SEND/RECEIVE states of conversing transactions. A transaction issuing a SEND INVITE is placed into the RECEIVE state and its conversation partner enters the SEND state.

7. *How does a transaction determine its SEND/RECEIVE state?*

A transaction can test the EIB to determine its SEND/RECEIVE state. If EIBRECV is set on (X'FF'), then the transaction is in the RECEIVE state. If this field is set off (X'00'), this indicates the SEND state.

8. *What is the purpose of the CONFIRM option of the SEND command? What does it do to the conversation partner's EIB?*

The CONFIRM option of the SEND command enables a transaction to request a confirmation from its conversation partner. Issuing a SEND CONFIRM causes the conversation partner's

EIBCONF field to be set on to indicate the request for confirmation.

9. *What does the SYNCPOINT command cause to happen during a distributed transaction?*

In this context a SYNCPOINT initiates commit protocols for the conversation. However, for LUTYPE 6.2 the synchronization level must support SYNCPOINTing.

10. *Why must programs that execute as parts of a distributed transaction be coordinated with each other?*

Programs that process as distributed transactions are essentially performing a single application unit of work even though it is being done by separate tasks in disperate systems. As such there must be coordination about what has to be done and the nature of data exchanged between them. However, further coordination is required because the programs must anticipate each other. If, for example, PIP data is sent, it must be obtained and understood by the Back-End Transaction. If one transaction uses the SEND CONFIRM to request private confirmation of processing, the other program must check EIB-CONF. The same situation applies to the use of other commands. The context and meaning of a conversation partner using a command such as ISSUE ERROR or ISSUE ABEND must be understood.

3

SNA — An Overview

3.1 INTRODUCTION

SNA is IBM's master plan for building communication-related products. As such it serves as a definition of the formats and protocols that are to be used by IBM product developers so that compatible products can be built. Communication-related products include online control systems such as CICS or IMS; telecommunication access methods such as ACF/VTAM or ACF/TCAM, host processors, communication controllers, software for communication controllers such as the Network Control Program, terminals, modems, control units, and so forth — in other words, all of the vast range of hardware and software that is used to construct a data communication network.

3.2 WHAT IS SNA?

What sets an SNA network apart from any old Brand X data communication network? SNA defines the formats and protocols used by communication-related products down to the bit level so that users of SNA products are assured a high degree of compatibility. This is important because networks are constantly growing, and if a new product is SNA-compatible, we can easily incorporate it into an SNA network. So, SNA defines all the rules and regulations for communication products. What exactly is it? SNA is an architecture or abstract plan that governs the development of SNA products.

In the last paragraph we defined SNA as an abstract plan. You can't buy a "can" of SNA, open it up, and have an SNA network. You can, however, pick and choose among SNA products according to your needs and requirements and from those products build an SNA network. Figure 3-1 illustrates a sample data communication network built with SNA products. There are three host processors, each of which has ACF/VTAM and a CICS/VS region. The host processors are channel attached to a communication controller, and each controller contains software labeled NCP, standing for *Network Control Program*. The communication controllers are connected to each other by remote data communication links. A communication link consists of some type of carrier facility, such as a telephone circuit and special equipment such as a modem which transforms the signal leaving the communication controller into a suitable format for transmission on the communication line. This sample network represents an implementation of SNA. But SNA has a life beyond this specific network or any particular products illustrated in it. SNA is an abstract plan or architecture.

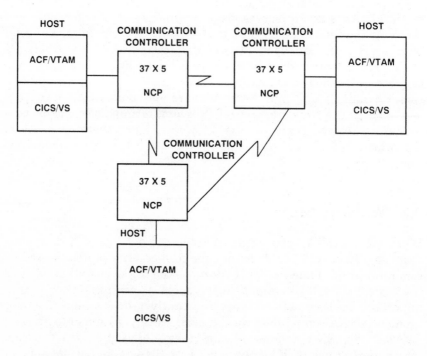

Figure 3-1 Sample SNA network.

3.3   SNA — NETWORK DEFINITION AND NAUS

According to SNA a network consists of two types of entities: *nodes* and *links*. A node is a machine such as a host, a communication controller, or a control unit. The links connect SNA nodes. Each SNA node has intelligence within it, and this intelligence is called a *Network Addressable Unit*, or *NAU*. What is a NAU? It is a unit of intelligence that is addressable by the network. In SNA there are three varieties of NAUs: the *SSCP*, the *PU*, and the *LU*.

3.4   THE SYSTEM SERVICE CONTROL POINT (SSCP)

The SSCP is a type of NAU that is in charge of a portion of the network called a *domain*. The SSCP, as its name implies, is a central control point for system services. What type of services? Activation, deactivation, and connection services are provided by the SSCP. The SSCP resides in an SNA access method. CICS, when it desires connection services, goes to VTAM, and VTAM acting as the SSCP aids CICS in establishing connections. To this end **the SSCP is a centralized place where control information is kept.**

3.5   THE PHYSICAL UNIT (PU)

The Physical Unit is the intelligence that manages the node's role with regard to the network. For example, nodes must be activated or brought online during network bringup. Nodes must also be deactivated during network shutdown. The PU is responsible for those sorts of functions. Basically **the PU is responsible for managing the node and its resources (such as links) in a network sense.**

3.6   THE LOGICAL UNIT (LU)

The Logical Unit, or LU, is the end user's port of access into the SNA network. For example, CICS application programs need to gain access to the SNA network so that they can send data in response to terminal operator queries. The program "plugs" into an LU. What exactly is an LU? Well, in the CICS Terminal Control Table there are definitions for terminals or other systems. For a CICS-VTAM environment, these definitions are Logical Units. So, input comes in from a terminal connected to CICS, and CICS initiates a task and anchors the task to an LU in the TCT. The LU in this context is a memory control area. However, an LU is more than that. For example, an application program conversing with a remote program to perform distributed transaction processing under CICS has different needs and requirements than an application program conversing with a dumb terminal such as a 3270. For distributed transaction processing we need coordinated commit/backout protocols to cite an example. This service is not required (it's not even relevant) for a program to 3270 "conversation."

3.7 TYPES OF LOGICAL UNITS

An SNA network can be viewed as a general purpose network that end users connect to. However, there are different kinds of end users. An end user can be a terminal, a terminal operator, or a program. Programs vary considerably in terms of their communication requirements. For example, a program may require very little service beyond basic send/receive correlation. Or a program performing distributed transaction processing may require many more services. The way that SNA "tailors" the general purpose network to specific end user requirements is by defining different kinds of Logical Units. So, the Logical Unit or end user's port varies based upon the end user's requirements. The synchronization service that we spoke of above is part of the support for LUTYPE6. The end user's port is a software port with a defined collection of services that are available. We will return to the types of Logical Units later in this chapter. For now we must deal with other matters.

3.8 SESSIONS BETWEEN NAUS

NAUs interact with each other to manage and control the SNA network and to provide connectivity between end users. In order for NAUs to exchange messages related to network management and control or in support of end user exchanges there must be a logical (as well as physical) connection between them. The logical connection is called a *session*. SNA defines five types of sessions: *SSCP-PU, SSCP-LU, PU-PU, SSCP-SSCP* and *LU-LU*. The first four types of sessions have to do with exchanges of SNA-defined commands between Network Addressable Units.

Figure 3-2 is a different mapping of the sample network depicted in Figure 3-1. Here, instead of seeing individual products, we see

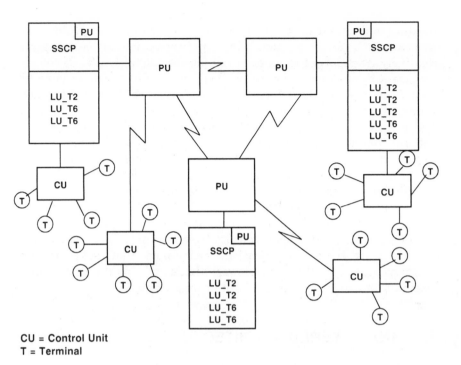

CU = Control Unit
T = Terminal

Figure 3-2 SNA Network with NAUs.

NAUs placed within six of the nodes in the network. We've also added some control units and terminals to the network. The control units are labeled "CU" and the terminals are labeled "T." Before a terminal user can log on to CICS or before a CICS program can engage in a distributed conversation with a remote CICS program, the network must first be activated. The access methods in the respective hosts are told to ACTivate the network. The SSCP within the access method responds by attempting to establish sessions with each of the PUs and LUs that it is responsible for.

An SSCP and all of its PUs and LUs (i.e., the LUs and PUs that the SSCP is responsible for) constitute a network domain. So we have three domains in our sample network. The SSCP-PU and SSCP-LU sessions serve to activate the resources within a domain and these sessions are used for network management and control functions. SSCP-SSCP sessions are performed in support of Cross-Domain communication. For example, if there is a need for a distributed conversation between two CICS programs residing in different hosts, the creation of the connection would begin with an SSCP-SSCP session. These "network-oriented" sessions are relatively transparent to us from the perspective of CICS. Of course, if these sessions cannot be established and if NAUs cannot perform their functions, we don't have a network. But we don't see the network-oriented sessions from CICS.

The sessions between Logical Units, or the LU-LU sessions, are not transparent to us. The LU-LU session is a logical connection and a collection of services without which our application programs would not be able to use the SNA network. We don't do anything to directly build these sessions. CICS takes care of that for us. When a session is needed to service a program's request, CICS can use an existing LU-LU session, if one is available, or it can *BIND* or initiate a session (with a little help from its friend VTAM). The LU-LU session is thus the communication mechanism that supports our programs accessing the SNA network. Let's end this discussion for a bit and talk about how SNA is built or organized.

3.9 SNA LAYERED ARCHITECTURE

The SNA network provides connectivity to end users such as application programs, enabling them to communicate with other end users. However, SNA is implemented as a highly functionalized architecture. This means that the services and facilities of an SNA network are provided in a highly functionalized and structured manner. SNA is not one large entity that provides all of the services required. Rather SNA is composed of a collection of layers. Each layer provides services, and it is the fact that a layer provides a particular set of services that is important. Each layer is largely insulated from other layers so that the "how to" of providing services does not impact other layers. This means that SNA is relatively easy to enhance and change.

The layers of SNA are illustrated in Figure 3-3. The five SNA layers are sandwiched in the middle and are bounded by continuous lines. Below what is architected in SNA is a physical interface layer. This layer describes things like electrical voltages used for signaling between connected devices, size of connectors, and the physical aspects of communication. SNA does not define this "layer" as there are industrywide standards that are developed by standards organizations. An example of a physical interface is RS-232, which is used to physically connect and define the signaling between devices.

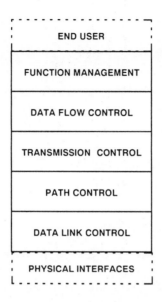

Figure 3-3 SNA layered architecture.

At the very top is the end user. Sometimes this is called the application layer. SNA also does not define the application layer. Rather, it provides services to the end user. The services are provided by each of the layers of SNA. Through the services of the five layers of SNA, end users have a reliable error-free connection with other end users.

3.10 DATA LINK CONTROL — THE LOWEST LAYER OF SNA

The scope of the *Data Link Control Layer* of SNA is depicted in Figure 3-4. Data Link Control is responsible for managing data links so that messages can be transmitted successfully between nodes. Data Link Control is responsible for transmit/receive functions between nodes, the detection of communication errors, recovery from communication errors by retransmitting corrupted messages, and generally making sure that messages are not lost. **The work of this layer transforms a physical communication circuit into a virtually error-free connection between nodes.**

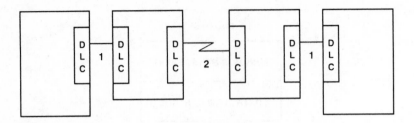

1 = Channel Protocol
2 = Synchronous Data Link Control (SDLC)

Figure 3-4 Data Link Control Layer.

Therefore, the other layers of SNA and the end user as well need not be concerned with message transmission. This service provided by Data Link Control is important in the SNA network because without it we would not have a basis for passing messages between nodes. However, how Data Link Control manages this service is not important to the higher layers. Data Link Control has its own protocols or means of performing its role in SNA. In Figure 3-4 we have four nodes connected and three "links" between them. This illustration might represent two hosts and two communication controllers between them. Data Link Control protocols are: the IBM channel protocol for channel attached devices and a link control protocol called *Synchronous Data Link Control* or *SDLC*, which is used on remote data links.

3.11   PATH CONTROL LAYER — THE ROUTING LAYER

Data Link Control takes care of data links. However, we also need to have messages routed source to destination. That is the role of the *Path Control Layer* of SNA. Path Control intelligence in a source node constructs a routing header (called a *Transmission Header*) which is appended to messages. In each intervening node, Path Control intelligence looks at this header and makes a routing decision until the destination node and ultimate destination are reached. Path Control manages the routes through the SNA network. This includes ensuring that messages leave the SNA network in the order that they entered it. So if one end user sends five messages to another end user, those messages will arrive and be presented in order rather than higgledy-piggledy. Network congestion is also

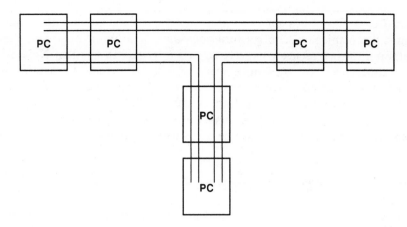

Figure 3-5 Path Control Layer of SNA.

managed by Path Control. Figure 3-5 illustrates the scope of the Path Control Layer. Note that there are no links depicted in this diagram. That's because Path Control doesn't worry about links. It doesn't have to because that function is managed by a lower layer. Well, in the same way, the layers above Path Control do not worry about network routing.

3.12   THE PATH CONTROL NETWORK

The *Path Control Network* consists of the two lowest layers of SNA. The Path Control Network can be thought of as a general purpose delivery system. Its services are not oriented toward any particular end user. Rather, the Path Control network is concerned with providing a fast and efficient delivery system between any connected Network Addressable Units, including LUs and the end users who access the SNA network through their Logical Units. The role of providing specific services as needed by end users is the role of the higher layers.

3.13   TRANSMISSION CONTROL

The *Transmission Control Layer* is responsible for providing the transmission services needed by NAUs during their sessions. Each different type of NAU, including Logical Units, requires Transmission Control services for the messages exchanged during their sessions. Transmission Control functions as a "mailman" ensuring that outgoing messages are correctly routed to the Path Control Network and that incoming messages are correctly directed. Transmission Control also ensures that *session level pacing* is used so that end users are not overrun with data. **Transmission Control services are session specific** so that, based upon session requirements customized Transmission Control services can be provided.

3.14 DATA FLOW CONTROL

It is the role of *Data Flow Control* to control the flow of data within sessions so that the session partners have a "connection" that is meaningful to their exchange. They may, for example, require a correlation between SEND/RECEIVE functions so that their network connection appears to be a half-duplex connection. If so, Data Flow Control provides the mechanisms to enforce a half-duplex logical connection for the session. In that case, only one of the end users can send at a time. However, if the session partners don't need such a service, they can both send and receive at any time or have a logical full duplex connection. It is important to point out that the Data Flow Control Send/Receive Mode makes a network connection "appear" half-duplex, for example, but this does not mean that the underlying Path Control Network is operating in a half-duplex transmission mode.

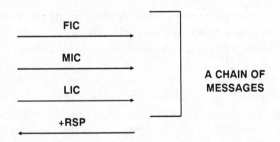

FIC = FIRST IN CHAIN
MIC = MIDDLE IN CHAIN
LIC = LAST IN CHAIN

Figure 3-6 A message chain is a group of messages that are related for recovery purposes.

Data Flow Control can group related messages flowing in one direction in a process referred to as *"chaining."* Chains are used to transmit multiple messages that are related and should be treated as a single unit for recovery purposes. If something goes wrong with one of the messages in a chain, all of the chained messages are to be discarded. Figure 3-6 illustrates chaining.

Another flow control mechanism provided within Data Flow Control is *Bracket Protocol*. Bracket Protocol involves the bracketing off of a collection of messages in both directions as one unit of work. A bracket may involve a chain in one direction followed by a chain in the other direction. But the point is that the seemingly unrelated transmissions from the network perspective are viewed as a part of a unit of work from the data flow control perspective. Figure 3-7 illustrates Bracket Protocol. The Bracket begins with a *Begin Bracket (BB) Indicator*. All messages that follow the Begin Bracket until the bracket is ended with the *End Bracket (EB) Indicator* are perceived to be a related unit of work.

For example, in program-to-program communication, program one may send several messages containing data records to be saved in a queue or database. After updating protected resources, program two sends back confirmations of updates. The programs which are processing in different SNA nodes then commit their modifications to protected resources by exchanging SYNCPOINT Indicators. At this point the unit of work is complete, and the End Bracket Indicator

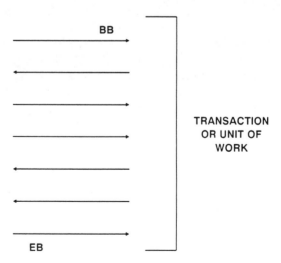

Figure 3-7 Bracket protocol.

terminates the bracket. **Bracket Protocol is normally used by transaction processing systems such as CICS as a way of correlating and keeping track of the separate data flows that make up a transaction.** The layers which we've spoken about up to but not including Data Flow Control are provided within the telecommunication access method or within the Network Control Program. However, Data Flow Control is managed by CICS or an equivalent online control system.

3.15   FUNCTION MANAGEMENT

Function Management is a rather complex layer of SNA which provides a variety of services. The Function Management services that we are concerned with from the vantage point of CICS and especially CICS InterSystem Communication are called *End User Services*, and Logical Units are the mechanism by which End User Services are provided.

End User Services allow Logical Units, to provide services for end user exchanges of information. End User Services are of two major varieties. First there are *Session Presentation Services*, which encompass data formatting, mapping, compaction, or compression if appropriate to the end user requirements. In other words, Session Presentation Services can perform data transformations to facilitate or optimize end user communication.

Second, there are *Application-to-Application Services*, which support facilities provided in LU-LU connections between Transaction Processing Systems such as CICS or IMS. Application-to-Application Services have three functions. 1) They enable application programs running in Transaction Processing Systems to access databases, files, queues or other resources without regard for where the resources are located within the SNA Network. 2) They coordinate SYNCPOINT or backout across the execution of separate programs executing in joined Transaction Processing Systems to ensure the consistency of protected resources. 3) They provide facilities that permit application programs to communicate with each other to perform distributed units of work without being concerned about network communication protocols.

Of course, these things sound familiar because we've discussed CICS Function Shipping, which permits CICS programs to access resources without regard for the location of the resource within the SNA network. We've discussed the fact that CICS provides coordination of SYNCPOINT processing across regions. And we've also discussed the CICS Distributed Transaction Processing facility which permits programs to communicate with each other without regard for network communication protocols. These end user services are provided within the LUTYPE 6 support in CICS.

3.16 SESSIONS BETWEEN LOGICAL UNITS

We have defined a session as a logical connection between two Network Addressable Units, and we described two classes of sessions, those that are oriented toward network functionality and those that are oriented toward end user connections. We identified this latter category as LU-LU sessions. Since there are different kinds of end users, there must be flexibility in the creation of LU-LU sessions so that the **appropriate Transmission Control, Data Flow Control, and Function Management services can be provided** according to the requirements of the particular end users in sessions.

Flexibility in the creation of LU-LU sessions is accomplished through three mechanisms. First, there are different types of Logical Units suited to different kinds of end users. A program communicating with a 3270 video terminal uses one type of LU. A program running in a Transaction Processing System such as CICS that communicates with another program also executing in a Transaction Processing System to accomplish Distributed Transaction Processing uses another type of LU. Why different LUTYPEs? Because the end users described above have different functional requirements which must be derived from their LUs or access ports into the SNA Network. Associated with different LUTYPEs are different sets of functional capabilities. An LU-LU session can only be bound between like LUTYPEs; so, an LU-LU session represents the joining of matched ports.

The second mechanism used to provide flexibility for LU-LU sessions is the use of NAU Services profiles. The profiles are used to define sets of Transmission Services, Function Management Services, Data Flow Control Services, and Presentation Services that are appropriate to different types of NAU sessions and different types of LU-LU sessions. Through the use of these profiles, sessions between Logical Units are tailored based upon LUTYPE to the precise needs of the session partners.

The third mechanism used in providing flexibility for LU-LU sessions can be found in the actual session initiation or BINDing. When a BIND or session initiation request is sent, it is accompanied by a data area that identifies the particular Transmission Services, Function Management and Data Flow Control services for the session as well as other information that defines the specific rules governing session communication protocols. BINDs can be *negotiable* or *non-negotiable*. For a negotiable BIND request, the BIND receiver is able to override certain session options defined during BINDing.

3.17   LUTYPEs

There are six different types of Logical Units: *LUTYPE 0, LUTYPE 1, LUTYPE 2, LUTYPE 3, LUTYPE 4,* and *LUTYPE 6*. LUTYPE 6, which comes in different flavors (LUTYPE 6.1 or LUTYPE 6.2), we will treat as a single LUTYPE for our purposes in this section of the text. Sessions are only possible between like LUTYPEs. So, for example, a session can be bound between LUTYPE 0-to-LUTYPE 0 or between LUTYPE 1-to-LUTYPE 1. However, a session cannot be bound between different LUTYPEs. There can never be, therefore, a session between an LUTYPE 1 and an LUTYPE 6. Why? Because an LUTYPE corresponds to a particular functional set of services, facilities, requirements, and session operational capabilities. Different LUTYPEs are used in support of different devices and/or data streams.

3.17.1   LUTYPE 0 or LU_T0

LUTYPE 0 is defined as a general catchall LU, intended for situations where a particular device and/or communication data stream are not suited to the remaining LUTYPEs.

3.17.2   LUTYPE 1 or LU_T1

LUTYPE 1 is used for sessions between a Logical Unit and another Logical Unit with multiple logical devices or I/O destinations such as printers and data storage devices. This type of session controls the different types of I/O devices associated with the Logical Unit.

3.17.3   LUTYPE 2 or LU_T2

LUTYPE 2 sessions allow an application program and a display device utilizing the 3270 Data Stream to communicate.

3.17.4   LUTYPE 3 or LU_T3

LUTYPE 3 sessions permit communication between an application program and a printer utilizing the 3270 Data Stream.

3.17.5   LUTYPE 4 or LU_T4

LUTYPE 4 sessions are used in several contexts. Such sessions support communication 1) between two terminals, 2) between an application program and a single device terminal, or 3) between an application program and a multi-device terminal. In Data Processing applications, LUTYPE 1 sessions and LUTYPE 4 sessions resemble each other. The LUTYPE 4 session can also be used for word processing applications.

3.17.6   LUTYPE 6 or LU_T6

LUTYPE 6 sessions support program-to-program communication in a distributed processing environment. Such sessions are used to connect Transaction Processing Systems such as CICS or IMS. The session is used to connect the Transaction Processing Systems in question. Within the Transaction Processing Systems, as a feature of LUTYPE 6 support, functionality is implemented to provided support for application program access to distributed resources. This ability to access remote resources permits files, queues, databases, and other resources distributed throughout an SNA network to be made available to application programs in connected systems.

Another LUTYPE 6 function which may be provided in Transaction Processing Systems is a conversational capability between distributed application programs. In this context, the application programs converse over an LUTYPE 6 session. The session is temporarily allocated for the conversation between the distributed programs so that they can perform a distributed transaction. **Distributed transactions take place within a single bracket.** Within a bracket, there is support for synchronization of modifications to protected resources. The termination of the program dialog is indicated by the End Bracket (EB) indicator. The session between the Transaction Processing Systems can then be used for other purposes such as other distributed transactions. As part of the architectural definition of the LUTYPE 6, there is support for *parallel sessions*. Parallel sessions enable two LUTYPE6s to have multiple sessions so that their communication capacity is enhanced without incurring the overhead of having multiple LUs. LUTYPE 6 sessions typically take place in multi-domain SNA networks.

3.18   LUTYPE 6.2 ADVANCED PROGRAM-TO-PROGRAM COMMUNICATION

As mentioned before, there are several flavors of the LUTYPE 6. The LUTYPE 6.2 is one of those variants. The LUTYPE 6.2 represents the fullest architectural functionality for program-to-program communication. The unique features of the LUTYPE 6.2 include: a true any-to-any connection, the use of Parallel Sessions between LUs, an application interface or *protocol boundary* between application programs and their Logical Units, the ability to pass Process Initialization Parameters, and varying synchronization levels. There is greater flexibility for sessions between system level products, and there is also support for non–system level products or LUTYPE 6.2 terminals.

3.18.1   Support Peripheral Node Programs

LUTYPE 6.2 is the only LUTYPE 6 that permits conversations peer-to-peer between programs executing in hosts, programs executing in less intelligent or peripheral nodes, or a program executing in a host and a program executing in a peripheral node. As such the LUTYPE 6.2 provides an any-to-any connection so that programs can engage in *Advanced Program-to-Program Communication (APPC)*. The term APPC is thus synonymous with LUTYPE 6.2. In contrast, the LUTYPE 6.1 supports sessions only between system level products.

3.18.2   LUTYPE 6.2 Protocol Boundary

In order to obtain application-to-application services, it is necessary for an application program or, as it is called in this context, a Transaction Processing Program to be able to request such services. To this end, SNA defines a protocol boundary between Transaction Processing Programs and the LUTYPE 6.2. The protocol boundary provides the mechanisms by which services are requested by Transaction Processing Programs. This protocol boundary consists of a defined set of service verbs or commands. Not only are protocol boundary verbs/commands defined, but command options and data values returned as a result of command execution are likewise defined in SNA. This architected language is documented in detail in the IBM Reference Manual entitled *Systems Network Architecture Transaction Programmer's Reference Manual for LU Type 6.2* GC30-3084.

This, however, does not mean that an application programmer developing an LUTYPE 6.2 Transaction Processing Program needs to code the protocol boundary verbs/commands. A Transaction Processing System may, in fact, provide a set of commands built in accordance with SNA's LUTYPE 6.2 protocol boundary. In CICS, for example, EXEC CICS commands are utilized in application programs. The EXEC CICS commands correspond functionally to the application interface provided by the LUTYPE 6.2 protocol boundary.

To provide a flavor of the LUTYPE 6.2 protocol boundary, we will consider an example. An application program is activated in a Transaction Processing System. As part of the program's function it needs to engage in a distributed dialog with a remote program. The program requires temporary use of an intersystem session. In the LUTYPE 6.2 there is a differentiation between a session which is a system resource and a *conversation* which is a distributed transaction that takes place between SNA brackets over an intersystem session. As a part of the architected protocol boundary of the LUTYPE 6.2 a command to request the use of an intersystem connection is provided. If an appropriate session is already in place, it can be utilized by the Transaction Processing System to fulfill the request. Otherwise, a session is initiated.

Once use of a session has been allocated to a Transaction Processing Program, it needs to cause its conversation partner, a remote program, to be activated. Again, the protocol boundary provides a mechanism for accomplishing this. There is also a facility for passing initialization information when a program is activated. (This is discussed below in the section on Process Initialization Parameters.) Subsequent to the activation of the remote process, the protocol boundary defines commands to be used by the conversing programs. They need to send/receive data, signal each other about respective status, and because their conversation is taking place over a half-duplex flip-flop connection in which brackets are used, they need to be able to indicate when a change of direction is needed. The protocol boundary provides verbs/commands to accomplish these things. The protocol boundary also provides commands to commit distributed modifications to protected resources and to end the conversation and thereby free the session. When the conversation is over, the session between the Transaction Processing Systems can be utilized for other conversations.

3.18.3 Process Initialization Parameters or PIP Data

As part of the conversational capability architected for the LUTYPE 6.2, initialization parameters can be passed to a remote program being initiated. These parameters are called Process Initialization Parameters or PIP data.

3.18.4 Base and Mapped Conversations

There are two types of conversations that can be conducted over an LUTYPE 6.2 session, and there are verbs/commands associated with each. Base conversations use a set of verbs that require a program to build and interpret headers called Generalized Data Stream (GDS) headers. Mapped conversation verbs make the SNA data stream transparent to the program. Thus the *mapped conversation* is a higher level conversation. *Base conversation* verbs would be used for Transaction Processing Programs whose conversation partner's LU does not support the mapped interface. Functionally, the two command sets are similar.

3.18.5 Synchronization Levels

Synchronization is also more flexible for LUTYPE 6.2 sessions. For peripheral node programs, which may not be able to support protected resource definition and SYNCPOINT/backout processing, the synchronization level can be determined when the session is bound. There are three levels of synchronization: no synchronization, private synchronization between the application processes and full SYNCPOINT synchronization. Full SYNCPOINT synchronization means that the Logical Units support the definition of protected resources and provide both backout and commit services. Mainframe Transaction Processing Systems such as CICS or IMS provide these application services.

If these application-to-application services are not available in both Logical Units, the session can still be bound but with a lower level of synchronization. Private synchronization means that the Transaction Processing Programs can exchange status information regarding their ability to complete the unit of work. The LUTYPE 6.2 protocol boundary provides commands for such confirmation requests and responses. However, any backout processing, if required, is the responsibility of the application processes. No synchronization means exactly that; neither syncpointing nor private confirmations are exchanged during conversations over the session. The maximum synchronization is determined when the session is bound and conversations using the session cannot exceed the maximum synchronization level. They can, however, have a lower synchronization level.

3.18.6   Minimum Function Set for LUTYPE 6.2 Implementation

SNA is an architecture and is, therefore, more encompassing than a particular implemented product. For example, product developers may not need or desire to support all of the architected functionality of the LUTYPE 6.2. As part of the LUTYPE 6.2 architecture there is a minimum functional set defined. For a product to support LUTYPE 6.2 it must implement this minimum set. Support for the base conversation verbs described above is included in this minimum functional set. Beyond the minimum functional set, there are optional functions which product developers may or may not elect to implement. The mapped conversation verbs are included in the optional functions.

3.19   SUMMARY

In the first two chapters of this text we examined the functionality of CICS Intercommunication. In this chapter we looked at IBM's Systems Network Architecture so that the reader could become acquainted with SNA concepts that will be helpful in using CICS ISC. Additionally, the reader gained perspective about where CICS Inter-System Communication fits in the grand scheme of things. CICS ISC is an implementation of SNA ISC. At first glance that sounds like CICS ISC is not some great and unique thing. Well, thank goodness it's not. Since CICS ISC is built upon SNA, it can communicate with other products that implement a compatible set of SNA ISC functionality.

REVIEW EXERCISES

Provide a short answer to each of the following.

1. What is SNA?
2. What role does Data Flow Control play in end user communication?
3. Cite three SNA Application-to-Application Services.
4. What is the Path Control Network, and what is its role?

Match each of the following terms with a definition below.

____ 1. LU
____ 2. NAU
____ 3. node
____ 4. SSCP
____ 5. Bracket Protocol
____ 6. PU
____ 7. APPC
____ 8. Protocol Boundary
____ 9. Parallel sessions
____ 10. Session

A. Another name for LUTYPE 6.2.
B. A unit of intelligence contained in an SNA node.
C. The end user's port into the SNA network. This "port" provides services needed by the end user.
D. A way of marking the message flows that constitute a transaction.
E. A logical pairing or connecting of two NAUs.
F. A machine in an SNA network.
G. A mechanism which permits multiple connections between LUTYPE 6s.
H. The manager of an SNA domain. This unit of intelligence provides activation, deactivation, and connection services.
I. A unit of intelligence that manages a node and the node's resources in a network sense.
J. A defined set of verbs or commands that are provided for a program's interface with the LUTYPE 6.2.

ANSWERS TO REVIEW EXERCISES

Provide a short answer to each of the following.

1. *What is SNA?*

    SNA is an architecture or master plan developed by IBM. The
    role of SNA is to provide a cohesive and detailed set of formats
    and protocols for SNA compatible communication related
    products. Thus SNA serves as a blueprint for IBM product
    developers.

2. *What role does Data Flow Control play in end user communica-
    tion?*

    Data Flow Control controls the flow of data to end users. For
    example, if they require a send/receive correlation that is half-
    duplex, this is enforced by Data Flow Control. Data Flow Con-
    trol also manages Bracket Protocol, which is a mechanism for
    bracketing off the separate messages that constitute a unit of
    work.

3. *Cite three SNA Application-to-Application Services.*

    a. Access to resources without regard to the location of such
        resources in the SNA Network.

    b. Synchronization services so that a distributed unit of work
        can be jointly committed or backed out.

    c. A conversational capability that permits programs to
        engage in a conversation without regard for network com-
        munication protocols.

4. *What is the Path Control Network, and what is its role?*

    The Path Control Network is composed of the two lowest layers
    of SNA: Data Link Control and Path Control. The role of the
    Path Control Network is to provide a reliable and effective
    message delivery service between source and destination nodes.

Match each of the following terms with a definition below.

C	1.	LU
B	2.	NAU
F	3.	node
H	4.	SSCP
D	5.	Bracket Protocol
I	6.	PU
A	7.	APPC
J	8.	Protocol Boundary
G	9.	Parallel sessions
E	10.	Session

4

CICS Installation and Link Definitions

4.1 INTRODUCTION

In this and subsequent chapters, we will examine in depth the Intercommunication facilities of Transaction Routing, Function Shipping, Asynchronous Processing, and Distributed Transaction Processing. This examination will include a discussion of the CICS mechanisms that are utilized in providing these services, application programming considerations for utilizing each of these facilities, and the system requirements and resource definitions needed. The latter category of system requirements and resource definitions can be viewed from two perspectives. There are general requirements for Intercommunication. There are also specific resource definition requirements for Transaction Routing, Function Shipping and Asynchronous Processing.

The general requirements are applicable to *all* types of Intercommunication. The general requirements are threefold: 1) installing CICS correctly so that it can utilize Intercommunication; 2) making appropriate external definitions in MVS and ACF/VTAM regarding CICS Intercommunication; 3) defining the Links and Sessions which serve to interconnect CICS to its Intercommunication partner. The Intercommunication partner may be: 1) for MRO, another CICS region/address space within the same machine; 2) for ISC LUTYPE 6.1 Links, another CICS system or an IMS system connected via an SNA network; or 3) for ISC LUTYPE 6.2 Links, another CICS system, or any other system level or device level product connected via an SNA network. For LUTYPE 6.2, prospective session partners must support a subset of LUTYPE 6.2 protocols that are compatible with CICS LUTYPE 6.2 protocols. Compatibility in this case means that other system/device support for LUTYPE 6.2 does not preclude the BINDing of sessions with CICS. Compatibility does not mean that the exact same subsets of LUTYPE 6.2 functionality are provided in non-CICS products. We will address the general requirements first and then proceed with a discussion of each of the Intercommunication Facilities of Transaction Routing, Function Shipping, and Asynchronous Processing.

4.2   INSTALLATION REQUIREMENTS

There are separate installation requirements to support MRO and ISC. For MRO, it is necessary to 1) link edit the CICS Type 2 SVC to the MVS nucleus; 2) ensure that CICS is defined as an MVS subsystem; 3) place DFHIRP into the Link Pack Area (LPA); 4) include the appropriate management facilities in CICS; and 5) establish a procedure for the CICS logon to InterRegion Communication.

For ISC, it is necessary to 1) ensure that CICS is properly defined to ACF/VTAM; and 2) include the appropriate management facilities in CICS.

4.2.1   MRO Installation — The Type 2 SVC

CICS Terminal Control Facility provides the interface between a CICS region and the passing of data to another region in support of MRO. The process by which such information is exchanged by CICS regions is termed InterRegion Communication. MRO InterRegion Communication (IRC) can take place in one of two ways: 1) utilizing MVS cross memory services, or 2) invoking the interregion program (DFHIRP). Cross memory services involves sharing storage across the separate address spaces. This is accomplished via cross-memory instructions and is subject to storage key protection.

The alternative to cross-memory services is to use InterRegion Communication modules which execute in supervisory state and transmit data between the CICS regions. This process is initiated by invoking DFHIRP via a supervisor call to an SVC routine. The SVC routine is provided with CICS, is named DFHCSVC, and has the SVC number 216. This SVC routine must be link edited to the MVS nucleus so that DFHIRP can be invoked. However, the Type 2 SVC is used in support of other CICS facilities as well. For example, CICS support for standard label tape journals, page fixing, anticipatory paging, eXtended Recovery Feature (XRF), subtask authorization used for VSAM, monitoring, external security, and other features require the Type 2 SVC. So this is not something that has to be done solely to support MRO.

In order to use MRO it is necessary for CICS to log on to the InterRegion Communication Access Method. This effectively opens the IRC link. DFHIRP is called to do this. Therefore, even if cross-memory services are used for actual data transfers, the Type 2 SVC is required so that the IRC link can be opened (and subsequently closed when no longer needed or CICS is coming down).

4.2.2 MRO Installation — CICS Definition as MVS Subsystem

MRO requires that CICS be defined as an MVS subsystem. The recommended method for accomplishing this is to place a record defining CICS in the system data set containing initialization information for MVS. This data set is called SYS1.PARMLIB. The record for CICS is 12 characters long and contains CICS followed by 8 spaces. This record is placed in a member of SYS1.PARMLIB called IEFSSNss where the lower case "ss" indicates a suffix. MVS obtains general initialization information from another member of SYS1.PARMLIB called IEASYSss. Again "ss" indicates a suffix which is normally "00." MVS looks for initialization information in IEASYS00 but can be directed to obtain additional initialization information from another SYS1.PARMLIB member named IEASYSss where the suffix is other than "00." However, the suffix of an extra IEASYSss must be provided at IPL time. Information in IEASYS00 or another IEASYSss must point to the IEFSSNss member containing the CICS record. This is accomplished by including the parameter SSN= in IEASYSss. The SSN= parameter provides the suffix name of the IEFSSNss member containing the CICS record. This procedure enables CICS to obtain the MVS SubSystem Interface (SSI) support required for Multi-Region Operation.

Although the method described above is the recommended procedure for defining CICS as an MVS subsystem, there are two other procedures that can be followed as well. One of these is to identify CICS as a subsystem in the MVS system generation SCHEDULR macro. This macro includes a SUBSYS parameter, and CICS can be named therein. The final method is to use AMASPZAP to zap a member of SYS1.LINKLIB. This member, IEFJSSNT, is a nonexecutable load module with a limited number of null table entries. One of the null entries can be super zapped to contain "CICS" followed by 8 spaces. The non-null entries of IEFJSSNT are used to supplement sysgen SUBSYS information during MVS initialization.

4.2.3 MRO Installation — Installing DFHIRP into the LPA

The MVS Link Pack Area or LPA is a protected storage area that can be shared by multiple regions. DFHIRP, the CICS InterRegion Program, must be placed therein. There is read-only access to modules in the LPA so any programs that are installed therein must be reentrant and link edited with the RENT attribute. The pregenerated version of DFHIRP is link edited correctly for LPA installation. Another InterRegion module, DFHCRC (used as the Intercommunication ESTAE exit for handling task abends) may also be placed in the LPA. This, however, is recommended only if the computer facility is using only release consistent CICS systems. The reason for this is that downward compatibility is not ensured. As an alternative, each separate region can have a private copy of DFHCRC which is placed in the CICS address space in protected storage. A module is placed in the LPA by naming it in a member of SYS1.PARMLIB called LPALSTss.

4.2.4 MRO Installation — Required CICS Management Modules

In support of MRO Function Shipping, Asynchronous Processing, and Distributed Transaction Processing, the command level EXEC Interface is required. If the EXEC Interface is not included, the only Intercommunication facility available is Transaction Routing, which is supported for both command and macro level programs.

MRO also requires the InterSystem communication program, DFHISP, and the Terminal Control Program. The Terminal Control Program must provide support for the InterRegion Communication access method. In the CICS pregenerated system all versions of Terminal Control provide this support. If generating a new version of Terminal Control, the IRC access method must be included in the generation options for ACCMETH=. Lastly, the System Recovery Program, DFHSRP, is required also.

These modules, the EXEC Interface, the InterSystem communication Program, Terminal Control Programs, and System Recovery

Program can be included in a CICS system by 1) coding appropriate System Initialization Table (SIT) options: EXEC=, ISC=, TCP=, ZCP= and SRT= or 2) providing such values during CICS startup. TCP and ZCP options provide identifying information about the Terminal Control Programs.

4.2.5   MRO Installation — CICS Connection to IRC

In order for CICS to use MRO connections, it is first necessary to connect to the IRC access method. As described above, this requires the Type 2 SVC. This connection can be established automatically during system initialization of CICS or subsequently by manual use of CEMT. To connect CICS during initialization, code IRCSTRT=YES in the System Initialization Table (SIT) or include IRCSTRT=YES as an initialization override. Otherwise, a master terminal operator can use the command: CEMT SET IRC OPEN to establish the connection.

4.2.6   ISC Installation — Defining CICS to ACF/VTAM

An application program major node, in this case CICS, must be defined to ACF/VTAM via an *APPL statement* that is included with other ACF/VTAM resource definition statements. The APPL statement is used to provide ACF/VTAM with information about CICS. This task is part of generating ACF/VTAM resource definitions and is not done within CICS. It is, however, necessary to know the *AP-PLID* or VTAM name given to CICS via the APPL statement as this APPLID must be provided in the CICS System Initialization Table. The following represents a sample APPL statement to define a CICS system:

```
S001CICS APPL   AUTH=(ACQ,PASS,SPO,VPACE),EAS=1000,         X
                HAVAIL=YES,SONSCIP=YES,VPACING=10,          X
                PARSESS=YES
```

S001CICS is the APPLID of this CICS system. The APPLID provided in the CICS System Initialization Table connects CICS to the information provided in the APPL statement defined to VTAM. It is also necessary to ensure that the information provided in the APPL statement correctly reflects CICS's requirements.

The APPL statement is used to define the number of sessions with other NAUs that CICS can have, and this includes parallel LUTYPE 6 sessions. This value is supplied with the EAS=number parameter. If CICS has more concurrent sessions than the number defined in EAS=, then the execution path in VTAM is increased. PAR-SESS=YES is also required if CICS is to engage in parallel sessions. Since the default is "NO," this option should be included to ensure that CICS can have parallel sessions. SONSCIP=YES is included so that CICS is notified of session failures. If this is coded, VTAM ends the session and sends CICS an RU or message that describes the failure.

During the process of session initialization, VTAM in its role as SSCP is given a logon mode name which corresponds to an entry in a logon mode table. This table entry contains a subset of BIND options that are applicable for the session being initiated. CICS may require entries in a logon mode table, and there are two ways that this can be done. VTAM comes with an IBM-supplied default table to which CICS's entries can be added, or a separate logon mode table with CICS's entries can be created. If this latter course is elected, the logon mode table with CICS's entries must be named with the MODETAB= parameter of the APPL statement. The primary purpose of logon mode table entries for CICS InterSystem Communication is to identify a VTAM *class of service* for LUTYPE 6.2 sessions. These sessions are defined in session groups, and each group can specify a MODENAME which relates to a Logon Mode Table Entry.

Class of service is based upon a Virtual Route/Priority within the Path Control Network. VTAM has a class-of-service table identifying Virtual Routes appropriate to a particular classes of service. A logon mode table entry identifies the appropriate class-of-service table entry. CICS uses the BIND information in the logon mode table entry for automatic installation of LUTYPE 6.2 terminals. Otherwise, for LUTYPE 6 connections this information is not utilized.

Control options are identified via the APPL statement AUTH= parameter. Values can be coded to permit CICS to acquire sessions (AUTH=ACQ), have session level pacing on intersystem flows (AUTH=VPACE), and pass terminal sessions to other VTAM applications (AUTH=PASS). The VPACING=number option is used to indicate CICS's pacing count or the number of normal flow RUs or message units that can be sent to it over sessions without CICS providing a pacing response. VPACING is an important value because if it is too high CICS will require large amounts of storage to accommodate all of the input. On the other hand, if VPACING is too low, CICS is forced to send more pacing responses which result in network data flows and thereby, impact throughput. Valid VPACING values are from 0 through 63. No pacing is performed if this option is omitted or if set to 0.

There are two more things that can be coded on the APPL statement that are pertinent to utilizing the *eXtended Recovery Facility (XRF)* of CICS 2.1. These are AUTH=SPO and the HAVAIL option. In XRF there is a pair of CICS systems. The "active system" is up and running and handling CICS transactions. There is also an "alternate system," which is partially initialized and waiting in the event that the active CICS fails. When a failure occurs, the alternate system detects the failure and performs an emergency restart and takes over the CICS workload. Some terminals are XRF-capable, and these terminals benefit from XRF because when the alternate system takes over and becomes the active CICS, it can take over their sessions without operator intervention.

Separate APPL statements define both the active and alternate CICS systems providing them with unique APPLIDs that define them to VTAM. When XRF is supported the APPL statements include AUTH=SPO and HAVAIL=YES. HAVAIL allows a system to support XRF sessions. The currently active CICS system has active sessions. The alternate CICS system has a backup session with any XRF capable terminals that are logged on to the active CICS. The backup session is used after a failure and ensuing takeover so that CICS can reestablish the terminal session without operator intervention. So, for CICS systems using XRF, it is necessary to include HAVAIL=YES on the APPL statement since the default is NO.

The only potential glitch with XRF is that it would be undesirable for end users and other systems to have to know which of the CICS systems, in the XRF pair, is currently active for logon/session initiation purposes. This is resolved internally. Both CICS systems (in their respective SITs) are given a generic APPLID and a specific APPLID. The generic APPLIDs are the same but the specific APPLIDs are different, based upon the names provided on the VTAM APPL statements used to define the respective CICS systems.

The generic APPLID is defined in a VTAM USERVAR table. The generic APPLID is thus a variable or symbol which can be set to an actual APPLID. The actual value (or real APPLID) of the USERVAR variable can be altered by a program defined as a Secondary Program Operator, or SPO. This definition is given to CICS on the APPL statement by specifying AUTH=SPO. SPO, thus, permits CICS to modify the specific APPLID associated with the USERVAR generic APPLID and is required for both CICS systems in an XRF pair. In this way, regardless of which of the CICS systems is active, the user can enter the same logon message requesting connection to the generic APPLID. Likewise, systems seeking sessions with the XRF pair use the generic APPLID. Since the active CICS system sets the generic APPLID to point to itself, end users and other systems are connected to the active CICS.

The good news is that XRF permits a faster restart of CICS. The bad news is that ISC and MRO sessions are generally not XRF-capable. The only possible exception is a single-session LUTYPE 6.2 terminal. However, subsequent to takeover, CICS reestablishes ISC and MRO sessions that are defined to it as requiring AUTOCONNECTion during system initializtion.

4.2.7   ISC Installation — Required CICS Modules

The CICS modules required for InterSystem Communication include the EXEC Interface programs, the InterSystem Communication Programs, and the Terminal Control Programs. These are included via System Initialization Table parameters or startup overrides. The SIT parameters/startup overrides are: EXEC=YES, ISC=YES, and the Terminal Control options TCP and ZCP.

4.3   SYSTEM AND LINK DEFINITIONS

The systems and links that provide the connectivity required for MRO or ISC must be defined to CICS. There are two methods that can be used to define these resources. The first, which is interactive from a CICS terminal is known as *Resource Definition Online* or *RDO*. The second involves creating source statements consisting of macro instructions specifying resource definitions.

4.3.1   Resource Definition Online

Resource Definition Online, or RDO, utilizes CICS-supplied transactions to manage resource definition online. CEDA is the most powerful of the RDO transactions. CEDA permits resource information to be entered interactively, and it also permits such resource information to be dynamically installed into an executing CICS system. CEDB provides a subset of CEDA functionality which permits resource definition but does not allow resource installation. CEDC permits read-only access to RDO resource information. Using RDO it is possible to DEFINE, ALTER, DELETE, or INSTALL resource information during CICS execution. The information defined in this way is kept in a VSAM file that is defined in the File Control Table. The DDNAME of this file, DFHCSD, and the file is known as the CICS System Definition file, or CSD. Only a subset of CICS resources can be defined with RDO. Namely, these are PCT entries, PPT entries, and VTAM network resources. For the other CICS tables the older macro method must be used.

4.3.2   Macro Resource Definition

All CICS tables can be defined using macro instructions unique to the different resource categories. For example, the DFHPCT macro is used to define Program Control Table entries, the DFHFCT macro is used to define File Control Table entries, and the DFHPPT macro is used to define Processing Program Table entries. The macro instructions are used to code assembler language source statements defining collections of resources. Typically, the source statements used to define a collection of resources are contained within a member of a partitioned data set, or in some other form of source statement library. So, one member of a PDS may contain all of the PPT macro source statements; another member may contain the source statements for the FCT; and yet another member, the PCT definitions.

After the source statements for a category of resources (all of the programs or all of the files or all of the transactions) are complete, a CICS JCL procedure is used to assemble the source code and create a load module which is link edited into the CICS load library. The CICS load library is a partitioned data set that has the DDNAME of DFHRPL in the CICS execution JCL. The "table" load modules are brought into CICS during system initialization.

Using macro definitions alone, it is not possible to provide resource information while CICS is up and running. In order to replace, for example, an FCT load module, it is necessary to "bounce" CICS (bring it down and back up again). However, for resources supported by RDO, it is possible to do online definition and installation in addition to any macro definition tables brought in by CICS initialization.

4.3.3   Getting All the Names Straight

In defining resources for MRO/ISC, we have to provide names for other systems and other connected systems need to provide a name for the local CICS. Keeping track of the names can be a job for a politician. Therefore, we're going to explain the relationships between all the names that CICS calls itself and the names by which CICS knows other systems. This has become a little more complex since the advent of the eXtended Recovery Facility (XRF) in CICS 2.1. Since using XRF makes getting the names straight a little more difficult, let's start with a single CICS system that does not use XRF.

A CICS system not utilizing XRF has two names: one name by which it is known internally, its SYSIDNT, and another name by which it is known externally, or its APPLID to VTAM and NETNAME to the rest of the world according to CICS and VTAM. The internal SYSIDNT is convenient for certain table generation functions, which we will discuss in a little bit. The most important things to remember about the SYSIDNT, in order of importance, are 1) it is internal to a CICS system and known by no one outside of that system; 2) it is a 1- to 4-character name; and 3) it is defined in the System Initialization Table.

CICS's APPLID is also named in the System Initialization Table. It is a 1- to 8-character name, and it is also the name specified on the VTAM APPL statement. The APPLID is the name by which the CICS system is known globally. In a System Initialization Table coding example, we might find the following:

```
DFHSIT
          .
          .
       XRF=NO,
       APPLID=DCCICS01,
       SYSIDNT=CIC1
          .
          .
```

The dots (.) are used to indicate the absence of the other DFHSIT parameters which would be needed in a real SIT. The above example indicates that the CICS system is *not* using XRF (XRF=NO). CICS's APPLID is DCCICS01, and this name was provided on a VTAM APPL statement and serves as this CICS's NETNAME as far as outside systems are concerned. This is the only name that outside systems need to know about this CICS.

Now let's tackle XRF. XRF means that we have a CICS pair consisting of an active CICS and an alternate CICS that is standing by in the event of a failure of the active CICS. As we discussed above, the alternate CICS "takes over" when the active CICS fails. The CICS pair have a global or generic name by which they are known to network end users. In this context we are including terminal operators and other systems who will have connections with the CICS pair. Of course, since only one of the pair is active at any time, any active sessions with the CICS pair are always with one CICS at a time.

The generic CICS name is associated with both CICS systems that make up the XRF pair. This generic name is defined in a VTAM USERVAR table as a variable. The actual value of the generic name USERVAR variable is modified by the active CICS so that it correctly points to the specific one of the pair that is active. In other words, when one of the XRF pair becomes active it plugs its own unique APPLID into the USERVAR variable.

External references, as in session initiation requests, use the generic CICS name. VTAM picks up the specific CICS system name from the USERVAR variable. Thus, outside of the XRF pair, other systems "see" the XRF pair as one system. Outside system definitions referencing connections to the XRF pair are always known by the generic name. Thus, when we define outside CICS systems, we are interested in the generic name. It is transparent to us whether this is a generic name that represents an XRF pair or the APPLID of a single CICS.

In XRF pairs, the generic name is specified in the System Initialization Table as the first of two APPLIDs. The CICS systems comprising an XRF pair also need unique APPLIDs. This is because the alternate CICS is partially initialized and connected with the network in support of backup sessions that it has to XRF-capable terminals while the active CICS is up and running and likewise connected to the network in active sessions. Because of this each CICS system in the XRF pair needs its own APPLID. This is defined with the second of two APPLIDs named in the System Initialization Table. The CICS systems will also have a SYSIDNT, and this SYSIDNT must be uniform for the XRF pair. Therefore, the following might be coded in the two System Initialization Tables for an XRF pair:

```
DFHSIT
       .
       .
APPLID=(DCCICS02,UNCICS01),
SYSIDNT=CIC2,
XRF=YES,
```

.
.
.
.

and

```
DFHSIT
       .
       .
APPLID=(DCCICS02,UNCICS02),
SYSIDNT=CIC2,
XRF=YES,
       .
       .
       .
       .
       .
       .
```

Once again, the dots (.) indicate missing SIT parameters not shown in these examples. Note that both CICS systems in the XRF pair have the same generic APPLID. This name is defined in the VTAM USERVAR table as a variable. The separate systems have their own unique APPLIDs of UNCICS01 and UNCICS02. These are both defined on VTAM APPL statements also specifying AUTH=SPO and HAVAIL=YES. The SYSIDNTs of both systems are the same (CIC2).

Our CICS system needs the NETNAME of every system with which it is going to connect. This will enable our system to establish either an SNA session or an InterRegion session. Although MRO uses a private CICS mechanism rather than the SNA network for communicating across regions, the concepts and terminology are largely the same. The generic name (1st APPLID in the other system's SIT) is the name by which our system knows other CICS systems for connection purposes.

If this name were used to define all of the resources associated with the remote system, then a change of NETNAME would result in potentially massive amounts of maintenance. All references to that system's resources in tables, including the Terminal Control Table, File Control Table, Temporary Storage Table, Destination Control Table, and Program Control Table would have to be altered. Furthermore, application programs that used the SYSID option would have to be altered as well. This is obviously undesirable.

Therefore, what CICS really does is use the NETNAME only in the system or connection definition in the Terminal Control Table. In this definition a SYSIDNT is associated with the NETNAME. Any sessions defined in the TCT identify the SYSIDNT and are therefore tied to the appropriate connection. Furthermore, the 1- to 4-character SYSIDNT is used in resource definition tables and in application programs naming the SYSID option. This means that if a NETNAME changes, only the TCT definition of the connection or system need be altered to reflect the new NETNAME.

The SYSIDNT by which CICS knows other systems is used solely for internal purposes by a CICS system. However, each connected system must have a unique SYSIDNT in order to correctly associate resources with their appropriate systems. Having gotten the name business straight, we are ready to start defining Terminal Control Table connections for Intercommunication.

4.3.4   Defining Intercommunication Connections

As with other select resources, one can utilize RDO or macro definitions to define Intercommunication connections. We will examine both methods. Which one is chosen is based upon the preference of the individual performing resource definition because the same definitions can be supplied with either mechanism. The option/parameter keywords are, however, different. Before we start looking at a comparison of options and defining them in the context of MRO, ISC LUTYPE 6.1, and so forth, we are going to examine the panel image that appears on a terminal screen (such as a 3270 display) for RDO. This is done to give the reader a flavor of what RDO is like. In all subsequent discussion of resource definitions, the RDO and macro options will be illustrated and discussed. However, we will not examine RDO panels for each of them.

Examples of all RDO panels and an explanation of panel options can be found in the IBM Manual *CICS/MVS Version 2.1 Resource Definition (Online)* SC33-0508. All of the resource definition macros and parameter explanations can be found in *CICS/MVS Version 2.1 Resource Definition (Macro)* SC33-0509. The reader is advised to obtain the IBM references before proceeding with CICS resource definition. Also, note the version and release information for the CICS manuals listed above. If you are using a different version or release of CICS these manuals may be inappropriate for performing resource definition in your environment. There are comparable IBM manuals for different versions/releases of CICS.

Figure 4-1 illustrates the actual RDO panel used to define CONNECTIONs. This panel is used to define MRO connections, ISC LUTYPE 6.1 connections, ISC LUTYPE 6.2 connections, and a fourth type of connection which we haven't mentioned before, the Indirect Link. Therefore, there are options contained on the panel for all of these different cases, and no one case is going to define all of the options. In the discussions of each type of connection we will discuss those items that are relevant on a case by case basis.

Figure 4-1 illustrates the RDO panel to DEFINE a CONNEC-TION. Under RDO the definition of a link to another system involves defining a CONNECTION and defining SESSIONS associated with the connection. So the panel illustrated in Figure 4-1 represents the first step. The second step is to define the SESSIONS. The panel for defining SESSIONS is illustrated in Figure 4-2. Also, you will recall that defining resources with RDO merely places the definitions in the CICS System Definition File. Such resources must be INSTALL-ed before they become part of realtime CICS.

4.3.5 Defining MRO Connections

Defining MRO connections always assumes that we are connecting CICS to CICS. Appropriate values to define an MRO link are listed

```
     Connection   ==>  ....
     Group        ==>  ........

     CONNECTION IDENTIFIERS
     Netname      ==>  ........
     INDsys       ==>  ....

     CONNECTION PROPERTIES
     ACcessmethod ==> Vtam        Vtam | IRc | INdirect | Xm
     Protocol     ==>             Appc | Lu61
     SInglesess   ==> No          No | Yes
     Datastream   ==> User        User | 3270 | SCs | STrfield | Lms
     Recordformat ==> U           U | Vb

     OPERATIONAL PROPERTIES
     AUtoconnect  ==> No          No | Yes | All
     INService    ==> Yes         Yes | No

     SECURITY
     SEcurityname ==> ........
     ATtachsec    ==> Local       Local | Identify | Verify
     Bindpassword ==>             PASSWORD NOT SPECIFIED
```

Figure 4-1 RDO Panel to define connections. Reprinted by permission from *CICS/MVS Version 2.1 Resource Definition (Online)* © 1987, 1988 by International Business Machines Corporation.

```
      Sessions     ==> ........
      Group        ==> ........

      SESSION IDENTIFIERS
      Connection   ==> ....
      SESSName     ==> ....
      NETnameq     ==> ........
      MOdename     ==> ........

      SESSION PROPERTIES
      Protocol     ==>                  Appc | Lu61
      MAximum      ==> 00000 , 00000     0-32767
      RECEIVEPfx   ==> ..
      RECEIVECount ==> No                No | 1-999
      SENDPfx      ==> ..
      SENDCount    ==> No                No | 1-999
      SENDSize     ==>                    1-30720
      RECEIVESize  ==>                    1-30720

      OPERATOR DEFAULTS
      OPERId       ==> ...
      OPERPriority ==> 000                0-255
      OPERRsl      ==> 0                  0-24,...
      OPERSecurity ==> 1                  1-64,...
      USERId       ==> ........

      SESSION USAGES
      Transaction  ==> ....
      SESSPriority ==> 000                0-255

      OPERATIONAL PROPERTIES
      Autoconnect  ==> No                No | Yes | All
      INservice    ==>                   No | Yes
      Buildchain   ==> Yes               Yes | No
      USERArealen  ==> 000               0-255
      IOarealen    ==> 00000 , 00000     0-32767
      RELreq       ==> No                No | Yes
      Discreq      ==> No                No | Yes
      NEPclass     ==> 000               0-255

      RECOVERY
      RECOVOption  ==> Sysdefault        Sysdefault | Clearconv | Releasesess
                                         | Uncondrel | None
      RECOVNotify  ==> None              None | Message | Transaction
```

Figure 4-2 RDO Panel to define sessions. Reprinted by permission from *CICS/MVS Version 2.1 Resource Definition (Online)* © 1987, 1988 by International Business Machines Corporation.

in Figure 4-3. Both the RDO and Macro definition options are included. Options for both are aligned horizontally to indicate which RDO options relate to macro equivalents. Note that the macro level definition utilizes one macro DFHTCT TYPE=SYSTEM to accomplish the total definition. Therefore, some of the options of both RDO commands are comparable to the single macro definition. We begin our discussion with the DEFINE CONNECTION command options listed in Figure 4-3.

The CONNECTION option is used to name the 1- to 4-character SYSIDNT. This is **an internal name assigned to the remote sys-**

tem for use in identifying its resources. The definifion of the
NETNAME is associated with this SYSIDNT in the DEFINE CON-
NECTION. In all subsequent references to the resources owned by a
remote system, only the SYSIDNT is used. Each connected system
requires a unique SYSIDNT but the importance of the SYSIDNT as
a symbolic system identifier is strictly within the local system.

The GROUP option associates this definition with a control group
that is used to associate a collection of RDO resources definitions for
INSTALL purposes. This makes the task of installing a collection of
related resources much easier because the entire group can be installed as a unit. Therefore, this option is relevant to RDO but has
nothing inherent to do with the characteristics of the CONNEC-
TION. Since this is not applicable to macro resource definition, there
is no equivalent shown for the DFHTCT TYPE=SYSTEM.

```
RDO Definition              Macro-Level Definition


DEFINE                      DFHTCT  TYPE=SYSTEM
  CONNECTION(sysidnt)         ,SYSIDNT=sysidnt
  GROUP(groupname)
  ACCESSMETHOD(IRC|XM)        ,ACCMETH={IRC|(IRC,XM)}
  NETNAME(name)               ,NETNAME=name
  SECURITYNAME(name)          ,XSNAME=name
  INSERVICE(NO)

DEFINE
  SESSIONS(csdname)
  GROUP(groupname)
  CONNECTION(sysidnt)
  PROTOCOL(LU61)
  RECEIVEPFX(prefix1)         ,RECEIVE=(prefix1,number1)
  RECEIVECOUNT(number1)
  SENDPFX(prefix2)            ,SEND=(prefix2,number2)
  SENDCOUNT(number2)


  OPERPRIORITY(number)        ,OPERPRI=number
  OPERRSL(number)             ,OPERRSL=number
  OPERSECURITY(number)        ,OPERSEC=number
  IOAREALEN(value)            ,TIOAL=value
  SESSPRIORITY(number)        ,TRMPRTY=number
  INSERVICE(NO)               ,TRMSTAT='OUT OF SERVICE'
```

Figure 4-3 Link definition for MRO in RDO and via the DFHTCT macro. Reprinted by permission from *CICS/MVS Version 2.1 Intercommunication Guide* ©
1987, 1988 by International Business Machines Corporation.

The ACCESSMETHOD option definition for MRO is either IRC or XM. If IRC is used, than the data transfer between the CICS systems is performed by the Type 2 SVC which invokes the InterRegion Program (DFHIRP) discussed earlier. If XM is specified, then MVS cross memory services are utilized for actual data exchanges. However, the CICS SVC is still needed so the link can be opened/closed.

The NETNAME option provides the first or only APPLID specified in the System Initialization Table of the CICS system we are using MRO to connect to.

SECURITYNAME provides a name for the remote system for security checking purposes. This name is used for link sign-on purposes. If the SECURITYNAME is desired for sign on security, the SECURITYNAME selected should be represented by a USERID entry in the local Sign oN Table. The SECURITYNAME is from 1 to 8 alphameric or national characters. If link sign on is used (via the SECURITYNAME field and Sign oN Table) then transaction and resource security keys are obtained from the SNT entry. This is known as link security. Link security can also be directly defined via the OPERSECURITY and OPERRSL options of the DEFINE SESSIONS command which define transaction and resource security keys, respectively. Link security can, thus, be accomplished by either method.

There is an additional option that is not shown in Figure 4-3. For RDO it is the ATTACHSEC option and the values that can be entered are LOCAL or IDENTIFY. If LOCAL is selected or allowed to default then individual requests that result in the attaching of a task are tested for security based upon the security values associated with the link itself. LOCAL checks security requirements against link security, and all users coming in over the link are identified with the link. So where LOCAL is specified or allowed to default, link security values are used for transaction and resource security checks. The system is thus not able to check security on an individual user basis so all users are associated with the link.

An ATTACHSEC value of IDENTIFY indicates that incoming attach requests are to provide a USERID. In this case, there should be a Sign oN Table entry in the local CICS for individual users (USERID). This SNT entry is located and security is checked against the individual SNT entry security information. So, ATTACHSEC(IDENTIFY) enables the local CICS system to differentiate among different users in the connected system and determine security individually. This means, however, that individual user requests must be checked uniquely. Also, Sign oN Table entries have to be provided for all users in the connected system.

In most cases it is probably safe to assume that the other CICS system has already checked security requirements before forwarding requests over the MRO connection. The macro equivalent of ATTACHSEC is USERSEC=LOCAL or USERSEC=IDENTIFY.

INSERVICE is specified as NO for MRO.

Next, we must define the MRO sessions associated with this connection. Defining MRO sessions involves defining both *SEND* and *RECEIVE* sessions. A SEND session is used for the local CICS to use for requests to the connected system. Responses regarding such requests are sent back over the SEND session. Requests from the remote system come in over RECEIVE sessions and they are responded to over the RECEIVE sessions. In this way CICS can readily correlate requests and responses.

There must be at least one SEND and one RECEIVE session between the systems, although based upon the anticipated traffic and direction of the traffic more SEND and/or RECEIVE sessions can be defined. In MRO, part of the functionality of the SNA bracket protocol is used to initiate and end "transactions." The connected CICS systems generate Begin Bracket and End Bracket Indicators. However, the SNA BID protocol used by a contention loser to request permission to initiate a bracket is not implemented. Therefore, in MRO, there are RECEIVE and SEND sessions.

Returning to Figure 4-3, we will next examine the options associated with the DEFINE SESSIONS command.

The SESSIONS option is used to provide a 1- to 8-character name for use in the CICS System Definition file used by RDO. Other than naming the sessions within the CSD, this name is not utilized in CICS.

GROUP is used to associate the sessions with a resource group for RDO INSTALLation purposes as discussed above under the DEFINE CONNECTION command.

CONNECTION names the SYSIDNT defined in the CONNECTION option of the DEFINE CONNECTION command. This option identifies the system with which the sessions are to be established.

PROTOCOL should be specified as LU61 on the DEFINE SESSIONS command.

RECEIVEPFX is required for MRO and is specified as 1 or 2 characters. The prefix is used in the construction of unique session IDs for each of the receive sessions.

RECEIVECOUNT specifies the number of RECEIVE sessions to be created between the systems. Each of the receive sessions is given a unique name. The combination of the prefix defined in the RECEIVEPFX and a number from one to the RECEIVECOUNT value are concatenated to create the unique session names for each of the RECEIVE sessions. So, if RECEIVEPFX=AB and RECEIVECOUNT=10 there will be 10 sessions and their names will be AB01, AB02, AB03, AB04, AB05, AB06, AB07, AB08, AB09, and AB10. The end result of the concatenation to build the session names cannot exceed 4 characters. With a 2-character prefix, the maximum number of sessions is 99. If the prefix is 1 character, then the maximum number of sessions is 999.

SENDPFX is used in the same manner as RECEIVEPFX except that the prefix is for the SEND sessions.

SENDCOUNT is likewise used in the same manner as RECEIVECOUNT except that this is the count of SEND sessions. Again, the SENDPFX and SENDCOUNT values are concatenated to build unique session names.

Operator information is provided with the next three options. These options define priority (OPERPRIORITY), transaction security (OPERSECURITY) and resource security (OPERRSL) for the "operator" associated with the link. This is an alternative to link "sign on" utilizing the userid named in the SECURITYNAME option of the DEFINE CONNECTION command and an entry in the local Sign oN Table. We ought to explain just a bit how these fields are used during the initiation or attaching of a task and during actual task execution.

OPERPRIORITY provides the priority value associated with tasks initiated on behalf of the "operator." During task attach processing, CICS calculates an executing priority for an initiated task. A task's priority is developed by adding together the operator's priority, the terminal's priority, which in this case is the SESSPRIORITY (4 options down from OPERPRIORITY in Figure 4-3), and the transaction priority obtained from the Program Control Table. Each of these values can be from 0 to 255 with 255 being the highest priority.

CICS uses task priority to order its active task list, and high priority tasks are provided greater opportunity to execute. It is normally, however, not a good idea to mix priority values. Rather, it is best to define priority for only one of the above options and leave the rest at 0. CICS performance is more easily tuned if only one of these values is used for task prioritization. In most cases priority is provided by the transaction definition. At any rate a user task's priority should never exceed 250 because this could well throw off internal operations in CICS such as loading programs into CICS owned storage. Normally user tasks are given low priorities, and small increments distinguish high priority functions from lower priority ones.

OPERRSL defines the operator's security key used for resource security level checking during Function Shipping and Distributed Transaction Processing. The OPERRSL can be defined as 0 or multiple values in the range of 1 through 24 can be defined. An OPERRSL of 2–5,8,22 defines an operator security key of 2,3,4,5,8,and 22. These values are mutually exclusive so an operator is not allowed to access a resource with a security level not defined in his/her resource security key. An OPERRSL of 0 indicates that a resource security key is not being defined for the operator.

Resources including files, temporary storage queues, transient data queues, journals, transactions, and programs can be defined with resource security levels. This definition is made in the specific resource definition tables, so a journal could be given a resource security level in the Journal Control Table. A resource security level can be 0, a number from 1 to 24, or PUBLIC. The default resource security level is 0.

Resource security level checking tests are made *only* if the task's TRANSID is defined as requiring resource security level checking in the Program Control Table definition (RSLC=YES). If RSLC=NO is indicated for a TRANSID, then the resource access tests are *not* made. Such tasks have access to all resources. If a transaction is defined as requiring resource security checking, each resource access is tested in all tasks performing the TRANSID. If the resource level is PUBLIC or the OPERRSL contains the resource level defined for the resource, then the access is allowed. However, if the operator's resource security key does not contain the exact resource security level, then the access is not allowed.

If the operator does not have a resource security key as would happen for an OPERRSL of 0 and resource security level checking is performed, only PUBLIC resources can be accessed. In the event of a resource access failure, CICS raises the NOTAUTH condition. A resource defined with a resource security level of 0 (and this is the default unless otherwise defined) cannot be accessed by a task requiring resource security level checking.

OPERSECURITY is used to define the operator's security key. The operator's security key is tested against a transaction's security level (as defined in the PCT) before CICS initiates a task. As with OPERRSL discussed above, multiple values can be defined. Valid values for transaction security are from 1 through 64. Transaction security values are mutually exclusive so an operator's transaction security key *must* contain the exact number specified as a transaction security level in order to use the TRANSID. If an operator's transaction security key does not contain the exact transaction security level,

CICS detects a transaction security violation and does not initiate the requested transaction. Transaction security testing is made prior to task attachment. Resource security checking is performed during a task's execution if requested (RSLC=YES) for the TRANSID.

If operator values (OPERPRIORITY, OPERRSL, or OPERSECURITY) are defined in the DEFINE SESSIONS command or the macro level equivalent, this precludes link sign on via the SECURITYNAME and Sign oN Table described above in the discussion of the DEFINE CONNECTION command.

IOAREALEN is used to define terminal input output area size used to pass data to an application program.

SESSPRIORITY defines the task initiation priority associated with the session. The use of SESSPRIORITY in developing a task's priority was discussed above in the paragraphs on OPERPRIORITY.

INSERVICE is defined as NO for MRO sessions.

The following code represents a sample MRO link definition:

```
          DEFINE

1                 CONNECTION(CIC2)
2                 GROUP(MROLINK)
3                 ACCESSMETHOD(IRC)

4                 NETNAME(DCCICS02)

          DEFINE

5                 SESSIONS(MROSESS)
6                 GROUP(MROLINK)
7                 CONNECTION(CIC2)
8                 PROTOCOL(LU61)
9                 RECEIVEPFX(AB)
10                RECEIVECOUNT(6)
11                SENDPFX(CD)
12                SENDCOUNT(4)
13                IOAREALEN(512)
```

Line 1 defines the SYSIDNT of the remote CICS system. This name is used only within the local CICS system so that resources associated with the remote system can be identified by a "logical" name rather than the NETNAME specified in line 4. The DEFINE CONNECTION thus associates the NETNAME and the SYSIDNT.

Line 2 identifies an RDO group name which is used to INSTALL all of the resources defined within the group.

Line 3 indicates that the CICS SVC is to be used for data transfer over the link.

Line 4 provides the NETNAME of the remote system. In that system this name is defined in the System Initialization Table as follows:

```
DFHSIT
    .
    .
    APPLID=(DCCICS02,UNCICS01),                            X
    XRF=YES
    .
    .
    .
    .
    .
```

Line 5 specifies an RDO name for the sessions. This has no use outside of RDO.

Line 6 names the RDO group for this resource. As mentioned above, this pertains only to the RDO INSTALL function which installs all resources in a group.

Line 7 relates the sessions back to the CONNECTION defined for the sessions.

Line 8 is coded LU61 for IRC and LUTYPE 6.1 sessions.

Line 9 defines a prefix for the RECEIVE sessions. These sessions are used to receive Requests from the remote system.

Line 10 specifies the number of RECEIVE sessions. The six sessions are named as follows: AB01, AB02, AB03, AB04, AB05, and AB06.

Line 11 defines a prefix for the SEND sessions. These sessions are used to send Requests to the remote system.

Line 12 specifies the number of SEND sessions. The four sessions are named as follows: CD01, CD02, CD03, and CD04.

Line 13 defines a Terminal Input Output Area (TIOA) size for the sessions.

The information provided above is one half of the MRO connection. A link must also be defined in the other system and in some cases the information specified in both systems must relate. The following is a sample of the information defined in the remote system.

```
        DEFINE

1               CONNECTION(CICX)
2               GROUP(LINKSX)
3               ACCESSMETHOD(IRC)
4               NETNAME(DCCICS01)
```

NOTES:

Line 3 defines the access method which must be the same for both systems. They must both use either cross memory services or IRC.

Line 4 specifies the remote system NETNAME. This must correspond to the other system's APPLID from its System Initialization Table.

```
        DEFINE

5               SESSIONS(SESS01)
6               GROUP(LINKSX)
7               CONNECTION(CICX)
8               PROTOCOL(LU61)
9               RECEIVEPFX(EF)
10              RECEIVECOUNT(4)
11              SENDPFX(GH)
12              SENDCOUNT(6)
13              IOAREALEN(512)
```

NOTES:

Line 10 defines the RECEIVE Sessions. This must correspond to the SENDCOUNT of the other system's SESSIONS definition.

Line 12 defines the SEND Sessions. This must correspond to the RECEIVECOUNT of the other system's SESSIONS definition.

4.3.6   Defining ISC LUTYPE 6.1 Connections

LUTYPE 6.1 links can be defined between two CICS systems or between a CICS system and an IMS system. The format of the RDO DEFINE CONNECTION is basically similar but IMS system definitions must be coordinated with IMS requirements. Figure 4-4 illustrates the definition format for LUTYPE 6.1 links.

```
RDO Definition                  Macro-Level Definition


DEFINE                          DFHTCT   TYPE=SYSTEM
   CONNECTION(sysidnt)           ,SYSIDNT=sysidnt
   GROUP(groupname)
   NETNAME(name)                 ,NETNAME=name
   ACCESSMETHOD(VTAM)            ,ACCMETH=VTAM
   PROTOCOL(LU61)
   DATASTREAM(USER|3270|         ,DATASTR={USER|3270|
              SCS|STRFIELD|                 SCS|STRFIELD|
              LMS)                          LMS}
   RECORDFORMAT(U|VB)            ,RECFM={U|VB}
   AUTOCONNECT(NO|YES|)          [,CONNECT=AUTO]
   SECURITYNAME(name)            ,XSNAME=name
   INSERVICE(YES)


DEFINE
   SESSIONS(csdname)
   GROUP(groupname)
   CONNECTION(sysidnt)
   PROTOCOL(LU61)
   RECEIVEPFX(prefix1)           ,RECEIVE=(prefix1,number1)
   RECEIVECOUNT(number1)
   SENDPFX(prefix2)              ,SEND=(prefix2,number2)
   SENDCOUNT(number2)
   SENDSIZE(size)                ,BUFFER=size
   RECEIVESIZE(size)             ,RUSIZE=size
   BUILDCHAIN(Y)                 ,CHNASSY=YES
   OPERID(operator-id)           ,OPERID=operator-id
   OPERPRIORITY(number)          ,OPERPRI=number
   OPERRSL(number)               ,OPERRSL=number
   OPERSECURITY(number)          ,OPERSEC=number
   IOAREALEN(value)              ,TIOAL=value
   SESSPRIORITY(number)          ,TRMPRTY=number
                                 ,TRMSTAT=TRANSCEIVE
```

Figure 4-4 Link definition for ISC LU_T6.1. Reprinted by permission from *CICS/MVS Version 2.1 Intercommunication Guide* © 1987, 1988 by International Business Machines Corporation.

The CONNECTION, GROUP, and NETNAME options are used in the same way as explained above in the MRO link description.

The ACCESSMETHOD option definition names VTAM.

The PROTOCOL option is coded as LU61.

DATASTREAM should be left to default to USER for CICS-CICS LUTYPE 6.1 links.

RECORDFORMAT of U is appropriate for CICS-CICS LUTYPE 6.1 links.

AUTOCONNECT specification of YES indicates automatic session initiation is to be attempted during CICS system initialization. If the attempt fails because, for example, the remote system is not available or if AUTOCONNECT(NO) is specified, then the master terminal command CEMT SET CONNECTION(sysidnt) INS ACQ can be used to subsequently initiate connection.

SECURITYNAME provides a name for the remote system for security checking purposes. The SECURITYNAME is used during link "sign on." An entry in the Sign oN Table relates the SECURITYNAME to a USERID defined in the table. CICS obtains link security values from the SNT entry. Link security is the only type of security for CICS-CICS LUTYPE 6.1 links. That is, attach security (ATTACHSEC) described above under MRO is not available for LUTYPE 6.1.

INSERVICE(YES) indicates that the link is to be in service as differentiated from it being out of service and not available for use.

Before we begin our discussion of the DEFINE SESSIONS command, it is necessary to understand the differences between SEND and RECEIVE LUTYPE 6.1 sessions. CICS to CICS sessions over an LUTYPE 6.1 link can be described as SEND and RECEIVE sessions. For LUTYPE 6.1 CICS BINDs sessions as a *contention loser*. This means that the CICS system that sends the BIND, although considered the "primary" because it is the BIND sender, binds sessions as a contention loser.

The contention loser must obtain permission from the contention winner to initiate a bracket and, therefore, the contention-losing CICS BIDs when it wants to initiate a transaction over a session that is a contention loser. This type of session is a RECEIVE session for the BIND-sending CICS. For the CICS that is receiving the BIND, or is the "secondary," the session is a contention winner. Since the bind receiver is the contention winner, it can initiate a bracket without going through the BID protocol. This type of session is a SEND session for the BIND-receiving CICS.

For CICS-to-CICS sessions, a pool of sessions is defined with the DEFINE SESSIONS command. From the vantage point of one of the CICS systems, some of the sessions in the pool are SEND sessions (no need to BID), and the remaining sessions are RECEIVE sessions (must BID before initiating a bracket). SEND sessions for the local CICS are RECEIVE sessions for the remote CICS. RECEIVE sessions for the local CICS are SEND sessions for the remote CICS.

CICS always uses bracket protocol to coordinate and synchronize work across LUTYPE 6 sessions, and in fact this is an architectural feature of these sessions. The bracket is initiated by the system that is making a request. Using SEND sessions for initiating work is preferable. The reason for this is fairly apparent when you realize that having to BID creates extra data flow and is less efficient. The BID would be required to initiate a bracket, i.e., make a request over a RECEIVE session. Therefore, when CICS is preparing to allocate a session for InterSystem Communication, it first checks to see if a contention winner is available for use.

If there are none available, then CICS uses a contention loser and BIDs for permission to initiate a bracket. To this end, in defining the SEND/RECEIVE sessions between two CICS systems, it is important to take into account the anticipated direction of request flows. If request traffic is going to initiate largely from one system, it would be more efficient to provide that system with more SEND sessions from the session pool. The result of this would be less overhead because the requesting CICS would have more contention winner sessions available for request initiation.

Returning to Figure 4-4, the DEFINE SESSIONS command defines the sessions associated with the CONNECTION.

The SESSIONS option is used to provide a 1- to 8-character name for use in the CICS System Definition file used by RDO. Other than naming the sessions within the CSD, this name is not utilized in CICS.

The GROUP and CONNECTION options are used in the same manner as described earlier in the DEFINE SESSIONS for MRO.

PROTOCOL should be specified as LU61.

RECEIVEPFX, RECEIVECOUNT, SENDPFX, and SENDCOUNT are used in accordance with the description of these options under MRO. Specification of these options must be matched across the systems such that one system's RECEIVECOUNT matches the other system's SENDCOUNT and vice versa.

SENDSIZE and RECEIVESIZE define the buffer and Request/Response Unit size (RUSIZE). A buffer of at least 256 bytes must be specified. A larger buffer size results in fewer message transmissions between the connected systems but does use more storage. Again, these options should be coordinated across the systems so that one system's SENDSIZE should correspond to the other system's RECEIVESIZE. If there is a mismatch, CICS negotiates the sizes at BIND time.

BUILDCHAIN(Y) indicates that RU chain assembly is to be performed before input is given to the application task.

As with MRO, link security can be accomplished by using the SECURITYNAME option of the DEFINE CONNECTION command and a Sign oN Table entry. Specifying operator security information in the DEFINE SESSIONS command prevents link sign-on. The OPERPRIORITY, OPERRSL, and OPERSECURITY options are used in the same manner as described above in the discussion of MRO. For LUTYPE 6.1 connections, security is always tested based upon link security values. In other words, USERIDs are not passed over LUTYPE 6.1 links, and CICS cannot differentiate among different users within the remote system. For CICS-to-CICS connections, where individual remote user security is a concern, LUTYPE 6.2 links should be used because USERIDs can be passed and individual user security testing is supported.

OPERID provides the 3-character CICS operator ID.

IOAREALEN is used to define terminal input output area size used to pass data to an application program.

SESSPRIORITY defines the task initiation priority associated with the session (instead of the TRMPRTY). This was discussed above under OPERPRIORITY.

4.3.7   Defining ISC LUTYPE 6.2 Connections

In order to define LUTYPE 6.2 connections it is necessary to define an RDO CONNECTION and specify a DEFINE SESSIONS for each group of sessions. A group of sessions shares a common LOGMODE name. So, for each different LOGMODE utilized for a particular connection it would be necessary to specify a DEFINE SESSIONS command. For macro definition the DFHTCT TYPE=SYSTEM defines the connection and is immediately followed by one or more DFHTCT TYPE=MODESET macros to define each session group. The DFHTCT TYPE=MODESET macros must be placed directly after the appropriate DFHTCT TYPE=SYSTEM macro. Note that when defining an LUTYPE 6.2 terminal which supports only a single session, the macro definition includes only the DFHTCT TYPE=SYSTEM macro. However, in this context, the DFHTCT TYPE=SYSTEM macro can include appropriate options from the DFHTCT TYPE=MODESET macro. All of the macro options listed in Figure 4-6 with the exception of MAXSESS may be included. Optionally, an LUTYPE 6.2 terminal can also be defined as a terminal and be a candidate for AUTOINSTALL.

Figure 4-5 illustrates the DEFINE CONNECTION and DFHTCT TYPE=SYSTEM macro for defining an LUTYPE 6.2 connection.

The CONNECTION and GROUP options are used as described above.

ACCESSMETHOD names VTAM.

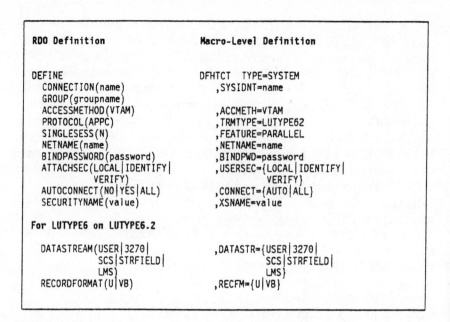

```
RDO Definition                    Macro-Level Definition


DEFINE                            DFHTCT  TYPE=SYSTEM
   CONNECTION(name)                  ,SYSIDNT=name
   GROUP(groupname)
   ACCESSMETHOD(VTAM)                ,ACCMETH=VTAM
   PROTOCOL(APPC)                    ,TRMTYPE=LUTYPE62
   SINGLESESS(N)                     ,FEATURE=PARALLEL
   NETNAME(name)                     ,NETNAME=name
   BINDPASSWORD(password)            ,BINDPWD=password
   ATTACHSEC(LOCAL|IDENTIFY|         ,USERSEC={LOCAL|IDENTIFY|
           VERIFY)                           VERIFY}
   AUTOCONNECT(NO|YES|ALL)           ,CONNECT={AUTO|ALL}
   SECURITYNAME(value)               ,XSNAME=value

For LUTYPE6 on LUTYPE6.2

   DATASTREAM(USER|3270|            ,DATASTR={USER|3270|
              SCS|STRFIELD|                   SCS|STRFIELD|
              LMS)                            LMS}
   RECORDFORMAT(U|VB)               ,RECFM={U|VB}
```

Figure 4-5 Connection/system definition for ISC LU_T6.2. Reprinted by permission from *CICS/MVS Version 2.1 Intercommunication Guide* © 1987, 1988 by International Business Machines Corporation.

PROTOCOL must be specified as APPC (Advanced Program-to-Program Communication).

SINGLESESS(N) indicates that this is an LUTYPE 6.2 to another system as opposed to an LUTYPE 6.2 terminal. SINGLESESS(N) indicates that parallel sessions are to be used between the connected systems. For an LUTYPE 6.2 terminal code is SINGLESESS(Y).

NETNAME specifies the APPLID of the connected system.

BINDPASSWORD is used to name an optional BIND time password. If provided, CICS performs a security check during the BIND process. If a remote system does not possess an identical password, the session cannot be bound and therefore identical values must be defined in both systems. Up to 16 hexadecimal digits can be specified. If fewer hex characters are entered, the password is padded with hex 0s to the left. Prior to being stored, the password is encrypted so don't f-o-r-g-e-t i-t! The password itself is not exchanged between the systems, rather it is used as an encryption factor for security exchanges.

ATTACHSEC indicates the level of security checking to be performed when remote system requests result in attaching work in the local CICS. LOCAL indicates that user security is to be equated with link security. Therefore, all incoming requests are checked against the link security values. IDENTIFY indicates that the communicating system is able to send a USERID with all attach requests and that CICS is to locate the user's entry in the local Sign oN Table. The user's SNT security information is then used to check security for the request.

This requires that the local CICS have an SNT entry for all remote users whose requests will be forwarded. VERIFY indicates that CICS is to locate the remote user's SNT entry and verify the password in addition to using the security information in the SNT entry to check security. VERIFY cannot be used in CICS to CICS connections and is applicable to remote systems that do not have an internal sign on facility but are able to forward USERIDs and PASSWORDs with attach requests.

AUTOCONNECT indicates system initialization BINDing of sessions. The BINDing of LUTYPE 6.2 sessions between systems is a two-stage process. First the connection must be established. This is accomplished by BINDing LU services manager sessions. After this connection is established, the actual LUTYPE 6.2 sessions can be established. AUTOCONNECT in the DEFINE CONNECTION command specifies initialization processing of the connection (LU services manager sessions). AUTOCONNECT is also specified in the DEFINE SESSIONS and this defines which user sessions are to be initiated during initialization.

Note that the LU services manager sessions must be in place prior to user sessions. RDO AUTOCONNECT(NO) is the equivalent of omitting CONNECT= in the DFHTCT TYPE=SYSTEM macro. AUTOCONNECT(YES) is the equivalent of CONNECT=AUTO in the macro definition. AUTOCONNECT(ALL) is the equivalent of CONNECT=ALL. This mapping (command to macro) applies to both RDO commands/macro definitions.

For AUTOCONNECT in the DEFINE CONNECTION command, NO indicates that the LU services manager sessions are not to be bound during system initialization; YES specifies that CICS is to attempt to bind such sessions during initialization. However, if the other system is not available, the sessions cannot be bound. CEMT could subsequently be used to initiate session BINDing when the remote system becomes available. For DEFINE CONNECTION, ALL is the equivalent of YES.

SECURITYNAME is used as described above to provide a userid for link sign on. See the discussion of the SECURITYNAME option under MRO.

RDO Definition	Macro-Level Definition

DEFINE
   SESSIONS(csdname)
   GROUP(groupname)
   PROTOCOL(APPC)
   CONNECTION(name)
   MODENAME(name)
   MAXIMUM(m1,m2)
   AUTOCONNECT(NO|YES|ALL)
 	
   SENDSIZE(size)
   RECEIVESIZE(size)
   OPERID(operator-id)
   OPERPRIORITY(number)
   OPERRSL(number)
   OPERSECURITY(number)
   USERAREALEN(value)
   SESSPRIORITY(number)
   TRANSACTION(name)
	DFHTCT TYPE=MODESET
	
	,SYSIDNT=name
	,MODENAM=name
	,MAXSESS=(m1,m2)
	,CONNECT={AUTO|ALL}
	
	[,BUFFER=size]
	[,RUSIZE=size]
	[,OPERID=operator-id]
	[,OPERPRI=number]
	[,OPERRSL=number]
	[,OPERSEC=number]
	[,TCTUAL=value]
	[,TRMPRTY=number]
	[,TRANSID=name]
	[,TRMSTAT=TRANSCEIVE]

Figure 4-6 Session definition for ISC LU_T6.2. Reprinted by permission from *CICS/MVS Version 2.1 Intercommunication Guide* © 1987, 1988 by International Business Machines Corporation.

The DATASTREAM and RECORDFORMAT options are used in support of upward migration for applications implemented on LU-TYPE 6.1 links. These options are discussed above under LUTYPE 6.1 links.

Figure 4-6 illustrates the DEFINE SESSIONS and DFHTCT TYPE=MODESET used to define a group of sessions.

SESSIONS and GROUP options are used as described above.

PROTOCOL is specified as APPC.

The use of CONNECTION is described above.

MODENAME defines a 1- to 8-character VTAM LOGMODE name. Based upon the class of service associated with the LOGMODE name, a virtual route is selected for the session.

MAXIMUM is used to specifiy the maximum number of sessions in the group (m1) and the maximum number of contention winners (m2). The number specified for m2 cannot exceed m1. For single-session LUTYPE 6.2 terminals, m1 must equal 1, and it is recommended that CICS m2 also be set to 1. CICS will then attempt to bind the session as a contention winner, but this is negotiable during BIND processing.

AUTOCONNECT defines system initialization BIND processing for this session group. NO indicates that session BINDing is not to be attempted. YES indicates that contention winner sessions are to be bound if possible. ALL indicates that CICS is to attempt to BIND all sessions (contention losers and contention winners). ALL permits CICS to BIND contention losing sessions for a remote system that is unable to send BIND requests. However, for CICS-to-CICS connections ALL can result in BIND races and hung logical units.

SENDSIZE, RECEIVESIZE, OPERID, OPERPRIORITY, OPER-RSL, and OPERSECURITY are discussed above.

USERAREALEN specifies a TCTUA size which can be from 0–255.

Use of SESSPRIORITY is described above.

TRANSACTION defines a 1- to 4-character TRANSID that is always to be used to initiate tasks when there is input from the sessions. A remote CICS system sends an appropriate architected process name (TRANSID) to initiate work.

As with MRO and LUTYPE 6.1 connections, the information defined in systems to be joined should be consistent with regard to session definitions and data sizes. However, discrepancies across systems for values defined for MAXIMUM, SENDSIZE, and RECEIVESIZE can be negotiated at BIND time. CICS writes messages regarding LUTYPE 6.2 session initiations or failures to the CSMT destination. When there is a cross system problem, this destination should be read in both systems.

4.4 SUMMARY

All types of CICS Intercommunication require that the appropriate CICS installation requirements, external definitions, and connection resources are defined properly. For Multi-Region Operation, it is important to coordinate definitions and requirements with the MVS systems programmer. For InterSystem Communication, it is likewise important to determine that the appropriate VTAM resource definitions and table entries have been made. In terms of cross system connections, it is necessary to coordinate CONNECTION and SESSION definitions in linked CICS systems so that such definitions are consistent.

In creating the CONNECTIONs or SYSTEM definitions and subsequently defining the SESSIONs or TERMINALs/MODESETs, it is important to be guided by the appropriate IBM reference material. The examples given in this chapter are designed to provide an overview of what has to be done so that the IBM reference material can be readily utilized.

REVIEW EXERCISES

Provide a short answer for each of the following.

1. What are the general requirements for Intercommunication?
2. What are the installation requirements for supporting CICS MRO?
3. How does VTAM know about a CICS region?
4. What is XRF and how does it affect the NETNAME assigned to CICS.
5. What is a SYSIDNT and why is it important?
6. What two methods may be used to define CICS resources? Can all resources be defined by either method?
7. What is a contention winner?
8. What is a contention loser?
9. When CICS has parallel sessions with other LUTYPE6 systems including other CICS systems, we define some of the sessions as SEND or contention winning sessions and others as RECEIVE or contention losing sessions. Why do we do this? What factor should be borne in mind when deciding on these values?
10. What types of Intercommunication require link definitions?

ANSWERS TO REVIEW EXERCISE

Provide a short answer for each of the following.

1. *What are the general requirements for Intercommunication?*

   The general requirements for Intercommunication include installing CICS correctly so that it can use Intercommunication; making external definitions in MVS and/or VTAM; and defining the connections and sessions with each remote system.

2. *What are the installation requirements for supporting CICS MRO?*

   It is necessary to: link edit the CICS Type 2 SVC to the MVS nucleus; to define CICS as an MVS subsystem; to install DFHIRP into the Link Pack Area; to include the required CICS management modules; and to set up a procedure for the CICS IRC logon.

3. *How does VTAM know about a CICS region?*

CICS is defined to VTAM via an APPL statement that is included with other VTAM resource definitions.

4. *What is XRF and how does it affect the NETNAME assigned to CICS?*

The eXtended Recovery Facility enables an installation to have two CICS regions, one which executes and the other which waits, partially initialized, so that it can take over in the event of the failure of the executing CICS. Some terminals are XRF capable and the 'backup' CICS can take these terminals over during a restart without requiring an operator to log back on.

Each of the CICS systems within the XRF pair has its own unique VTAM APPLID and is defined via a VTAM APPL statement. They also share a common generic APPLID which is really a VTAM USERVAR variable. The active CICS modifies the USERVAR variable so that it contains the actual APPLID of the currently active system. All users and other systems external to the XRF pair know the pair by the generic APPLID.

5. *What is a SYSIDNT and why is it important?*

The SYSIDNT is a logical name by which a CICS system is known. In the Terminal Control Table, the connection or system definition specifies the actual NETNAME of a remote system. Tied to this definition is a logical name or SYSIDNT. The SYSIDNT is used in all subsequent references to the system in question. In this way, if a system's NETNAME changes only the TCT connection or system definition needs to be altered. However, the scope of the SYSIDNT is only significant within the local CICS in which it is defined.

6. *What two methods may be used to define CICS resources? Can all resources be defined by either method?*

Some CICS resources (TRANSIDs, PROGRAMs and VTAM network resources) can be defined via Resource Definition Online, or RDO. RDO uses CICS supplied transactions to define resources in a VSAM file called the CICS System Definition file or CSD. Resources defined in the CSD can likewise be installed using RDO. There are three RDO TRANSIDs. CEDA permits resources to be defined and installed. CEDB permits resources to be defined but does not do the install function. CEDC permits read-only access.

All CICS resources can be defined using resource specific MACRO instructions. The MACROs defining resources are then assembled to create load modules and brought into CICS at system initialization. New MACRO-generated tables can be brought into CICS only when it is initialized. RDO performs resource installation while CICS is up and running.

7. *What is a contention winner?*

A contention winner is a session partner that can begin a bracket or transaction without seeking permission. The contention winner merely places a begin bracket (BB) indicator on the message flow and the bracket is begun.

8. *What is a contention loser?*

A contention loser is a session partner that cannot begin a bracket or transaction without seeking permission from its contention winning session partner. In order to do this a contention loser sends an SNA defined BID request to seek permission to begin a bracket.

9. *When CICS has parallel sessions with other LUTYPE6 systems including other CICS systems we define some of the sessions as SEND or contention winning sessions and others as RECEIVE or contention losing sessions. Why do we do this? What factor should be borne in mind when deciding on these values?*

There is less network traffic if a system can use a contention winner session to initiate a bracket or transaction. In order to use a contention loser a BID has to be sent and a response received to grant bracket permission. We want to give both connected systems some sessions on which they can begin brackets without having to BID. When deciding on how many of each to define for a particular connection, we must bear in mind the direction of requests.

10. *What types of Intercommunication require link definitions?*

ALL TYPES! If there is no link between systems there can be no Function Shipping, Asynchronous Processing, Transaction Routing, or Distributed Transaction Processing.

5

Defining IC TRANSIDs, Programs, and Profiles

5.1 INTRODUCTION

In the previous chapter we discussed the installation requirements for CICS in order to support Multi-Region Operation and Inter-System Communication, external definitions in MVS and VTAM, and the definitions of links to other systems. Link definitions are not, however, the only definitions that have to be made to run CICS Intercommunication. There are CICS programs and transactions that have to be incorporated into a CICS Region in order for CICS to support Multi-Region Operation or InterSystem Communication. Additionally, there may be an installation-specific requirement for Intercommunication Profiles. In this chapter we will discuss how CICS Intercommunication Programs and TRANSIDs can be defined in CICS and the use of Profiles.

5.2 CICS INTERCOMMUNICATION TRANSIDS AND PROGRAMS

The manner in which CICS programs and TRANSIDs get added to the CICS system depend upon whether RDO or macro level definitions are utilized to define system resources. In either case, ultimately, Process Program Table entries must be created for Intercommunication Programs, and Program Control Table entries are needed for TRANSIDs associated with Intercommunication. Since the methodology is different for RDO and macro level definition we will deal with each separately.

5.2.1   Macro Level Definition of CICS Programs and TRANSIDs

The table definitions required for Intercommunication are made through the use of GROUP macros, which obviate the need for coding individual DFHPPT or DFHPCT macros for each of the individual CICS Intercommunication Programs and TRANSIDs. As a matter of fact, the GROUP macros are used to include all of the CICS-required table entries on a facility-by-facility basis. So, in order to get table entries in support of activity keypointing or the Master Terminal Facility, or in this case Intercommunication, it is merely necessary to code an additional option in a GROUP macro.

In order to generate Intercommunication TRANSID entries in the Program Control Table, it is merely necessary to code the following:

```
DFHPCT TYPE=GROUP,FN=(ISC, . . . . )
```

The dots (.) indicate the remaining CICS TRANSIDs that are also to be generated by including a keyword in the GROUP macro. The TRANSID entries that are generated as a result of selecting Inter-System Communication on the GROUP macro include 1) CLS1 and CLS2, which are associated with the Logical Unit Type 6.2 services manager; 2) CRTE, which is a routing transaction discussed in the next chapter; 3) CSMI, CSM1, CSM2, CSM3, and CSM5, which map to the CICS Mirror Program (DFHMIR) that performs CICS Function Shipping services; 4) CSNC and CSIR, which are TRANSIDs for the IRC Connection Manager and IRC Session Recovery, respectively; 5) CRSR or the remote scheduler's TRANSID; 6) CMPX or the TRANSID of the local queuing shipper; and 7) CRSQ for the ATI Purge TRANSID. So, 13 different TRANSIDs are generated as a result of including ISC in the DFHPCT TYPE=GROUP macro.

The Program Control Table entries generated for the Mirror Program listed above under item number 3 are used in support of CICS Function Shipping. We will return to this topic again in the chapter on Function Shipping, but for now it is necessary only to understand that Function Shipping requests to remote systems/regions may be preceded by a CICS supplied TRANSID (CSMI, CSM2, CSM3, etc.). Different types of Function Shipping utilize different TRANSIDs as follows. CSMI is used for all types of Multi-Region Operation Function Shipping requests to CICS systems subsequent to release 1.6. CSMI is also the TRANSID used in support of File Control Function Shipping Requests for InterSystem Communication. CSM1 is used for receipt of system messages when CICS is connected to IMS. CSM2 is the TRANSID of a scheduler function that handles Interval Control Function Shipping Services. CMS3 is used for Temporary Storage and Transient Data Queue Function Shipping requests. CSM5 is used for DL/I requests. All of these Function Shipping TRANSIDs are serviced by DFHMIR, the CICS MIRror Program.

In the Program Control Table entries that are generated for ISC as a result of the TYPE=GROUP macro, Resource Security Level Checking is requested or, in other words, RSLC=YES is included. It is important to be aware of this for one simple reason. Function Shipping allows a task to access remote resources such as Files, TS Queues, and TD Queues. These items are defined as REMOTE and LOCAL resources. If in CICS1 we are supporting incoming Function Shipping, the above TRANSIDs will be sent to our system. We are currently discussing how to generate the Program Control Table entries necessary to recognize these incoming TRANSIDs and attaching a task to execute in DFHMIR to actually perform the resource access so that CICS1 supports Function Shipping. By default the mirror TRANSIDs specify resource security checking.

In addition to defining the mirror transactions, we will also be generating the usual local resource definitions in our CICS environment. Therefore, we will also be creating File Control Table and Destination Control Table entries and may well be creating Temporary Storage Table entries which define these resources.

The default Resource Security Level for such resources is 0. An RSL of 0 indicates that no task with RSLC=YES can access the resource. If we omit specification of RSL in local table definitions, then our Function Shipping TRANSIDs, as generated by default, are precluded from accessing those resources. We have two choices to select from in resolving this issue. We can explicitly code DFHPCT macros for the Mirror Program's TRANSIDs and not code RSLC=YES.

The second choice is that we can provide a Resource Security Level from 1 to 24 for each resource or we can select RSL=PUBLIC. PUBLIC makes the resource available unconditionally to all tasks. However, PUBLIC has global significance and should not be coded lightly. In addition to CICS resource security checking, an external security manager such as RACF, the Resource Access Control Facility, can be utilized for security checking. External Security is specified by coding options in the System Initialization Table. For example, if external security is to be used for operator sign on or resource access, it is necessary to code EXTSEC=YES in the System Initialization Table. If EXTSEC=YES is coded, each separate facility that qualifies for resource security checking can be defined as using external security. Again, this is accomplished via System Initialization Table options. The following sample code from the System Initialization Table shows the parameters that can be used in requesting external security. For each option, "YES" indicates that external security is to be utilized for determining if the resource access is to be allowed, and "NO" indicates that external security is not to be used for the specific class of resources.

```
1      DFHSIT TYPE=CSECT,                              X
2             EXTSEC=NO/YES,                           X
3             XDCT=YES/NO,                             X
4             XFCT=YES/NO,                             X
5             XJCT=YES/NO,                             X
6             XPCT=YES/NO,                             X
7             XPPT=YES/NO,                             X
8             XPSB=YES/NO,                             X
9             XTST=YES/NO,                             X
              .
              .
              .
              .
              .
              .
              .
              .
              .
```

Dots (.) indicate remaining DFHSIT Options

Notes:

Line 3   Defines external Security for Destination Control Table Entries.
Line 4   Defines external Security for File Control Table Entries.
Line 5   Defines external Security for Journal Control Table Entries.
Line 6   Defines external Security for Program Control Table Entries.
Line 7   Defines external Security for Processing Program Table Entries.
Line 8   Defines external Security for IMS Program Specification Blocks.
Line 9   Defines external Security for Temporary Storage Table Entries.

The problem with using a resource RSL=PUBLIC is that if you are utilizing an external security manager, the external security manager is not invoked to check PUBLIC resources. Therefore, setting RSL=PUBLIC is not a viable, all-purpose solution in systems where security mandates use of an external security manager. But if allowed to default, then RSL is 0 and the resource is unavailable for TRANSIDs defined as RSLC=YES. Thus, you could have a problem in terms of the mirror transactions being able to access default resources. Based upon an installation's need for CICS resource security, you can omit resource security testing (RSLC=NO) for the mirror TRANSIDs, you can define a resource security level for your resources, or you can define all of your resources as PUBLIC.

Resource Security Level Checking varies based upon the link connection with the remote system. For Multi-Region Operation and InterSystem Communication LUTYPE 6.2 links, ATTACH Security can be specified. This is accomplished by the ATTACHSEC (IDENTIFY) for RDO or USERSEC=IDENTIFY for macro level definition. In this case each request is accompanied by a USERID and the local CICS looks up the USERID in the Sign oN Table. From the user's SNT entry a resource security key is obtained and used for resource security level checking. Therefore, if using ATTACH security for MRO or ISC LUTYPE 6.2 links, it is necessary to ensure that remote operators are correctly defined in the Sign oN Table with regard to USERID and Resource Security Keys.

ATTACH security is not required and can be omitted by selecting ATTACHSEC(LOCAL) or USERSEC=LOCAL. In this case, Link Security Resource Security values are used. Link Security values are either 1) hard coded in the link definition (OPERRSL option) or 2) based on link sign on (SECURITYNAME RDO option or XSNAME= for macro level). Using Link Security means, however, that your CICS system cannot differentiate between different users (USERIDs) from the remote system. The good news is that each user does not require a Sign oN Table entry. However, some environments require a high degree of security so this issue must be evaluated. ATTACH security is not available with LUTYPE 6.1 links. Link security values are used for security purposes on LUTYPE 6.1 links, and there is no way to differentiate between individual users. It is therefore only necessary to ensure that resources and Link Security match up.

If your environment and the nature of reachable resources does not mandate Resource Security Level Checking, then for CICS-to-CICS connections you can consider making resources public or specifying RSLC=NO for the Mirror TRANSIDs. After all, in the

CICS system from which Function Shipping requests are coming, security checking can be performed. Certainly transaction security is typically used and REMOTE resource definitions in the File Control Table, Program Control Table and Destination Control Table can specify a resource security level. Therefore, resource security level checking can be dealt with in the requesting CICS system before Function Shipping Requests are sent.

If Transaction security is desired for the Mirror TRANSID entries generated as a result of the DFHPCT TYPE=GROUP macro, this can be accomplished in the coding of the DFHPCT TYPE=INITIAL macro. The following is a sample requesting a Transaction Security Level of 4 for Mirror Transaction Definitions in the Program Control Table.

```
       DFHPCT TYPE=INITIAL,                          *
              TRANSEC=(MIRROR(04), . . . . .)
```

Again, it is necessary to ensure that Sign oN Table entries are set up properly for transaction security values if ATTACH security is used for MRO and ISC LUTYPE 6.2 links. Otherwise, it is only necessary to be certain that link security values properly reflect security requirements.

To generate the Processing Program Table entries required in support of InterSystem Communication, the following GROUP macro is used.

```
       DFHPPT TYPE=GROUP,FN=(ISC, . . . . .)
```

The dots (.) indicate that more groups of CICS programs would normally be included in this macro. The Processing Program Table entries generated as a result of including ISC in the above macro include: 1) DFHMIR — the MIRror program 2) DFHRTE — the transaction routing program; 3) DFHCRP — the CICS Relay Program used in support of Transaction Routing; 4) DFHLUP — the LUTYPE 6.2 services manager program; 5) DFHCRR — the Inter-Region Communication session recovery program; 6) DFHCRNP — the connection manager program for InterRegion Communication; 7) DFHRSP — the startup program for InterRegion Communication; 8) DFHCRQ — the purge program for Automatic Transaction Initiation; 9) DFHCRS — the remote scheduler program; and 10) DFHMXP — the local queuing shipping program.

5.2.2   Resource Definition Online of CICS Programs/TRANSIDs

Using RDO it is not necessary to create the required resource definitions because you get them automatically. Where do they come from?
IBM. How do you get them? You define a VSAM CICS System
Definition file. You initialize the file with a CICS utility program
designed for that purpose. The initialized CSD file contains two lists
of resource groups: DFHLIST and DFHLIST2. DFHLIST2 contains
VTAM terminal models and TYPETERM definitions for defining
VTAM terminals online. Otherwise DFHLIST2 contains everything
that DFHLIST contains. DFHLIST contains resource groups defining
all of the CICS Programs and TRANSIDs needed for all of the
facilities of CICS that require such PPT and PCT definitions. The
resource group containing definitions for Intercommunication is
named DFHISC. This group contains the programs and TRANSIDs
described above for the PPT and PCT macro definitions.

It is not even necessary to use CEDA INSTALL to install these
GROUP definitions individually into CICS. It is merely necessary to
define a list into which you will ultimately ADD your installation-
specific groups of resources and APPEND DFHLIST or DFHLIST2 to
your list. (Use DFHLIST2 for RDO support for VTAM terminals.)
Then, in the System Initialization Table you provide the name of the
list which includes the installation specific resource groups with
DFHLIST/DFHLIST2 appended to it. The name of this list is defined
with the GRPLIST parameter of DFHSIT.

5.3   PROFILES FOR INTERCOMMUNICATION

Profiles are used in two contexts in CICS. Before Resource Definition
Online, a transaction's requirements for Terminal Control options
were defined as part of the TRANSID's PCT entry. Such options included message protection, message journaling, provision of an error
category for an installation-specific Node Error Program (NEP), a
Receive TIMe OUT (RTIMOUT), device support, and what if any
Function Management Headers were to be passed to the application
program. In order to facilitate RDO transaction definitions,
PROFILEs are used to define these transaction-related requirements. Then, when defining TRANSACTIONs using RDO, a
PROFILE may be named and the options built into the profile are
incorporated into the transaction's definition. There are default
profiles, and the RDO DEFINE PROFILE command can be used to
build any installation-specific profiles required. So, in that sense, a

profile is a named set of Terminal Control Options that govern a transaction's interaction with its Principal Facility (usually a terminal). And, in this sense of the term, a profile is not used when defining TRANSIDs with macro definitions. The items that are specified for an RDO profile are coded or allowed to default in each DFHPCT TYPE=ENTRY definition.

The second context in which profiles are used is in CICS Intercommunication. In Intercommunication profiles are used to describe or govern the interaction of a transaction and its alternate facility, which is a session with a remote system/LUTYPE 6.2 terminal. All tasks that use Intercommunication services have an alternate facility.

In an earlier chapter we briefly discussed an ALLOCATE command which is used to request use of an alternate facility. This is done within application programs that perform Distributed Transaction Processing, and in this context the application programmer is aware of the acquisition of an alternate facility. In the ALLOCATE command, a PROFILE option permits the specification of an alternate facility profile name. If one is not specified explicitly because ALLOCATE command does not include the PROFILE option, a default CICS Profile named DFHCICSA is used.

When a program issues a command against a remotely defined file or queue, an alternate facility is acquired by CICS. The alternate facility is used for the data flows between the local and remote systems in support of Function Shipping. When a user enters a TRANSID at a terminal and that TRANSID is defined as remote, CICS acquires an alternate facility for use in cross-system exchanges in support of Transaction Routing. In utilizing Asynchronous Processing, the application program may or may not be aware of an alternate facility. If the START command is utilized, CICS acquires the alternate facility and performs Function Shipping to send the transaction initiation request to the appropriate system. In this context, Asynchronous Processing is a special case of Function Shipping. If the SEND LAST technique is used to implement Asynchronous Processing, then the application program uses ALLOCATE to acquire a connection over which to SEND LAST. In this context, Asynchronous Processing is a subset of Distributed Transaction Processing.

Whether or not the application program explicitly acquires the use of a session or one is obtained by CICS, the fact is that all application tasks that use Intercommunication services have alternate facilities.

A profile defines the task's interaction with its alternate facility. For Function Shipping requests, CICS always uses a default profile named DFHCICSF. For Transaction Routing CICS uses a profile named DFHCICSS unless an alternate profile name is defined in the Program Control Table definition of the remote transaction. This is accomplished with the Transaction Routing PROFile or TRPROF PCT option. For Asynchronous Processing, the profile used is dependent upon whether we utilize Function Shipping or a subset of Distributed Transaction Processing.

There are a number of default profiles that come with CICS. These profiles are generated automatically at the end of the Program Control Table if macro definition is used and for RDO they are contained in two groups within DFHLIST and DFHLIST2. By and large, the IBM-supplied profiles are sufficient for most installations. However, there may be a need to create additional installation specific profiles or modify one or more of the IBM profiles. The actual Resource Definitions in groups within DFHLIST/DFHLIST2 cannot be altered, but copies can be made, altered, and used in place of the IBM profile resource definitions. To alter the PCT derived via macro definitions, it is merely necessary to code a DFHPCT TYPE=PROFILE and specify the PROFILE name of the CICS profile to be replaced. Duplicated profile names are not generated in the assembled PCT load module, so this allows an installation to replace a particular IBM Profile in the PCT generated from macro definitions.

First, we are going to identify the IBM profiles and then we will tackle how and why installation-specific profiles are created. After going over what is in a profile, we will list the characteristics of the various IBM-supplied profiles.

5.3.1   IBM Default Profiles

In the RDO List, DFHLIST/DFHLIST2, the Group DFHISC contains three profiles: DFHCICSF, DFHCICSR and DFHCICSS. As you will note from our discussion above, DFHCICSF is used for all Function Shipping requests and DFHCICSS is the default profile for Transaction Routing requests. Another Group within DFHLIST/DFHLIST2, DFHSTAND, contains four more profiles: DFHCICSA, DFHCICSE, DFHCICST, and DFHCICSV. DFHCICSA is the default profile for Distributed Transaction Processing over LUTYPE 6.2 connections. All of these profiles are automatically generated at the end of a macro-generated PCT.

5.3.2   Installation-Specific Profiles for Intercommunication

The primary reason for creating unique installation profiles for Intercommunication is so that they are available for use by application programs performing Distributed Transaction Processing over LUTYPE 6.2 connections. In this context, the region containing the Front-End Transaction, the one that does the ALLOCATE command and subsequently CONNECTs the remote PROCESS, can name a PROFILE in the ALLOCATE command. The main reason for doing so is that one of the characteristics a profile can specify is a MODENAME (RDO) or MODENAM (macro definition).

The MODENAME specified in the profile definition relates to a MODENAME specified for a group of LUTYPE 6.2 sessions. MODENAME, as you will recall, is applicable only for LUTYPE 6.2 sessions. In the context of SESSION definition the MODENAME relates to a VTAM LOGMODE or name of an entry in VTAM's Logon Mode Table. A Class Of Service (COS) designation in the Logon Mode Table is resolved into a collection of Virtual Routes which are appropriate to SESSION requirements. The Virtual Route represents a prioritization in terms of network traffic flows. At each intermediate routing node along a Virtual Route, the priority associated with the Virtual Route results in message prioritization.

Another reason why multiple MODENAMEs might be used to define different SESSION groups from a system's point of view is to provide an alternate routing capability for different sets of sessions between connected systems. Alternate routing means that different Virtual Routes can be used and these Virtual Routes can be via different network paths. Thus if a Virtual Route fails, CICS still has potentially another route to the connected system.

If we are using multiple routing, one of the Virtual Routes may be more direct and provide a better response time rate. Or, if a single physical (explicit) route exists, multiple Virtual Routes can be used to prioritize flows. Thus different MODENAMEs can relate to different Virtual Routes and different priorities. An application program performing Distributed Transaction Processing over an LUTYPE 6.2 can obtain a particular Class of Service by naming a PROFILE that defines a MODENAME associated with that Class of Service. It goes without saying, however, that the MODENAME used in a profile *must* be defined as a MODENAME in one of the SESSION groups with the connected system. If the application program can connect with one of several systems based upon application requirements and determined at program execution time, it is neces-

```
PROFile      ==> ........
Group        ==> ........
Scrnsize     ==> Default       Default | Alternate
MOdename     ==> ........
PRIntercomp  ==> No            No | Yes

JOURNALLING
Journal      ==> No            No | 1-99
MSGJrnl      ==> No            No | INPut | Output | INOut

PROTECTION
MSGInteg     ==> No            No | Yes
Onewte       ==> No            No | Yes
PROtect      ==> No            No | Yes

PROTOCOLS
Dvsuprt      ==> All           All | Nonvtam | Vtam
Inbfmh       ==> No            No | All | Dip | Eods
RAq          ==> No            No | Yes
Logrec       ==> No            No | Yes

RECOVERY
Nepclass     ==> 000           0-255
RTimout      ==> No            No | 1-7000
```

Figure 5-1 Panel used for RDO of PROFILES. Reprinted by permission from *CICS/MVS Version 2.1 Resource Definition (Online)* © 1987, 1988 by International Business Machines Corporation.

sary to ensure that SESSIONS using the MODENAME are defined for *all* of the possible systems that the program may connect to.

To define a PROFILE, RDO or macro definition may be used. Figure 5-1 illustrates the panel used for online PROFILE definition. The profile is given a name with the PROFILE option and this name is referenced in ALLOCATE commands by application programs. The MODENAME is specified with the MODENAME option. The DFHPCT TYPE=PROFILE macro contains comparable options.

5.4   DEFAULT IBM PROFILE CHARACTERISTICS

The information provided in this section is not important to an understanding of Intercommunication. It is included for those folks who are involved with the business of defining or altering Intercommunication profiles. In most cases, installations use the default profiles that come from IBM. However, for the sake of textual completeness, the following material is included to document the IBM profiles (for those who are interested.)

The profile DFHCICSF is used for all Function Shipping Requests. The characteristics of this profile are as follows: SCRNSIZE is DE-

FAULT; PRINTERCOMP is NO; MSGJRNL is NO; MSGINTEG is NO; ONEWTE is NO; PROTECT is NO; DVSUPRT is ALL (meaning VTAM and NONVTAM devices are supported); INBFMH is ALL (meaning that ALL INBound Function Management Headers, except those processed by CICS such as ATTACH and SYNCPOINT, are passed to the program); RAQ is NO; LOGREC is NO; and NEPCLASS is 0. This profile does not specify a MODENAME. However, the profile can be copied and altered to include a MODENAME. This allows specification of a Class of Service for Function Shipping requests. However, if you do this, you must be sure to provide a SESSION group to *every* connected system over which Function Shipping requests are to be passed, with the appropriate MODENAME.

The profile DFHCICSS is the default profile for Transaction Routing requests. This can be altered via the REMOTE PCT definition of the TRANSID by inclusion of the TRPROF naming a different Transaction Routing PROFile. DFHCICSS is used as the profile for the Intercommunication link in the CICS region/system which owns the terminal. Another Transaction Routing Profile named DFHCICSR is utilized in the system/region owning the transaction. The characteristics of DFHCICSR are listed below. The characteristics of DFHCICSS are as follows: SCRNSIZE is DEFAULT; PRINTERCOMP is NO; MSGJRNL is NO; MSGINTEG is NO; ONEWTE is NO; PROTECT is NO; DVSUPRT is ALL (meaning VTAM and NONVTAM devices are supported); INBFMH is ALL (meaning that ALL INBound Function Management Headers, except those processed by CICS such as ATTACH and SYNCPOINT, are passed to the program); RAQ is NO; LOGREC is NO; and NEPCLASS is 0.

The profile DFHCICSR is used in Transaction Routing in the CICS region/system which owns the TRANSID. The characteristics of this profile are: SCRNSIZE is DEFAULT; PRINTERCOMP is NO; MSGJRNL is NO; MSGINTEG is NO; ONEWTE is NO; PROTECT is NO; DVSUPRT is ALL (meaning VTAM and NONVTAM devices are supported); INBFMH is ALL (meaning that ALL INBound Function Management Headers, except those processed by CICS such as ATTACH and SYNCPOINT, are passed to the program); RAQ is NO; LOGREC is NO; and NEPCLASS is 0.

The profile DFHCICSA is the default profile for use on ALLOCATE commands. The characteristics of this profile are as follows: SCRNSIZE is DEFAULT; PRINTERCOMP is NO; MSGJRNL is NO; MSGINTEG is NO; ONEWTE is NO; PROTECT is NO; DVSUPRT is ALL (meaning VTAM and NONVTAM devices are supported); IN-

BFMH is ALL (meaning that ALL INBound Function Management Headers, except those processed by CICS such as ATTACH and SYNCPOINT, are passed to the program); RAQ is NO; LOGREC is NO; and NEPCLASS is 0. This profile specifically defines INBFMH as ALL. However, over LUTYPE 6.2 connections no Function Management Headers are *ever* passed to an application program. The fact that the profile specifies this is not a problem, but you should be aware of the fact that regardless of what is said in the profile Function Management Headers are not going to be passed to tasks executing in LUTYPE 6.2 application programs.

The remaining IBM-supplied profiles are DFHCICST, DFHCICSV, and DFHCICSE. These profiles are used between a transaction and its principal facility and are not of concern to us in the context of CICS Intercommunication. Their characteristics are defined in Appendix B of the *CICS/MVS Version 2 Release 1 Resource Definition (Online)*, IBM Reference Number SC33-0508.

5.5 SUMMARY

Having 1) installed CICS Correctly; 2) made external definitions as needed in MVS and VTAM; 3) defined links with remote systems; 4) ensured that the proper CICS PCT and PPT definitions for Intercommunication TRANSIDs and programs have been generated and installed; 5) reviewed the IBM-supplied profiles for use with Intercommunication and potentially defined our own profiles for use in programs that perform Distributed Transaction Processing over LUTYPE 6.2 Links, we are now ready to deal with each of the individual facilities of Intercommunication.

As we go through each facility, there will be more resource definitions that need to be created. However, these are specific to facilities such as Function Shipping Resources or Transaction Routing Resources and do not have the global sweep of the resources discussed up to this point. In the next chapter, we will be discussing Transaction Routing in depth.

6

Transaction Routing

6.1 INTRODUCTION

In the previous chapters we defined the CICS installation requirements for utilizing Multi-Region Operation and InterSystem Communication. We also examined the Terminal Control Table "link"
definitions that are needed in support of Intercommunication. These
link definitions are required in support of Transaction Routing,
Function Shipping, Asynchronous Processing and Distributed Transaction Processing. We also examined the CICS programs and
TRANSIDs required to support Intercommunication and looked at
profiles used for Intercommunication functions. In this chapter we
will examine Transaction Routing in depth. We will examine how it
works, the resource definitions that are specifically required to support Transaction Routing and the application programming/design issues involved with using Transaction Routing.

6.2 TRANSACTION ROUTING — HOW IT WORKS

Transaction Routing is supported over InterRegion Communication
links (MRO) and LUTYPE 6.2 links. However, there is no support for
Transaction Routing over LUTYPE 6.1 connections. Transaction
Routing enables a CICS system to send a transaction, defined to it
as remote, to another CICS system for actual processing. Thus, there
are two CICS sytems involved in the coordination necessary for
Transaction Routing: the *Terminal Owning* region and the *Transac-*

tion Owning region. **In support of Transaction Routing both the transaction and the terminal must be defined in both systems.** The following represents resource definition information in a Terminal-Owning CICS system. Our example uses an LUTYPE 6.2 connection between the systems but an IRC link could have been used as well.

```
                              CIC1


Program Control Table


DEFINITION OF REMOTE TRANSACTION

    DFHPCT TYPE=REMOTE,SYSIDNT=CIC2,TRANSID=XX01,                  X
           RTIMOUT=015,DTIMOUT=015,TRANSEC=8,  . . .


DEFINITION OF ISC TRANSIDS NEEDED IN SUPPORT OF ISC

    DFHPCT TYPE=GROUP,FN=(ISC, . . . )


Processing Program Table


DEFINITION OF ISC PROGRAMS WHICH ARE GENERATED AS A GROUP IN THE PPT.
           DFHPPT TYPE=GROUP,FN=(ISC, . . . )


Terminal Control Table
DEFINITION OF THE CONNECTION WITH THE REMOTE CICS SYSTEM
           DFHTCT TYPE=SYSTEM,ACCMETH=VTAM,NETNAME=DCCICS02,       X
                  SYSIDNT=CIC2,TRMTYPE=LUTYPE62,BUFFER=256,        X
                  FEATURE=PARALLEL, . . .                          X


DEFINITION OF A SET OF SESSIONS WITH THE REMOTE CICS SYSTEM
           DFHTCT TYPE=MODESET,SYSIDNT=CIC2,MAXSESS(4,2),          X
                  MODENAM=M1CICS,CONNECT=AUTO, . . .               X


DEFINITION OF A LOCALLY OWNED 3270 TERMINAL
           DFHTCT TYPE=TERMINAL,ACCMETH=VTAM,TRMIDNT=NO57,         X
                  TRMTYPE=LUTYPE2,TRMMODL=2,DEFSCRN=(24,80),       X
                  FEATURE=(AUDALARM,UCTRAN),TRMSTAT=(TRANSCEIVE),  X
                  NETNAME=LU37N057,BUFFER=1526,TIOAL=(200,4000),   X
                  CONNECT=AUTO, . . .                              X
```

Note that the Program Control Table contains a definition of a remote TRANSID, which is owned by a CICS system known locally through its SYSIDNT of CIC2. The DTIMOUT and RTIMOUT options are used in this PCT entry to force a timeout if the task is suspended waiting for a session to the remote system or if the remote system does not respond. Since this task is initiated by a terminal operator, TRANSEC or transaction security is specified. The Terminal-Owning CICS will thus check operator security prior to initiating the local task.

The PPT entry for the ISC group of programs creates the table entries for the ISC programs including a *CICS Relay Program (DFHCRP)* which is utilized in the Terminal-Owning region to relay messages between a terminal and a remote task initiated to accomplish Transaction Routing.

In the Terminal Control Table, the remote system is defined with the DFHTCT TYPE=SYSTEM macro. This macro associates this SYSIDNT with a NETNAME of DCCICS02. The DFHTCT TYPE=MODESET defines one group of sessions with that system. Additionally, the TCT contains a definition of a locally owned 3270 terminal. These table definitions are facsimiles and are not intended to be complete definitions, as indicated by the trailing dots (.) following the macro definitions. There are more options for all of the macros coded, and such options have to be examined on a case-by-case basis when doing actual resource definitions.

A terminal operator signed on to terminal NO57 enters the TRANSID XX01 and some initial data. An examination of the Program Control Table determines that the transaction is remotely owned by a CICS system with the SYSIDNT of CIC2. The local CICS checks security for the transaction as defined with the TRANSEC option in the PCT definition. A task is initiated in the local CICS and connected to the Terminal Control Table Terminal Entry (TCTTE) for terminal NO57. This task has the characteristics defined in the PCT entry for XX01. However, the task executes in a CICS program called the CICS Relay Program (DFHCRP). A session with the remote system is acquired for Transaction Routing purposes and a transaction initiation request is sent. The transaction to be initiated is, of course, XX01. Figure 6-1 illustrates the task created in the Terminal Owning region.

In the Transaction Owning CICS system, the following table definitions have been specified.

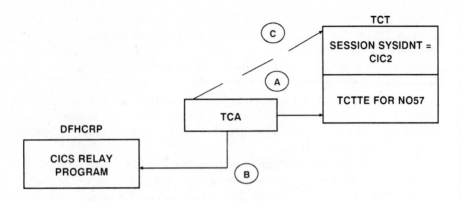

Figure 6-1 Terminal-owning region. A) A user task is initiated with the characteristics of the "remote" TRANSID's PCT definition. This task is connected to the terminal from which the remote TRANSID was entered. B) The task executes in a CICS program named DFHCRP, and provides the communication mechanism between the remote task and the locally owned terminal. C) A session to the remote system is allocated to the task and a transaction initiation request is sent over the session.

```
                              CIC2


Program Control Table
DEFINITION OF THE LOCAL TRANSACTION
    DFHPCT TYPE=ENTRY,TRANSID=XX01,PROGRAM=XX01P01,              X
        TRNPRTY=5, . . .                                        X
DEFINITION OF ISC TRANSIDS NEEDED IN SUPPORT OF ISC
    DFHPCT TYPE=GROUP,FN=(ISC, . . . )


Processing Program Table
DEFINITION OF THE PROGRAM WHICH SERVICES THE LOCAL
TRANSACTION
        DFHPPT TYPE=ENTRY,PROGRAM=XX01P01,PGMLANG=COBOL,        X
            RES=YES, . . .                                      X


DEFINITION OF THE BMS MAPSET USED BY PROGRAM XX01P01
    DFHPPT TYPE=ENTRY,PROGRAM=XX01M01,PGMLANG=ASSEMBLER,        X
        RES=YES


DEFINITION OF THE ISC GROUP OF PROGRAMS
    DFHPPT TYPE=GROUP,FN=(ISC, . . . )
```

```
Terminal Control Table
DEFINITION OF THE TERMINAL OWNING CICS SYSTEM CONNECTION
     DFHTCT TYPE=SYSTEM,ACCMETH=VTAM,NETNAME=DCCICS01,            X
          SYSIDNT=CIC1,TRMTYPE=LUTYPE62,BUFFER=256,               X
          FEATURE=PARALLEL, . . .                                 X


DEFINITION OF ONE SET OF SESSIONS WITH THE TERMINAL-OWNING
  CICS SYSTEM
     DFHTCT TYPE=MODESET,SYSIDNT=CIC1,MAXSESS(4,2),               X
          MODENAM=M1CICS,CONNECT=AUTO, . . .                      X


REMOTE TERMINAL DEFINITION
     DFHTCT TYPE=REMOTE,ACCMETH=VTAM,TRMIDNT=NO57,                X
          TRMTYPE=LUTYPE2,TRMMODL=2,DEFSCRN=(24,80),              X
          SYSIDNT=CIC1,BUFFER=1526,TIOAL=(200,4000), . . .        X
```

In the Transaction-Owning region, the TRANSID XX01 is used to initiate a task which executes in the program XX01P01. The characteristics of this user task are derived from its local PCT definition. This program and the BMS map that it utilizes for terminal output data formatting are defined in the Transaction Owning CICS's Processing Program Table. As part of initiating the application task, the Transaction Owning CICS builds a control block referred to as a *Surrogate TCTTE*. The task is given this Surrogate TCTTE as its principal facility. Figure 6-2 illustrates the user task initiated in CIC2. The Surrogate TCTTE, to all intents and purposes, looks like a real TCTTE as far as the task is concerned. However, operator security information is not available in the Surrogate TCTTE, and therefore an ASSIGN command to obtain operator security informa-

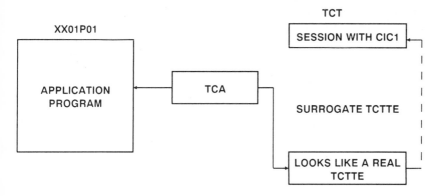

Figure 6-2 Transaction-owning system.

tion (OPSECURITY and OPERKEYS) will not return meaningful results. The 1- to 3-character operator ID, or OPID, is potentially available if the operator did in fact sign on to the terminal in the Terminal-Owning region. Therefore, in a secure CICS environment where operator sign-on is required, this value is available for audit trails or other purposes and can be obtained with the ASSIGN command.

The task executing in program XX01P01 performs a RECEIVE command to obtain initial data entered by the terminal operator at the remote terminal, does its application processing which may involve reading local and remote files, builds an output terminal display using a BMS map, and issues a SEND MAP command. The mapping operation is performed by BMS and then Terminal Control is invoked. Terminal Control recognizes the ouput request against the Surrogate TCTTE and directs the output to the appropriate LUTYPE 6.2 session with CIC1. This data is received by the Relay Task executing in the Terminal-Owning region, which in turn directs the output to the terminal. When the transaction in the Transaction Owning region completes processing and RETURNs control to CICS, an indication is sent to the CICS Relay Task and it likewise ends.

6.3   RESOURCE DEFINITIONS FOR TRANSACTION ROUTING

The resource definitions required for Transaction Routing are distributed between the Terminal-Owning and the Transaction Owning CICS systems. For both the Terminal-Owning and Transaction Owning systems, there are general requirements. These include the ISC Transactions and programs which are defined as a group in the PCTs and PPTs, respectively. Also, the Terminal Control Tables in both systems are used to define connections and one or more session groups for interconnection between the systems. These are general requirements in the sense that they are needed to support Transaction Routing with the remote system.

6.3.1   Resource Definitions for the Terminal Owning System

In the Terminal Owning CICS, there must be a local definition of the terminal. Not all terminals, however, can be utilized for Transaction Routing. **Ineligible terminals include APPC terminals (LUTYPE 6.2 single session devices), the MVS operator con-**

sole, IBM 7770 Audio Response Unit, IBM 2260 terminals, pooled TCAM terminals, and pooled 3600 or 3650 pipeline logical units.

Additionally, there must be a remote definition of the specific TRANSID to be routed. Therefore, the Program Control Table in the Terminal Owning system must contain an entry for the remote transaction. The definition of the remote transaction in the Terminal-Owning CICS provides information about the characteristics required for the CICS Relay Task. These should reflect the "real" transaction's requirements for things like security and priority. Any characteristics to be defined for the application task that runs in the Transaction Owning CICS are defined in that system's Program Control Table. In the example provided above, macro-level definition was illustrated, but RDO could also have been utilized. Figure 6-3 illustrates the RDO DEFINE TRANSACTION command with options that are related to Transaction Routing. Most of the options are fairly self-explanatory, but a couple of them require some comment.

For remote Transactions, i.e., those with remote attributes such as REMOTESYSTEM, the PROGRAM option is forced to DFHCRP. The TWASIZE is set to 0 since DFHCRP does not utilize a Transaction Work Area. The REMOTENAME option allows a transaction to be defined differently in the Terminal Owning system (with a TRANSACTION name) but relate to a different TRANSID or REMOTENAME in the Transaction-Owning system. This serves as a transaction alias in the Terminal Owning system. *LOCALQing*, which permits requests to be queued if a system or session is not available, should not be used for Transaction Routing where a human being is sitting at a terminal awaiting a response. This option may be pertinent to automatically initiated transactions, i.e., Interval Control STARTed TRANSIDs used to accomplish Asynchronous Processing, but is not appropriate for transactions defined as remote in support of Transaction Routing. TRANSEC or TRANsaction SECurity should be defined for operator-initiated tasks to be routed to a remote system. A Deadlock TIMe OUT or DTIMOUT should also be defined so that the CICS Relay Task does not wait indefinitely for a session to become available or a response to be received from the remote system.

The PROFILE option provides the name of a profile of Terminal Control processing options that are to be used to govern the interaction between the operator's terminal and the task executing in DFHCRP or the CICS Relay Transaction. The definition and use of this PROFILE option are explained in the previous chapter. The TRPROF under "Remote Attributes" defines a profile used for the

```
    DEFINE
    TRANSACTION(name)
    [GROUP(groupname)]
    [PROGRAM(name)]
    [TWASIZE({0|value})]
    [PROFILE({DFHCICST|name})]
    [PARTITIONSET(name)]
    [STATUS({ENABLED|DISABLED})]

Remote attributes
    REMOTESYSTEM(name)
    [REMOTENAME({local-name|remote-name})]
    [TRPROF({DFHCICSS|name})]
    [LOCALQ({NO|YES})]

Scheduling
    [PRIORITY({1|value})]
    [TCLASS({NO|value})]

Aliases
    [TASKREQ(value)]
    [XTRANID(value)]

Recovery
    [DTIMOUT({NO|value})]
    [INDOUBT({BACKOUT|COMMIT|WAIT})]
    [RESTART({NO|YES})]
    [SPURGE({NO|YES})]
    [TPURGE({NO|YES})]
    [DUMP({YES|NO})]
    [TRACE({YES|NO})]

Security
    [EXTSEC({NO|YES})]
    [TRANSEC({1|value})]
    [RSL({0|value|PUBLIC})]
    [RSLC({NO|YES|EXTERNAL})
```

Figure 6-3 RDO DEFINE TRANSACTION options for defining TRANSIDs for Transaction Routing. Reprinted by permission from *CICS/MVS Version 2.1 Intercommunication Guide* © 1987, 1988 by International Business Machines Corporation.

session connecting the relay transaction and the remote system. If a TRPROF is not defined, its value defaults to DFHCICSS, and the characteristics of this IBM-supplied Intercommunication profile are enumerated in the previous chapter. The reason why an installation defined TRPROF might be named is to provide a Class of Service for Transaction Routing of this transaction. However, if this done, it is necessary to ensure that the appropriate MODENAMEs are used for

LUTYPE 6.2 connections with the system to which this TRANSID is routed. An example of using the TRPROF and its accompanying resource definitions follows.

```
Program Control Table
DEFINITION OF THE REMOTE TRANSACTION
    DFHPCT TYPE=REMOTE,SYSIDNT=CIC2,TRANSID=XX01,              X
           TRNPRTY=5,TRANSEC=8,TRPROF=UPROF1,                 X
           DTIMOUT=015,RTIMOUT=015, . . .                     X


DEFINITION OF PROFILE FOR TRANSACTION ROUTING - HIGH
    PRIORITY CLASS OF SERVICE
    DFHPCT TYPE=PROFILE,PROFILE=UPROF1,MODENAM=M1CICS,        X
           . . . . .


DEFINITION OF PROFILE FOR TRANSACTION ROUTING - LOW
    PRIORITY CLASS OF SERVICE
    DFHPCT TYPE=PROFILE,PROFILE=UPROF2,MODENAM=M2CICS,        X
           . . . . .


DEFINITION OF PROFILE FOR DISTRIBUTED TRANSACTION PROCESSING
    DFHPCT TYPE=PROFILE,PROFILE=UPROF3,MODENAM=M3CICS, ·      X
           . . .


Terminal Control Table
DEFINITION OF THE CONNECTION TO THE TRANSACTION-OWNING CICS
    DFHTCT TYPE=SYSTEM,ACCMETH=VTAM,NETNAME=DCCICS02,         X
           SYSIDNT=CIC2,TRMTYPE=LUTYPE62,BUFFER=256,          X
           RUSIZE=256,FEATURE=PARALLEL,. . . . .              X


DEFINITION OF FIRST SET OF SESSIONS WITH THE
    TRANSACTION-OWNING CICS SYSTEM
    DFHTCT TYPE=MODESET,SYSIDNT=CIC2,MAXSESS(4,2),            X
           MODENAM=M1CICS,CONNECT=AUTO, . . .                 X
DEFINITION OF SECOND SET OF SESSIONS WITH THE TRANSACTION-
    OWNING CICS SYSTEM
    DFHTCT TYPE=MODESET,SYSIDNT=CIC2,MAXSESS(4,2),            X
           MODENAM=M2CICS,CONNECT=AUTO, . . .                 X


DEFINITION OF THIRD SET OF SESSIONS — USED FOR
    DISTRIBUTED TRANSACTION PROCESSING WITH THE OTHER SYSTEM
    DFHTCT TYPE=MODESET,SYSIDNT=CIC2,MAXSESS(4,2),            X
           MODENAM=M3CICS,CONNECT=AUTO, . . .                 X
```

In the Program Control Table there are three PROFILEs defined. The only processing option that we are interested in for our PROFILEs is providing a connection to a MODENAM. The absence of other options of DFHPCT TYPE=PROFILE is indicated by the dots (.). There are three installation-specific MODENAMs used in the TCT MODESETs which define session groups, and therefore, there are three PROFILEs defined in the PCT. The appropriate Transaction Routing PROFile (TRPROF) is defined in the transaction's PCT entry.

In the Terminal Control Table, a SYSTEM CONNECTION is defined with the remote system. Subsequent to the connection definition, there are three sets of sessions defined via DFHTCT TYPE=MODESETs. The session sets are identical except that they specify different MODENAM values. These three MODENAM names represent VTAM LOGMODE names and are defined as entries in the Logon Mode Table. These external definitions are REQUIRED in this context!

6.3.2 Definitions In the Transaction-Owning System

In the Transaction-Owning system the transaction is defined as a local TRANSID in the Program Control Table. There are several options regarding the terminal definition: RDO or macro definitions can be used in the Transaction-Owning region to define remote terminals. In RDO a DEFINE TYPETERM command is used to create a named collection of terminal attributes, or an IBM-supplied default type terminal definition can be utilized. The TYPETERMs supplied by IBM are contained within the list DFHLIST2 which we discussed in the previous chapter. The RDO DEFINE TYPETERM accommodates the entry of a TYPETERM name; resource/device information; mapping and paging characteristics; operational, session, and message-receiving properties; diagnostic display, recovery and application features.

Once the TYPETERM definition is created or selected from the IBM defaults, the DEFINE TERMINAL can be used to define individual terminals. As with TYPETERMs, there are TERMINAL models provided by IBM, and these resource definitions are also contained in DFHLIST2. The DEFINE TERMINAL panel is illustrated in Figure 6-4. The information entered into this panel for a remote terminal includes the TERMinal ID, the appropriate TYPETERM name, a SYSIDNT of the REMOTESYSTEM, and a REMOTENAME

```
TErminal      ==> ....
Group         ==> ........
AUTINSTModel  ==> No           No | Yes | Only
AUTINSTName   ==> ........

TERMINAL IDENTIFIERS
TYpeterm      ==> ........
Netname       ==> ........
Console       ==> No           No | 0-99
REMOTESystem  ==> ....
REMOTEName    ==> ....
Modename      ==> ........

ASSOCIATED PRINTERS
PRINTER       ==> ....
PRINTERCopy   ==> No           No | Yes
ALTPRINTEr    ==> ....
ALTPRINTCopy  ==> No           No | Yes

PIPELINE PROPERTIES
POol          ==> ....
TAsklimit     ==> No           No | 1-32767

OPERATOR DEFAULTS
OPERId        ==> ...
OPERPriority  ==> 000          0-255
OPERRsl       ==> 0            0-24,...
OPERSecurity  ==> 1            1-64,...

Userid        ==> ........

TERMINAL USAGES
TRansaction   ==> ....
TErmpriority  ==> 000          0-255
Inservice     ==> Yes          Yes | No

SESSION SECURITY
SEcurityname  ==> ........
ATtachsec     ==> Local        Local | Identify | Verify
Bindpassword  ==>              PASSWORD NOT SPECIFIED
```

Figure 6-4 The DEFINE TERMINAL Panel. Reprinted by permission from *CICS/MVS Version 2.1 Resource Definition (Online)* © 1987, 1988 by International Business Machines Corporation.

if the TERMID in the Transaction Owning system is different from its real name (TERMID) in the Terminal Owning region.

One word of caution about using RDO for VTAM terminal definitions, the TYPETERM definition(s) to be used for terminals must be installed prior to the installation of the terminals. The CEDA INSTALL command is used for these purposes. Also, if a TYPETERM is altered and reinstalled, it is necessary to reinstall all of the terminals referencing the TYPETERM definition in order to obtain the new values for each of the terminals.

For macro definition, a DFHTCT TYPE=REMOTE may be coded to specify remote terminal information. Figure 6-5 illustrates the format of this macro.

```
DFHTCT   TYPE=REMOTE
        ,ACCMETH=access-method
        ,SYSIDNT=name
        ,TRMIDNT=name
        [,RMTNAME=name]
        ,TRMTYPE=terminal-type

        [,ALTPGE=(lines,columns)]
        [,ALTSCRN=(lines,columns)]
        [,ALTSFX=number]
        [,DEFSCRN=(lines,columns)]
        [,ERRATT={NO
           |([LASTLINE][,INTENSIFY][,color][,highlight])}]
        [,FEATURE=(feature[,feature],...)]
        [,OPERRSL={0|(number[,...]}]
        [,OPERSEC={1|(number[,number],...)}]
        [,PGESIZE=(lines,columns)]
        [,TCTUAL=number]
        [,TIOAL={value|(value1,value2)}]
        [,TRMMODL=numbercharacter]

     Non-VTAM

        [,DISMSG=name]
        [,LPLEN={132|value}]
        [,STN2980=number]
        [,TAB2980={1|value}]

     VTAM and TCAM SNA Only

        [,BMSFEAT=(FMHPARM,NOROUTE,NOROUTEALL,OBFMT,OBOPID)]
        [,HF={NO|YES}]
        [,LDC={listname|(aa[=nnn],bb[=nnn],cc[=nnn],...)}]
        [,SESTYPE=session-type]
        [,VF={NO|YES}]

     VTAM Only

        [,FF={NO|YES}]
```

Figure 6-5 The DFHTCT TYPE=REMOTE macro format. Reprinted by permission from *CICS/MVS Version 2.1 Intercommunication Guide* © 1987, 1988 by International Business Machines Corporation.

For those individuals who adore CICS table maintenance and take great glee in duplicating their efforts, RDO or macro definition can be used to redundantly define terminals in Terminal-Owning and Transaction-Owning regions. However, for other folks who do not quite fit into this category, there is another choice. As a matter of fact, this other choice may well result in a better operational environment because there will be no inconsistencies between local and remote terminal definitions. With both RDO and macro definition there is a way to generate the required remote and local table entries from one set of definitions. In a Multi-Region environment, it is normal for connected CICS systems to share a common CICS System Definition file (CSD). RDO defined TYPETERMs and TERMINALs can be installed into multiple CICS systems. When the definitions are installed into the Terminal Owning region, the one whose SYS-IDNT is the same as the REMOTESYSTEM name, a full local definition is created. However, when installed into another system, with a different SYSIDNT, a remote definition is created. Please bear in mind that RDO terminal definition is available *only* for VTAM terminals. Other types of terminals must be defined through macro definition.

If the two CICS systems are not able to share a common CSD, as may well be the case with ISC LUTYPE 6.2 connections, then the RDO terminal definitions in the Terminal Owning system can be defined as shippable. This is applicable only to RDO defined VTAM terminals, and terminal definitions *cannot* be shipped to releases of CICS prior to 1.7. The SHIPPABLE option is selected in the TERM-TYPE definition. If a terminal used for Transaction Routing is defined as shippable, a "shippable definition" flag is set and sent to the Transaction-Owning region along with the transaction initiation request. If the Transaction-Owning region already possesses a definition of the terminal, then the flag is ignored. However, if no terminal definition is present then the Transaction-Owning CICS requests that the Terminal-Owning CICS ship the terminal definition. The terminal definition need not be reshipped with each request because it is retained until CEDA INSTALL is used to alter or remove the terminal definition in/from the Terminal-Owning CICS or the Terminal Owning CICS is cold started.

There is one other case when CICS loses a shipped definition. A terminal may be defined through RDO as a candidate for AU-TOINSTALL. Such terminals are dynamically added to CICS when a successful terminal logon is processed and dynamically removed from CICS when logoff occurs. If the terminal is an AUTOINSTALL terminal in the Terminal-Owning region, a logoff results in the terminal definition being removed from the Terminal-Owning system and from the Transaction-Owning system. There is one note of caution about AUTOINSTALL and terminal definition shipping. If a terminal can be defined in two CICS systems that are connected by Transaction Routing, caution must be observed. If in one region the terminal were not defined through AUTOINSTALL and the same terminal was defined with AUTOINSTALL in the other system, a serious problem could ensue. For example, the user is logged onto the CICS system with a fixed shippable definition. The user performs a remote TRANSID and the terminal definition is shipped to the other CICS system. The user then logs off but since the definition is not via AUTOINSTALL, the terminal definition is not removed upon logoff, nor is the shipped definition removed from the Transaction Owning CICS. If the user then attempts to logon to the Transaction Owning region directly, this causes a problem. Therefore, the way around this is to define AUTOINSTALL for both systems or for neither system.

In macro definition it is likewise possible to share source code. A copy member can be created in a source statement library containing standard terminal definitions. These definitions can include CICS macros that generate line information for BTAM terminals as well as all of the actual DFHTCT TYPE=TERMINAL macros to define the terminals. The copy member is copied into multiple Terminal Control Tables subsequent to a DFHTCT TYPE=REGION macro. The purpose of the DFHTCT TYPE=REGION macro is to indicate whether a local or remote definition is being assembled. The following source code could be contained in a TCT GEN of local resources.

```
DFHTCT TYPE=INITIAL,SYSIDNT=CIC1, . . .
DFHTCT TYPE=REGION,SYSIDNT=LOCAL
             - OR -
             SYSIDNT=CIC1
COPY SHRTERMS
DFHTCT TYPE=FINAL
```

The purpose of the SYSIDNT option of the DFHTCT TYPE=INITIAL macro is solely so that the table assembles correctly. Because the SYSIDNTs match on the TYPE=INITIAL and second choice of the TYPE=REGION or because of a SYSIDNT of LOCAL on the TYPE=REGION macro, the definitions within the copy member SHRTERMS are assembled as locally owned terminal definitions. However, in the example below, remote entries would be generated.

```
DFHTCT TYPE=INITIAL,SYSIDNT=CIC2, . . .
DFHTCT TYPE=REGION,SYSIDNT=CIC1
COPY SHRTERMS
DFHTCT TYPE=FINAL
```

The TYPE=REGION macro can be used to toggle on/off what is assembled. In the following example, the contents of the first copy member are processed as a collection of remote entries, whereas the definitions in the second copy member are assembled as local resources.

```
DFHTCT TYPE=INITIAL,SYSIDNT=CIC3,  . . .
DFHTCT TYPE=REGION,SYSIDNT=CIC1
COPY SHRTERMS
DFHTCT TYPE=REGION,SYSIDNT=CIC3
             - OR -
             SYSIDNT=LOCAL
COPY ALLMINE
DFHTCT TYPE=FINAL
```

Another option for sharing macro definition source code is to code terminal definitions using the DFHTCT TYPE=REMOTE macro and providing a complete definition. This is possible because parameters from DFHTCT TYPE=TERMINAL can also be code for the TYPE=REMOTE macro. The TYPE=REMOTE macro names a SYSIDNT. When assembled in a TCT in which the DFHTCT TYPE=INITIAL macro specifies the SYSIDNT named on the TYPE=REMOTE macros, local resource definitions are created. However, if the SYSIDNTs are different during assembly, the TYPE=REMOTE macros result in the assembly of remote resource definitions. The advantages of using the same source code are twofold: There is less table maintenance to perform and this ensures that there are no discrepancies between the terminal definitions in the joined systems.

6.4 AUTOMATIC TRANSACTION INITIATION AND TRANSACTION ROUTING

A request for Automatic Transaction Initiation (ATI) can specify a remote terminal resource. This can be done via a START command in which a remote terminal is defined in the TERMID option, or a trigger level defined for an Intrapartition Transient Data Queue can be reached. A TRANSID named in the Destination Control Table *must* be local to the queue owning region. However, a terminal named in the queue's DCT entry can be remote. When an ATI request occurs for a remote terminal, the local CICS system sends the request to the Terminal-Owning region. In the Terminal-Owning region, when the terminal becomes available, a CICS Relay Task executing in DFHCRP is attached to the terminal. The Relay Task uses a session to the Transaction-Owning region and sends a request for transaction initiation. Thus, aside from the fact that the Transaction-Owning region forwards the ATI request to the Terminal-Owning region, the processing of ATI requests for remote terminals is the same as for normal Transaction Routing. Of course, there are two potential sources of delay. The Transaction Owning CICS may have to wait for a session to the Terminal Owning System. Second, once received in the Terminal Owning CICS, it may be necessary to wait until the terminal becomes available.

There is one point that needs to be remembered for Automatic Transaction Initiation and remote terminals. The ATI request is first processed in the Transaction-Owning region, which must be cognizant of the SYSIDNT of the Terminal-Owning region so that the ATI request can be forwarded properly. If there is no definition of the remote terminal in the Transaction-Owning region when the ATI request is first processed, then CICS does not know where to send the ATI request. Thus, terminal definition shipping cannot be relied upon when Transaction Routing is used in the context of Automatic Transaction Initiation. If the processing of a prior routed transaction caused shipment of a terminal definition for the appropriate terminal, then the Transaction Owning region is able to utilize the shipped terminal definition and forward the ATI request accordingly. However, this may not have occurred. Therefore, it is probably best not to depend upon shipped terminal definitions in a situation where such terminals are candidates for cross system ATI requests.

6.5   TRANSACTION ROUTING — APPLICATION PROGRAM CONSIDERATIONS

The application programming considerations for programs to be utilized in a Transaction Routing environment are negligible. Existing programs can readily be used in Transaction Routing and normally require no alteration. Application programs can be written in assembler, COBOL, or PL/I, and both the command level and macro level programs are supported. The macro level support provides upward compatiblity for older existing CICS applications as new applications are not written in macro level.

Both conversational and pseudo-conversational transactions are supported for Transaction Routing. Obviously, however, pseudo-conversational programming is preferable. We use pseudo-conversational programming so that storage resources are not held during operator processing of screen data in a single-system environment. In a Transaction Routing environment, storage resources in multiple

CICS systems would be held during operator processing if conversational programs were utilized. Also, a session is reserved exclusively for routing terminal input/output between the Relay Task in the Terminal-Owning region and the user transaction in the Transaction-Owning region during the lifetime of these tasks. To hold a session or connection between two systems as an exclusive resource of a conversational application is not a good thing to do. As a matter of fact some might call it evil!

For pseudo-conversational transactions RETURN with TRANSID is supported. The TRANSID named in the RETURN command can be local to the same system that the original routed transaction processed in, or it can be local to the Terminal Owning region. Care should be exercised to ensure that a TRANSID named in a RETURN command is uniquely defined as remote in the Terminal Owning CICS unless the next transaction is intended to process in the Terminal Owning region.

Application programs may utilize native mode Terminal Control Commands, Basic Mapping Support, or the Batch Data Interchange Facility to communicate with a remotely owned terminal. BMS mapsets or partition sets must be defined in the Transaction-Owning region along with the programs that utilize them. Mapping operations are performed in the Transaction-Owning region before the terminal data stream is forwarded to the Terminal-Owning region.

BMS paging services can also be utilized. With BMS paging a series of pages are built until a logical message is complete. The ACCUM and PAGING options are used in a BMS output command such as SEND MAP to indicate that output data are to be accumulated in pages and complete pages are to be stored in Temporary Storage as opposed to being directed to a terminal. The application program uses a SEND PAGE command to indicate that a logical message is complete. Subsequent to the SEND PAGE command, the CICS paging transaction CSPG is invoked and a terminal operator can enter paging commands to review various stored pages. When the operator has completed examination of the output, the Temporary Storage queue is purged. Building of logical pages takes place in the Transaction Owning region. Such pages are saved in Temporary Storage until the logical message is complete. At that time, the queue of BMS pages is forwarded to the Terminal Owning system where they are saved in Temporary Storage and available for the paging transaction, "CSPG," which is handled in the Terminal Owning region. After forwarding, the BMS page queue is deleted from Temporary Storage in the Transaction Owning CICS.

The RETAIN option of the SEND PAGE command allows an application task to obtain control back at the next sequential instruction after the SEND PAGE command, when the paging operation is complete (i.e., the operator is through reviewing Temporary Storage pages). This option should be avoided for paging operations in a Transaction Routing environment.

BMS Routing can be utilized to route messages to terminals in remote systems. The BMS ROUTE command is used for this purpose. The ROUTE command can name a route list defining terminals and/or operators (OPID) to receive the routed message. Additionally the ROUTE command can specify an OPCLASS or class of operators (as defined in the Sign oN Table) who are to receive the message. There are restrictions regarding the use of operator qualifying information in cross system message routing. If no route list is named and the OPCLASS information is omitted, the message is routed to all remotely defined terminals in the connected Terminal-Owning region. If, on the other hand, no route list is included and the OPCLASS is specified, the message is not sent to any remote operators at all. Unless specific terminals are named in a route list, operator-qualifying information cannot be used cross systems. Thus, OPCLASS or OPID (as defined within the route list) cannot be specified independently as they can within a single-system environment.

A transaction initiated as a result of Transaction Routing is able to use remote resources through CICS Function Shipping. Such remote resources can be located in any connected CICS including the Terminal-Owning region. However, Function Shipping requests back to the Terminal-Owning region require the use of an additional session because the one utilized for Transaction Routing is dedicated to that process. If this were to occur frequently because the routed transaction is heavily used, the need for cross system sessions might increase.

6.6   CRTE — THE ROUTING TRANSACTION

There is a CICS-supplied routing transaction, "CRTE," that can be used on LUTYPE 6.2 or MRO links between CICS systems. CRTE cannot be used on LUTYPE 6.1 connections, however. This routing transaction can prove very handy in several contexts. First, in a multi-system environment, it may be desirable for a Master Terminal Operator to occasionally use CEMT or CSMT against one or more remote systems. This could be accomplished in several ways.

First, for local CICS systems, the MTO's terminal could be defined in all regions and the MTO could simply logon to the appropriate CICS systems.

The next scenario is that the CICS region to which the MTO logs on can have defined within it, alias TRANSIDs for CSMT and CEMT in each of the other CICS regions. The REMOTENAME option of the RDO DEFINE TRANSACTION Command or its macro equivalent can specify CSMT or CEMT and the TRANSACTION option provide a local alias name. If there is one connected system, this is a plausible choice. It is merely necessary to make the appropriate table definitions and inform the Master Terminal Operator of the alias TRANSIDs. However, it might get cumbersome to relate different alias names for CEMT and CSMT for multiple connected systems.

The third choice is to use CRTE, the CICS routing transaction. CRTE can be used from any 3270 display station except an MVS console. CRTE establishes a "session" between the CRTE terminal and a remote system. After this "session" is established, all TRANSIDs entered from the terminal are routed to the named CICS system. CEOT and CSOT, the terminal status transactions cannot be used over a CRTE "session." The format of the route command to establish a terminal "session" with a remote system is:

```
CRTE SYSID=sysidnt
```

The SYSID option names the remote system's SYSIDNT as it is known in the CICS region to which the MTO is logged on. Optionally, a TRPROF parameter can be used to name a CICS profile for use during the routing "session." The format of CRTE in this context is:

```
CRTE SYSID=sysidnt,TRPROF=profname
```

If TRPROF is omitted, a default IBM profile is used. Subsequent to entering CRTE a message confirms that the "session" is established and TRANSIDs can be entered for the remote system. However, if the remote system is a secure CICS requiring sign on, then a sign on has to be performed. Any terminal operators using CRTE against a secure CICS system will require SNT entries in the remote system. Once in and signed on to the remote system, a terminal operator can utilize CEMT or CSMT or any other transactions (limited by his/her security key) except CSOT and CEOT, as mentioned above. In order to terminate the "session" with the remote CICS, the terminal operator must enter:

CANCEL

A message is then displayed informing the operator of the termination of the routing "session." CRTE can be entered repeatedly, meaning that, once in a routing "session" with a remote CICS, it is possible to enter another CRTE TRANSID and request connection to yet another CICS system. A separate CANCEL request is required for each iteration of CRTE.

CRTE is useful to application programmers because it permits use of EDF across systems so that the CICS Execute Diagnostic Facility can be used to test program execution in remote regions. Also, CRTE can be used to provide an ad hoc Transaction Routing capability without requiring table definitions. In conclusion, CRTE is oriented toward making transaction routing available without requiring PCT definitions. However, it should be relied upon only for Transaction Routing of lightly used transactions. For heavy use transactions, the table definitions should be defined.

6.7   INDIRECT LINKS FOR TRANSACTION ROUTING

Transaction Routing is possible between two CICS systems that are not directly connected to each other. The pathway between such systems can involve one or more intermediate CICS systems. So, if CICS1 is connected to CICS2, and CICS2 is connected to CICS3, then an Indirect Link for Transaction Routing purposes can be defined between CICS1 and CICS3 even though there is no direct link between them. This is termed an Indirect Link, and there can be multiple intermediate CICS systems between the Terminal-Owning and Transaction-Owning CICS regions. Figure 6-6 illustrates an Indirect Link between two CICS systems. Note that in this example there are three intermediate systems between CIC1 and CIC5. Indirect Links are applicable only to Transaction Routing. They are not used for other types of Intercommunication.

Resource definitions for the Transaction and Terminal must be contained in all of the CICS systems along an Indirect Link. So in Figure 6-6, all five of the CICS systems would require definitions for both the TRANSID and Terminal. An Indirect Link cannot turn back on itself or Transaction Routing requests abend. In addition to the transaction and terminal definitions a definition of the Indirect Link is required in the systems along an Indirect Link with the exception

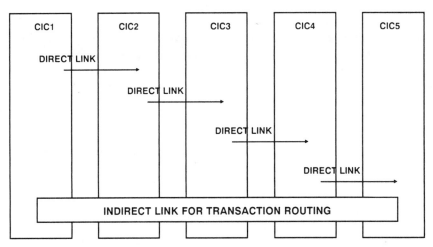

Figure 6-6 Indirect link between CIC1 and CIC5. Indirect links can be defined for Transaction Routing.

of the Terminal-Owning CICS system and the next CICS system along the link that is directly connected to the Terminal-Owning region. In Figure 6-6, Indirect Link definitions would be required in CIC3, CIC4 and CIC5.

The terminal definitions in each system identify the SYSIDNT of the true Terminal-Owning CICS. The TRANSID definitions in the PCT, however, define the adjacent CICS system as the owner of the TRANSID. Adjacent in this context starts with the Terminal-Owning CICS. In that system the TRANSID is defined as being owned by the next CICS system along the Indirect Link. And this is carried forth across the pathway. So, relating back to Figure 6-6, if CIC1 were the Terminal-Owning region and CIC5 were the Transaction-Owning system, the following definitions would be required.

CIC1 would contain a definition of the terminal as a locally owned resource and a definition of the transaction which defines CIC2 as its owner.

CIC2 would contain a definition of the terminal as a remote terminal owned by CIC1 and a transaction definition defining CIC3 as the owner.

CIC3 would contain a definition of an indirect link to CIC1 through CIC2, a definition of the terminal as remote and owned by CIC1, and a definition of the transaction indicating that CIC4 is the owner.

CIC4 would contain a definition of an indirect link to CIC1 through CIC3, a definition of the terminal as remote and owned by CIC1, and a definition of the transaction indicating that CIC5 is the owner.

CIC5 would contain a definition of an indirect link to CIC1 through CIC4, a definition of the terminal as remote and owned by CIC1, and a definition of the transaction as a locally owned resource.

In order to define an Indirect Link the RDO DEFINE CONNECTION command or the DFHTCT TYPE=SYSTEM macro can be used. An example of RDO definition is:

```
DEFINE CONNECTION(Terminal Owner sysidnt)
       GROUP(RDO control group name)
       ACCESSMETHOD(INDIRECT)
       NETNAME(netname of Terminal Owning CICS)
       INDSYS(sysidnt)
```

The SYSIDNT named in the INDSYS option is that of the adjacent directly connected CICS that goes toward the Terminal Owning region. An example of macro definition is:

```
        DFHTCT TYPE=SYSTEM,ACCMETH=INDIRECT,              X
               SYSIDNT=(Terminal Owner sysidnt),          X
               NETNAME=(netname of Terminal Owning CICS), X
               INDSYS=(sysidnt)
```

Again, the SYSIDNT specified in the INDSYS parameter names the next directly connected CICS system along the path going toward the Terminal Owning region. No SESSIONS are defined subsequent to the DEFINE CONNECTION for an Indirect Link and no TYPE=MODESET macros follow the TYPE=SYSTEM macro in this context. The actual sessions used for cross system communication are the sessions of the Direct Links between the connected systems. A direct connection (DEFINE CONNECTION and DEFINE SESSIONS) underlying an Indirect Link must be installed when RDO is used, prior to the installation of the Indirect Link.

REVIEW EXERCISES

Provide a short answer to each of the following.

1. Is there a limitation for ISC Transaction Routing in terms of how the LUTYPE 6 systems are connected?
2. What is a "surrogate TCTTE" and how is it used?
3. What is the function of the DFHTCT TYPE=REGION macro?
4. What is meant by a "shippable" terminal definition?
5. Is it a good idea to define TIMEOUTs for Remote Transactions and, if so, why?
6. What is LOCALQing and why is it not appropriate for transaction routing?
7. What is the CICS Relay Program (DFHCRP) and what is its role in transaction routing?
8. What is CRTE and how may this TRANSID be useful to an application programmer?
9. Why are conversational transactions particularly inappropriate for Transaction Routing?
10. Can BMS be used in a transaction routing environment? If so, where are mapsets defined?
11. The routing transaction, CRTE, initiates a "session" with a remote system. How does one get out of the "session"?

ANSWERS TO REVIEW EXERCISES

Provide a short answer to each of the following.

1. *Is there a limitation for ISC Transaction Routing in terms of how the LUTYPE 6 systems are connected?*

    Transaction Routing is supported ONLY on LUTYPE 6.2 LINKS.

2. *What is a "surrogate TCTTE" and how is it used?*

    A surrogate TCTTE is used during Transaction Routing. In the Transaction-Owning region, a routed transaction causes a user task to be created which executes in a user program. CICS creates a surrogate TCTTE which serves as the task's TCTTE. To all extents and purposes the surrogate looks like the real thing. The only thing is that operator security information is not available.

3. *What is the function of the DFHTCT TYPE=REGION macro?*

The purpose of this macro is to allow the sharing of copy books with TCT macro resource definitions across the TCT gens for multiple systems. Based upon the SYSIDNT defined in the TYPE=REGION, the subsequent copy code can generate local definitions or remote definitions as appropriate.

4. *What is meant by a "shippable" terminal definition?*

VTAM RDO terminals can be defined as shippable. This is done in the terminal's TYPETERM specification. If a terminal definition is shippable, the Terminal-Owning CICS sets a flag to indicate this in the Transaction Routing request sent to the remote Transaction-Owning region. If the Transaction-Owning region already has a definition for the terminal, then the flag is ignored. Otherwise, the Transaction-Owning region can request that the terminal owning CICS ship the terminal's definition.

5. *Is it a good idea to define TIMEOUTs for Remote Transactions and, if so, why?*

Yes. A human being is sitting and waiting for a response. If a session is not available or there is no response from the remote region, it would be nice if the task timed out and let the user go. Otherwise, the task could wait until a session/response is obtained.

6. *What is LOCALQing and why is it not appropriate for Transaction Routing?*

LOCALQing is when CICS queues requests for a system that is not available. This is obviously not something that we would want for Transaction Routing because we don't want a user hung. However, this might be handy for remotely directed START requests.

7. *What is the CICS Relay Program (DFHCRP) and what is its role in Transaction Routing?*

The CICS Relay Program serves as the communication mechanism between a terminal and a remote user task. When a remote transaction is requested, the Terminal-Owning region initiates a task to run in the CICS Relay Program. DFHCRP acquires a session to the remote system and sends the Transaction Routing request. When a response is received from the remote transaction, DFHCRP sends the data to the terminal.

8. *What is CRTE and how may this TRANSID be useful to an application programmer?*

CRTE is the CICS-supplied routing transaction. Using CRTE a terminal user can name a remote SYSIDNT and have CICS establish a "session" with the remote system. During the session all TRANSIDs are directed to the remote system. This is handy for an application programmer because it permits the remote testing of programs via CEDF.

9. *Why are conversational transactions particularly inappropriate for Transaction Routing?*

Storage resources in two CICS regions would be tied up waiting for a terminal operator's response. Plus, Transaction Routing involves the exclusive use of a session during the lifetime of the relay task and the user task. That means that an IRC or ISC session would likewise be tied up waiting for a terminal operator's response.

10. *Can BMS be used in a Transaction Routing environment? If so, where are mapsets defined?*

Yes. The BMS mapsets are defined in the Transaction-Owning region along with the transaction's program.

11. *The routing transaction, CRTE, initiates a "session" with a remote system. How does one get out of the "session"?*

One enters: CANCEL.

7

Function Shipping

7.1 INTRODUCTION

CICS Function Shipping permits application programs executing under CICS to access resources of other connected CICS systems. A CICS application program may access remote: VSAM and BDAM files; Intrapartition or Extrapartition Transient Data Queues; and Temporary Storage Queues. Additionally, DL/I databases managed by a remote CICS can also be accessed via Function Shipping. It is merely necessary to code regular CICS commands to gain access to remote resources. Therefore, all of the CICS File commands listed in Figure 7-1, Transient Data commands listed in Figure 7-2, and Temporary Storage commands listed in Figure 7-3 can be used to access remote files, Transient Data Queues, and Temporary Storage Queues, respectively. Additionally, the Interval Control START Command can be used to initiate a remote TRANSID but, we will consider this a "special case" and discuss the START Command in the chapter on Asynchronous Processing.

A SYSID option can be used in resource access commands to name the SYSIDNT of a remote system, but more typically the SYSID is not included and CICS determines that the resource being accessed is remote from an examination of the local resource definition table (i.e., the File Control Table, Temporary Storage Table, or Destination Control Table). If the SYSID option is included, the local CICS does

```
TO READ A REMOTE RECORD:
    EXEC CICS READ FILE(ddname) UPDATE
         INTO(data-area-name)  *  or  *  SET(pointer)
         LENGTH(2-byte-binary-field-name)
         RIDFLD(data-area-name)
         RBA  *  or  RRN
         KEYLENGTH(key-size)
         GENERIC
         GTEQ  *  or  *  EQUAL
         DEBKEY  *  or  *  DEBREC
         SYSID(sysidnt)

TO REWRITE A RECORD PREVIOUSLY READ FOR UPDATE:
    EXEC CICS REWRITE FILE(ddname)
         FROM(data-area-name)
         LENGTH(record-length)
         SYSID(sysidnt)

TO ADD A RECORD TO A FILE:
    EXEC CICS WRITE FILE(ddname)
         FROM(data-area-name)
         LENGTH(record-length)
         RIDFLD(data-area-name)
         RBA  *  or  RRN
         KEYLENGTH(key-size)
         MASSINSERT
         SYSID(sysidnt)

TO DELETE A VSAM KSDS/RRDS RECORD:
    EXEC CICS DELETE FILE(ddname)
         RIDFLD(data-area-name)
         RBA  *  or  *  RRN
         KEYLENGTH(key-size)
         GENERIC
         NUMREC(2-byte-binary-field)
         SYSID(sysidnt)

TO RELEASE A VSAM CI LOCK WITHOUT UPDATING:
    EXEC CICS UNLOCK FILE(ddname)
         SYSID(sysidnt)
```

Figure 7-1 File control commands.

not examine the resource definition table but simply ships the request to the named system unless Resource Security Level Checking is specified in the TRANSID's PCT definition. If RSLC=YES is selected, then the NOTAUTH condition occurs for commands which include the SYSID option.

```
TO INITIATE A BROWSE:

    EXEC CICS STARTBR FILE(ddname)
        REQID(request-identifier)
        RIDFLD(data-area-name)
        RBA  *  or  RRN
        KEYLENGTH(key-size)
        GENERIC
        GTEQ  *  or  *  EQUAL
        DEBKEY  *  or  *  DEBREC
        SYSID(sysidnt)

TO READ THE NEXT SEQUENTIAL RECORD:
    EXEC CICS READNEXT FILE(ddname)
        INTO(data-area-name)  *  or  *  SET(pointer)
        LENGTH(2-byte-binary-field-name
        RIDFLD(data-area-name)
        RBA  *  or  RRN
        KEYLENGTH(key-size)
        REQID(request-identifier)
        SYSID(sysidnt)

TO READ THE PREVIOUS RECORD:
    EXEC CICS READPREV FILE(ddname)
        INTO(data-area-name)  *  or  *  SET(pointer)
        LENGTH(2-byte-binary-field-name)
        RIDFLD(data-area-name)
        RBA  *  or  RRN
        KEYLENGTH(key-size)
        REQID(request-identifier)
        SYSID(sysidnt)

TO END A BROWSE:
    EXEC CICS ENDBR FILE(ddname)
        REQID(request-identifier)
        SYSID(sysidnt)

TO RESET A BROWSE POINTER:
    EXEC CICS RESETBR FILE(ddname)
        RIDFLD(data-area-name)
        RBA  *  or  RRN
        KEYLENGTH(key-size)
        GENERIC
        REQID(request-identifier)
        GTEQ  *  or  *  EQUAL
        SYSID(sysidnt)
```

Figure 7-1 (continued) File control commands.

```
TO WRITE TO A TD QUEUE:
    EXEC CICS WRITEQ TD QUEUE(destid)
        FROM(name-of-data-area)
        LENGTH(size-of-item)
        SYSID(sysidnt)

TO READ A TD QUEUE ITEM:
    EXEC CICS READQ TD QUEUE(destid)
        INTO(data-area-name)  *  or  *  SET(pointer)
        LENGTH(2-byte-binary-field-name)
        NOSUSPEND
        SYSID(sysidnt)

TO DELETE A TD QUEUE:
    EXEC CICS DELETEQ TD QUEUE(estaid)
        SYSID(sysidnt)
```

Figure 7-2 Transient data commands.

7.1.1   Defining Remote Files For Function Shipping

The definition of a file as remote is made using a DFHFCT
TYPE=REMOTE macro instruction. Resource Definition Online
(RDO) is not available for file definitions. The format of the DFHFCT
TYPE=REMOTE macro is as follows.

```
        DFHFCT  TYPE=REMOTE,
                FILE=ddname,
                SYSIDNT=sysidnt,
                KEYLEN=key-size,
                LRECL=record-size,
                RMTNAME=remote-ddname,
                RSL=0
                - OR -
                PUBLIC
                - OR -
                (1-24)
```

The SYSIDNT= parameter provides the SYSIDNT of the file-
owning system as defined in its SYSTEM/CONNECTION definition
in the Terminal Control Table.

The FILE= option provides the 1- to 8-character DDNAME by
which the file is known locally. This is the name specified in the
FILE option of file access commands in application programs. The

```
TO WRITE TO A TS QUEUE:
    EXEC CICS WRITEQ TS QUEUE(dataid)
        FROM(name-of-data-area)
        LENGTH(size-of-item)
        MAIN  *  OR  *  AUXILIARY
        NOSUSPEND
        REWRITE
        ITEM(name-of-data-area)
        SYSID(sysidnt)

TO READ A TS QUEUE ITEM:
    EXEC CICS READQ TS QUEUE(dataid)
        INTO(data-area-name)  *  or  *  SET(pointer)
        LENGTH(2-byte-binary-field-name)
        NUMITEMS(2-byte-binary-field-name)
        ITEM(2-byte-binary-field-name)  *  or  *  NEXT
        SYSID(sysidnt)

TO DELETE A TS QUEUE:
    EXEC CICS DELETEQ TS QUEUE(dataid)
        SYSID(sysidnt)
```

Figure 7-3 Temporary storage commands.

FILE option is new in CICS release 2.1 and replaces the DATASET option. The DATASET option may still be used for upward compatibility but FILE is the preferred option name.

The remaining parameters are optional. The RMTNAME= parameter provides the 1- to 8-character DDNAME by which the file is known in the remote system. If this parameter is omitted, the remote DDNAME is assumed to be the same as the DDNAME specified in the FILE= option. The RMTNAME= parameter allows the FILE= parameter to be utilized as a local alias for the file's true DDNAME. This would be necessary if there were a local file defined in the File Control Table with the same DDNAME as a remote file.

The KEYLEN= option permits the specification of keylength information for keyed files such as a VSAM Key Sequenced Data Set. If KEYLEN is omitted from the File Control Table (FCT) definition of a remote keyed file, then application program commands must specify keylength information via the KEYLENGTH option of file access commands, where appropriate. If the file is not keyed, then the application program includes a qualifier, such as Relative Byte Address (RBA) or Relative Record Number (RRN), to indicate that the RIDFLD or Record IDentification FieLD does not contain a variable length key but rather a Relative Byte Address (RBA) or Relative

Record Number (RRN). RBAs are used to access VSAM Entry Sequenced Data Sets, and RRNs are used to access VSAM Relative Record Data Sets. Since RBAs and RRNs are of a fixed size, further length specification is unnecessary if either keyword is specified as a qualifier of the RIDFLD option.

The LRECL= parameter may be specified to provide fixed record length information for the file. If this option is not defined in the FCT, then application programs must provide length information via the LENGTH option of file access commands, where appropriate.

The Resource Security Level or RSL= parameter can be used to give the file resource security protection. Resource security checking is performed in the local CICS when an access request is made for a resource, in this case a file, from a command level task whose TRANSID is defined in the PCT as RSLC=YES. The RSL can be 0, or a number from 1 to 24, or PUBLIC. PUBLIC means that the resource is unconditionally available. If external resource security (via a product such as the Resource Access Control Facility or RACF) has been defined for file resources in the local CICS system, external resource security checking is bypassed if RSL=PUBLIC. If RSL=0, the resource *cannot* be accessed by any task executing a TRANSID defined as RSLC=YES in its PCT definition. If the RSL= is defined as a number from 1 through 24, the local CICS checks the operator's resource security key as defined in the Sign oN Table to ensure that access is permitted.

The following code illustrates a sample File Control Table definition for a remote file.

```
DFHFCT  TYPE=REMOTE,FILE=APPFILE,LRECL=80,        X
        SYSIDNT=CIC1,RMTNAME=EDFILE,              X
        KEYLEN=9,RSL=PUBLIC
```

The owning system is specified as "CIC1." "CIC1" is a SYSIDNT or CONNECTION name defined in the Terminal Control Table via a DFHTCT TYPE=SYSTEM macro or DEFINE CONNECTION RDO command.

The name by which this file is known locally is "APPFILE." Application programs will use this name in file access commands. However, "APPFILE" is but a local alias name for the file because the RMTNAME parameter is used to provide a different name. In CIC1, the file is known as "EDFILE" and there must be an FCT definition for a file named "EDFILE" in that system.

KEYLEN information is specified so local file access commands need not specify KEYLENGTH information.

Resource Security Level is declared as PUBLIC. No resource security checking is to be performed in the local CICS. If EXTernal SECurity is defined for files in the local CICS, it is bypassed for this FCT entry.

An application program command sequence to access and update this file from a Command Level COBOL Program is provided in Figure 7-4. Note that the coding to access this remote resource is identical to the coding that might be specified for access to a local resource. Figure 7-5 illustrates the same commands as they might be coded in a Command Level COBOL II Program. Figure 7-6 is the same old thing again but coded in assembler language. In our samples, we performed update access. In other words, we READ the

```
WORKING-STORAGE SECTION.
01  APP-ID              PIC X(9).
01  APP-RECL            PIC S9(4) COMP.
        .
        .
        .

LINKAGE SECTION.
01  BLL-CELLS.
        04  FILLER          PIC S9(8) COMP.
        04  APP-BLL         PIC S9(8) COMP.
01  APP-RECORD.
        04  APP-KEY-FIELD   PIC X(9).
        04  APP-NAME        PIC X(30).
        04  APP-REST        PIC X(41).
        .
        .
        .

PROCEDURE DIVISION.
        .
        .
        .

    EXEC CICS READ UPDATE FILE('APPFILE')
            SET(APP-BLL) RIDFLD(APP-ID)
            LENGTH(APP-RECL)
    END-EXEC.
        .
        .       statements to update record fields.
        .
    EXEC CICS REWRITE FILE('APPFILE')
            FROM(APP-RECORD)
            LENGTH(APP-RECL)
    END-EXEC.
```

Figure 7-4 COBOL function shipping sample.

```
WORKING-STORAGE SECTION.
01  APP-ID              PIC X(9).
01  APP-RECL            PIC S9(4) COMP.
    .
    .
    .

LINKAGE SECTION.
01  APP-RECORD.
    04  APP-KEY-FIELD   PIC X(9).
    04  APP-NAME        PIC X(30).
    04  APP-REST        PIC X(41).
    .
    .
    .

PROCEDURE DIVISION.
    .
    .
    .

    EXEC CICS READ UPDATE FILE('APPFILE')
            SET(ADDRESS OF APP-RECORD) RIDFLD(APP-ID)
            LENGTH(APP-RECL)
    END-EXEC.
    .
    .    statements to update record fields.
    .
    EXEC CICS REWRITE FILE('APPFILE')
            FROM(APP-RECORD)
            LENGTH(APP-RECL)
    END-EXEC.
```

Figure 7-5 COBOL II function shipping sample.

FILE for UPDATE purposes and subsequently used the REWRITE command to update the file record.

CICS provides the mechanisms to coordinate local and remote updates such that protected resource modifications in both local and remote systems are committed together upon task SYNCPOINT or normal RETURN. A normal RETURN results in CICS taking a SYNCPOINT on behalf of the RETURNing task. All tasks that RETURN to CICS normally always result in a SYNCPOINT being taken inherently by CICS. The only way to avoid this SYNCPOINT is to ABEND the task using the ABEND command.

The local CICS, upon task SYNCPOINT or RETURN sends a message to the remote system requesting that it SYNCPOINT to commit modifications to protected resources. The remote system performs this process and sends back a message indicating its success or failure. If the remote SYNCPOINT is successful, the local CICS then

```
DFHEISTG DSECT
APPREC    DS    0CL80
APPKEY    DS    CL9
APPNAME   DS    CL30
APPREST   DS    CL41
            .
            .
            .
APPRID    DS    CL9
APPLEN    DS    H
APPGM     CSECT
            .
            .
            .
          EXEC CICS READ UPDATE FILE('APPFILE')                    *
              INTO(APPREC) RIDFLD(APPRID) LENGTH(APPLEN)
            .
            . code to update APPREC data.
            .
          EXEC CICS REWRITE FILE('APPFILE') FROM(APPREC)           *
              LENGTH(APPLEN)
            .
            .
            .
```

* Indicates continuation indicated by non blank character
in column 72. The continued line must begin in column 16.

Figure 7-6 Assembler function shipping sample.

processes the SYNCPOINT. If, on the other hand, the remote
SYNCPOINT fails, the modifications to protected resources by the
remote task are backed out in the remote system and a negative
response is forwarded to the local CICS. The local CICS then abends
the local task and performs backout of local modifications to
protected resources. If, on the other hand, a failure occurs in the
local system such as a task ABEND, the local CICS notifies the
remote system of the need for backout and modifications to remote
protected resources are then backed out.

Please note that the remote File Control Table (FCT) definition of
a file cannot be used to make a remote file a protected resource. The
only place where a file can be defined as protected is in the file
owning CICS system's File Control Table (FCT). So, in the file-
owning system, resource protection status is defined. It is, after all,
the remote system which is indeed protecting the resource. A file is
declared a protected resource by including the LOG=YES option in
its DFHFCT TYPE=FILE definition.

7.2   DEFINING REMOTE TRANSIENT DATA QUEUES

The format of the DFHDCT TYPE=REMOTE macro is as follows.

```
DFHDCT TYPE=REMOTE,DESTID=dest-name,
       SYSIDENT=sysidnt,
       LENGTH=record-size,
       RSL=0
       - or -
       1-24
       - or -
       PUBLIC,
       RMTNAME=remote-destid
```

This macro is utilized to define remote Intrapartition or Extrapartition Transient Data Queues.

The DESTID= parameter is used to name the 1- to 4-character Transient Data DESTination IDentifier by which the queue is locally known. This then is the name provided in the QUEUE option of Transient Data access commands coded in application programs within the local system.

The SYSIDNT= parameter names the SYSIDNT of the remote queue owning system as defined in the local Terminal Control Table.

The remaining parameters of the DFHDCT TYPE=REMOTE are optional. The LENGTH= parameter can be used to provide record length information for fixed length queues. If this option is omitted, then application program access commands must provide record length information via the LENGTH command option where appropriate.

The RMTNAME= and RSL= parameters are used as described above in the discussion of the DFHFCT TYPE=REMOTE macro. The following is a sample DCT entry for a remote Transient Data Queue.

```
DFHDCT TYPE=REMOTE,DESTID=Q001,SYSIDNT=CIC1,    X
       LENGTH=80,RSL=PUBLIC
```

In this sample entry the RMTNAME= is not used. The Queue Name or DESTID is the same in the local and remote systems. The following illustrates sample COBOL code to read a record from the remote queue.

```
WORKING-STORAGE SECTION.
01 Q-REC-AREA.
    04 .... detail of record format
01 Q-LEN     PIC S9(4)    COMP    VALUE +80.
PROCEDURE DIVISION.
    .
    .
    EXEC CICS READQ TD QUEUE('Q001')
        INTO(Q-REC-AREA) LENGTH(Q-LEN)
    END-EXEC.
    .
    .
```

The COBOL code in this example is fairly generic, meaning that it could be contained in a VS COBOL or COBOL II program. The following illustrates an example of writing to the remote queue in an assembler language program.

```
DFHEISTG DSECT
QREC        DS    0CL80
QFLD1       DS    CL20
QFLD2       DS    CL20
            DS    CL40
QLEN        DS    H
QPGM        CSECT
  .
  .
        MVC QLEN,=H'80'
        EXEC CICS WRITEQ TD QUEUE('Q001')              *
            FROM(QREC) LENGTH(QLEN)
```

7.3 DEFINING REMOTE TEMPORARY STORAGE QUEUES

The DFHTST TYPE=REMOTE macro is used to create definitions of remote Temporary Storage Queues in the Temporary Storage Table. The format of this macro is as follows.

```
        DFHTST TYPE=REMOTE,DATAID=dataid,              *
            SYSIDNT=sysidnt,RMTNAME=dataid
```

The DATAID= parameter provides the 1- to 8-character Temporary Storage Queue name or DATA IDentifier. The value coded for this option is named with the QUEUE option of Temporary Storage commands that are used in local application programs to gain access to the queue.

The SYSIDNT= option names the remote system as it is defined in the Terminal Control Table.

RMTNAME= allows the specification of a remote DATAID for the queue. This optional parameter is used as discussed above under the DFHFCT TYPE=REMOTE macro.

Note that in the case of Temporary Storage remote queue definition, there is no provision for defining a Resource Security Level, or RSL.

7.4   DEFINITIONS OF LOCAL PROTECTED RESOURCES

In addition to defining remote resources in resource tables, these resources must also be defined within the resource owning CICS regions/systems. **It is via the local definitions that resources can be made protected.** The local definition of a file can make the file a protected resource. Temporary Storage AUX (disk) queues can be protected via a definition in the local Temporary Storage Table. Intrapartition Transient Data Queues can be protected in the queue's Destination Control Table entry. There is no CICS recovery or protection status for Extrapartition Transient Data Queues.

CICS recovery for protected resources means backout. If a unit of work or task is inflight or logically incomplete because it has not issued a SYNCPOINT command or a normal RETURN, CICS recovery reverses modifications to protected resources if the individual task or the entire CICS system abends. **Each separate CICS region/system recovers its own protected resources and to this end CICS systems exchange messages with regard to task normal or abnormal completion and SYNCPOINTs.** In this way separate CICS systems are able to coordinate their management of protected resources.

One thing that the application designer/programmer should be aware of with regard to using Intrapartition Transient Data or Temporary Storage Queues is that there is no mechansim built into CICS to perform forward recovery in the event that DFHINTRA or DFHTEMP suffer physical damage which makes them unreadable. What does that mean to the user of remote queues? It means that you should not save data that is critical in a remote queue unless you are prepared to save and resend it. Otherwise, you run the risk (very, very slight) of losing your data if the remote system were, for example, to take a head crash on DFHINTRA or DFHTEMP. In rare cases CICS users build their own forward recovery (the ability to rebuild DFHINTRA or DFHTEMP). However, things change, and perhaps it would be wiser to either not save critical information in one of these queues or to JOURNAL copies of critical data so that it can be resent to the remote system. It might be safer to control your own recovery planning.

7.5 FUNCTION SHIPPING — HOW IT WORKS FOR ISC

As we know, CICS Function Shipping is an implementation of SNA Application-to-Application Services. One of the SNA Application-to-Application Services architected for LUTYPE 6 is application program access to remote resources without the program needing to be concerned with the location of resources distributed throughout the SNA Network. That is exactly the service which CICS Function Shipping provides. In SNA there are three model programs which serve as an architectural basis for product implementations of remote resource access support programs. There is a queue model, a scheduler model, and a database model. As stated above, the model programs provide a common basis for various products when implementing this feature of SNA. In CICS the architected model programs were the basis for the implementation of the *CICS Mirror Program, DFHMIR*. DFHMIR is the CICS program that executes in remote regions/systems and performs the services needed to support remote access of resources. Thus, DFHMIR actually runs in a remote resource-owning CICS region/system and executes Function Shipped commands. In addition to serving as an implementation of the SNA model programs, DFHMIR contains support for remote file access. There is no file access model defined in SNA, so this aspect of DFHMIR is CICS product–specific.

In a previous chapter we discussed the CICS PCT entries required in support of Function Shipping. We named five TRANSID entries that are created within the PCT, which all map to DFHMIR. These TRANSIDs are CSMI, CSM1, CSM2, CSM3, and CSM5. These are called *"process names"* and CSM1, CSM2, CSM3 and CSM5 are *architected process names*, meaning that the functions supported in association with these CICS TRANSIDs are SNA architected processes, implemented within DFHMIR. CSMI is the process name used for

Function Shipping File Control requests. CSM3 is the process name for Temporary Storage and Transient Data Queue access. CSM2 is the process name for Interval Control START requests. CSM1 is the process name for IMS messages, and CSM5 is the process name for DL/I database access via a remote CICS system.

Assuming that all of the local and remote resource definitions are in place in two connected CICS systems, Function Shipping as an Intercommunication facility is available for application programs. Let's review an example and see how it actually works. In Figure 7-7 task number 125 is executing in an application program. The task's principal facility is a TCTTE representing the terminal that caused the task to be initiated. The application program issues a command against a resource. In our sample a file access command is utilized. The application program command causes the Execute Interface to be invoked. This is illustrated in Figure 7-8.

The TCA number 125 is now executing within the Execute Interface. The Execute Interface determines that the resource is remote based upon the resource definition in the File Control Table. Because the resource is remote, the Execute Interface calls a CICS program called *DFHXFP, the CICS Transformer Program.* The purpose of the call to the Transformer Program is to have the file access request transformed into a format suitable for transmission through the SNA network. The transformed request is returned to the Execute Inter-

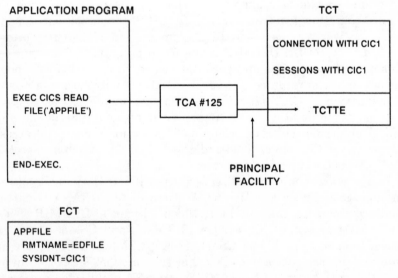

Figure 7-7 Task executing in CICS.

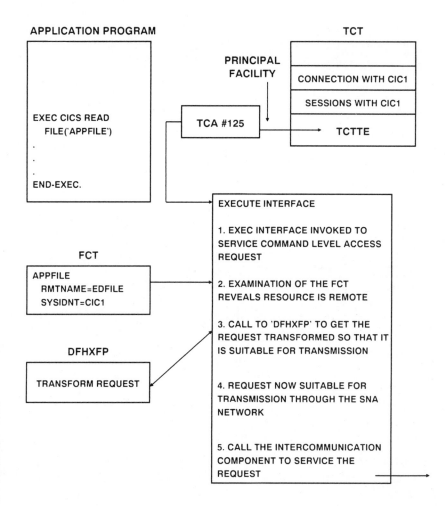

Figure 7-8 TASK access request for remote resource invokes the Execute Interface.

face, which then invokes the Intercommunication Component within CICS. An alternate facility, namely, a session to the remote system, is acquired by the Intercommunication Component. The default Function Shipping Profile (DFHCICSF) governs this task's interaction with its alternate facility.

Figure 7-9 illustrates the task executing in the Intercommunication Component. The Intercommunication Component recognizes that this is the first Function Shipping request to this particular remote system for this particular task. It is going to be necessary to have a DFHMIR task attached in the remote system. To this end,

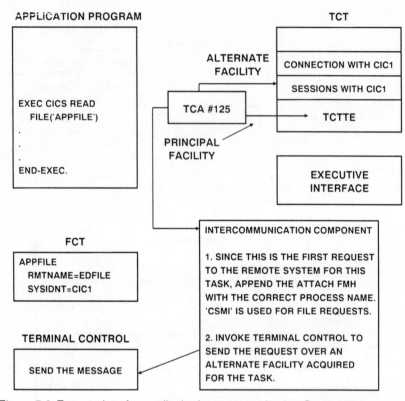

Figure 7-9 Execute Interface calls the Intercommunication Component.

the Intercommunication Component appends the correct process name ("CSMI" since this is a file access request) to the transformed request. The process name is actually contained in an *ATTACH Function Management Header*, which is concatenated to the transformed request. Function Management Headers are SNA-defined data areas which are used to coordinate Function Management Services.

In this case CICS uses an ATTACH type header which the remote system recognizes as such. One of the data items in the ATTACH header is the process name to be attached. When the remote system receives the request, it recognizes that the ATTACH header is a request to initiate a task and it will do so. However, the ATTACH header and transformed request must first be sent off to the remote system. The Intercommunication Component invokes the services of Terminal Control to SEND the request over the task's alternate facility.

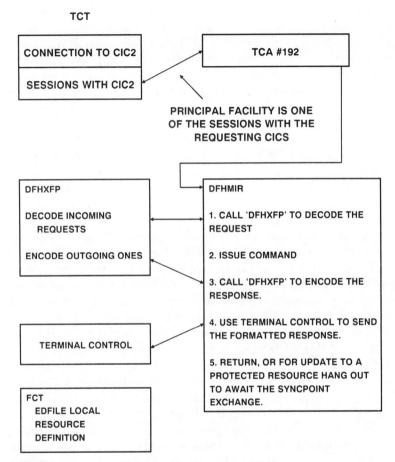

Figure 7-10 The Mirror Task in the remote system.

In the remote system, a task is attached which executes in the Mirror Program. DFHMIR is invoked based upon the attach header containing the process name which accompanies the Function Shipping request. The task executing within DFHMIR is attached to the session or connection to the originating CICS region/system. Figure 7-10 illustrates the mirror task in the remote system.

At point number 1, DFHMIR calls the Transformer Program, DFHXFP, to decode the received request. After decoding, DFHMIR attempts to execute the request shown in the illustration at point number 2. The Mirror Program utilizes command level facilities and executes the appropriate command. In our example the mirror task executes an EXEC CICS READ command against the EDFILE.

When command execution is complete, DFHMIR prepares to issue its response. The response will contain a return code and possibly a data record retrieved from the EDFILE. The response has to be placed into the suitable format and, therefore, at point number 3 DFHMIR calls the Transformer Program again and the response is encoded for transmission. The Mirror Program SENDs back the encoded response to the requesting CICS system at point number 4.

The mirror task will now either end or wait for further requests. If the mirror task serviced a READ UPDATE it would have to remain alive to perform the REWRITE. This is necessary whether or not the file is protected because the same task has to do the READ UPDATE and subsequent REWRITE. If a mirror task did a READ UPDATE and terminated, the exclusive control and record pointer for REWRITE purposes would be gone.

If the Mirror Task updates a protected resource, it likewise cannot end even after the update is physically complete. In this case, the Mirror Task must await a SYNCPOINT request from the requesting system. In our example, however, a simple READ was requested and there was no prior work done by the Mirror Task that would necessitate its remaining in the system. Therefore, the Mirror Task ends.

The Intercommunication Component in the requesting CICS region keeps track of this Mirror Task status. Because the mirror ended, any subsequent Function Shipping requests against CIC1 by task 125 will be preceded by a process name in accordance with the function being shipped. Had the mirror remained alive to complete processing or SYNCPOINTing, the Intercommunication Component would, likewise, be aware of this. Any subsequent Function Shipping requests done by a task with a waiting mirror do not cause a "new" Mirror Task to be initiated in the remote system. The mirror thus becomes a remote extension of the application task.

Furthermore, when the local application task requests a SYNCPOINT explicitly or implicitly by RETURNing to CICS, the Intercommunication Component sends the waiting Mirror Task a SYNCPOINT request. The Intercommunication Component receives the SYNCPOINT response from the Mirror Task and, based upon whether that response is positive or negative, either allows the local task SYNCPOINT to proceed or ABENDs the task and thereby causes Dynamic Transaction Backout to occur locally. Any TRANSID that updates local and remote resources should therefore be defined as requiring Dynamic Transaction Backout as should the TRANSID definitions for the Mirror Task.

The response from the Mirror Task is received in CIC2 or the requesting CICS system. This is illustrated in Figure 7-11. The Inter-

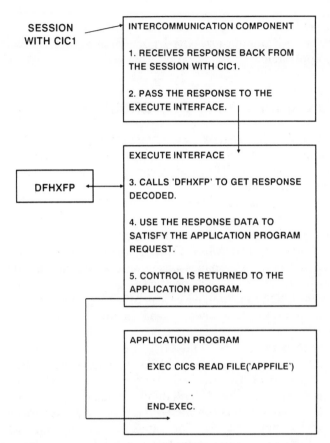

Figure 7-11 Response received back in CIC2.

communication Component receives the response at point number 1. It passes the response to the Execute Interface at point number 2. The Execute Interface calls the Transformer Program, DFHXFP, to get the response decoded. At point 4 the Execute Interface uses the decoded response to satisfy the application program's command and at point 5, control is returned to the application program. The Function Shipping service is now complete. All of the behind-the-scenes programs that enable CICS to perform Function Shipping are part of the LUTYPE 6 implementation in CICS.

These CICS programs enable CICS to provide the SNA architected application-to-application service of making remote resources available to application programs. The CICS implementation of remote resource access is architected functionally in SNA, as are the formats and protocols used in intersystem exchanges. The CICS programs that manage Function Shipping are based upon SNA-defined model programs where applicable.

7.6   FUNCTION SHIPPING — MRO VERSUS ISC

From a general overview perspective Function Shipping in MRO is handled in a similar manner as that described above in the discussion on ISC Function Shipping. However, there are several differences that should be pointed out.

In order to optimize execution of MRO Function Shipping, a Short Path Transformer Program is used for MRO requests to CICS systems after release 1.6. Therefore, if an installation is using CICS at a later release than 1.6, the *Short Path Transformer Program, DFHXFX*, is used for request/response encoding and decoding. The Short Path Transformer uses a CICS-specific (as opposed to SNA-architected) format for TIOAs exchanged across MRO regions. In such cases, the process name, CSMI is always used for all MRO Function Shipping requests.

Another difference between ISC and MRO Function Shipping is that Mirror Tasks can be suspended in MRO instead of being terminated as they are in ISC. An ISC Mirror is terminated or DETACHed when it has completed a read-only request and has no further work to do or when it has completed SYNCPOINT exchanges for protected resource modifications. The same rules hold for MRO tasks except that instead of being terminated or DETACHed, MRO Mirror Tasks may be SUSPENDed.

The CICS Task Dispatcher maintains two internal lists of tasks. One list contains a control block called a Dispatch Control Area, or DCA, for each active task in the system. The other task list likewise is comprised of DCAs, but these represent tasks that are suspended and not eligible for dispatching.

Normally tasks are on the active task DCA chain. This is true even if they are not immediately dispatchable or capable of running. For example, a task might be waiting for a VSAM file read to complete before it can again be dispatched. Such a task waits on the active DCA chain with an indicator set to reveal that it is waiting for this type of event. The task's DCA also has a pointer to an Event Control Block, or ECB, which will be posted when the event it is waiting for has completed. So most tasks live out their lives in CICS residing on the active chain, being either dispatchable or nondispatchable, while awaiting the completion of a service.

The Dispatch Control Area, or DCA, is used only by the Task Dispatcher, and it is a logical extension of the Task Control Area, or TCA, that everybody else in the CICS world uses to keep track of tasks. A Task's DCA and its TCA point to each other, so if you have one, you know where the other is located and can get to it. The purpose of the DCA is to use a small control block as opposed to the large TCA for task dispatching. This keeps the working set of the task dispatcher small. This minimizes paging during task dispatching, and task dispatching is constantly going on in CICS. Therefore, it is critical that this function is done as efficiently as possible and with as little paging as possible.

Some task waits, however, unlike I/O waits, are not controlled by system software processing, and CICS has no way of determining the duration of such waits. For example, a task performs an unconditional GETMAIN and CICS doesn't have the storage to satisfy the request. The availability of storage within the CICS Dynamic Storage Area is dependent upon when application tasks free up storage by RETURNing to CICS or issuing FREEMAINs. A task waiting for storage as a result of an unconditional GETMAIN is moved off of the active DCA chain and placed upon the suspended task DCA chain. Other reasons why tasks might be suspended include waiting for a CICS ENQueue which another application task currently owns, waiting to RECEIVE conversational terminal input, waiting for availability of a session to a remote system, waiting to WRITEQ TS to Temporary Storage AUX when there is no space in DFHTEMP, and the like.

Why the suspended DCA chain? Task dispatching must be efficient or CICS performance degrades dramatically. Remember, the task dispatcher is performing dispatching or task switches at least every runaway task interval amount of time and normally much more frequently. CICS does not want the Task Dispatcher to spend time examining DCAs for tasks that are in for long waits. This would increase the working set of the dispatcher and increase its execution path length. Therefore, when a task is in for a potentially long wait, the task is unhooked from the active DCA chain and moved to the suspended chain. When the resource, whatever it is that the task is waiting for, becomes available, the task is RESUMEd back onto the active DCA chain. Only tasks that are on the suspended DCA chain are candidates for CICS timeouts, such as the DTIMOUT or RTIMOUT.

These timeouts can be defined for PCT entries. And, by the way, the command EXEC CICS SUSPEND does *not* cause a task to be placed on the suspended DCA chain. The EXEC CICS SUSPEND command leaves the task on the active chain in a dispatchable state and returns control to the Task Dispatcher. The task issuing the EXEC CICS SUSPEND may be in fact be again dispatched by the dispatcher if is still the highest priority active task on the active DCA chain.

When we say that a Mirror Task is suspended we mean specifically that it is disconnected from the IRC link and moved to the suspended DCA chain with a timeout of 2 seconds. The Mirror Task thus waits in limbo in the event that another Function Shipping request comes in. A suspended Mirror Task can be used to satisfy any need for a mirror task that results from a Function Shipping request coming across an IRC link. Why SUSPEND and RESUME or activate Mirror Tasks? Because the CICS processing to terminate or DETACH tasks is extensive, just as the processing to ATTACH or create new tasks is extensive.

If a Mirror Task is going to be required imminently, CICS saves this overhead by "reusing" MRO Mirror Tasks. The 2-second timeout that is used for suspended Mirror Tasks balances off the overheads of 1) keeping a task in the system in terms of its storage resource utilization and 2) having to DETACH a task and ATTACH a new one. This timeout is not alterable in an installation; it is hardwired into CICS.

When a Function Shipping request is received in CICS over an InterRegion Communication Link, CICS only needs to ATTACH a new Mirror Task if one is not currently available on the Suspended DCA chain. However, suspended Mirror Tasks do count toward the MaXimum Task (MXT) value and, therefore, it may be desirable to limit the number of suspended Mirror Tasks that we want in our CICS system. This can be accomplished via a System Initialization Table parameter, "MAXMIR."

A Mirror Task is suspended when it completes its processing only if it will not cause the number of suspended Mirrors to exceed MAXMIR. The default for MAXMIR if not coded is 999. If MAXMIR is reached, Mirror Tasks are DETACHed instead of being suspended. Other factors in the CICS environment might also result in Mirror Tasks being ended. For example, if CICS reaches the Maximum Task limit (MXT) or goes Short-on-Storage, Mirror tasks are ended. Closing the IRC link (CEMT SET IRC CLOSED) also ends Mirror Tasks.

In Release 2.1 of CICS there is provision for using long-running mirror Tasks. This is accomplished via another System Initialization Parameter, "MROLRM," which can be coded as MROLRM=NO or MROLRM=YES. If MROLRM=NO is elected, then Mirror Tasks are handled as described above for ISC except that they may be

SUSPENDed instead of being terminated. Suspending or terminating Mirror Tasks is advantageous in one way because it frees up sessions so that they can be used for subsequent InterRegion requests. However, in certain kinds of environments, this can have a negative impact.

Suppose, for example, that most of the application programs that request MRO Function Shipping do multiple accesses against the remote system. Once an update access is made cross region or cross system, the Mirror Task waits for SYNCPOINT notification. However, if many tasks do repeated READ-only access to resources, the normal course of action in ISC is to terminate the Mirror Tasks and in MRO to either terminate or SUSPEND the Mirrors. In ISC, we have no choice, that is the way it is. In MRO, however, we can elect to use MROLRM=YES. In systems with MROLRM=YES coded in the SIT, Mirror Tasks wait for SYNCPOINT notification even if there are no protected resources involved. Therefore, once attached, a Mirror Task remains active on the IRC link and waits for subsequent requests from the remote task.

From the vantage point of the requesting system it is not necessary to go through session allocation for each separate read-only request. In the region supporting MRO, it is not necessary to RESUME a suspended Mirror or ATTACH a new one. Therefore, in an environment where most tasks make repeated read only requests, MROLRM=YES can be used to minimize the overheads described above. However, bear in mind that MRO sessions thus become reserved for an ongoing dialog between a single requesting task and a single Mirror. If read only activity does not warrant use of MROLRM=YES, this can actually be disadvantageous.

There is one last SIT option pertinent to MRO that ought to be mentioned, even though it is not specifically oriented toward Function Shipping. This option is the MROBTCH option, which is new in release 2.1 of CICS. MROBTCH is specified as a number from 1 up to 255. The default is 1. MROBTCH greater than one causes incoming MRO requests (Function Shipping and all other types as well) to be batched up to the MROBTCH number.

In other words, a single MRO request does not cause the MRO region to be posted or awakened. Rather requests are batched and the region is posted when the MROBTCH limit is reached or when the Region Exit Time (SIT-specified ICV value) has expired. When using MROBTCH, the objective is to batch up multiple requests before incurring the overhead of awakening the MRO region. Ideally, the MRO region is awakened and handles the MROBTCH number with less overhead than were it posted and awakened for each individual request. Furthermore, the Region Exit Time can be set low enough in time duration so that periods of light MRO activity (which would not result in the MRO region being posted due to MROBTCH) do not excessively delay processing of MRO requests.

7.7 MULTIPLE MIRROR SITUATIONS

Up to this point we have considered Function Shipping between only two CICS systems: a requesting region in which an application resource access request results in the Function Shipping of a command to a remote system and the remote system in which Function Shipping is actually serviced. However, a task is not limited regarding the number of local or remote access requests that can be performed. Likewise, task requests can be made against multiple systems.

Therefore, it is quite possible that a single application task may indirectly result in the attachment of multiple remote Mirror Tasks in different systems/regions. Some of these Mirror Tasks can be servicing purely read-only access requests and therefore be of short duration. Other Mirror Tasks may be called upon to perform update access and therefore of longer duration since they are required to await SYNCPOINTing. If a Mirror remains attached to the Inter-System/InterRegion session, it services any subsequent requests made by the application task for that system's resources.

The Intercommunication Component keeps track of the status of all remote Mirror Tasks (whether they have terminated or are waiting for SYNCPOINT notification). The Intercommunication Component also engages in SYNCPOINT exchanges with all appropriate Mirrors. When multiple Mirrors exist for an application task, this is called a *Multiple Mirror Situation*.

7.8 CHAINED MIRRORS

Function Shipping requests can be chained through one or more intermediate CICS systems. Figure 7-12 illustrates a *chained mirror*. In this diagram an application task represented by TCA number 431 in CIC1 executes an EXEC CICS READ FILE("APPFILE") command. The Execute Interface gains control, determines that the file is owned by CIC2, calls DFHXFP to encode the READ request, and

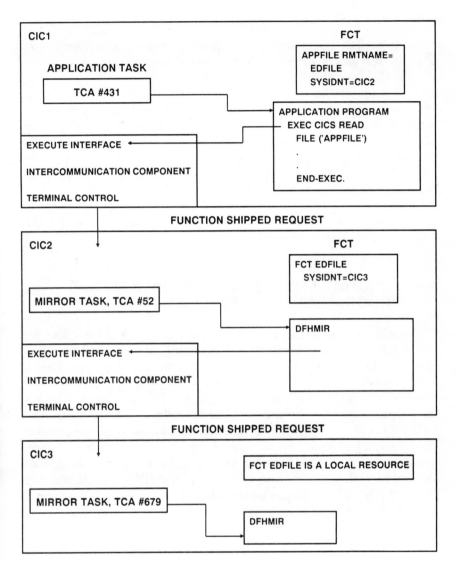

Figure 7-12 Chained mirror.

invokes the Intercommunication Component. Using the services of Terminal Control, the request is Function Shipped to CIC2.

In CIC2 a Mirror Task is ATTACHed. The Mirror Task invokes DFHXFP to get the request decoded and then executes the request using the normal command level facilities of CICS. The Execute Interface is invoked, determines that the resource is remote, calls

DFHXFP to encode the request for transmission, and calls the Inter-communication Component. The Intercommunication Component uses the services of Terminal Control to ship the request to CIC3.

In CIC3 a Mirror Task is ATTACHed. The Mirror Task invokes DFHXFP to get the received request decoded and executes the appropriate CICS command. The result of the read against the local resource is then encoded using the services of DFHXFP and sent to CIC2 to satisfy its Function Shipping. In CIC2, the response is decoded and presented to the Mirror Task. The Mirror calls DFHXFP to encode the response and forwards it along to CIC1 as the response to its Function Shipping request. In CIC1 the response is decoded by DFHXFP and used to satisfy the application program READ command. Chained mirrors should be used solely for READ-only access of remote resources.

7.9   FUNCTION SHIPPING — APPLICATION PROGRAMMING ISSUES

The application programming issues that should be addressed for use of CICS Function Shipping are minimal from a coding perspective. Standard CICS commands are used in the same manner as in a single system environment. The application programmer should be aware of the additional unusual conditions that can occur in an Intercommunication environment. These include ISCINVREQ and SYSIDERR. The ISCINVREQ condition indicates an error that occurred during remote system processing of a Function Shipping request which cannot be classified as one of the other error categories associated with the command issued. The SYSIDERR indicates that either the remote system is unknown or that a link to it is unavailable. In both cases the default course of action is to terminate the task.

From a program design point of view, it is particularly important for application programs that are performing distributed updating to do so in the most efficient manner possible. In a single-system environment, we normally code CICS programs such that all up-front work, such as editing and validation, are performed before accessing files with update intent. Once file processing has commenced, we code as efficiently as possible so that file updates can be completed in as tight an execution sequence as can be achieved. This type of program design is more critical in a multi-system environment for very obvious reasons.

Another thing that should be pointed out is that programs using Function Shipping should not use the SYNCPOINT ROLLBACK command. The reason for this is because Function Shipping can be supported on MRO InterRegion Communication, LUTYPE 6.1, or LUTYPE 6.2 links. The LUTYPE 6.1 does not support the SYNCPOINT ROLLBACK. If a an application program utilizing an LUTYPE 6.1 link uses SYNCPOINT ROLLBACK, local resources are backed out but remote protected resources are *not* backed out. Therefore, if the ROLLBACK function is required, it is best to ABEND the task and invoke Dynamic Transaction Backout. Backout is then performed in both the local and remote systems universally for IRC, LUTYPE 6.1, and LUTYPE 6.2 links.

The final item to be mentioned is that EXEC CICS INQUIRE and EXEC CICS SET commands cannot be used across Intercommunication Connections. Therefore, file open/close functions are not supported cross systems/regions.

7.10 FUNCTION SHIPPING — DESIGN CONSIDERATIONS

There are several issues that need to be considered regarding the design of a CICS system utilizing Function Shipping. These issues include evaluating and dealing with the INDOUBT period, ensuring that timeouts are used appropriately, and developing standards to avoid cross system deadly embraces.

7.10.1 The INDOUBT Period

Any transactions that update remote and local resources should be defined to CICS as requiring Dynamic Transaction Backout. In a multi-system environment there is another consideration, and this may require some thinking and perhaps planning. We know that CICS systems coordinate SYNCPOINT exchanges to commit modifications to protected resources. If there is a session, task, or system failure prior to SYNCPOINT exchanges, all is well because connected systems will perform required back out. Even if one of the systems fails, the CICS emergency restart will backout uncommitted modifications. If there is failure subsequent to SYNCPOINT exchanges, again there is no problem because the connected systems have either committed or backed out if SYNCPOINTing was unsuccessful.

However, a problem occurs if there is a system or session failure after SYNCPOINT flows have been initiated but before they complete. Let's consider an example to illustrate this problem. In CIC1, task number 157 READs for Update a local protected file. A dynamic backout log is allocated in CICS storage for task 157 and a before update image of the record is saved in this storage area along with the control information such as the file DDNAME and RIDFLD. Task 157 REWRITEs the record to the file. Task 157 then READs for UPDATE a remote file. The request is Function Shipped to CIC2 and a Mirror Task is initiated.

The Mirror executes the READ UPDATE and a dynamic backout log is allocated in storage for the Mirror Task. A before-update image of the record along with file DDNAME and RIDFLD are saved in the task unique memory log. The Mirror Task sends the response back to CIC1. Task 157 updates the record and REWRITEs. This request is Function Shipped to the Mirror Task in CIC2. The Mirror Task performs the REWRITE and returns a response to CIC1. Task 157 takes a SYNCPOINT either explicitly through program execution of a SYNCPOINT Command or inherently by RETURNing to CICS.

The CICS Intercommunication Component gains control and sends a SYNCPOINT request to CIC2. In this context, CIC1 is the INITIATOR of the SYNCPOINT and CIC2 is a SYNCPOINT SLAVE. CIC1 now enters the twilight zone of SYNCPOINTing referred to as the *INDOUBT period*. If all goes well CIC1 will get either a positive or negative response to its SYNCPOINT request. A positive response results in local SYNCPOINTing to commit local updates. A negative response results in task 157 being abended and local updates being backed out. However, if no response is received because of 1) a session failure or 2) a system failure, CIC1 has no way of knowing if 1) the SYNCPOINT request was received and processed before the failure or 2) the SYNCPOINT request was not processed. This is why the INDOUBT period bears its name. CIC1 is INDOUBT.

If the intersystem connection is via an LUTYPE 6.2 link, CIC1 will attempt to clarify the situation and resynchronize processing on another session with the remote system. This is accomplished through a comparison of Unit of Recovery Descriptors (URDs) maintained by the two CICS systems. However, this may not be successful because the remote system may have failed. If LUTYPE 6.2 resynchronization is not successful or if the remote system is connected via another type of link, there is the potential for a loss of synchronization between the systems and as a result protected resources may be left in an inconsistent state. The default course of action in this case is when INDOUBT, BACKOUT. For MRO this is the only choice supported.

However, for ISC links, CICS can be requested (in the PCT definition of a transaction) to COMMIT protected resources when IN-DOUBT. Either course, BACKOUT or COMMIT, can result in protected resources being inconsistent across systems. Before we deal with this issue, it is necessary to mention one more possible specification for the INDOUBT period. For ISC sessions CICS can be requested to lock up resources and WAIT until the session can be recovered. When a session with the remote system can be reestablished, the systems exchange status information and the local system decides whether to COMMIT or BACKOUT.

This option, however, has very limited scope. The lock and WAIT only occur if 1) there is only one remote system connected to the SYNCPOINTing task; 2) only local protected resources have been modified; and 3) the only protected modifications result from EXEC CICS WRITEQ TS to add one or more new elements to a TS queue or an EXEC CICS START PROTECT was performed. In any other circumstances, lock up and WAIT becomes BACKOUT.

What to do about the potential for a loss of resource synchronization? Messages regarding session failures and the resulting possibility of resource problems are written to a Transient Data Destination named CSMT. Therefore, this destination can be examined to determine if a further investigation is required if a connected system fails. If loss of integrity has occurred, installation-specific procedures (manual or programmatic) can be used to reestablish resource synchronization. The system designer must evaluate the significance of CICS being INDOUBT and, if necessary, establish procedures for dealing with potential resource inconsistencies.

7.10.2   Timeouts

It is important to ensure that tasks using CICS Function Shipping services are defined to CICS with timeout values. In particular the Deadlock TIMe OUT or DTIMOUT is important to use so that tasks do not wait indefinitely for sessions to become available for the sending of Function Shipping requests. This is particularly important for tasks that interact with a terminal operator and use Function Shipping. If a task is strictly an internal task, running without connection to a terminal, and there is an application reason for not using a timeout, this is acceptable.

However, leaving a person sitting at a terminal for an indeterminate wait should be avoided. The Receive TIMe OUT or RTIMOUT may also be specified so that a task does not wait indefinitely for a terminal response. The need for timeouts should be conveyed to the systems programmer performing CICS table maintenance by identifying the TRANSIDs that will be using Function Shipping and therefore require them.

7.10.3   Avoid Cross-System Deadly Embraces

In designing a CICS system to operate in a single-system environment, it is a good idea to develop programming standards that minimize the likelihood of deadly embraces. This form of task "lockout" is a danger particularly in a system in which multiple tasks perform updates against multiple files. Conventional wisdom dictates that one file at a time is read with update intent and updated before the next file update is attempted. Also, there should be a prescribed sequence of multiple file updates. All tasks that update common files should do so in a defined order. If possible, multiple updates within the same file should likewise occur in a given order such as ascending/descending sequence of prime key. These measures do not preclude a deadly embrace, but they certainly minimize the likelihood of an occurrence.

If avoiding task deadlocks in a single system environment is desirable, it is even more so in a multi-system environment where things like interregion/intersystem sessions can be held by deadlocked tasks. Therefore, the development of standards to avoid lockouts is particularly important in a multi-system environment where tasks will perform multiple updates to cross-system resources. Because multiple systems often transcend a single department or group, this effort can, unfortunately, be more difficult to coordinate.

REVIEW EXERCISES

Provide a short answer to each of the following.

1. What does a resource security level of 0 imply about a resource's ability to be accessed by tasks for whom CICS has been requested to perform resource security level checking (PCT definition of RSLC=YES)?

2. The following represents a Destination Control Table definition for a remote queue:

```
DFHDCT TYPE=REMOTE,DESTID=D001,SYSIDNT=CIC1
```

    a. Can you tell if this is an extrapartition or intrapartition queue from the local information about this resource?

    b. Can you tell if this a protected resource from the local information about this resource?

    c. How can one define a remote resource as a protected resource of CICS?

    d. From the DCT macro shown above, how can you determine the NETNAME of the remote system?

3. What is the role of DFHFXP in Function Shipping?
4. Why doesn't ISC Function Shipping use the short path transformer program, DFHXFX? After all, it has a shorter path.
5. What is the role of DFHMIR in Function Shipping?
6. For ISC Function Shipping, what happens to a mirror task after it has serviced a read-only access request?
7. For ISC Function Shipping, what happens to a Mirror Task which has serviced an update access against a protected resource?
8. Why is it not a particularly good idea to save critical data in remote Temporary Storage queues without first journaling a copy of such data?
9. What advantage is there in the suspension of MRO Mirror Tasks?
10. What is MAXMIR?
11. What factors cause a Mirror Task to be terminated in MRO aside from reaching MAXMIR?
12. What is a chained mirror and why is it recommended that chained mirrors be used for read-only access?
13. What is a function management header?
14. What is a multiple mirror situation?
15. Why is it not a good idea to use a SYNCPOINT ROLLBACK command in a program that does Function Shipping?
16. What is the INDOUBT period?

ANSWERS TO REVIEW EXERCISES

Provide a short answer to each of the following.

1. *What does a resource security level of 0 imply about a resource's ability to be accessed by tasks for whom CICS has been requested to perform resource security level checking (PCT definition of RSLC=YES)?*

   A resource security level of 0 implies that RSLC=YES tasks will not be able to access the resource.

2. *The following represents a Destination Control Table definition for a remote queue:*

   ```
   DFHDCT TYPE=REMOTE,DESTID=D001,SYSIDNT=CIC1
   ```

   a. *Can you tell if this is an extrapartition or intrapartition queue from the local information about this resource?*

   No.

   b. *Can you tell if this a protected resource from the local information about this resource?*

   No.

   c. *How can one define a remote resource as a protected resource of CICS?*

   Impossible! However, you can ask the people in charge of the remote system to define the resource in that manner in the remote system.

   d. *From the DCT macro shown above, how can you determine the NETNAME of the remote system?*

   You can't. You would have to go to the TCT and look for a DEFINE CONNECTION or DFHTCT TYPE=SYSTEM and relate the SYSIDNT back to the NETNAME.

3. *What is the role of DFHFXP in Function Shipping?*

The role of DFHFXP is to encode/decode Function Shipping requests and responses into/out of the SNA format so that they can be transmitted over an SNA network.

4. *Why doesn't ISC Function Shipping use the short path transformer program, DFHXFX? After all, it has a shorter path.*

DFHXFX can only be used for MRO because MRO is CICS product–specific. DFHXFX transforms requests and responses for MRO but the format that is used is not consistent with SNA architecture and, therefore, CICS cannot utilize DFHXFX's services for ISC Function Shipping.

5. *What is the role of DFHMIR in Function Shipping?*

DFHMIR is the mirror program which actually executes in a remote CICS region. When a Function Shipping request is received in a remote region, DFHMIR is attached to service the request.

6. *For ISC Function Shipping, what happens to a Mirror Task after it has serviced a read-only access request?*

The Mirror Task is detached or terminated.

7. *For ISC Function Shipping, what happens to a Mirror Task which has serviced an update access against a protected resource?*

The Mirror Task remains in the remote system to await SYNCPOINT processing.

8. *Why is it not a particularly good idea to save critical data in remote Temporary Storage queues without first journaling a copy of such data?*

There is no built-in forward recovery for DFHTEMP or for DFHINTRA, for that matter. This means that in the unlikely event that there is a head crash or some other disaster that damages the disk containing one of these files, all of the data in the queues is A) gone or B) user-recoverable. If your information is critical, it really doesn't belong in temporary storage.

However, if you journal the data record, at least you can recover the information.

9. *What advantage is there in the suspension of MRO Mirror Tasks?*

A suspended Mirror Task can service any incoming Function Shipping request. This means that if CICS has a suspended mirror task, it merely has to RESUME the task as opposed to going through the overhead of ATTACHing a new one. Also, by suspending mirrors CICS avoids the overhead associated with DETACHing or ending a task.

10. *What is MAXMIR?*

MAXMIR is a System Initialization Table parameter that defines a maximum number of suspended Mirror Tasks for a CICS system supporting MRO Function Shipping. When the MAXMIR limit is reached, CICS terminates mirrors rather than suspending them.

11. *What factors cause a Mirror Task to be terminated in MRO aside from reaching MAXMIR.*

When a Mirror Task is suspended, CICS sets a 2-second time limit. If a subsequent request does not hit the system and cause the mirror to be reinvoked, the mirror is timed out. Also, if CICS goes Short-on-Storage, if maximum task is reached, or if the IRC link is closed Mirror Tasks are ended.

12. *What is a chained mirror and why is it recommended that chained mirrors be used for read-only access?*

A chained mirror involves Function Shipping to a remote CICS system wherein the desired resource is also defined as remote. Therefore, the remote system Function Ships an access request to yet another remote system. Obviously, if you update in such a situation, there is a high risk.

13. *What is a function management header?*

A function management header is an SNA defined header or data area that is used to coordinate function management services. As an example of a function management service, systems like CICS provide remote resource access. In order to accomplish this, somebody has to actually do the access service. An ATTACH function management header is used to initiate this somebody (DFHMIR task).

14. *What is a multiple mirror situation?*

A multiple mirror situation is when a task has two or more remote mirror tasks in two or more remote CICS systems. The mirror tasks, in ISC, are generally hanging out waiting for SYNCPOINT processing so that they can safely commit and end.

15. *Why is it not a good idea to use a SYNCPOINT ROLLBACK command in a program that does function shipping?*

ISC function shipping is supported over LUTYPE6.1 and LUTYPE6.2 links. We have no way of knowing what is coded in the TCT. LUTYPE 6.1 does not support the ROLLBACK. Therefore, if a task did a SYNCPOINT ROLLBACK, its local resource modifications would be backed out but a remote mirror connected over an LUTYPE6.1 link would not perform backout.

16. *What is the INDOUBT period?*

The INDOUBT period occurs after a SYNCPOINT exchange has begun. A SYNCPOINT initiator sends a SYNCPOINT request. If, at this point, the remote system crashes or the session is lost, CICS does not know whether the SYNCPOINT was received and acted upon or if it wasn't. Therefore, the SYNCPOINT initiating CICS is in doubt as to what has happened.

8

Asynchronous Processing

8.1 INTRODUCTION

Asynchronous Processing is a type of CICS Intercommunication in
which multiple tasks perform distributed but nonsynchronized units
of work. From the vantage point of application design and implementation, the programs that perform Asynchronous Processing are
synchronized in the sense that their processing is coordinated. One
program's execution is meant to trigger the next asynchronous task
and in all likelihood pass application-dependent parameters and
data. The work performed by the asynchronous task fulfills a specific
application function. However, from CICS's point of view
asynchronous tasks are separate unrelated units of work.

Any work done by one asynchronous task is unrelated to processing done by the other from CICS's point of view. There is no coordination between asynchronous tasks with regard to recovery. If an
asynchronously started task abends, there is no notification to the
initiating task and there is no backout recovery provided. CICS sees
no relationship between Asynchronous Tasks — that's why they are
called asynchronous. Therefore, Asynchronous Processing is not applicable to cross-region/cross-system processing in which CICS
recoverability is required for distributed updates to protected resources. If asynchronous tasks perform updates, it is up to the application developer to ensure that work is successfully accomplished and
that proper application checks are in place to ensure that all required updates are carried out. In this regard, there is no support
from CICS.

Since there is no relationship between asynchronous tasks, CICS does not coordinate a request to be handled by an asynchronous task with a response back to the requesting task. As a matter of fact, there is no support for direct task to task exchanges in Asynchronous Processing. Any coordination between one task's "request" and another task's "response" is the responsibility of the application developers. Therefore, Asynchronous Processing is not applicable to a situation where a person waits at terminal for a response. When Asynchronous Processing is utilized to service a terminal operator's request, the request should be forwarded to the remote system and then the operator should be informed that the response will be available later. The operator can then continue performing other transactions. If this approach is not suitable to the application being implemented, then do not use Asynchronous Processing. Rather, Distributed Transaction Processing should be utilized.

Asynchronous Processing can be used to initiate remote tasks in a remote CICS or IMS/VS system. There are special considerations and limitations in Asynchronous Processing between CICS and IMS/VS systems. These differences and special considerations are discussed in the chapter on CICS-to-IMS InterSystem Communication. In this chapter we will consider only CICS-to-CICS Asynchronous Processing.

8.2   TWO TYPES OF ASYNCHRONOUS PROCESSING

Asynchronous Processing can be implemented in two ways. The first involves use of the Interval Control START Command to start a remote task and pass it data. The STARTed task uses the RETRIEVE Command to obtain the data passed from the starting task. In this type of Asynchronous Processing, the TRANSID which is to be STARTed on a remote system is normally defined as remote in the Program Control Table. CICS Function Ships the START request to the remote system and the Mirror Task executes the START Command. The second way in which Asynchronous Processing can be implemented does not involve Function Shipping, but rather a subset of Distributed Transaction Processing. In this second type of Asynchronous Processing the SEND LAST is used in place of the conversational techniques of Distributed Transaction Processing. Regardless of which technique is used, Asynchronous Processing is quite efficient in terms of CICS resources; a session is not held while the remote process is performing its function. The session is held only while the START Command is being Function Shipped or until the SEND LAST request has been sent and the session freed.

8.3   SYSTEM DEFINITIONS REQUIRED FOR ASYNCHRONOUS PROCESSING

The general system definitions discussed in earlier chapters are, of course, required for Asynchronous Processing. These include the Terminal Control Table link definitions in both the local and remote systems. Additionally, if the START Command is used to initiate a remote TRANSID, a remote transaction definition is normally required in the Program Control Table. Since this table definition is specific to the START/RETRIEVE type of Asynchronous Processing, we will discuss the parameters required for remote transaction definition in the next section dealing with this type of asynchronous processing.

8.4   ASYNCHRONOUS PROCESSING — START AND RETRIEVE COMMANDS

The START command can be used to start a remote task and pass it data. When the remote task is initiated, the RETRIEVE command is used to obtain the passed data. This type of Asynchronous Processing requires that the TRANSID named in the START command be defined as a remote resource or that the SYSID option of the START command be used to name the sysidnt of the remote system.

8.4.1   Remote Transaction Definition

Defining a transaction for use in Asynchronous Processing involves fewer parameters than would be required to define a transaction for use in Transaction Routing. The reason for this is that in Asynchronous Processing, the table definition merely has to support getting the START request Function Shipped to the correct remote region/system. Transaction definitions for Transaction Routing define task characteristics of an application task that runs in the Terminal-Owning region. Even though this task executes in the CICS Relay Program, it still has application-dependent characteristics defined in the PCT definition. Figure 8-1 illustrates the in-

```
RDO Definition              Macro-Level Definition


DEFINE                      DFHPCT TYPE=REMOTE
  TRANSACTION(name)                ,TRANSID=name
  GROUP(groupname)
  REMOTESYSTEM(sysidnt-name)       ,SYSIDNT=name
  REMOTENAME(name)                 [,RMTNAME=name]
  LOCALQ(NO|YES)                   [,LOCALQ={NO|YES}]
  RSL(0|number|PUBLIC)             [,RSL={0|number|PUBLIC}]
```

Figure 8-1 Transaction definition options for Asynchronous Processing using the START command. Reprinted by permission from *CICS/MVS Version 2.1 Intercommunication Guide* © 1987, 1988 by International Business Machines Corporation.

formation that might be specified for a TRANSID that is to be used solely for Asynchronous Processing.

The TRANSACTION option names the 1- to 4-character transaction identifier or TRANSID.

The GROUP option associates this resource definition with a group of resources. Resource Groups are installed together under RDO and, therefore, there is no equivalent to GROUP for the macro level definition.

The REMOTESYSTEM option is used to identify the SYSIDNT of the remote system as specified in the Terminal Control Table link definition (DEFINE CONNECTION RDO command or DFHTCT TYPE=SYSTEM macro).

The REMOTENAME option permits the definition of an alternate name for the transaction identifier. The REMOTENAME is the name by which the TRANSID is known in the remote system. Through the use of this option, the TRANSACTION option can be used to provide an alias name for a remote TRANSID.

The LOCALQ option can be used to request *local queueing* of START requests. Local queueing enables CICS to store a START request for subsequent forwarding to the remote system. If LOCALQ(YES) is specified, then a START request is stored in the local CICS if a link to the remote system is not available when the START request is made. A link may not be available because the remote system is down or because a hardware or circuit problem precludes immediate establishment of a session between the systems. When LOCALQ(YES) is specified, START commands to be queued must include the NOCHECK option discussed below. The LOCALQ(YES) option thus requests queueing of STARTs for this TRANSID.

However, a more global type of local queueing can be implemented in an installation if a *global user exit* is created for the CICS program DFHISP. The global user exit can selectively choose transactions to be queued regardless of the LOCALQ option in the PCT. The global user exit program must be written in assembler language, and it requires a standard Processing Program Table definition. Details as to register conventions, parameters passed to the exit program, and the meaning of return codes passed back to DFHSIP by the exit program are contained in the IBM Reference Manual *CICS/MVS Customization Guide* SC33-0507. Once the exit program has been assembled and link edited into the CICS Relocatable Program Library (DFHRPL), it can be activated as an exit. The exit point in DFHISP is named XISLCLQ.

A command level program executes an EXEC CICS ENABLE command to enable the exit program as an exit for XISLCLQ. The EXEC CICS DISABLE command is used to disable an active exit if it is no longer desired. The formats of both the ENABLE and DISABLE commands are provided in the *CICS/MVS Customization Guide*. The logical place to ENABLE a global user exit is from a postinitialization program. Postinitialization programs are named in a Program List Table for Program Initialization (PLTPI). Any user programs named in a PLTPI are given control automatically subsequent to CICS initialization. If a PLTPI program is used to ENABLE the global user exit, then this becomes an automatic function when CICS initializes.

LOCALQ(NO) indicates that this TRANSID is not to be queued if a START request is made when a link to the remote sytem is unavailable.

The RSL option can be used to provide a Resource Security Level for this TRANSID. A complete discussion of this option is provided above in the discussion of RSL options in the previous chapters.

Figure 8-2 is an example of a remote transaction definition for use in asynchronous processing. Command level facilities are required for STARTing remote TRANSIDs; a macro level request (DFHIC TYPE=INITIATE or DFHIC TYPE=PUT) to initiate a remote transaction is not processed successfully. Therefore, the START command must be used.

```
M A C R O       D E F I N I T I O N
------------------------------------------

    DFHPCT TYPE=REMOTE,TRANSID=XX01,SYSIDNT=CIC2,        X
           LOCALQ=YES
```

```
R D O     C O M M A N D
-------------------------------

    DEFINE TRANSACTION(XX01)
           GROUP(CIC2GP)
           REMOTESYSTEM(CIC2)
           LOCALQ(YES)
```

Figure 8-2 Transaction definition for START of Remote TRANSID.

8.4.2   The START Command

The START command format is:

```
EXEC CICS START
          TRANSID(tran-id)
          TERMID(term-id)
          INTERVAL(interval-info)
          -OR- TIME(time-info)
          FROM(data-area)
          LENGTH(from-data-area-length)
          FMH
          RTRANSID(return-tran)
          RTERMID(return-termid)
          QUEUE(q-name)
          REQID(request-name)
          SYSID(sysidnt-from-TCT-link-definition)
          NOCHECK
          PROTECT
```

The TRANSID option names the Transaction identifier to be initiated. This option may name a 4-byte field containing the TRANSID, or an actual TRANSID may be expressed as a literal value. Since we are concerned with Asynchronous Processing and the START command, this TRANSID would normally be defined as

Remote in the local PCT. Otherwise, the SYSID option would be required in the START command.

The TERMID option names a terminal to be associated with the STARTed task. This option may name a 4-byte field containing the TERMID, or an actual TERMID may be expressed as a literal value. For Asynchronous Processing it is atypical to use the TERMID option. If TERMID is specified, the terminal must be available before CICS can initiate the task. In addition to providing a terminal ID, the TERMID option can specify a SYSIDNT. In this case CICS acquires a session with the remote system as the STARTed task's principal facility.

Time information is provided to tell the remote CICS when to initiate the STARTed task. The time information can be provided as an INTERVAL or as an actual TIME. If omitted, time information defaults to INTERVAL(0). INTERVAL or TIME specification is in the format of HHMMSS where HH or hours may be from 00 to 99, MM or minutes may be from 00 to 59, and SS or seconds may be from 00 to 59. TIME or INTERVAL options may also name a 4-byte packed field, such as a COBOL field defined as PIC S9(7) COMP-3, in which the time information is represented in packed decimal format as X'0HHMMSS+'. Most commonly, an INTERVAL(0) is used for Asynchronous Processing, but time information can certainly be specified. Time information determines when the remote task is to be STARTed, and not when the request is to be shipped to the remote system.

Figure 8-3 illustrates a cross system START request. The command specifies time information as an INTERVAL of 1 hour and 15 minutes. The request is shipped to the remote system and executed immediately by the Mirror Task. The Mirror Task execution of the START request results in the creation of an Interval Control Element (ICE) in the remote system. In the figure, the Interval of 1 hour and 15 minutes is added to the local clock in CIC2 to derive an expiration time for the request. At 11:15 the ICE melts or expires and the task will be started. It is best to use INTERVALs rather than TIMEs for remote START requests. As a matter of fact, our example would have worked differently if the START command in Figure 8-3 were coded to request a TIME(111500) intending the remote task to be initiated at 11:15. The local CICS, CIC1, would have converted the TIME request to an INTERVAL based upon the local clock, which is illustrated as 11:00 in the drawing. As a result, an INTERVAL of 15 minutes would have been developed and the START request would have carried the INTERVAL of 15 minutes. Since the local clock in CIC2 is 1 hour behind the clock of CIC1, the

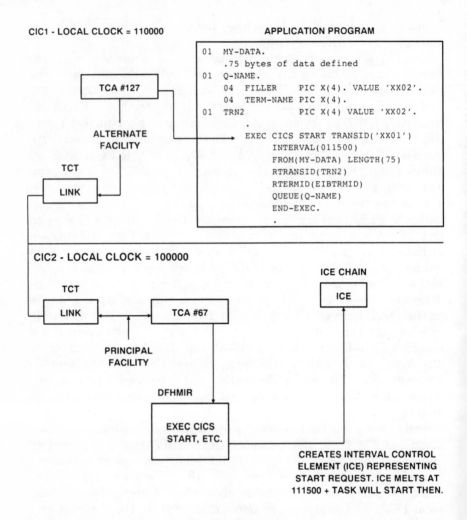

Figure 8-3 Function Shipping of START Request is a special case of Function Shipping called Asynchronous Processing.

remote task would have been initiated at 10:15, or 15 minutes later than the START request as opposed to the INTERVAL of 1 hour and 15 minutes actually desired. To avoid this, code INTERVAL for remote STARTs.

The FROM option names a program data area containing parameters/data to be passed to the STARTed task. This area is free form but, of course, must agree with the field delineation and field formats expected by the STARTed task. Optionally, a Function

Management Header can be contained in this data area. Normally Function Management Headers are not used.

The LENGTH option defines the size of the FROM data area. This can be expressed as a numeric literal or as a 2-byte binary field named by the LENGTH option.

FMH indicates the presence of a Function Management Header within the FROM data area.

The RTRANSID option names a TRANSID. This field is normally used to pass a TRANSID to be STARTed back in the STARTing task's local system. The purpose of this task piggybacking is to provide a mechanism to locally process the results or data created by the remote Asynchronous Task. This option would typically be used in Asynchronous Processing, although a TRANSID (or anything else) could also be placed in the FROM area as a data field.

The RTERMID option names a TERMID. In Asynchronous Processing the RTERMID is typically used to name a terminal required when the remote Asynchronous Task does the START for the RTRANSID back to the local system.

The QUEUE option can contain up to 8 bytes of queue name. The queue can be local or remote to the STARTing task. The queue is used in a manner defined by the application. It can contain data that the STARTed task is to read and process or it can be used as a storage facility for data selected by the remote task and subsequently read and processed back in the local system. The queue can be a Transient Data Queue or a Temporary Storage Queue.

The REQID option allows the programmer to provide an 8-character name for this START request. This is useful if it is anticipated that the START request may subsequently need to be cancelled using the CANCEL command.

The SYSID option can be used to provide a SYSIDNT so that the local PCT is not checked for a TRANSID definition. The SYSIDNT names the remote system as it is defined in the Terminal Control Table link definition.

The NOCHECK option indicates that the STARTing Task does not need to be notified of the correct receipt of the Function Shipped request. If NOCHECK is omitted, the remote system sends a confirmation to the local CICS. All this confirmation indicates is that a remote Mirror Task received the START request. Omitting the NOCHECK causes extra network traffic and does not inform the application program about whether or not the STARTed task was correctly initiated and properly executed, which is really what we would want to know. Therefore, the use of NOCHECK is recommended as it optimizes network traffic. Also, the NOCHECK option is required if LOCALQueuing is to be used for a START request. When NOCHECK is used, CICS does not actually Function Ship the START request until the STARTing task SYNCPOINTs, ends normally, or issues a subsequent Function Shipping request for the same remote system.

The PROTECT option indicates that the START request is not to be processed until the requesting task takes a SYNCPOINT or ends successfully. If the requesting task fails subsequent to a START PROTECT request, the START is not processed. If PROTECT and REQID are specified, the value used for the REQID should be defined as a recoverable Temporary Storage DATAID on the remote system. This is done in the Temporary Storage Table in the remote system.

8.4.3   Unusual Conditions Associated with the START Command

The unusual conditions associated with the START command include INVREQ, IOERR, ISCINVREQ, NOTAUTH, SYSIDERR, TERMIDERR, and TRANSIDERR.

The INVREQ signifies that the START command is invalid or references information that is invalid.

The IOERR occurs if a START command references data to be passed to the STARTed task and there is no room in Temporary Storage to save the data or there is a problem with the Temporary Storage data set (DFHTEMP).

The ISCINVREQ indicates that an error occurred during the processing of a START command in a remote system and the error does not relate to one of the other unusual conditions.

The NOTAUTH indicates a resource security failure. This indicates that the terminal operator's resource security key (as defined in the Sign oN Table) does not contain the resource security level defined for the TRANSID being initiated. NOTAUTH can also occur if the executing task's TRANSID is defined in the PCT as requiring Resource Security Level Checking (RSLC=YES) and the program contains a START command utilizing the SYSID option.

The SYSIDERR indicates that either the remote system defined as owning the TRANSID is not defined in the Terminal Control Table or that a link to the remote system is currently not available. If LOCALQueuing is used for the TRANSID then the SYSIDERR does not occur because a link is unavailable. In that case the START request is stored until a link becomes available.

The TERMIDERR indicates that the TERMID option names an undefined terminal.

The TRANSIDERR indicates that the TRANSID named is not defined in the PCT.

The conditions raised for a START command used in an Intercommunication environment are dependent upon whether the NOCHECK option is included in the command coding and whether or not LOCALQueuing is utilized. If START NOCHECK is included, then none of the conditions are raised except possibly the SYSIDERR. The SYSIDERR does not occur, however, if LOCALQueuing is used. You will recall that NOCHECK is a required command option if LOCALQueuing is utilized. If NOCHECK is omitted then all of the unusual conditions can occur and, additionally, the task can be abended if the connected Mirror Task abends. The abend code associated with a Mirror Task abend is dependent upon the link type. For an InterSystem Communication link the abend code is "ATNI"; for an MRO InterRegion Communication link, the abend code is "AZI6." The default action for all of the unusual conditions associated with the START command is to abend the task.

8.4.4   The RETRIEVE Command

The RETRIEVE command is used by a STARTed task to obtain the data passed to it in the START request. The format of the RETRIEVE command is:

```
EXEC CICS RETRIEVE
      INTO(data-area-name)
      -OR-
      SET(pointer)
      LENGTH(2-byte-binary-field)
      RTRANSID(4-byte-data-area-name)
      RTERMID(4-byte-data-area-name)
      QUEUE(8-byte-data-area-name)
      WAIT
```

INTO names a data area into which the START command FROM data is to be placed. SET names a pointer that is to be SET to the address of the FROM data. If a Function Management Header is present (as indicated by the inclusion of the FMH option of the START command), the EIBFMH flag is set to high values (X'FF'). Otherwise EIBFMH is set to low values (X'00').

The LENGTH option names a 2-byte binary field into which CICS places the length of the Start command FROM data. If INTO is used then the LENGTH field must be preset with the length of the INTO data area before the RETRIEVE command is executed.

RTRANSID, RTERMID, and QUEUE name data fields which are to receive the data specified by those options of the START command.

The WAIT option can only be used by a terminal-oriented task — one that is attached to a network resource. This option permits a task to WAIT for more data from START commands for the same combination of TERMID and TRANSID. CICS queues up expired Interval Control START requests in an Automatic Initiator Descriptor (AID) chain. The AID chain is sequenced by TERMID and then TRANSID. This allows a task to perform multiple RETRIEVE requests to obtain successive data from multiple START requests for the same combination of TERMID and TRANSID. When there are no more expired Interval Control STARTS (and therefore no more data) for the same combination of TERMID and TRANSID, CICS raises the ENDDATA condition. As an alternative, WAIT can be used. This indicates that the task wants to wait for another START to expire and then its data satisfies the WAIT. However, if you reread the first sentence of this paragraph, you will note that this is a dangerous option. Do we want a terminal operator sitting and WAITing for another Interval Control Element, or ICE, to melt? If the Interval Control STARTed task is attached to a system, do we want a session to another system/region tied up waiting for ICE to melt? Also, the task could conceivably WAIT forever, so there would have to be some way of getting rid of it after a certain amount of time. The best way to get rid of a task stuck in this type of WAIT is to define a Deadlock TIMe OUT, or DTIMOUT, for the TRANSID in its PCT definition. Otherwise, the task could conceivably wait until CICS is asked to shut down. At that point CICS awakens the sleeping beauty and the task should then RETURN to CICS. All in all, the WAIT option should probably be avoided, and the program can deal with the ENDDATA condition. When there is no more data, the best policy is probably to finish up processing and RETURN to CICS.

8.4.5   Unusual Conditions of the RETRIEVE Command

The unusual conditions associated with the RETRIEVE command include ENDDATA, ENVDEFERR, INVREQ, INVTSREQ, IOERR, LENGERR, NOTAUTH, and NOTFND. There are no special considerations for use of the RETRIEVE command to obtain data sent by a remote START command. The RETRIEVE is, after all, being done in the region where the Mirror Task executed the START command. So even though the original request came from another region, to all purposes, it makes no difference whether the START was executed locally by an application program or the Mirror Program.

The ENDDATA condition means there is no more data to RETRIEVE. This can be because the task has RETRIEVEd all of the data associated with START requests for this combination of TERMID and TRANSID. It can also occur because the task was not initiated via an Interval Control START request or the START request did not pass data.

The ENVDEFERR condition means that the RETRIEVE command data options do not match the data options specified in the START command.

The INVREQ indicates that the RETRIEVE command is invalid.

The INVTSREQ indicates that Temporary Storage is not generated properly in the system. This problem is resolved through the systems programming staff.

The IOERR indicates an Input/Output ERRor during a read of Temporary Storage. The application task can retry the request and abend if the reissued request is unsuccessful.

The LENGERR occurs with use of the INTO option when the data area named is not large enough to accommodate the data passed in the START command FROM area. The data is truncated.

The NOTAUTH indicates a resource security failure.

The NOTFND means that CICS cannot find the data. This can occur because another task deleted it directly from Temporary Storage or the REQID named in the START command was not unique.

The default action is to abend the task unless the unusual condition is programmatically processed.

8.5 ASYNCHRONOUS PROCESSING — SEND LAST AND RECEIVE

This type of Asynchronous Processing is actually a subset of Distributed Transaction Processing. However, in this case, the normal conversational capability is not utilized. Rather a session/conversation is acquired and used to SEND one or more messages, and the only or last SEND specifies the LAST option. **The SEND LAST**

causes CICS to generate an End Bracket (EB) indicator which means that no more data can be sent on the session and no data can be RECEIVEd on the session. The program then frees the session/conversation. The session or conversation can be acquired in one of two ways. The Front-End asynchronous task can be initiated via a START command that names a SYSIDNT or a remote system in the TERMID option. Intrapartition Transient Data ATI can also be used to initiate a task with a connection to a remote system. In either case of ATI, the task is started up with the connection to the remote system as its principal facility. Otherwise, the Front-End asynchronous task can acquire a session/conversation with the ALLOCATE command. However, the coding of the ALLOCATE command is dependent upon the type of link connecting the systems. The ALLOCATE command format is discussed in the subsequent chapters dealing with Distributed Transaction Processing. If the link is an MRO InterRegion Communication link or an LUTYPE 6.1 link or an LUTYPE 6.2 link, consult the command description in the appropriate chapter.

Once the session/conversation is allocated and the session-ID or conversation-ID has been saved, the initiation of the remote Asynchronous Process must be achieved. There are several options for this. A TRANSID can be placed in the first 4 bytes of the output area referenced by the SEND command. This is probably the simplest way to initiate the remote process. Otherwise, if MRO or LUTYPE6.1, a BUILD ATTACH command can be used to build an attach Function Management Header. If the cross-system link is an LUTYPE 6.2 the CONNECT PROCESS can be used prior to the first send. Once remote task initiation has been dealt with, the SEND command is used to SEND data. In the last or only SEND command the LAST option is used. If the session/conversation was acquired through the ALLOCATE command, the FREE command can be used to free the session or the task can RETURN immediately to CICS.

The remote asynchronous task is started and performs one or more RECEIVEs until it has acquired the data. The task cannot use the session over which its data was sent because the remote SEND LAST command ended the bracket state. The data is processed, and if it is necessary to send back some sort of response to the requesting system the asynchronous task can acquire a session/conversation to the remote system and perform a SEND LAST or perform a START for a remote TRANSID defined in the other system.

8.6   SUMMARY

Regardless of the way in which Asynchronous Processing is implemented, using Interval Control or Terminal Control, there are a couple of common issues that might need to be addressed. If it is necessary for the task to determine how it was started up, the ASSIGN command can be used to obtain the task's STARTCODE. The STARTCODE is a 2-byte field which CICS sets to indicate how the task was inititated. "TD" indicates that terminal input initiated the task. "S" indicates a START command without data, and "SD" indicates a START command with data resulted in task initiation. An example of how this might be coded follows.

```
01 STRT-CD PIC XX.
       88 TERMINAL-INPUT-INITIATION VALUE TD'.
       88 INTERVAL-CONTROL-START VALUE 'SD'.
       .
       .
       EXEC CICS ASSIGN STARTCODE(STRT-CD) END-EXEC.
       IF TERMINAL-INPUT-INITIATION
           .
           .
       ELSE
           IF INTERVAL-CONTROL-START
               .
```

Other values for STARTCODE include "QD" for a task initiated as a result of the Intrapartition Transient Data Trigger level being reached and "U" for a user-initiated task. Bear in mind, however, that a task initiated because of an Intrapartition Transient Data Queue is initiated in the queue owning region, because the QUEUE and its TRANSID must be local to the same CICS region. It would be possible to use Function Shipping to WRITEQ TD to a remote queue, but any task started as a result of the trigger level is local to the queue-owning region.

Another common requirement is passing the APPLID of the originating CICS system. This, for example, would be needed if an asynchronous task could be initiated from two or more CICS regions. In that case we need to know which region is to receive the asynchronous "reply." A task can obtain its system's APPLID via the ASSIGN command. The format of this request is:

```
01 MY-APPLID PIC X(8).
     .
     .
     EXEC CICS ASSIGN APPLID(MY-APPLID) END-EXEC.
```

If your system is using the eXtended Recovery Facility, or XRF, the APPLID is the generic APPLID representing the XRF pair. However, that is the APPLID that you want, because all the other systems know only that name. If your system is not using XRF, then the ASSIGN for APPLID returns the specific APPLID of your CICS region. The APPLID can then be included in the data sent to the asynchronous task. The asynchronous task can obtain the SYSIDNT of the originating CICS system by using the EXTRACT TCT command naming the passed APPLID. The format of EXTRACT TCT is:

```
EXEC CICS EXTRACT TCT
     NETNAME(remote-applid)
     SYSID(4-byte-field) - OR - TERMID(4-byte-field)
```

In this way, the remote task can obtain the SYSID for use in a START command or to subsequently acquire a session back to the originating system.

With Asynchronous Processing it is up to the application developer to design the application interfaces necessary to obtain and coordinate requests and subsequent data and responses. Also, the application design must address what happens if a remote task fails. Since these tasks are asynchronous, there is no notification from CICS. Design techniques that can be used were described in the introductory chapters when Asynchronous Processing was first discussed.

REVIEW EXERCISE

Provide a short answer for each of the following.

1. What significance is there in defining a transaction with the characteristic of LOCALQ(YES)?
2. For the PCT definition of a transaction routing TRANSID, a full definition of transaction characteristics is provided. This is not necessary for a transaction to be used to START a remote asynchronous task. Why?

3. Aside from defining transactions individually with LOCALQ(YES), there is another way to accomplish local queuing. What is the other way?
4. What does the NOCHECK option of the START command accomplish?
5. What does the PROTECT option of the START command accomplish?
6. What purpose does the INTERVAL or TIME option of the START command serve? Is this the time at which the request is shipped to the remote system? Or is it the time at which the remote task is initiated?
7. What is accomplished with the WAIT option of the RETRIEVE command?
8. What SNA indicator is generated by the LAST option of a SEND LAST command?
9. Under what circumstances is it not necessary for a Front-End Transaction to perform an ALLOCATE command?
10. How can a task obtain its local CICS system's APPLID so that it can be included in the data area named in the START command?
11. If a remote task has the NETNAME of the system from which its request originated, how can it obtain the local SYSIDNT associated with the originating system?
12. How may a task ascertain the mechanism that caused it to be initiated?

ANSWERS TO REVIEW EXERCISES

Provide a short answer for each of the following.

1. *What significance is there in defining a transaction with the characteristic of LOCALQ(YES)?*

   If LOCALQ(YES) is specified in a transaction's PCT definition, then CICS will queue a START request for the TRANSID if the remote system is unavailable.

2. *For the PCT definition of a transaction routing TRANSID, a full definition of transaction characteristics is provided. This is not necessary for a transaction to be used to START a remote asynchronous task. Why?*

With transaction routing a local task is to be initiated. That task executes in the CICS Relay Program but it has the characteristics defined in the PCT entry. For asynchronous processing, the task initiation request is shipped to another system and the only PCT information required is that which will enable CICS to correctly ship the START request.

3. *Aside from defining transactions individually with LOCALQ(YES), there is another way to accomplish local queuing. What is the other way?*

A global user exit program can be written for DFHSIP. Once the exit is activated, DFHSIP passes it control to determine if local queuing is to be performed.

4. *What does the NOCHECK option of the START command accomplish?*

The NOCHECK option optimizes message flows because it indicates that the application does not need a confirmation of the fact that the START was received and processed in the remote system. Actually, what we would normally be concerned with is whether or not the asynchronous task actually executed correctly. This information is not available whether or not NOCHECK is specified.

5. *What does the PROTECT option of the START command accomplish?*

The PROTECT option includes the START request within the PROTECTED resources of the task. In other words, if the task requesting the START PROTECT does not SYNCPOINT or end normally, the START is not processed.

6. *What purpose does the INTERVAL or TIME option of the START command serve? Is this the time at which the request is shipped to the remote system? Or is it the time at which the remote task is initiated?*

The time information provided on a START command defines the time at which the STARTed task is initiated.

7. *What is accomplished with the WAIT option of the RETRIEVE command?*

If there is no more data for the task's combination of TRANSID and TERMID, then the task waits for another START to expire and processes the data from that START. This, however, is a dangerous option because a task could wait a long time.

8. *What SNA indicator is generated by the LAST option of a SEND LAST command?*

The End Bracket indicator is generated. This effectively terminates the task's use of the session.

9. *Under what circumstances is it not necessary for a Front-End Transaction to perform an ALLOCATE command?*

A Front-End Transaction initiated via ATI may already have as its principal facility a connection with the appropriate remote system.

10. *How can a task obtain its local CICS system's APPLID so that it can be included in the data area named in the START command?*

The task can execute the ASSIGN command naming the APPLID option. CICS returns the APPLID in the 8-byte field named by the APPLID option.

11. *If a remote task has the NETNAME of the system from which its request originated, how can it obtain the local SYSIDNT associated with the originating system?*

The task executes the EXTRACT TCT command providing the NETNAME via the NETNAME option. CICS returns the 4-byte SYSIDNT.

12. *How may a task ascertain the mechanism that caused it to be initiated?*

The task performs an ASSIGN command requesting the STARTCODE option. CICS returns a code indicating how the task was initiated.

Chapter

9

Distributed Transaction Processing

9.1 INTRODUCTION

In this chapter we begin our discussion of Distributed Transaction Processing. Distributed Transaction Processing allows two separate tasks to engage in a synchronized exchange to accomplish a unit of work between them. DTP provides facilities so that two programs can communicate with each other, signal each other with regard to their status, and jointly commit modifications to protected resources.

There are, however, special considerations for writing DTP application programs based upon the type of Intercommunication link connecting them: MRO InterRegion Communication links, LUTYPE 6.1 links, or LUTYPE6.2 links. Within LUTYPE 6.2 there are two similar application programming command sets. There is a command set that enables application programs to engage in mapped conversations and another set of commands for use in unmapped conversations. Because there are significant differences between LUTYPE 6.2 mapped conversations, LUTYPE 6.2 unmapped conversations, and MRO/LUTYPE 6.1 conversations, we will examine each of these topics in separate chapters.

However, before we begin looking at these different subsets of DTP there are some common issues that need to be addressed. These include resource definitions for DTP; a basic review of definitions and concepts needed to understand and use DTP; and the programming

223

considerations involved with designing and implementing programs to perform DTP.

9.2   RESOURCE DEFINITIONS FOR DTP

Aside from the general system requirements for supporting Inter-communication, DTP requires almost no special resource definitions. The links to any interconnected systems must, of course, be defined in the Terminal Control Table, the appropriate CICS programs have to be generated, the table entries for CICS Intercommunication programs and TRANSIDs must be created, and the external definitions in MVS or VTAM must be defined. All of the general things that we've discussed in earlier chapters are required, but specific remote resource definitions for transactions, terminals, files, or queues are not needed for DTP.

The only specific resource that may be required is the definition of one or more PROFILEs in the Program Control Table. This is particularly so in the case of LUTYPE 6.2 conversations because a profile can be explicitly named when requesting use of a session for a distributed conversation over LUTYPE 6.2 links. The selected profile can name a modeset and thereby define a class of service for the conversation. So the only thing that the systems programmer has to do in support of DTP specifically is to define the local resources and perhaps a profile or two.

9.3   REVIEW OF DEFINITIONS AND CONCEPTS

In the introductory chapters we defined some of the terms used in the context of DTP. Since a clear understanding of these terms and their relationship to SNA is important in correctly designing and coding distributed transactions, a brief review is in order.

9.3.1   Conversation Versus Session

In order for two distributed application programs to communicate with each other and perform DTP, it is necessary for them to utilize a communication connection which links their respective systems. This communication connection is made through an SNA network and is called a session. **The session is, however, a resource of the systems that are joined by it and is only temporarily**

given over for the use of application programs. LUTYPE 6.2 distinguishes between the session, which is a connection resource between systems, and its use for a *conversation* by end users of the LUTYPE 6.2. Since the term LUTYPE 6.2 is synonomous with *Advanced Program-to-Program Communication (APPC)*, the end users in this case are the application programs engaging in a conversation. The conversation takes place within SNA brackets. SNA brackets are indicators which bracket off bidirectional flows such that these "separate" flows are seen as a transaction or unit of work. A distributed conversation begins a bracket and CICS generates the *Begin Bracket (BB)* indicator automatically to accompany the first cross system flow. The *End Bracket* is generated by CICS as a result of application program command execution or termination. Once the End Bracket (EB) has been transmitted, however, the conversation *is over!*

9.3.2   Front-End Transaction

The *Front-End Transaction* is the one that initiates the conversation. The Front-End Transaction is started as a result of normal transaction initiation — terminal operator input or Automatic Transaction Initiation (ATI). Automatic Transaction Initiation can be via an Interval Control START or as a result of an Intrapartition Transient Data Queue trigger level being reached. In the case of ATI, the task initiation process may well obtain the connection with the remote system. For example, a locally STARTed task obtains a network resource based upon the TERMID option of the START command. The TERMID option can be used to name a SYSIDNT of a remote system. In this case as a part of normal Automatic Transaction Initiation, CICS obtains the network resource or use of a session to the remote system. Assuming that a link to a remote system named "CIC1" has been defined, the following command would result in the initiation of a task that has use of a session to CIC1.

```
EXEC CICS START TRANSID('WMA1')
     TERMID('CIC1') FROM(MY-DATA) LENGTH(50)
     INTERVAL(0) END-EXEC.
```

A Destination Control Table definition of an Intrapartition Transient Data Queue specifies the DESTID or queue name; a trigger level or count of records; a locally owned TRANSID that is to be automatically initiated when the count of records hits the trigger level; a destination factor which can be SYSTEM (or TERMINAL or FILE); and the TERMID or SYSIDNT if the destination factor indicates that a network resource is required. The following Destination Control Table definition defines an intrapartition queue with a destination factor of SYSTEM and requires a connection to CIC1.

```
DFHDCT TYPE=INTRA,TRANSID=WMA2,TRIGLEV=5,              X
       DESTFAC=(SYSTEM,CIC1),DESTID=INT1
```

When the fifth record is written to the intrapartition queue named "INT1," a local task is started to process the transaction "WMA2." A session is allocated as the task's principal facility as part of task initiation.

In these two examples of ATI, a session with a remote system was allocated as part of transaction initiation, and that connection is the tasks principal facility. Of course, not all ATI tasks can be relied upon to have a session as a principal facility. Had the TERMID option been omitted from the START command above, the STARTED task would not have been connected to the remote system. Had DESTFAC=FILE been specified in the Destination Control Table definition, the triggered task would, likewise, not have been connected to the remote system. In the case of a task initiated as a result of terminal input, the terminal is the task's principal facility.

A task that does not have a session allocated to it is able to acquire one as an alternate facility. An alternate facility is acquired through an ALLOCATE command. Once a Front-End Transaction has a connection to a remote system allocated to it (either by transaction initiation or through execution of an ALLOCATE command), it is able to initiate a remote process or conversation partner.

9.3.3   Back-End Transaction

The *Back-End Transaction* is the one that is initiated by the Front-End Transaction. The Back-End Transaction is always connected to the session and the session is always its principal facility. LUTYPE 6 is designed for peer-to-peer communication. What that means is that the Logical Units are "peers." It does not mean that distributed transactions should be coded so that conversing programs are peers. As a matter of fact, the opposite is true. The simplest design for distributed transaction programs is for one of the modules to be the main process and for the other to be a submodule that does a limited function.

The reason for this is that interprogram coordination required in a "master-to-slave" type design is far simpler. If both programs are truly data processing peers, then many things could go awry at either end. It would be necessary for the application designer to build complex interprogram protocols so that they could signal each other about the various errors and coordinate their processing accordingly. In contrast, if one of the programs does the bulk of the processing and the other serves as a remote subroutine, there is less to coordinate between them. Normally, the Front-End Transaction is the "master" and the Back-End Transaction is the "slave," but this does not have to be the case.

9.3.4   Principal Versus Alternate Facility

A task's principal facility is the one that the task is born with and that caused it to be initiated. To this end any Terminal Control commands that are used in a program are automatically directed to the task's principal facility. If a task obtains an alternate facility, it must explicitly direct Terminal Control commands to the alternate facility by specifying a CONVersation ID or CONVID (for LUTYPE 6.2) or a SESSION ID (for MRO and LUTYPE 6.1). A task can only have one principal facility but it can have multiple alternate facilities. So it is possible for a conversation to involve multiple connected programs.

One possible configuration of a distributed transaction involving multiple programs is illustrated in Figure 9-1. This type of distributed transaction is complex and requires careful design of interprogram coordination. Also, it is necessary for one program to be the master or guiding force for the entire transaction. That role would logically belong to "A." However, Program "B" in its relationship with "C" would be the master or focal point of coordinating that conversation. Program "D" would be the point of coordination for both programs "E" and "F." Thus, when multiple programs are involved in a distributed transaction, a master/slave tree design is recommended. This is especially true if the transaction involves distributed updates to protected resources. In that case SYNCPOINTs are exchanged, and such exchanges must be controlled and coordinated from one place. So when it comes to designing distributed transactions, it is best to think in terms of master/slave relationships. Otherwise, the design and processing becomes unwieldly. Of course, the best case is to keep distributed transactions as simple as possible.

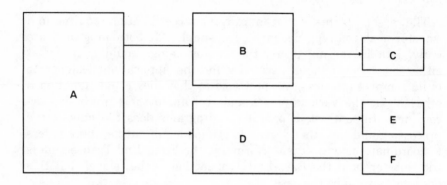

CONVERSATIONS:

A-to-B	A is the Front-End	B is the Back-End
B-to-C	B is the Front-End	C is the Back-End
A-to-D	A is the Front-End	D is the Back-End
D-to-E	D is the Front-End	E is the Back-End
D-to-F	D is the Front-End	F is the Back-End

Figure 9-1 A complex distribute transaction involving six programs.

9.3.5   SNA Indicators

Being aware of *SNA indicators*, what they mean, when they are generated, when they are transmitted, and how to test for their presence is critical to the successful design and implementation of programs that perform a distributed transaction. There are three SNA indicators that are important to the application programmer: a *Change-Direction Indicator*, an *End Bracket Indicator*, and a *Syncpoint Indicator*. If you don't know what causes them and you don't know how to test for them, you are in *big* trouble.

9.3.6   Change Direction Indicator

All distributed transactions take place over sessions whose send/receive flow control is the SNA *half-duplex flip-flop protocol*. This is architecturally required for LUTYPE 6. What does this mean to application programmers? It means that during a conversation only one of the transactions is allowed to send at time. When the distributed transaction is initiated with the birth of the Back-End Transaction, one of the transactions is in the *send state* and is allowed to send and the other is in the *receive state* and is not allowed to send. **The right to send flip-flops between them based upon the generation and transmission of an SNA Change-Direction Indicator.** Only a send state transaction can cause a state change in normal circumstances. Rule number 1 (hard and fast in stone) — "The Front-End Transaction is in the send state when the transaction is initiated." Rule number 2 — "The Back-End Transaction is in the receive state when the transaction is initiated." There are only certain things that a transaction can do while in the receive state so it is imperative to know the state you're in. A Change-Direction indicator is generated by the send state transaction performing a SEND INVITE command or a CONVERSE command. At this point it is not necessary to remember the exact commands because we will go over this in each of the successive chapters with regard to each type of distributed transaction program. Subsequent to the execution of a RECEIVE command, CICS informs the transaction of its SEND/RECEIVE state.

9.3.7   Bracket Indicators

When the distributed transaction is initiated, CICS automatically generates the Begin Bracket Indicator, which is carried on the first conversation flow. Aside from the fact of knowing that the Begin Bracket is there, the application programmer need not be concerned about it. The End Bracket Indicator is generated when the send state transaction performs a SEND LAST or frees the session. For ISC links CICS does not send the End Bracket Indicator immediately. The reason for this is that CICS optimizes the number of flows during a conversation by accumulating data and SNA indicators. This is not done for MRO, and in this regard MRO programs may have to be coded differently. Again, we will go over this again with regard to each type of distributed conversation. At this point it is sufficient to understand that once an End Bracket is transmitted, the conversation is over.

9.3.8   Syncpoint Indicators

A SYNCPOINT Indicator is generated when an MRO or LUTYPE 6.1 program executes a SYNCPOINT command or RETURNS normally to CICS prior to the transmission of an End Bracket Indicator. For LUTYPE 6.2 there are levels of synchronization and when the highest level of synchronization is used, a SYNCPOINT Indicator is generated in the same circumstances as for LUTYPE 6.1 or MRO. A SYNCPOINT command can only be issued when in the send state with regard to all conversation partners. Referring back to Figure 9-1, "A" could execute a SYNCPOINT if it were in the send state with regard to "B" and "D." A transaction receiving a SYNCPOINT indicator must respond to it. The response is dependent upon the type of conversation and will be addressed specifically in each of the subsequent chapters.

9.4   PROGRAMMING CONSIDERATIONS

DTP takes place between programs that are designed to be a matched pair. Their activities, command utilization, error protocols, and message formats must all be coordinated. This, of course, favors designing distributed transactions to be as simple as possible. In Figure 9-1 we have six programs within a distributed transaction. Each of the separate interactions must be defined. Commands used in program "C" that impact the "B"-to-"C" conversation must be understood and tested for in program "B." The same is true with regard to all of the other conversations listed in the figure. For each conversation it is necessary to define the program-to-program protocols. The following, which is by no means an exhaustive list of the issues that should be addressed for each program-to-program interaction, will clarify why it is recommended that DTP be kept as simple as possible.

1. Specify the conversation-oriented commands that will be used in both programs.
2. Define the context in which such commands are to be used, i.e., signaling various errors or establishing confirmation points for successful processing.
3. What messages are to be exchanged bidirectionally? Are message formats fixed or variable? When should send/receive states be reversed?
4. What processing is to be carried out in each of the programs? How do these processes potentially impact the conversation?
5. What errors can result, and what impact do they have on the conversation?
6. Which errors are recoverable and need not result in termination of the conversation?

7. Which errors are unrecoverable, and in each case who is to abort the conversation?
8. For recoverable errors, what if any responsibility does each process have for recovery?
9. What coordination is needed for recovery?
10. What sort of messages or confirmations are to be exchanged in the event of successful processing?
11. Is there a need for SYNCPOINTing to commit modifications to protected resources?
12. If SYNCPOINTing is required, who is to be the initiator of SYNCPOINT processing, and when is the SYNCPOINT appropriate?
13. What positive or negative responses are to be returned for SYNCPOINT requests?
14. If the conversation is terminated because of session/system failure, is it to be restarted? If so, how?
15. Is there a need for some sort of manual/programmatic recovery in the event of session failure during the INDOUBT period of SYNCPOINT exchanges?

If the major share of processing and control is contained in one program, the design of interprogram protocols and coordination is greatly simplified. Consequently, the recommendation is made for a master/slave program-to-program relationship. If the transaction is accomplished with two distributed programs, the design is simpler than if additional programs are needed. So, in designing distributed transactions, the KISS principle is the golden rule.

The programs that perform DTP are a matched pair that are designed and coded to fit together. Yet, they are, to all extents and purposes, separate entities that communicate through CICS. Therefore, it is necessary to know how CICS passes conversation information to the application program. This aspect of program coding is likewise dependent upon the flavor of Intercommunication utilized. For LUTYPE 6.2 mapped conversations, fields in the Execute Interface Block are set by CICS to reflect status information. For LUTYPE 6.1 and MRO, the EIB is also used but some of the fields utilized vary. For LUTYPE 6.2 unmapped conversations, the EIB is not used. An application program defined work area, referred to as the CONVDATA area, is used to pass status information to the application. **It is important to know in all cases when CICS sets indicators, what the indicators mean and what action is mandated for each indicator.**

To simplify the coding of distributed programs, IBM has created a collection of *state diagrams* unique to each conversation type. The state diagrams represent each of the possible states that a transaction can be in throughout a conversation. We will go over the state diagrams pertinent to each type of conversation in each of the subsequent chapters, but for now it is only necessary to understand the importance of the state diagrams. Each transaction involved in a conversation is in a defined state during the conversation and of course, states change based upon the actions (commands and command options) of the conversation partners.

So to take a simplified view of this, at one point or in one state the session is not yet allocated. If a session is allocated and both the Front-End and Back-End Transactions have been initiated, one of them is in the send state and the other is in the receive state. When the send state transaction causes a change direction indicator to be sent, it enters a state known as receive pending and then progresses to being in the receive state. In other words, there are a finite number of states for each transaction involved in distributed transaction processing, and these states are identified by conversation type.

For each identified state only certain commands and actions are valid and certain tests (for example of EIB indicators) might be required. For each conversational state, there is a state diagram. The state diagram for each conversational state defines the commands that may be issued, which tests would be recommended, and what if any state transition or change results from each possible command. The state diagrams are useful to the application programmer/designer because they identify processes that are valid at each point in a conversation. Using the state diagrams during the design phase aids the designer in developing valid sets of interactions for various conditions and problems that can occur during a distributed transaction. The application programmer is able to use the state diagrams as a reference during program coding so that valid command sequences can be constructed and appropriate tests made.

10

Initiating LUTYPE 6.2 Mapped Conversations

10.1 PROGRAMMING AND DESIGN CONSIDERATIONS

Using the application programming facilities provided for LUTYPE 6.2 mapped conversations, programs may be developed in COBOL, PL/I, or assembler language. As part of designing the application programs that comprise a distributed transaction, it is necessary to define the processing to be performed in the Front-End Transaction and the the Back-End Transaction. Some commands are appropriate to one transaction or the other, but most commands can be utilized by either. However, within the context of using mapped conversation commands, it is necessary to be aware of the transaction's state with regard to the conversation. Therefore, in our discussion of each command, we will relate the commands back to the conversation states.

10.2 CICS COMMANDS FOR LUTYPE 6.2 MAPPED CONVERSATIONS

The LUTYPE 6.2 CICS commands are an implementation of the protocol boundary verbs defined for LUTYPE 6.2 conversations within System Network Architecture. These CICS commands are listed in Figure 10-1.

USED BY THE FRONT-END TRANSACTION:

ALLOCATE - used to request use of a session so that the Front-End Transaction has an alternate facility over which a conversation can be held.

CONNECT PROCESS - used to initiate a remote process or, as we might call it, a conversation partner.

USED BY THE BACK-END TRANSACTION:

EXTRACT PROCESS - used to obtain conversation related information from the ATTACH Function Management Header which caused CICS to invoke the Back-End Transaction.

USED BY EITHER TRANSACTION IN ACCORDANCE WITH THE TRANSACTION'S CURRENT STATE AND THE CONVERSATION'S SYNCHRONIZATION LEVEL:

SEND - used to SEND data and/or SNA indicators.

CONVERSE - used to SEND, WAIT, and RECEIVE.

WAIT - used to force transmission of the buffer in which CICS has stored conversation data and SNA indicators.

ISSUE CONFIRMATION - used as a positive response to a CONFIRMation request.

ISSUE ERROR - used as a negative response to a CONFIRMation request or to signal an application-defined error.

ISSUE ABEND - used as a negative response to a CONFIRMation request or to signal an application-defined error. This command abends the conversation.

ISSUE SIGNAL - used by a RECEIVE STATE transaction to request that it be placed into the SEND STATE.

FREE - used to FREE the session.

ISSUE PREPARE - used to prepare an unreliable conversation partner for a SYNCPOINT. This would be used in complex conversations involving multiple transactions.

SYNCPOINT - used to initiate COMMIT protocols.

Figure 10-1 LUTYPE 6.2 mapped conversation commands.

STATE 1 MAPPED LUTYPE6.2 CONVERSATIONS		SESSION NOT ALLOCATED
Commands You Can Issue	What To Test (For EIBERRCD tests see the table on page 199)	New State
ALLOCATE [NOQUEUE] *	SYSIDERR	1
	SYSBUSY *	1
	Otherwise (obtain conversation identifier from EIBRSRCE)	2

* If you want your program to wait until a session is available, omit
the NOQUEUE option of the ALLOCATE command and do not code a HANDLE
command for the SYSBUSY condition.

If you want control to be returned to your program if a session is not
immediately available, either specify NOQUEUE on the ALLOCATE command
and test EIBRCODE for SYSBUSY (X'D3'), or code a HANDLE CONDITION SYSBUSY
command.

Figure 10-2 State 1 — SESSION NOT ALLOCATED diagram. Reprinted by permission from *CICS/MVS Version 2.1 Intercommunication Guide* © 1987, 1988 by International Business Machines Corporation.

10.3 THE ALLOCATE COMMAND

The ALLOCATE command is used by a Front-End Transaction that
does not already have use of a session to a remote system. The AL-
LOCATE command requests an alternate facility from CICS. The
conversation state for this transaction at this point in processing is
State 1 — *Session Not Allocated*. Figure 10-2 illustrates the state
diagram for state 1. According to this state diagram there is only one
command that can be used in state 1 and that is the ALLOCATE
command to obtain use of a session.

10.3.1 ALLOCATE Command Format

The format of the ALLOCATE command is as follows:

```
EXEC CICS ALLOCATE
    SYSID(sys-name)
    PROFILE(profile-name)
```

NOQUEUE

NOSUSPEND

The SYSID option is used to provide the SYSIDNT of the remote system. This is the name defined in the local CICS Terminal Control Table for the remote system. This option may name a 4-byte character field, or an actual SYSIDNT may be named as a literal.

The PROFILE option provides the 1- to 8-character name of a communication profile to use for the conversation. This option is coded only if an installation-specific profile is desired. Otherwise, if omitted, a default CICS Profile, "DFHCICSA," becomes the profile for the conversation. You will recall that a profile is used to name a collection of terminal control processing options. The one option in a profile that may interest us in coding the ALLOCATE command is the definition of a modeset name within the profile. The modeset name relates to a collection of sessions with the remote system. Associated with the modeset name is a VTAM class of service. By being able to name a profile, we are able to select a class of service or priority for this conversation. The use of profiles is installation-specific, however, and they may not be usable in your installation.

The NOQUEUE option indicates that CICS is not to queue the request for a session. If a session is available, CICS ALLOCATEs it to the task. If, however, an appropriate session is not currently available, CICS returns control back at the next sequential instruction with an indication in EIBRCODE (X'D3'in byte 0) that a session was not allocated. Subsequent to the execution of an ALLOCATE command with the NOQUEUE option, the EIBRCODE should be tested to determine if a session was indeed allocated. The reasons why a session might not be available can include 1) no active sessions with the remote system, 2) sessions currently available to the remote system are contention losers which would require that CICS BID or seek permission to begin a transaction or in SNA terms a bracket, or 3) all existing sessions are being used. The wait for a session could be of short or long duration.

The NOSUSPEND option is another name for the NOQUEUE option. Either option may be used and the meaning is identical.

10.3.2   Unusual Conditions and the ALLOCATE Command

The unusual conditions associated with the ALLOCATE command include CBIDERR, INVREQ, SYSBUSY, SESSBUSY, and SYSIDERR.

The CBIDERR indicates that the profile named in the PROFILE option of the ALLOCATE command is not known to CICS. If the profile name as you know it is spelled correctly, you should verify the profile's existence with the CICS system's programmer. The default course of action for CICS is to abend the task.

The INVREQ indicates that the Logical Unit is already allocated to the task. Check the command coding to ensure the SYSIDNT name is correct for this allocate command, or test interactively to be certain the command is not being executed repeatedly. By default, CICS terminates the task.

The SYSBUSY condition indicates that the requested system is busy. Unless the NOQUEUE/NOSUSPEND option has been included in the ALLOCATE command or the SYSBUSY has been programmatically handled, CICS queues the task until a session becomes available. Handling the condition SYSBUSY takes precedence over the NOQUEUE option. In other words, if you have coded HANDLE CONDITION SYSBUSY and included the NOQUEUE/NOSUSPEND option for purposes of overkill, control is returned to your program at the paragraph named in the HANDLE CONDITION for SYSBUSY.

The SESSBUSY condition is similar to the SYSBUSY condition and is handled in the same manner. The SESSBUSY indicates that the requested session group or modeset is busy.

The SYSIDERR indicates an error related to the SYSIDNT requested, which precludes CICS providing a session to the task. Sessions with the remote system may all be out of service, or the SYSIDNT named in the SYSID option may not be defined in the Terminal Control Table. This condition can occasionally happen because an incorrect modename is specified in the profile requested via the PROFILE option. This would occur if none of the session groups or modesets with the requested system corresponded with the modename defined in the named profile. Try removing the PROFILE option and if the ALLOCATE then works, the systems programmer should be apprised of the situation so that the profile definition can be compared against the sessions defined for the remote system. The default action is for CICS to abend the task.

The EIBRCODE can be checked to determine the nature of the SYSIDERR. When a SYSIDERR occurs, Byte 0 of EIBRCODE contains X'D0'. Byte 1 of the EIBRCODE contains an indication of why the SYSIDERR occurred.

10.3.3   Examples of ALLOCATE Command Coding

The following code is an example of an ALLOCATE command in a COBOL program.

```
IDENTIFICATION DIVISION.
PROGRAM-ID. SAMPLE.
ENVIRONMENT DIVISION.
DATA DIVISION.
WORKING-STORAGE SECTION.
01  WS-CONVID        PIC X(4).
.
.
PROCEDURE DIVISION

        EXEC CICS ALLOCATE
                SYSID('CIC1')
                NOQUEUE
        END-EXEC.
```

The task executing this ALLOCATE command will not wait until a session becomes available if CICS currently does not have one to allocate. Because NOQUEUE has been specified, we will receive control back at the next instruction whether or not the allocation was made. Therefore, it is important to test EIBRCODE to determine the outcome. The following statement should be included directly after the above ALLOCATE command.

```
IF EIBRCODE = LOW-VALUES
        MOVE EIBRSRCE TO WS-CONVID
        GO TO M100-SESSION-ALLOCATED
ELSE
        . abend or send a message
```

If EIBRCODE equals low values, then the session has been allocated. Once the session is allocated, it is imperative to save the conversation ID that CICS has assigned. In the sample code above, this is accomplished with the MOVE EIBRSRCE TO WS-CONVID statement.

The following code is an example of an ALLOCATE command in an assembler language program.

```
DFHEISTG DSECT
.
CONVID1    DS   CL4
.
SAMPLE     CSECT
           EXEC CICS ALLOCATE SYSID('CIC1') NOQUEUE
           CLC  EIBRCODE,=XL6'00'
           BNE  ABEND1
           MVC  CONVID1,EIBRSRCE
```

Again, we test EIBRCODE, and if the session is allocated, the CONVersation ID contained in EIBRSRCE is saved.

10.3.4   ALLOCATE Command Summary

If the ALLOCATE command is being performed by a terminal-oriented task — one that is communicating with a terminal operator, it would be important to include the NOQUEUE or NOSUSPEND option or HANDLE the CONDITION SYSBUSY so that the operator will not be forced to wait until a session becomes available. If the application design isolated the terminal operator interaction into a separate task and the distributed transaction processing is being done by a task that is independent of a terminal, then the nature of the application determines if we want to hang out and wait for a session to become available.

The ALLOCATE command provides a task with an alternate facility. By default all terminal control commands are directed to a task's principal facility unless a qualifier is used to redirect such commands to an alternate facility. In LUTYPE 6.2 commands, this qualifier is called a CONVersation ID or CONVID. CICS places the CONVID in the EIBRSRCE field within the Execute Interface Block. It is important to save the contents of EIBRSRCE in a program work area for use as the CONVID in terminal control commands directed to the alternate facility. The EIBRSRCE field is dynamic, meaning that it is constantly changing. It is an 8-byte field used to name the resource accessed in the last CICS command. Therefore, it is necessary to save this information immediately upon successful execution of the ALLOCATE command or at least before any other CICS command is executed. The CONVID is 4-bytes and is padded on the right with blanks when contained in the 8-byte EIBRSRCE field. If a transaction is to have multiple alternate facilities, then multiple CONVIDs will need to be saved subsequent to each ALLOCATE command.

The ALLOCATE command, if successful, alters the transaction's state with regard to the conversation. If we look at Figure 10-2, which is the state 1 diagram, we note that if the ALLOCATE command was successful (as indicated by the "Otherwise" entry to the right of the command), the transaction is in a new state, and this is state 2.

10.4   THE NEW STATE — STATE 2

Figure 10-3 is the state diagram for state 2. In state 2, the *session is allocated*. The Front-End Transaction may have acquired the session through the ALLOCATE command discussed above, or the session may have been allocated as a result of automatic transaction initiation as discussed in the previous chapter. A Front-End Transaction that has a session allocated to it via automatic transaction initiation is already in state 2 when initiated.

If we look at Figure 10-3, we see that there are two possible commands that can be validly executed when in state 2. The commands are FREE to free or release the session and CONNECT PROCESS to initiate a remote process. If the FREE command is executed, the new state as listed on the right side of the diagram is state 1, meaning that the session is no longer allocated. However, we're not ready to free this session, so we're going to look next at the CONNECT PROCESS command.

10.5   THE CONNECT PROCESS COMMAND

The CONNECT PROCESS command is used to initiate the Back-End Transaction. Additionally, CONNECT PROCESS can be used to pass initialization parameters to the Back-End Transaction and specify a required synchronization level for the conversation.

10.5.1   CONNECT PROCESS Command Format

The format of the CONNECT PROCESS command is as follows:

STATE 2 MAPPED LUTYPE6.2 CONVERSATIONS		SESSION ALLOCATED
Commands You Can Issue	What To Test (For EIBERRCD tests see the table on page 199)	New State
CONNECT PROCESS	TERMERR *	3
FREE	-	1
* The failure of a CONNECT PROCESS command (caused by such things as the unavailabilit⁄ of the remote process or mismatched sync levels) is usually indicated on a later command on the same conversation.		

Figure 10-3 State 2 — SESSION ALLOCATED diagram. Reprinted by permission from *CICS/MVS Version 2.1 Intercommunication Guide* © 1987, 1988 by International Business Machines Corporation.

```
EXEC CICS CONNECT PROCESS
          PROCNAME(name-of-process)
          PROCLENGTH(length-of-procname)
          CONVID(conversation-name)
          SYNCLEVEL(sync-level)
          PIPLIST(name-of-PIP-data-area)
          PIPLENGTH(total-length-piplist)
```

The PROCNAME option provides the name of the remote process. If the conversation partner is another CICS application program in a remote system, then the PROCNAME is a 1- to 4-character transaction identifier. CICS permits process names to be as long as 32 characters in support of other LUTYPE 6.2 products. User process names cannot begin with hex values in the range of X'00' through X'3F' as these are reserved for SNA-architected process names.

The PROCLENGTH defines the length of the PROCNAME. If the remote end is another CICS system, then the length is from 1 to 4 bytes. The length is expressed as a 2-byte binary value.

The CONVID option provides the CONVersation ID of the conversation to which this CONNECT PROCESS relates. If the session is an alternate facility, the CONNECT PROCESS and all subsequent session-oriented commands will require the CONVID option. If the transaction was initiated as a result of ATI (Interval Control START or Transient Data Trigger) with a session as its principal facility, then the CONVID option is not required. If the session is the transaction's principal facility, then the CONVID value can be obtained from the EIBTRMID field. This option names the 4-byte field containing the CONVID.

The SYNCLEVEL indicates the synchronization level required for this conversation. When a session is bound, a session *maximum synchronization level* is determined based upon the capabilities of the session partners. If the session partners are two CICS systems, then the session can operate at the highest SYNCLEVEL. However, if CICS's session partner is an LUTYPE 6.2 terminal, a lower SYNCLEVEL may be mandated. **The maximum session SYNCLEVEL reflects the synchronization processing support of the least capable session partner.** SYNCLEVELs are expressed numerically.

Level 0 is the lowest level. With level 0 there is no support for synchronization. If a CICS program modifies protected resources and SYNCPOINTs, the conversation is not affected. Furthermore, there is no Logical Unit support for private commands to exchange synchronization status. Any synchronization required is the responsibility of the application programs conversing. A program can, after all, use a SEND command to send a message that queries its conversation partner and RECEIVE back a message that says "Yeah, I'M OK." But at level 0 this is not supported within the Logical Units. So, if a conversation uses SYNCLEVEL 0, there is no built-in support for synchronization; if there is any synchronization managed via application program protocols, this is transparent to their respective Logical Units. Why have a SYNCLEVEL 0 when CICS can support synchronization, including SYNCPOINTs and SYNCPOINT ROLLBACKs? Because LUTYPE6.2 is an *any-to-any connection*, and some of those "anys" such as LUTYPE 6.2 terminals may not have the facilities of CICS.

Level 1 is a step up from level 0. With level 1 there is support for private synchronization exchanges. This means that using level 1, application programs can utilize commands based upon the LUTYPE 6.2 protocol boundary verbs that allow them to exchange synchronization status. These commands in CICS are the SEND command with a CONFIRM option which requests a confirmation, a positive response indicated via the ISSUE CONFIRMATION command, and a couple of commands that can give a negative response (ISSUE ERROR or ISSUE ABEND) to a request for confirmation. How does this differ from level 0? These commands are supported by the Logical Units so there is no need to develop the application-specific protocols described in the discussion of SYNCLEVEL 0.

CICS transactions engaged in a level 1 conversation have built-in commands that can be used for private confirmation exchanges.

What exactly does SEND . . . CONFIRM mean? What does an ISSUE CONFIRMATION in response mean? That is application-dependent and application-specific. The Logical Unit provides this functional capability. How you use it is defined by you. If a CICS program, engaged in a distributed covnersation at SYNCLEVEL 1, issues a SYNCPOINT to commit modifications to protected resources, there is no affect on the conversation.

Level 2 is the highest SYNCLEVEL. Level 2 supports the private confirmation commands described in level 1 and it also has full support for SYNCPOINT and SYNCPOINT ROLLBACK processing. If a program engaged in a SYNCLEVEL 2 conversation issues a SYNCPOINT command, the result is the generation of a SYNCPOINT indicator and cross-system message flows to coordinate commit processing between the systems. If a program is engaged in 10 level 2 conversations, the SYNCPOINT indicators are generated for all of the conversations and intersystem flows coordinate SYNCPOINTing of the entire distributed unit of work. However, a SYNCPOINT can only be taken in specific conversation states.

SYNCLEVEL(2) should be requested only when it is desired that conversation partners engage in a mutual SYNCPOINT. With SYNCLEVEL(2), a RETURN command, which causes an implicit SYNCPOINT, may effectively force a conversation partner to respond to a SYNCPOINT request not intended in the transaction design. If a conversation is not intended to include a mutual SYNCPOINT, the initiating CONNECT PROCESS command should request a SYNCLEVEL(1). In that way, one transactions's SYNCPOINT or RETURN does not initiate a transaction wide SYNCPOINT. This is actually safer because if a transaction is not expecting a SYNCPOINT request and therefore does not check to see if one is required, things can go awry. If a transaction is asked to SYNCPOINT and it does not do so, it abends.

If the SYNCLEVEL option is omitted from the CONNECT PROCESS command, the default SYNCLEVEL is the highest level allowed for the session.

The PIPLIST names a data area containing PIP data. PIP data consists of Process Initialization Parameters. CICS does not use the PIP data in any way. CICS merely passes any named PIP data along. So, if a conversation involves two CICS application programs, PIP data can be used to send transaction specific initialization parameters from the Front-End Transaction to the Back-End Transaction. However, non-CICS APPC systems may utilize PIP data in some way. To this end, if your CICS program is conversing with a program in a non-CICS APPC system, PIP data may have some significance to the other APPC system and you would have to format PIP data in accordance with the remote system's requirements. One or more process initialization parameters may be used. Each PIP is preceded by a 4-byte LLbb field, and the LL indicates the individual parameter length +4 to include the preceding LLbb field. A PIP list in COBOL might look like this:

```
01 MY-PIPS.
    04 PIPL1            PIC S9(4) COMP VALUE +16.
    04 FILLER           PIC S9(4) COMP VALUE +0.
    04 PIP1             PIC X(12).
    04 PIPL2            PIC S9(4) COMP VALUE +8.
    04 FILLER           PIC S9(4) COMP VALUE +0.
    04 PIP2             PIC X(4).
```

In assembler the PIP list layout might look like this. However, the length fields would have to be initialized assuming that they would be contained within the DFHEISTG DSECT.

```
MYPIPS      DS      0F
PIPL1       DS      H
PIP1R       DS      H
PIP1        DS      CL12
PIPL2       DS      H
PIP2R       DS      H
PIP2        DS      CL4
```

The PIPLENGTH defines the total length of PIP data. The PIP lists coded above are 24 bytes in length, so the PIPLENGTH would indicate a length of 24 in this case. As with other CICS length fields, the PIPLENGTH is a 2-byte binary field.

10.5.2 Unusual Conditions and the CONNECT PROCESS Command

The unusual conditions associated with the CONNECT PROCESS command include INVREQ, LENGERR, and NOTALLOC. The default action is for CICS to abend the task when one of these conditions occurs.

The INVREQ indicates that a CONNECT PROCESS command requested a SYNCLEVEL(2) for a session that does not support that level of synchronization. In other words, the requested SYNCLEVEL exceeds the maximum SYNCLEVEL for the session.

The LENGERR condition indicates a problem with the PIPLIST/PIPLENGTH specified in the CONNECT PROCESS. A PIPLENGTH value must be in the range of 0 to 32,763. CICS checks to ensure that the individual length fields specify a value of at least 4 bytes and that the lengths specified for all PIPs add up to the value defined in PIPLENGTH. The LENGERR occurs if PIPLIST/PIPLENGTH do not conform to the above.

The NOTALLOC condition indicates that the named facility (CONVID) has not been allocated to the transaction.

10.5.3   Examples of the CONNECT PROCESS Command

The following code is a COBOL sample of the CONNECT PROCESS command. For the sake of continuity in this example, we have incorporated the sample code from above so that the command coding can be seen in the appropriate context.

```
IDENTIFICATION DIVISION.
PROGRAM-ID. SAMPLE.
ENVIRONMENT DIVISION.
DATA DIVISION.
WORKING-STORAGE SECTION.
01   MY-PIPS.
      04   PIPL1          PIC S9(4) COMP VALUE +16.
      04   FILLER         PIC S9(4) COMP VALUE +0.
      04   PIP1           PIC X(12).
      04   PIPL2          PIC S9(4) COMP VALUE +8.
      04   FILLER         PIC S9(4) COMP VALUE +0.
      04   PIP2           PIC X(4).
01 PIP-LENGTH             PIC S9(4) COMP VALUE +24.
01 WS-CONVID              PIC X(4).
01 R-TRANSID              PIC X(4) VALUE 'WS02'.
01 RSP-FLD                PIC S9(8) COMP.
PROCEDURE DIVISION
        .
        .
        .
      EXEC CICS ALLOCATE
                SYSID('CIC1')
                NOQUEUE
      END-EXEC.
```

```
    IF EIBRCODE = LOW-VALUES
        MOVE EIBRSRCE TO WS-CONVID
        GO TO M100-SESSION-ALLOCATED
    ELSE
            EXEC CICS ABEND ABCODE('NSES') END-EXEC.
M100-SESSION-ALLOCATED.
    EXEC CICS CONNECT PROCESS
            PROCNAME(R-TRANSID) PROCLENGTH(4)
            CONVID(WS-CONVID)   SYNCLEVEL(1)
            PIPLIST(MY-PIPS)
            PIPLENGTH(PIP-LENGTH)
            RESP(RSP-FLD)
    END-EXEC.
    IF RSP-FLD = DFHRESP(NORMAL) NEXT SENTENCE
    ELSE
            EXEC CICS ABEND ABCODE('NCNP') END-EXEC.
M200-WS02-CONNECTED.
```

If the program execution falls through to M200-WS02-CON-NECTED, then the remote process has been initiated.

The following is a continuation of our assembler language example.

```
DFHEISTG DSECT
RSPFLD      DS   F
MYPIPS      DS   0F
PIPL1       DS   H
PIP1R       DS   H
PIP1        DS   CL12
PIPL2       DS   H
PIP2R       DS   H
PIP2        DS   CL4
PIPLEN      DS   H
CONVID1     DS   CL4
.
SAMPLE      CSECT
*
            EXEC CICS ALLOCATE SYSID('CIC1') NOQUEUE
            CLC   EIBRCODE,=XL6'00'
            BNE   ABEND1
            MVC   CONVID1,EIBRSRCE
            MVC   PIPL1,=H'16'
```

```
        MVC   PIP1R,=H'0'
        MVC   PIPL2,=H'8'
        MVC   PIP2R,=H'0'
        MVC   PIPLEN,=H'24'
        EXEC CICS CONNECT PROCESS PROCNAME('TRAN')          *
                   PROCLENGTH(4) CONVID(CONVID1)            *
                   SYNCLEVEL(1) PIPLIST(MYPIPS)             *
                   PIPLENGTH(PIPLEN)                        *
                   RESP(RSPFLD)
        CLC   RSPFLD,DFHRESP(NORMAL)
        BNE   ABEND2
* remainder of conversation code
ABEND1  DS    0H
        EXEC CICS ABEND ABCODE('NSES')
ABEND2  DS    0H
        EXEC CICS ABEND ABCODE('NCNP')
```

10.5.4   The CONNECT PROCESS Command — Summary

The CONNECT PROCESS command enables a Front-End Transaction to initiate a Back-End Transaction based upon a process name, or, as we know it in CICS, a TRANSID. PIP data can be passed in the CONNECT PROCESS and a synchronization level can be requested. What does the CONNECT PROCESS command really do? It causes CICS to build an attach Function Management Header, which is concatenated to data sent to the remote system. The attach FMH causes the remote system, CICS in this case, to attach a task. The attached task is connected to the conversation/session as its principal facility. The name of this principal facility is contained in the Back-End Transaction's EIBTRMID field.

10.6   THE NEW STATE — STATE 3

Looking back at Figure 10-3 we can see that as a result of the successful execution of the CONNECT PROCESS command a Front-End Transaction enters state 3, *the send state*. The state 3 diagram provided in Figure 10-4 defines the session-oriented commands that can be validly executed at this point in the transaction's life. However, before we forge on with a description of the commands that could be coded in this Front-End Transaction, let's first discuss the status of the Back-End Transaction when it is initiated.

STATE 3 MAPPED LUTYPE6.2 CONVERSATIONS		SEND STATE
Commands You Can Issue	What To Test (For EIBERRCD tests see the table on page 199)	New State
SEND	-	3
SEND INVITE	-	4
SEND INVITE WAIT	-	5
SEND LAST	-	9
SEND LAST WAIT	-	10
SEND CONFIRM (SYNCLEVEL 1 or 2 only)	See "Checking the Response to SEND CONFIRM" earlier in this chapter. New states assume that EIBERR is not set.	3
SEND INVITE CONFIRM (SYNCLEVEL 1 or 2 only)		5
SEND LAST CONFIRM (SYNCLEVEL 1 or 2 only)		10
CONVERSE Equivalent to: SEND INVITE WAIT RECEIVE	Go to the STATE 5 table and make the tests shown for the RECEIVE command	-
RECEIVE (INVITE is sent by CICS)	Go to the STATE 5 table and make the tests shown for the RECEIVE command	-
ISSUE PREPARE (SYNCLEVEL 2 only) Note: If a negative response is received, EIBERR and EIBERRCD will also be set	EIBSYNRB	8
	EIBFREE	10
	Otherwise	3
SYNCPOINT (SYNCLEVEL 2 only)	EIBRLDBK (or ROLLEDBACK condition)	5
	Otherwise (transaction will ABEND if SYNCPOINT fails)	3
SYNCPOINT ROLLBACK (SYNCLEVEL 2 only)	(transaction will ABEND if ROLLBACK fails)	3
WAIT CONVID	-	3
ISSUE ERROR	EIBRECV	5
	Otherwise	3
ISSUE ABEND	-	10
FREE Equivalent to: SEND LAST WAIT FREE	-	1

Figure 10-4 State 3 — SEND STATE diagram. Reprinted by permission from *CICS/MVS Version 2.1 Intercommunication Guide* © 1987, 1988 by International Business Machines Corporation.

10.7   THE BACK-END TRANSACTION — INITIATED IN STATE 5

The Back-End Transaction is initiated in state 5, *the receive state.* Figure 10-5 illustrates the state 5 diagram. Aside from dealing with conversation errors, the only valid command for a receive state transaction is to RECEIVE. Actually, the initiated Back-End Transaction can precede the RECEIVE command with an EXTRACT PROCESS command to obtain information from the attach Function Management Header received and processed in this CICS region.

10.8   THE EXTRACT PROCESS COMMAND

The EXTRACT PROCESS command allows a newly initiated Back-End Transaction to obtain conversation-related information. This is an optional command and is coded if the application deems the conversation-related information significant. For example, addressability to PIP data may be required, or perhaps the transaction needs to verify the SYNCLEVEL of the conversation.

10.8.1   The Format of the EXTRACT PROCESS Command

The format of the EXTRACT PROCESS command is:

```
EXEC CICS EXTRACT PROCESS
          PROCNAME(32-byte-field-name)
          PROCLENGTH(2-byte-binary-field-name)
          CONVID(4-byte-field-name)
          SYNCLEVEL(2-byte-binary-field-name)
          PIPLIST(pointer)
          PIPLENGTH(2-byte-binary-field-name)
```

The options of the EXTRACT PROCESS command mirror those of the CONNECT PROCESS command.

The PROCNAME option names a data field to receive the PROC-NAME defined in the CONNECT PROCESS. Because CICS supports process names up to 32 bytes in length, the field named by the PROCNAME option must conform to that size. Shorter process names are padded to the right with blanks. The PROCLENGTH option names a field which receives the process name length defined in the CONNECT PROCESS PROCLENGTH option.

STATE 5 MAPPED LUTYPE6.2 CONVERSATIONS		RECEIVE STATE
Commands You Can Issue	What To Test (For EIBERRCD tests see the table on page 199)	New State
RECEIVE [NOTRUNCATE] *	EIBCOMPL *	–
	EIBCONF (SYNCLEVEL 1 or 2 only)	6
	EIBSYNC (SYNCLEVEL 2 only)	7
	EIBSYNRB (SYNCLEVEL 2 only)	8
	EIBFREE	10
	EIBRECV	5
	Otherwise	3
SYNCPOINT ROLLBACK (SYNCLEVEL 2 only)	(transaction will ABEND if ROLLBACK fails)	3
ISSUE ERROR	EIBFREE	10
	Otherwise	3
ISSUE ABEND	–	10

* If NOTRUNCATE is specified, a zero value in EIBCOMPL indicates that the data passed to the application by CICS is incomplete (because, for example, the data-area specified in the RECEIVE command is too small). CICS will save the remaining data for retrieval by subsequent RECEIVE NOTRUNCATE commands. EIBCOMPL is set when the last part of the data is passed back. If the NOTRUNCATE option is not specified, overlength data is indicated by the LENGERR condition, and the remaining data is discarded by CICS.

Figure 10-5 State 5 — RECEIVE STATE diagram. Reprinted by permission from *CICS/MVS Version 2.1 Intercommunication Guide* © 1987, 1988 by International Business Machines Corporation.

The CONVID option, if specified, names a 4-byte data field which contains the contents of EIBTRMID. EIBTRMID is the name of the Back-End Transaction's principal facility.

The SYNCLEVEL option names a 2-byte binary field which can be tested to verify the SYNCLEVEL.

The PIPLIST option names a pointer. For COBOL, this would be a Linkage Section BLL-cell. For COBOL II this would be the address special register, meaning that no explicit BLLCELL is coded. For assembler this would be a register.

The PIPLENGTH option names a 2-byte binary field which receives the total length of passed PIP data or 0 if CICS did not receive any PIP data.

10.8.2   Unusual Conditions and the EXTRACT PROCESS Command

The unusual conditions associated with the EXTRACT PROCESS command are INVREQ and NOTALLOC. The default action is for CICS to abend the task in both cases.

The INVREQ condition indicates that data is invalid.

The NOTALLOC condition indicates that the session/conversation is not allocated to this transaction. Either omit the CONVID option or make sure that it is preset to the contents of EIBTRMID.

10.8.3   Examples of the EXTRACT PROCESS Command

The following code is a sample of the EXTRACT PROCESS command in a COBOL Program.

```
WORKING-STORAGE SECTION.
01 WS-PROCESS-NAME.
      04  WS-TRAN          PIC X(4).
      04  FILLER           PIC X(28).
01 WS-WORK-FIELDS.
      04  WS-PROCESS-LEN   PIC S9(4) COMP.
      04  WS-PIP-LEN       PIC S9(4) COMP.
      04  WS-SYNCL         PIC S9(4) COMP.
      04  WS-CONVID        PIC X(4).
LINKAGE SECTION.
01 BLL-CELLS.
      04  FILLER           PIC S9(8) COMP.
      04  PIP-BLL          PIC S9(8) COMP.
01 PASSED-PIPS.
      04  LEN-PIP1         PIC S9(4) COMP.
      04  FILLER           PIC S9(4) COMP.
      04  PIP-ONE          PIC X(12).
      04  LEN-PIP2         PIC S9(4) COMP.
      04  FILLER           PIC S9(4) COMP.
      04  PIP-TWO          PIC X(4).
```

```
PROCEDURE DIVISION.
    MOVE EIBTRMID TO WS-CONVID.
    EXEC CICS EXTRACT PROCESS
              PROCNAME(WS-PROCESS-NAME)
              PROCLENGTH(WS-PROCESS-LEN)
              PIPLIST(PIP-BLL)
              PIPLENGTH(WS-PIP-LEN)
              CONVID(WS-CONVID)
              SYNCLEVEL(WS-SYNCL)
    END-EXEC.

    IF WS-SYNCL = 1 NEXT SENTENCE
    ELSE
        EXEC CICS ISSUE ABEND END-EXEC
        EXEC CICS ABEND ABCODE('SYNC') END-EXEC.
```

To convert this example to COBOL II we merely remove the BLLCELLs and alter the pointer definition in the PIPLIST option as follows.

```
WORKING-STORAGE SECTION.
01  WS-PROCESS-NAME.
    04  WS-TRAN         PIC X(4).
    04  FILLER          PIC X(28).
 01 WS-WORK-FIELDS.
    04  WS-PROCESS-LEN  PIC S9(4) COMP.
    04  WS-PIP-LEN      PIC S9(4) COMP.
    04  WS-SYNCL        PIC S9(4) COMP.
    04  WS-CONVID       PIC X(4).
LINKAGE SECTION.
01 PASSED-PIPS.
    04  LEN-PIP1        PIC S9(4) COMP.
    04  FILLER          PIC S9(4) COMP.
    04  PIP-ONE         PIC X(12).
    04  LEN-PIP2        PIC S9(4) COMP.
    04  FILLER          PIC S9(4) COMP.
    04  PIP-TWO         PIC X(4).
PROCEDURE DIVISION.
    MOVE EIBTRMID TO WS-CONVID.
    EXEC CICS EXTRACT PROCESS
              PROCNAME(WS-PROCESS-NAME)
              PROCLENGTH(WS-PROCESS-LEN)
              PIPLIST(ADDRESS OF PASSED-PIPS)
```

```
                    PIPLENGTH(WS-PIP-LEN)
                    CONVID(WS-CONVID)
                    SYNCLEVEL(WS-SYNCL)
        END-EXEC.

     IF WS-SYNCL = 1 NEXT SENTENCE
     ELSE
            EXEC CICS ISSUE ABEND END-EXEC
            EXEC CICS ABEND ABCODE('SYNC') END-EXEC.
```

The following is an assembler language example of the above code.

```
DFHEISTG DSECT
PROCNM      DS    0CL32
TRN         DS    CL4
            DS    CL28
PLEN        DS    H
PIPLEN      DS    H
SYNCL       DS    H
CONV        DS    CL4
PIPPTR      EQU   8
BACKEND     CSECT
            MVC   CONV,EIBTRMID
            EXEC CICS EXTRACT PROCESS                    *
                  PROCNAME(PROCNM)                       *
                  PROCLENGTH(PLEN)                       *
                  PIPLIST(PIPPTR)                        *
                  PIPLENGTH(PIPLEN)                      *
                  CONVID(CONV)                           *
                  SYNCLEVEL(SYNCL)
            CLC   SYNCL,=H'1'
            BE    SYNCOK
            EXEC CICS ISSUE ABEND
            EXEC CICS ABEND ABCODE('SYNC')
SYNCOK      DS    0H
```

10.8.4   EXTRACT PROCESS Summary

The optional EXTRACT PROCESS command allows a Back-End Transaction to obtain conversation related information from the received attach Function Management Header. If obtaining addressability to PIP data or determining the conversation SYNCLEVEL is important, this information is available via the EXTRACT PROCESS command.

10.9 SUMMARY

In this chapter we have begun our examination of the LUTYPE 6.2 mapped conversation verbs. We have gone through the commands that are used to initialize the conversation. As such, we were guided by the information in the state diagrams that identify appropriate commands, tests and new states that result from command execution. In the next chapter we will look at the LUTYPE 6.2 mapped conversation verbs that enable the conversing transactions to exchange information, reverse their send state/receive state relationship, and generally coordinate their processing.

REVIEW EXERCISES

Provide a short answer to each of the following.

1. Under what circumstances would it not be necessary for a Front-End Transaction to use the ALLOCATE command to obtain use of a session?
2. What does the NOQUEUE option of the ALLOCATE command do?
3. Subsequent to a successful ALLOCATE command, what field in the EIB contains the conversation ID? What should be done to ensure that the CONVID is not overlayed and lost?
4. CICS uses a 4-byte TRANSID to initiate a task. Why does the PROCNAME option of the EXTRACT PROCESS command reference a 32-byte field?
5. What effect does a SYNCPOINT command have on a SYNCLEVEL(0) conversation? SYNCLEVEL(1)? SYNCLEVEL(2)?
6. If a transaction is initiated by Interval Control and has as its principal facility a session with a remote system over which it is going to initiate a Back-End Transaction, what is the initial conversation state?
7. What is the only thing that a transaction can do when in state 1 with regard to a conversation?

8. What is the conversation state of the Front-End Transaction after it has executed a successful CONNECT PROCESS?
9. What is the initial conversation state of the Back-End Transaction?

ANSWERS TO REVIEW EXERCISE

Provide a short answer to each of the following.

1. *Under what circumstances would it not be necessary for a Front-End Transaction to use the ALLOCATE command to obtain use of a session?*

   When the transaction was initiated via Automatic Transaction Initiation and possessed as its principal facility use of a session with the remote system.

2. *What does the NOQUEUE option of the ALLOCATE command do?*

   The NOQUEUE option of the ALLOCATE command informs CICS not to queue the request for use of a session. If a session is available, it is allocated to the task. However, if no session is available, then CICS sets an error code in the EIBRCODE and returns control to the requesting task.

3. *Subsequent to a successful ALLOCATE command, what field in the EIB contains the conversation ID? What should be done to ensure that the CONVID is not overlayed and lost?*

   The EIBRSRCE field contains the CONVID. Since EIBRSRCE is a volatile field the contents or CONVID should be saved directly after a successful ALLOCATE command.

4. *CICS uses a 4-byte TRANSID to initiate a task. Why does the PROCNAME option of the EXTRACT PROCESS command reference a 32-byte field?*

   In support of other LUTYPE 6.2 products CICS supports process names of up to 32 bytes. Therefore, it expects this size field.

5. *What effect does a SYNCPOINT command have on a SYNCLEVEL(0) conversation? SYNCLEVEL(1)? SYNCLEVEL (2)?*

A SYNCPOINT command has no effect whatsoever on a SYNCLEVEL(0) conversation. It also has no effect on a SYNCLEVEL(1) conversation. For a SYNCLEVEL(2) conversation, the SYNCPOINT command results in transaction-wide SYNCPOINT exchanges. All SYNCLEVEL(2) conversation partners are involved in the commit protocols managed by CICS.

6. *If a transaction is initiated by Interval Control and has as its principal facility a session with a remote system over which it is going to initiate a Back-End Transaction, what is the initial conversation state?*

Since the transaction already possesses use of a session, it is initiated in state 2.

7. *What is the only thing that a transaction can do when in state 1 with regard to a conversation?*

A state 1 transaction can request use of session via the ALLO-CATE command.

8. *What is the conversation state of the Front-End Transaction after it has executed a successful CONNECT PROCESS?*

Subsequent to a successful CONNECT PROCESS, the Front-End Transaction is in state 3 — the SEND State.

9. *What is the initial conversation state of the Back-End Transaction?*

The Back-End Transaction is in the RECEIVE state when initiated.

11

LUTYPE 6.2 Mapped Conversation Data Exchanges

11.1 INTRODUCTION

In the previous chapter we discussed the LUTYPE 6.2 mapped conversation commands used by both the Front-End and Back-End Transactions during conversation initialization. In this chapter we are going to examine the commands that enable the transactions to carry on their conversation.

11.2 THE SEND COMMAND

The SEND command for use in LUTYPE 6.2 mapped conversations can be used to send data and/or conversation indicators. However, before we get into a discussion of the SEND command options and resulting SNA indicators, it is necessary to understand how CICS handles the transmission of data during LUTYPE 6.2 conversations.

When using a CICS SEND command under any circumstances, CICS does not immediately drop everything and race off to send the output. Normally, output is batched up for an interval of time before the CICS terminal dispatcher actually sends off data. The reason for this is that it requires less system overhead than would sending each separate task output request individually. This represents an output scheduling technique, and the reason for this technique is to optimize the amount of system overhead incurred by CICS's interaction with the telecommunication access method. For LUTYPE 6.2 sessions, CICS also uses a scheduling technique, the purpose of which is to optimize the number of separate message flows through the SNA network.

Why is this important? The bulk of the time that is required for transaction processing is not spent executing instructions in a computer. Rather, the time it takes to physically transmit messages between communicating processes is far greater than execution time for processing the messages. Therefore, in order to optimize transaction processing time for distributed transactions, CICS attempts to batch up data and indicators into one transmission.

When an application program engaged in an LUTYPE 6.2 conversation says SEND to CICS, it takes any data and SNA indicators that derive from SEND command options and places them in an internal buffer. Successive SEND commands merely result in more data and possibly SNA indicators being placed into the buffer. Furthermore, if an LUTYPE 6.2 transaction is communicating over a conversation that is at SYNCLEVEL(2), the execution of a SYNCPOINT command adds a SYNCPOINT indicator to the buffered output. When the buffer is full or a transaction forces message transmission programmatically, CICS sends the buffer which may contain multiple application messages.

However, from a programming point of view some of this is relatively transparent. For example, a receiving transaction has to perform multiple RECEIVE commands to obtain data from multiple SEND commands. Each RECEIVE is satisfied by the data sent by one SEND command. In other respects, particularly with regard to certain SNA indicators, it necessary for a transaction to be aware of the deferral of transmission. We'll talk more about this later. For now, let's get on with the format of the SEND command.

11.2.1   Format of the SEND Command

The format of the SEND command for LUTYPE 6.2 is as follows.

```
EXEC CICS SEND
          CONVID(field-containing-CONVID)
          FROM(data-area-name)
          LENGTH(value-defining-FROM-area-size)
          INVITE * OR * LAST
          CONFIRM * OR * WAIT
```

The CONVID option names the data field which contains the CONVID obtained by the Front-End Transaction from EIBRSRCE subsequent to the ALLOCATE command. For the Back-End Transaction or a Front-End Transaction that was not required to ALLO-CATE a session, the specification of CONVID is optional. In the latter two cases, EIBTRMID contains the value to be specified for CONVID.

The FROM option names an application data area containing a message to be sent. The inclusion of the FROM area is optional in the SEND command for LUTYPE 6.2 conversations. The SEND command can be used without data in certain cases. The purpose of performing a SEND command without data is to cause CICS to generate one or more SNA indicators.

The LENGTH option is used to define the length of the data message contained in the area named with the FROM option.

The INVITE option is used to generate an SNA Change-Direction Indicator. The SEND STATE transaction is now inviting the RECEIVE STATE transaction to start sending. If you glance back to Figure 10-4 in the previous chapter, you will note that inclusion of the INVITE option impacts the transaction's state. Depending on which other command options, if any, are included along with SEND INVITE, the transaction's new state may be 4 or 5. State 4 is named *RECEIVE PENDING AFTER INVITE*, and Figure 11-1 illustrates the state 4 diagram. State 5 is the RECEIVE STATE, and that state diagram is illustrated in Figure 10-5. SEND INVITE may be used alone or with data, meaning that the FROM/LENGTH options may be included or omitted.

The transaction receiving a SEND INVITE is informed of its state change, from RECEIVE STATE to SEND STATE, via the EIBRECV field in the Execute Interface Block. EIBRECV is turned off (X'00') to indicate that the transaction is in the SEND STATE. Conversely, EIBRECV is set on (X'FF') to indicate that the transaction is in the RECEIVE state. CICS sets EIBRECV when a RECEIVE command is executed. Therefore, this field should be tested immediately after a RECEIVE command when you know it is meaningful. In other words, if you say SEND INVITE, CICS does not race in and alter EIBRECV. You know that you said SEND INVITE and, therefore, you are either in the RECEIVE STATE or RECEIVE is PENDING AFTER INVITE. It is only after you execute a RECEIVE command that CICS sets on EIBRECV. INVITE and the next option, LAST, are mutually exclusive.

The LAST option generates the SNA End Bracket (EB) Indicator. SEND LAST can be used with or without data. Again, if you look at

STATE 4 HAPPED LUTYPE6.2 CONVERSATIONS	RECEIVE PENDING AFTER INVITE	
Commands You Can Issue	What To Test (For EIBERRCD tests see the table on page 199)	New State
WAIT	-	5
RECEIVE Equivalent to: WAIT RECEIVE	Go to the STATE 5 table and make the tests shown for the RECEIVE command	-
ISSUE ERROR	EIBFREE	10
	Otherwise	3
ISSUE ABEND	-	10
SYNCPOINT (SYNCLEVEL 2 only)	EIBRLDBK (or ROLLEDBACK condition)	5
	Otherwise (transaction will ABEND if SYNCPOINT fails)	5
SYNCPOINT ROLLBACK (SYNCLEVEL 2 only)	(transaction will ABEND if ROLLBACK fails)	3

Figure 11-1 State 4 — RECEIVE PENDING AFTER INVITE. Reprinted by permission from *CICS/MVS Version 2.1 Intercommunication Guide* © 1987, 1988 by International Business Machines Corporation.

Figure 10-4, you will note that use of the LAST option alters the transaction's state to either state 9 or 10. State 9 is named *FREE PENDING AFTER SEND LAST*, and that state diagram is illustrated in Figure 11-2. State 10 is the *FREE SESSION STATE*, and that state diagram is shown in Figure 11-3. If we glance at Figures 11-2 and 11-3 for a moment, it becomes apparent that the LAST option (and, more specifically, the End Bracket Indicator that it causes CICS to generate) is ending the conversation. The difference between states 9 and 10 is that in state 9 the End Bracket has been generated but not yet sent, so it is still valid, for example, to request a confirmation with SEND CONFIRM or take a SYNCPOINT/SYNCPOINT ROLLBACK (if SYNCLEVEL is 2) or ABEND the conversation. In State 10, the End Bracket has been generated and transmitted. The only thing that you can do is FREE the conversation or RETURN immediately to CICS. From this you should begin to see why INVITE, which generates a Change-Direc-

STATE 9 MAPPED LUTYPE6.2 CONVERSATIONS	FREE PENDING AFTER SEND LAST	
Commands You Can Issue	What To Test (For EIBERRCD tests see the table on page 199)	New State
WAIT	–	10
FREE	–	1
SEND CONFIRM (no data) (SYNCLEVEL 1 or 2 only)	–	10
SYNCPOINT ROLLBACK (SYNCLEVEL 2 only)	–	10
SYNCPOINT (SYNCLEVEL 2 only)	–	10
ISSUE ABEND	–	10

Figure 11-2 State 9 — FREE PENDING AFTER SEND LAST. Reprinted by permission from *CICS/MVS Version 2.1 Intercommunication Guide* © 1987, 1988 by International Business Machines Corporation.

tion Indicator and thereby solicits input, and LAST, which slams the door, are mutually exclusive.

The CONFIRM option is used to request a private confirmation during LUTYPE 6.2 conversations at SYNCLEVELs 1 or 2. Including CONFIRM in a SEND command causes CICS to transmit the contents of the internal buffer. In this way the receiving process obtains the data and is able to realistically respond to the request for CONFIRMation.

STATE 10 MAPPED LUTYPE6.2 CONVERSATIONS	FREE SESSION	
Commands You Can Issue	What To Test (For EIBERRCD tests see the table on page 199)	New State
FREE	–	1

Figure 11-3 State 10 — FREE SESSION. Reprinted by permission from *CICS/MVS Version 2.1 Intercommunication Guide* © 1987, 1988 by International Business Machines Corporation.

Including CONFIRM in a SEND command causes the receiver of the SEND CONFIRM, the other transaction, to know that you wish an application-dependent confirmation. CICS conveys this information to the receiver of a SEND CONFIRM in the Execute Interface Block. The EIBCONF field is set on to high values or X'FF' when a CONFIRMation request has been received. Therefore, it is necessary for the two transactions to be coordinated in this. If a SEND CONFIRM is used but the conversation partner does not test EIBCONF, it does not realize that the confirmation has been requested.

The response to a SEND CONFIRM can be positive (ISSUE CONFIRMATION command) or negative (ISSUE ERROR or ISSUE ABEND). The CONFIRM option by itself does not necessarily result in a state change for the issuing transaction. If you glance at Figure 10-4 and look for the row with SEND CONFIRM solely, you will see that if no error is signaled (EIBERR is not set) then SEND CONFIRM new state is 3, meaning that we're still in the SEND STATE.

Remember that the CONFIRM option of the SEND command may only be used if the conversation is at the appropriate SYNCLEVEL (i.e., 1 or 2). If appropriate to the session's SYNCLEVEL, SEND CONFIRM can be used with or without data.

The WAIT option is used to force CICS to transmit the data and indicators accumulated within the internal buffer. The transaction receives control back at the next instruction after the SEND command after the data has been transmitted. The use of the WAIT option does not, in itself, cause a state change. SEND WAIT alone is not valid. If there are no data or other indicators, SEND WAIT cannot be used. There is, however, a WAIT command that suits the purpose. The CONFIRM and WAIT options are mutually exclusive. CONFIRM causes CICS to send a confirmation request and thereby flushes the buffer so WAIT is not needed with SEND CONFIRM.

11.2.2   Unusual Conditions and the SEND command

The unusual conditions of the SEND command include EOC, INVREQ, LENGERR, NOTALLOC, SIGNAL, and TERMERR.

The EOC condition occurs when an End Of Chain is detected by CICS. All this means is that a collection of related message units (called RUs or Request/Response Units in SNA terminology) have been received as a chain and that the chain is now complete. CICS ignores this condition in terms of affecting the application task, and you might as well ignore it also.

The INVREQ condition indicates that you attempted to do something invalid in the context of the session or the session state. For example, you might have tried to do a SEND CONFIRM but the SYNCLEVEL is 0. The default course of action is for CICS to abend the task.

The NOTALLOC condition indicates that the CONVID is not allocated to the transaction. The default course of action is for CICS to abend the task.

The SIGNAL condition indicates that the conversation partner has used an ISSUE SIGNAL to create an incoming signal for you. A RECEIVE STATE transaction is allowed to use the ISSUE SIGNAL command to inform its conversation partner of a need for a state change into the SEND STATE. This may reflect a local error or some other application-dependent condition which requires (from the RECEIVE STATE transaction's perspective) a need to send a message.

If your conversation partner is going to use the ISSUE SIGNAL command, you should anticipate this and understand the conditions under which the command will be used. When the condition occurs, CICS sets on EIBSIG (X'FF') in the Execute Interface Block. If you anticipate an incoming SIGNAL you can test EIBSIG after a SEND, RECEIVE, or CONVERSE. What you do when you detect that the SIGNAL has been received is application-dependent. You might accede to the SIGNAL and execute a SEND INVITE or just ignore the situation until a convenient point in your processing. However, in making such a decision, you should know what the SIGNAL means when it comes from your conversation partner! The default course of action for CICS is to set on EIBSIG and ignore the situation beyond that.

The TERMERR condition is not good news. This means that either the session has failed or that your conversation partner has abended the conversation by executing an ISSUE ABEND command. The default course of action for CICS is to abend the task (ATNI abend code). If you elect to HANDLE this condition, it is normally necessary to FREE the session immediately when the condition occurs. **Failure to do so may result in an INVREQ and an ensuing abend (ATCV abend code).**

11.2.3   Summary of the SEND Command

The SEND command can only be used when in the appropriate state. The use of the state diagrams is critical to determine what you can validly do during the different states of a transaction's life. The SEND command is actually a multifaceted command in the context of LUTYPE 6.2. It is not merely a way of sending data. Functionally, the SEND command allows the SEND STATE transaction to generate an SNA Change-Direction Indicator and thereby perform a flip-flop in states so that both conversational partners get a turn to SEND. The Change-Direction Indicator is generated with the IN-VITE option of the SEND command.

A SEND command with the LAST option generates an SNA End Bracket Indicator, and as we know a conversation takes place within brackets. Therefore, once the End Bracket is generated and sent, the conversation is over and the only thing that can be done in terms of the session is to FREE it.

The CONFIRM option of the SEND command can be used to request a confirmation from a conversation partner. Upon receipt of a confirmation request, CICS sets on EIBCONF which must be interrogated by a transaction that anticipates receipt of a request for confirmation. In order to use the CONFIRM option, the conversation SYNCLEVEL must be 1 or 2.

The INVITE, LAST, and CONFIRM options can be used alone in a SEND command or with other options, including data. The WAIT option which forces CICS to transmit accumulated data and indicators cannot, however, be used alone. INVITE and LAST are mutually exclusive, as are WAIT and CONFIRM.

Some of the SEND command options impact fields in the Execute Interface Block, and the testing of EIB fields is critically important. As we examine more of the mapped conversation commands, you will see that there are still more EIB fields that may require testing. EIB fields are volatile, meaning that they change, potentially after the next CICS command. It is, therefore, a good programming practice to save the contents of EIB fields that are relevant to a conversation in program dynamic storage areas subsequent to CICS commands relating to the conversation. Failure to test EIB fields will mean that your transaction will not work properly with its conversation partner and very well may mean that the transaction will abend.

11.2.4 Examples of the SEND Command

The following examples of the SEND command use different options, and a programmer coding the SEND command needs to be mindful of any state change as a result of options chosen.

1. ```
   EXEC CICS SEND CONVID(WS-CONVID)
        FROM(OUTPUT-MESSAGE)
        LENGTH(M-LEN)   END-EXEC.
   ```

   EXAMPLE 1: In this example, the SEND command is used to send data. Checking Figure 10-4, which is the SEND STATE diagram, we note that the transaction remains in state 3, the SEND STATE.

2. ```
   EXEC CICS SEND CONVID(WS-CONVID)
        CONFIRM FROM(OUTPUT-MESSAGE)
        LENGTH(M-LEN) END-EXEC.
   ```

   EXAMPLE 2: In this example, the SEND command is used to send data and to request a confirmation. The conversation partner may use the ISSUE CONFIRMATION to indicate a positive confirmation or an ISSUE ERROR or ISSUE ABEND command to indicate a negative response. If a negative response is returned, CICS sets on this task's EIBERR field, which should be tested subsequent to the SEND command. Note in Figure 10-4 that a SEND CONFIRM that is positively responded to (EIBERR is not set) leaves the SENDing transaction in the SEND STATE as indicated by the new state of 3.

3. ```
   EXEC CICS SEND CONVID(WS-CONVID)
        CONFIRM INVITE
        FROM(OUTPUT-MESSAGE)
        LENGTH(M-LENGTH) END-EXEC.
   ```

   EXAMPLE 3: In this example, the SEND command is used to send data, request a confirmation, and generate an SNA Change-Direction Indicator. The INVITE option causes CICS to generate the Change-Direction Indicator. The CONFIRM option flushes CICS's buffer, forcing CICS to transmit accumulated data and indicators. Therefore, this task is now in the RECEIVE STATE as indicated in Figure 10-4. The next thing for this task to do is to check EIBERR and RECEIVE.

4. ```
   EXEC CICS SEND CONVID(WS-CONVID)
        INVITE END-EXEC.
   ```

EXAMPLE 4: In this example, the SEND command is used to generate an SNA Change-Direction Indicator. According to Figure 10-4 the task is now in state 4. This task would in all probability next execute a RECEIVE command. The state 4 diagram is illustrated in Figure 11-1, if you wish to examine the other options.

5. EXEC CICS SEND CONVID(WS-CONVID)
        LAST WAIT END-EXEC.

EXAMPLE 5: In this example, the SEND command is used to generate the SNA End Bracket Indicator. Furthermore, the WAIT option forces transmission. As a result the End Bracket Indicator is sent and the task, according to Figure 10-4, is now in state 10. The state 10 diagram is illustrated in Figure 11-3 and the only valid thing for this task to do is to FREE the session and get on with its processing.

This set of SEND command options can be used to prevent conversation syncpointing for conversations at SYNCLEVEL(2). Once a SEND LAST WAIT is executed, nothing further is sent on the session. Therefore, a subsequent RETURN command which implicitly takes a SYNCPOINT will not result in a SYNCPOINT indicator being sent to the remote system. In contrast, had the command been SEND LAST without the WAIT, the End Bracket would be generated but *not* transmitted. Therefore, a subsequent RETURN command with its implicit SYNCPOINT would add the SYNCPOINT indicator to the accumlated data, and this would be sent to the remote system. In the remote system, the conversation partner's RECEIVE command would receive among other things the SYNCPOINT indicator in the EIB (EIBSYNC). If the remote task fails to take a SYNCPOINT, it abends because when EIBSYNC is set on the task takes a SYNCPOINT or DIES! If SYNCPOINTing is genuinely never needed, this potential problem could be resolved by requesting a SYNCLEVEL(1) for the conversation. As an alternative or when SYNCPOINTing is to be avoided for SYNCLEVEL(2) conversations, the SEND LAST WAIT may be used.

6. EXEC CICS SEND CONVID(WS-CONVID) INVITE WAIT
        END-EXEC.

EXAMPLE 6: In this example, the SEND command is used to force an immediate Change-Direction. The INVITE option generates the SNA Change-Direction Indicator and the WAIT option causes immediate transmission. Therefore, Figure 10-4 indicates that in this case the new state is 5, the RECEIVE STATE. One context in which this command would prove useful is if a Front-End Transaction does not have data to SEND upon conversation initiation. Regardless of whether or not it is desirable, the Front-End Transaction is in the SEND STATE and the Back-End Transaction is in the RECEIVE STATE. SEND INVITE WAIT can be used by a Front-End Transaction to immediately toggle the SEND/RECEIVE relationship upon conversation initiation.

```
7.  EXEC CICS SEND CONVID(WS-CONVID) LAST
        FROM(OUTPUT-MESSAGE) LENGTH(M-LEN)
        END-EXEC.
```

EXAMPLE 7: This SEND command sends data and causes CICS to generate the SNA End Bracket Indicator. However, transmission is not forced so the End Bracket is not transmitted. A subsequent RETURN or SYNCPOINT command adds the SYNCPOINT indicator to the accumulated data if the conversation is at SYNCLEVEL(2). The distributed transaction is thus forced through SYNCPOINT processing.

11.3 THE RECEIVE COMMAND

The RECEIVE command is used to receive data and obtain, via Execute Interface Block Fields, conversation status information. The EIB fields important to an application program are to some degree dependent upon the commands and command options that the conversation partner may potentially use. To this extent both conversation partners must be coordinated. Beyond the commands and options that are specific to a particular conversation, there are certain EIB fields that should routinely be tested subsequent to a RECEIVE command.

The EIB is volatile, CICS changes it subsequent to EVERY CICS command. Therefore, it is a good idea to know when you code a RECEIVE, or for that matter any other command, what EIB fields can possibly be set as a result. If the command sets no EIB fields, fine. But if EIB fields are set, those that are significant to your application should be saved in work fields in dynamic storage. In many contexts the RECEIVE command may require that multiple EIB flags be tested. There is an order of precedence for such testing and some flags require immediate execution of certain CICS commands. Therefore, it is not feasible to make all the tests at once, and to this end, it is advisable to save the important EIB fields. We will discuss this in more depth when we discuss other APPC mapped conversation commands, but for now it is important to recognize that these tests need to be made. The EIB fields that may need to be tested subsequent to a RECEIVE are listed in Figure 10-5, the RECEIVE STATE diagram. These fields include EIBCOMPL, EIBCONF, EIB-SYNC, EIBSYNCRB, EIBFREE, and EIBRECV.

11.3.1   The Format of the RECEIVE Command

The format of the RECEIVE command for APPC mapped conversations as follows.

```
EXEC CICS RECEIVE
          CONVID(field-name)
          INTO(data-area-name)
             OR
          SET(pointer)
          MAXLENGTH(2-byte-binary-field)
          LENGTH(2-byte-binary-field)
          NOTRUNCATE
```

The CONVID option names the data field containing the CONVersation ID.

The mutually exclusive INTO or SET options allow the application to obtain incoming data. When SET is used the application program obtains addressability to data that is actually located in a CICS work area. CICS may release this area when the next EXEC CICS command is exeuted. So, you can think of the CICS work area as something that is temporarily loaned to your task and not something that your task owns. INTO copies the data into your dynamic work area (COBOL WORKING-STORAGE or assembler DFHEISTG DSECT). As such you have your data as long as the task lives.

The MAXLENGTH option names a 2-byte binary field which is used to define maximum length information. When used in a command specifying RECEIVE INTO, this field indicates the maximum size that the program can accommodate in terms of its defined input work area size. A RECEIVE SET command that does not include the MAXLENGTH option results in CICS providing addressability to all of the input data. With RECEIVE SET, the MAXLENGTH option defines the maximum amount of data that the program is willing to accept.

If the actual data length exceeds the MAXLENGTH field specification, CICS raises the LENGERR error condition and truncates the remaining data. However, if the RECEIVE command includes the NOTRUNCATE option that is listed above in the RECEIVE command format, truncation is not performed and the task may do successive RECEIVEs to obtain the remaining data. If MAXLENGTH is omitted from a RECEIVE command, CICS looks to the LENGTH option to provide any required data length information for RECEIVE INTO.

The LENGTH option names a 2-byte binary field which is used to provide length information when the MAXLENGTH option described above is not included in a RECEIVE command. When LENGTH is used with RECEIVE INTO, the LENGTH field indicates the size of the INTO area. This represents the maximum amount of information that the program can accommodate as a result of a single RECEIVE command. Subsequent to the RECEIVE, CICS updates the length field to indicate the actual size of the data. When used in a RECEIVE SET, CICS returns the actual data length in the LENGTH field. RECEIVE INTO LENGTH can result in a length error if the application program area is not large enough to accommodate all of the input. Again CICS truncates the data and raises the LENGERR condition unless the NOTRUNCATE option is included in the RECEIVE command.

The NOTRUNCATE option is explained fairly well in the discussion of MAXLENGTH and LENGTH. If NOTRUNCATE is included in a RECEIVE command, CICS does not raise the LENGERR condition and does not truncate data. The application program can then do successive RECEIVE commands and obtain any remaining data. When all data has been passed to the application program, CICS sets on EIBCOMPL (X'FF' is on). Therefore, an application program RECEIVEs until EIBCOMPL is equal to high values. If you omit the NOTRUNCATE option, EIBCOMPL is always set on.

11.3.2   Unusual Conditions and the RECEIVE Command

The unusual conditions of the RECEIVE command include EOC, LENGERR, NOTALLOC, SIGNAL, and TERMERR.

The EOC condition is explained in the discussion of the unusual conditions of the SEND command.

The LENGERR condition can only occur for a RECEIVE command which does not specify NOTRUNCATE and which uses the INTO option. When LENGERR occurs, CICS truncates any remaining data and by default abends the task. You can programmatically avoid the abend by dealing with the condition, but the data is truncated.

The NOTALLOC, SIGNAL, and TERMERR conditions were discussed previously in the section dealing with unusual conditions of the SEND command.

11.3.3   Examples of the RECEIVE Command

The following are examples of the RECEIVE command. Note that in each case fields are moved from the EIB to the task's dynamic copy of WORKING-STORAGE or DFHEISTG DSECT. This COBOL example is generic enough to be appropriate for COBOL or COBOL II.

```
WORKING-STORAGE.
01  T-I-AREA         PIC X(250).
01  WORK-FIELDS.
    04 T-LEN         PIC S9(4) COMP VALUE +250.
    04 WS-CONVID     PIC X(4).
    04 SV-SYNC       PIC X.
        88 TAKE-A-SYNCPOINT       VALUE HIGH-VALUES.
    04 SV-FREE       PIC X.
        88 FREE-SESSION           VALUE HIGH-VALUES.
    04 SV-RECV       PIC X.
        88 MY-TURN-TO-SEND        VALUE LOW-VALUES.


PROCEDURE DIVISION.
* NOTE: USE OF CONVID IS OPTIONAL FOR TASK'S PRINCIPAL
*       FACILITY. IF IT IS CODED IN SUCH A CASE, THE
*       CONVID VALUE COMES FROM EIBTRMID.
    EXEC CICS RECEIVE CONVID(WS-CONVID)
        INTO(T-I-AREA) LENGTH(T-LEN)
    END-EXEC.
    MOVE EIBSYNC TO SV-SYNC.
    MOVE EIBFREE TO SV-FREE.
    MOVE EIBRECV TO SV-RECV.
    IF TAKE-A-SYNCPOINT
        EXEC CICS SYNCPOINT END-EXEC
```

```
                . etc
       IF FREE-SESSION
          EXEC CICS FREE CONVID(WS-CONVID) END-EXEC
          . etc
       IF MY-TURN-TO-SEND
          . go to it!
```

The following is an assembler language version of the above coding.

```
DFHEISTG DSECT
TIAREA    DS   CL250
TLEN      DS   H
CONVID1   DS   CL4
SVSYNC    DS   CL1
SVFREE    DS   CL1
SVREC     DS   CL1
               .
*NOTE: USE OF CONVID IS OPTIONAL FOR TASK'S PRINCIPAL
*
*      FACILITY. IF IT IS CODED IN SUCH A CASE, THE
*
*      CONVID VALUE COMES FROM EIBTRMID.
*
          EXEC CICS RECEIVE CONVID(CONVID1)             *
               INTO(TIAREA) LENGTH(TLEN)
*
          MVC  SVSYNC,EIBSYNC
          MVC  SVFREE,EIBFREE
          MVC  SVREC,EIBRECV
          CLI  SVSYNC,X'FF'
          BNE  TSTFREE
          EXEC CICS SYNCPOINT
TSTFREE   DS   0H
          CLI  SVFREE,X'FF'
          BNE  TSTREC
          EXEC CICS FREE CONVID(CONVID1)
          EXEC CICS RETURN
TSTREC    DS   0H
          CLI  SVREC,X'FF'
          BE   STLRCV
* CAN START SENDING SINCE NOW IN SEND STATE
               .
```

```
STLRCV DS    0H
* CONTINUE RECEIVING SINCE STILL RECEIVE STATE
```

11.4   THE CONVERSE COMMAND

The CONVERSE command functionally combines a SEND INVITE
WAIT and RECEIVE. Actually, if this is the function that is desired,
one CONVERSE command has a shorter execution path than the
processing of the separate commands. CICS generates an SNA
Change-Direction Indicator, and if you check Figure 10-4, you will
note that the transaction enters the RECEIVE STATE subsequent to
a CONVERSE command.

11.4.1   The Format of the CONVERSE Command

The format of the CONVERSE command is as follows.

```
EXEC CICS CONVERSE
          CONVID(field-containing-convid)
          FROM(data-area-name)
          FROMLENGTH(from-length-info)
          INTO(data-area-name)
             * OR *
          SET(pointer)
          TOLENGTH(input-length-info)
          MAXLENGTH(max-length-info)
          NOTRUNCATE
```

The options of the CONVERSE command are a subset of options
that can be defined on the SEND and RECEIVE commands. Since
we've gone over these options, we'll curtail the discussion of them
and merely point you in the direction of the appropriate command if
you wish to review the options.

The CONVID option is used as described above for the SEND and
RECEIVE commands.

The FROM option names the data area containing the output message to be sent as in the SEND command.

The FROMLENGTH option specifies the length of the FROM data
area — the output message length as in the SEND command.

The mutually exclusive INTO or SET options are used as described above in the RECEIVE command.

The MAXLENGTH and TOLENGTH options are used as the MAXLENGTH and LENGTH options of the RECEIVE command.

The NOTRUNCATE option is used as described in the discussion of the RECEIVE command.

11.4.2   Unusual Conditions Associated with CONVERSE

The unusual conditions associated with the CONVERSE command are EOC, LENGERR, NOTALLOC, SIGNAL, and TERMERR. The EOC, NOTALLOC, SIGNAL, and TERMERR conditions were described in the section dealing with unusual conditions of the SEND command. The LENGERR is discussed above in the section on unusual conditions and the RECEIVE command.

11.4.3   Example of the CONVERSE Command

The following is an example of the CONVERSE command in a generic COBOL program.

```
WORKING-STORAGE SECTION.
01  OUTPUT-MESSAGE        PIC X(250).
01  INPUT-MESSAGE         PIC X(250).
01  WORK-FIELDS.
    04 I-LEN       PIC S9(4) COMP VALUE +250.
    04 O-LEN       PIC S9(4) COMP VALUE +250.
    04 WS-CONVID   PIC X(4).
    04 SV-COMPL    PIC X.
       88 FINITO              VALUE HIGH-VALUES.

PROCEDURE DIVISION.

* NOTE: USE OF CONVID IS OPTIONAL FOR TASK'S PRINCIPAL
*       FACILITY. IF IT IS CODED IN SUCH A CASE, THE
*       CONVID VALUE COMES FROM EIBTRMID.
    .
    .

    EXEC CICS CONVERSE CONVID(WS-CONVID)
         FROM(OUTPUT-MESSAGE) FROMLENGTH(O-LEN)
         INTO(INPUT-MESSAGE) TOLENGTH(I-LEN)
```

```
            NOTRUNCATE END-EXEC.
       MOVE EIBCOMPL TO SV-COMPL.
  M000-RECEIVE-MORE.
          .
  * INSTRUCTIONS PROCESS OR SAVE DATA RECEIVED.
          .
       IF FINITO GO TO M100-RECEIVED-ALL.
       MOVE +250 TO I-LEN.
       EXEC CICS RECEIVE CONVID(WS-CONVID)
            INTO(INPUT-MESSAGE) LENGTH(I-LEN)
            NOTRUNCATE END-EXEC.
       MOVE EIBCOMPL TO SV-COMPL.
       GO TO M000-RECEIVE-MORE.
  M100-RECEIVED-ALL.
```

11.5   THE WAIT COMMAND

The WAIT command can be used to force CICS to transmit the internal buffer with data and control indicators before the task continues its execution.

11.5.1   The Format of the WAIT Command

The format of the WAIT command is as follows.

```
  EXEC CICS WAIT CONVID(data-area-name)
```

The CONVID option is used as in all the other APPC mapped conversation commands.

11.5.2   Unusual Conditions of the WAIT Command

The only unusual condition that can occur for the WAIT command is the NOTALLOC condition, which indicates that the named CONVID is not allocated.

11.6   SUMMARY

In this chapter we have examined the APPC mapped conversation commands used to SEND and RECEIVE data between conversation partners. In the next chapter we will examine the remaining APPC mapped conversation commands.

REVIEW EXERCISE

Match the following SEND Command options with a description below.

___ 1.   CONVID
___ 2.   CONFIRM
___ 3.   LAST
___ 4.   WAIT
___ 5.   INVITE

A. Causes the SNA Change-Direction indicator to be generated.
B. Used by the Front-End Transaction so that the output of the SEND command is properly directed to the appropriate conversation.
C. Requests a confirmation of a SYNCLEVEL(1) or SYNCLEVEL(2) conversation partner.
D. Causes CICS to generate the SNA End Bracket Indicator.
E. Causes CICS to transmit the data and SNA indicators contained in the task's buffer.

In the following SEND Commands describe the indicators generated and whether or not CICS will transmit the data and indicators in the task's output buffer.

1. `EXEC CICS SEND CONVID(WS-CONV) LAST WAIT`
2. `EXEC CICS SEND CONVID(WS-CONV) FROM(MSG-OUT)`
   `                LENGTH(200) WAIT`
3. `EXEC CICS SEND CONVID(WS-CONV) CONFIRM`
4. `EXEC CICS SEND CONVID(WS-CONV) INVITE WAIT`
5. `EXEC CICS SEND CONVID(WS-CONV) FROM(MSG-OUT)`
   `                LENGTH(200)`
6. `EXEC CICS SEND CONVID(WS-CONV) INVITE CONFIRM`

For each of the SEND commands listed above, examine the SEND STATE diagram provided in the previous chapter and indicate the transaction's state subsequent to command execution.

1.

2.

3.

4.

5.

6.

Provide a short answer to each of the following.

1. How does a conversation partner know that CICS has received a CONFIRMation request?
2. How does a Back-End Transaction know when it has been placed into the SEND state?
3. What restriction is there upon use of the SEND CONFIRM and ISSUE CONFIRMATION commands during a LUTYPE 6.2 conversation?
4. Why are INVITE and LAST mutually exclusive options of the SEND command?
5. Why are WAIT and CONFIRM mutually exclusive options of the SEND command?
6. What is the conversation state of the Back-End Transaction when initiated?
7. You are coding a Front-End Transaction. The ALLOCATE and CONNECT PROCESS commands have been successfully executed. You have no data to send and want to place your conversation partner into the SEND state. What command do you use? List any appropriate command options.
8. When is a good time to test EIBRECV to determine if a transaction has been placed into the SEND state?
9. What EIB fields should be tested subsequent to a RECEIVE command and how does one know the order in which these tests should be made?

10. Why is it a good idea to save EIB fields in WORKING-STORAGE or the DFHEISTG DSECT area?

ANSWERS TO REVIEW EXERCISE

Match the following SEND command options with a description below.

B 1. CONVID
C 2. CONFIRM
D 3. LAST
E 4. WAIT
A 5. INVITE

In the following SEND commands describe the indicators generated and whether or not CICS will transmit the data and indicators in the task's output buffer.

1. *EXEC CICS SEND CONVID(WS-CONV) LAST WAIT*

   The LAST option generates the End Bracket Indicator and the WAIT option forces the transmission. Therefore, there is nothing to do but free the session. This set of SEND command options can terminate a conversation to prevent a SYNCPOINT exchange when a task RETURNs to CICS.

2. *EXEC CICS SEND CONVID(WS-CONV) FROM(MSG-OUT)*
   LENGTH(200) WAIT

   This command generates no SNA indicators but the transmission is forced by the WAIT option. However, any indicators generated by one or more previous SEND commands would indeed be transmitted at this point.

3. *EXEC CICS SEND CONVID(WS-CONV) CONFIRM*

   This command requests a confirmation of the conversation partner.

4. *EXEC CICS SEND CONVID(WS-CONV) INVITE WAIT*

The INVITE option generates the Change-Direction option and the WAIT option forces the transmission.

5. *EXEC CICS SEND CONVID(WS-CONV) FROM(MSG-OUT)*
   LENGTH(200)

This command generates no SNA indicators. The data contained in MSG-OUT is placed into the internal buffer. However, transmission does not take place immediately.

6. *EXEC CICS SEND CONVID(WS-CONV) INVITE CONFIRM*

The INVITE option generates the Change-Direction Indicator and the CONFIRM option requests a confirmation.

For each of the SEND commands listed above, examine the SEND STATE diagram provided in the previous chapter and indicate the transaction's state subsequent to command execution.

1. The conversation state is 10, FREE SESSION.
2. The conversation state is 3, SEND STATE.
3. The conversation state is 3, SEND STATE if EIBERR is not set on. So, if EIBERR=X'00', the conversation remains in the SEND state.
4. The conversation state is 5, RECEIVE STATE.
5. The conversation state is 3, SEND STATE.
6. The conversation state is 5, RECEIVE STATE if EIBERR is not set on. So, if EIBERR=X'00', the conversation is in the RECEIVE state.

Provide a short answer to each of the following.

1. *How does a conversation partner know that CICS has received a CONFIRMation request?*

   EIBCONF is set on (X'FF') by CICS when it receives a CONFIRMation request on behalf of a conversation.

2. *How does a Back-End Transaction know when it has been placed into the SEND state?*

   EIBRECV is tested. If EIBRECV=X'FF', the transaction is still in the RECEIVE state and should issue another RECEIVE command when it can accommodate more input. EIBRECV should be tested or saved for subsequent testing after the RECEIVE command.

3. *What restriction is there upon use of the SEND CONFIRM and ISSUE CONFIRMATION commands during a LUTYPE 6.2 conversation?*

The CONFIRM option of the SEND command and the ISSUE CONFIRMATION command may only be used on SYNCLEVEL(1) or SYNCLEVEL(2) conversations.

4. *Why are INVITE and LAST mutually exclusive options of the SEND command?*

INVITE requests a response and LAST generates the End Bracket Indicator. Once the End Bracket is transmitted, the conversation partner cannot SEND because the conversation is over.

5. *Why are WAIT and CONFIRM mutually exclusive options of the SEND command?*

WAIT causes a transmission of the buffer as does CONFIRM. CONFIRM also requests a confirmation request.

6. *What is the conversation state of the Back-End Transaction when initiated?*

State 5 — RECEIVE STATE.

7. *You are coding a Front-End Transaction. The ALLOCATE and CONNECT PROCESS commands have been successfully executed. You have no data to send and want to place your conversation partner into the SEND State. What command do you use? List any appropriate command options.*

EXEC CICS SEND INVITE WAIT

8. *When is a good time to test EIBRECV to determine if a transaction has been placed into the SEND state?*

Directly after the execution of the RECEIVE command.

9. *What EIB fields should be tested subsequent to a RECEIVE command and how does one know the order in which these tests should be made?*

In the State 5 Diagram, EIBCOMPL, EIBCONF, EIBSYNC, EIBSYNRB, EIBREE and EIBRECV are listed as the fields to be tested. The tests should be made in the order in which they are listed in the state diagram.

10. *Why is it a good idea to save EIB fields in WORKING-STORAGE or the DFHEISTG DSECT area?*

The EIB is volatile and changes. When there are multiple tests to be made, they have to be made one at a time and there may be other commands that have to be executed as a result of certain tests. By saving the EIB fields for subsequent testing, valuable indicators are not overlayed.

Chapter

12

Conclusion of LUTYPE 6.2 Mapped Conversations

12.1 INTRODUCTION

In this chapter we will conclude our examination of APPC mapped conversation commands. This includes a discussion of how these commands can be used to exchange status information between conversing transactions and how the use of such commands can be detected by you and your conversation partner. The EIB contains fields that are set on for certain commands, so these fields must be tested. This means that you must know what commands will be used by your conversation partner so that you can make the appropriate tests and similarly your conversation partner must know what commands you are going to utilize.

12.2 THE ISSUE CONFIRMATION COMMAND

The ISSUE CONFIRMATION command is used to provide a positive response to a request for CONFIRMation. However, use of the CONFIRM option of the SEND command and its accompanying positive response with the ISSUE CONFIRMATION requires that a conversation be operating at a SYNCLEVEL of 1 or 2. The CONFIRM option and ISSUE CONFIRMATION are not allowed at SYNC-LEVEL(0).

The requirement to ISSUE CONFIRMATION is defined within the application design. In application "X," there is a need for establishing periodic confirmations that things are going well. Perhaps the application involves queue transfer. The Front-End Transaction is essentially reading a queue of records and sending them to the Back-End Transaction. The Back-End Transaction does not have data to send back. So by and large the Front-End Transaction is going to be in the SEND STATE and the Back-End Transaction is going to be in the RECEIVE STATE. Why do we want to be bothered with confirmations? Suppose that something goes wrong at the back end. Perhaps the Back-End Transaction is saving records in Temporary Storage for future processing. It is conceivable that the system could run out of space within the AUX Temporary Storage data set. We do not want to just send off data records and have no way of ensuring that they are being correctly disposed of. There are other options aside from a CONFIRMation exchange for dealing with something going wrong, but the application designers elected to use the CONFIRMation exchange. The design specifies that after sending five records, a confirmation will be requested.

What special requirements does this design decision involve? The conversation must take place at a SYNCLEVEL of 1 or 2. Therefore, the Front-End Transaction must specify one of these SYNCLEVELs in the CONNECT PROCESS command. Furthermore, it is probably a good idea for the Back-End Transaction to do an EXTRACT PROCESS upon invocation and verify the SYNCLEVEL. Additionally, both programs know that confirmations are used. Therefore, appropriate EIB tests can be conducted in the application programs. The Front-End Transaction SENDs four records with a SEND command that does not include the CONFIRM option. The fifth record is sent via the following command:

```
EXEC CICS SEND CONVID(WS-CONVID) FROM(Q-REC)
     LENGTH(Q-LEN) CONFIRM END-EXEC.
```

This SEND command results in the CICS buffer being transmitted to the remote system. The remote CICS uses the data received to satisfy a RECEIVE command executed by the Back-End Transaction. In addition to providing data to the Back-End Transaction, CICS sets EIBCONF on (X'FF') to signal the confirmation request. Looking at Figure 10-5, the RECEIVE STATE diagram, we find that RECEIVE with EIBCONF set on indicates a new state. The new state is 6, and that state name is *RECEIVER ISSUE CONFIRMA-*

STATE 6 MAPPED LUTYPE6.2 CONVERSATIONS	RECEIVER ISSUE CONFIRMATION	
Commands You Can Issue	What To Test (For EIBERRCD tests see the table on page 199)	New State
ISSUE CONFIRMATION	EIBFREE (saved value)	1θ
	EIBRECV (saved value)	5
	Otherwise	3
ISSUE ERROR	EIBFREE (saved value)	3
	Otherwise	3
ISSUE ABEND	-	1θ

Figure 12-1 State 6 — RECEIVER ISSUE CONFIRMATION. Reprinted by permission from *CICS/MVS Version 2.1 Intercommunication Guide* © 1987, 1988 by International Business Machines Corporation.

TION. Figure 12-1 illustrates this state diagram. The Back-End Transaction tests EIBCONF and recognizes that it is now in state 6. You will note that after executing the ISSUE CONFIRMATION it will be necessary to test saved EIB fields. Therefore, before responding to the confirmation request, EIBFREE and EIBRECV should be saved for subsequent testing. Now, suppose that EIBCONF is set on and the contents of EIBFREE and EIBRECV have been saved. We can now respond positively to the confirmation request. The positive response is the execution of the ISSUE CONFIRMATION command.

12.2.1   The Format of the ISSUE CONFIRMATION Command

The format of the ISSUE CONFIRMATION command is as follows.

```
EXEC CICS ISSUE CONFIRMATION CONVID(field-name)
```

The CONVID option is not required and in the context of a Back-End Transaction would not be needed because the conversation is the back-end's principal facility.

12.2.2   Subsequent Tests After Positive Response

After executing the ISSUE CONFIRMATION command, the saved contents of EIBFREE and EIBRECV should be tested. The test of EIBFREE is used to determine if the conversation partner performed a SEND CONFIRM LAST. In this case the CONFIRM caused our EIBCONF to be set on. The LAST option caused EIBFREE to be set on (X'FF'), and that has placed us in state 10, which is illustrated in Figure 11-3. The only valid thing to do at this point is to FREE the session. This can be accomplished by executing a FREE command or by immediately RETURNing to CICS so that it can FREE the session.

If the saved contents of EIBFREE do not indicate the need for a FREE (X'00') the next test is of the saved contents of EIBRECV. If EIBRECV is set on (X'FF') the transaction is still in the RECEIVE STATE and should do another RECEIVE. Otherwise the transaction is in the SEND STATE and can begin SENDing data. **The tests that are listed in the State diagrams should be conducted or conversation errors can result. The tests should also be conducted in the order in which they are listed in the diagrams.** For example, if we had tested the saved contents of EIBRECV first and acted in accordance with what we found there, a conversation error might have ensued because the conversation is over if EIBFREE is on and, in that case, the only valid thing to do is FREE the session.

If you know exactly what your conversation partner is going to be doing, it is possible to bypass some of the EIB testing. For example, if we look at Figure 10-5, you will note that subsequent to the RECEIVE, fields are tested in the following order: EIBCOMPL, EIBCONF, EIBSYNC, EIBSYNRB, EIBFREE, and EIBRECV. If you did not include the NOTRUNCATE option in your RECEIVE command, obviously you don't want to test EIBCOMPL. If you know for a fact that your conversation partner is never going to ask for a confirmation or that your conversation is at SYNCLEVEL (0), the test of EIBCONF can be bypassed. We could continue on down the list and come up with reasons/rationalizations for not performing EIB tests. However, remember that it's better to be safe and know that your program is going to work. People do maintenance and it is possible for programs to change such that unanticipated EIB fields can be set on. In some cases we can be pretty certain that bypassing certain tests won't cause a problem. For example, if a transaction verifies a SYNCLEVEL of 0 subsequent to an EXTRACT PROCESS command then there is, indeed, no point in testing EIBCONF, EIBSYNC or

EIBSYNRB. But when in doubt, it's better to perform an extra test or two and know the transaction's state definitively.

12.2.3   Unusual Conditions of the ISSUE CONFIRMATION Command

The unusual conditions associated with the ISSUE CONFIRMA-TION command are NOTALLOC, TERMERR, and INVREQ.

The NOTALLOC condition indicates that the conversation is not allocated.

The TERMERR condition indicates a session-related error or possibly a conversation partner's execution of an ISSUE ABEND.

The INVREQ condition indicates that the command is invalid in the context of the session. For example, a conversation is at SYNCLEVEL(0) and an ISSUE CONFIRMATION is not allowed due to the SYNCLEVEL.

12.2.4   Testing the Response to a SEND CONFIRM

After performing a SEND CONFIRM, the SENDing transaction's data is transmitted to the remote system. When control is given back to the application program at the next instruction after the SEND command, it is necessary to test for the response. The ISSUE CON-FIRMATION command does not turn on an EIB field. However, a negative response to a confirmation request, such as the execution of an ISSUE ERROR command, turns on EIBERR (X'FF'). Therefore, the transaction should now test EIBERR to determine if a positive or negative response was returned to the confirmation request. If you look back at Figure 10-4 which illustrates the SEND STATE diagram, you will note that the transaction is still in the SEND STATE as long as EIBERR is not set on. Therefore, the following might be coded immediately after the SEND CONFIRM command.

```
WORKING-STORAGE SECTION.
01   WORK-FIELDS.
     04 SV-ERR         PIC X.
        88 PROCESSING-CONFIRMED         VALUE LOW-VALUES.

PROCEDURE DIVISION.

     EXEC CICS SEND CONFIRM . . . etc. END-EXEC.
```

```
MOVE EIBERR TO SV-ERR.
IF PROCESSING-CONFIRMED
    . . . continue with normal processing
ELSE
    . . . error processing
```

12.3   THE ISSUE ERROR COMMAND

The ISSUE ERROR command can be used as a negative response to a CONFIRMation request. However, unlike the ISSUE CONFIRMA-TION, ISSUE ERROR can be used at any SYNCLEVEL. Therefore, it can be utilized for any purpose devised by the application designer to indicate that an error has occurred which necessitates the conversation partner's attention. ISSUE ERROR is also permitted for a RECEIVE STATE transaction.

12.3.1   Format of the ISSUE ERROR Command

The format of the ISSUE ERROR command is:

```
EXEC CICS ISSUE ERROR CONVID(field-name)
```

12.3.2   Unusual Conditions and the ISSUE ERROR Command

The unusual conditions of the ISSUE ERROR command are NOTAL-LOC and INVREQ.

12.3.3   ISSUE ERROR Programming Considerations

The receipt of an ISSUE ERROR causes CICS to turn on the EIBERR field (X'FF'). CICS receives an ISSUE ERROR on behalf of your conversation, but does not post EIBERR until the next conver-sation-related command. Therefore, if your conversation partner uses ISSUE ERROR to inform you of error conditions, EIBERR should be tested after each conversation-related command. This is not always indicated in the state diagrams, but if an application makes use of ISSUE ERROR and one can be received, it is recommended EIBERR be tested.

EIBERR actually gets set on for other things as well so it is necessary to verify the cause. This can be performed by testing EIBERRCD, which is set to X'08890000' for receipt of an ISSUE ERROR. ISSUE ERROR is a way of signaling an error and typically a transaction that has detected an error also needs to send some type of qualifying message. In recognition of this fact, the execution of an ISSUE ERROR by a RECEIVE STATE transaction causes that transaction to be placed into the SEND STATE.·

Conversely, receiving an ISSUE ERROR while in the SEND STATE normally places a transaction into the RECEIVE STATE. Figure 10-5 is the RECEIVE STATE diagram. Note that when an ISSUE ERROR is executed, the transaction's new state is 3 or the SEND STATE unless EIBFREE is set on. EIBFREE would be set on because your conversation partner said SEND LAST or FREE. If EIBFREE is on, the session must be FREEd. So generally speaking, the transaction that says ISSUE ERROR is placed into the SEND STATE and the one that receives ISSUE ERROR is placed into the RECEIVE STATE. However, this is not an absolute rule, and it is therefore necessary to conduct the EIB tests indicated in the state diagram.

If two transactions are designed to use ISSUE ERROR to signal each other about conversation-related errors, there is always the possibility that both of them could ISSUE ERROR so that their ISSUE ERRORs cross each other. This is called an *ISSUE ERROR race*. As with most races, the winner is not known until the finish line is crossed. So, which transaction will be the ISSUE ERROR race winner and which one will be the ISSUE ERROR race loser? Results are not predictable. In other words, you must test the EIB to determine if your ISSUE ERROR came in first.

Therefore, after executing an ISSUE ERROR, EIBRECV should be tested. If EIBRECV indicates that the transaction is in the SEND STATE, EIBRECV=X'00', then A) there was no ISSUE ERROR race or B) the transaction is the ISSUE ERROR race winner. If the transaction is in the SEND STATE, the conventional thing to do is to SEND INVITE an error message or code and then execute a RECEIVE. This sends error information to the conversation partner and generates an SNA Change-Direction Indicator. This series of commands would be as follows:

```
EXEC CICS ISSUE ERROR CONVID(WS-CONVID) END-EXEC.
IF EIBFREE = LOW-VALUES NEXT SENTENCE
    ELSE GO TO FREE-SESSION.
IF EIBRECV = LOW-VALUES
```

```
EXEC CICS SEND CONVID(WS-CONVID)
     INVITE FROM(ERR-MSG1) LENGTH(25)
END-EXEC
EXEC CICS RECEIVE INTO(INP-MSG)
     LENGTH(T-LEN) END-EXEC
          . . . save and test EIB fields
ELSE
     . . . save and test EIB fields appropriate to
          the conversation and go on from there.
```

12.4   THE ISSUE ABEND COMMAND

The ISSUE ABEND command can be used to signal an application error. Like ISSUE ERROR, ISSUE ABEND can be used by a RECEIVE STATE transaction and ISSUE ABEND causes EIBERR to be set on. However, ISSUE ABEND aborts the conversation. The transaction performing the ISSUE ABEND is not terminated but the conversation is. Subsequent to an ISSUE ABEND, it is necessary to free the session. This can be done with a FREE command or by RETURNing to CICS.

If ISSUE ABEND is performed by a transaction in the SEND STATE, CICS transmits any data waiting in the internal buffer prior to sending the ISSUE ABEND. If a RECEIVE STATE transaction ISSUEs ABEND, incoming data is purged but the SNA indicators are not. If CICS detects an End Bracket in the received buffer, EIBFREE is set on and it is mandatory to FREE the session as described above. In this case, CICS does not send your ISSUE ABEND indication to the remote system because the conversation is finished.

Since ISSUE ABEND is like pulling the plug, it is normally used in the context of indicating a severe error. For example, if a transaction requires operation at a SYNCLEVEL(2) and the result of an EXTRACT PROCESS reveals an improper SYNCLEVEL, it might be appropriate to ISSUE ABEND. However, the manner in which one uses ISSUE ABEND is determined in the application design.

12.4.1   The Format of the ISSUE ABEND Command

The format of the ISSUE ABEND command is as follows.

```
EXEC CICS ISSUE ABEND CONVID(field-name)
```

The CONVID option need not be used when the conversation is the transaction's principal facility.

12.4.2   Unusual Conditions of the ISSUE ABEND Command

The unusual conditions of the ISSUE ABEND command are the same as those defined for the ISSUE ERROR command.

12.4.3   Detecting ISSUE ABEND by a Conversation Partner

Detecting the ISSUE ABEND executed by a conversation partner is relatively simple. When the conversation is abended, CICS raises the TERMERR condition. If receiving an ISSUE ABEND is anticipated because the use of ISSUE ABEND has been defined in the transaction's design, there are two choices. Don't deal with the TERMERR condition, in which case the transaction abends along with the conversation. The other case is to handle the TERMERR condition. When TERMERR occurs, it normally necessary to immediately FREE the session. Then you can verify the cause of TERMERR by inspecting the EIB. If ISSUE ABEND gave rise to the TERMERR, EIBERR is set on (X'FF') and EIBERRCD equals X'08640000'.

12.5   THE ISSUE SIGNAL COMMAND

The ISSUE SIGNAL command is used by a RECEIVE STATE transaction to indicate its need to have a state change. In other words, a RECEIVE STATE transaction can request being placed into the SEND STATE by executing an ISSUE SIGNAL. CICS turns on EIB-SIG (X'FF') to indicate receipt of an ISSUE SIGNAL. The transaction receiving the ISSUE SIGNAL is not required by CICS to do anything specific. However, in the context of application design, the use of ISSUE SIGNAL has specific meaning and the transaction must act in accordance with the application requirements. The receiver of an ISSUE SIGNAL may immediately execute a SEND INVITE or it may continue processing until a more convenient time and then SEND INVITE.

If you can receive an ISSUE SIGNAL because the protocols of your application provide for its use, EIBSIG should be tested after each command.

12.5.1   The Format of The ISSUE SIGNAL Command

The format of the ISSUE SIGNAL command is as follows.

```
EXEC CICS ISSUE SIGNAL CONVID(field-name)
```

The CONVID option is not required for a transaction whose principal facility is the conversation over which ISSUE SIGNAL is to flow.

12.5.2   Unusual Conditions Of ISSUE SIGNAL

The unusual conditions of the ISSUE SIGNAL are NOTALLOC and TERMERR. These conditions are discussed for other commands in this chapter.

12.6   THE FREE COMMAND

The FREE command is used to FREE a session. This may be used as a normal part of conversation termination as follows.

```
EXEC CICS SEND CONVID(WS-CONVID) LAST WAIT
EXEC CICS FREE CONVID(WS-CONVID)
```

In this case, the End Bracket Indicator is generated by the LAST option. The End Bracket and any deferred data are transmitted by the WAIT option. The session is then freed by the FREE command.

However, the FREE command can be executed by a SEND STATE transaction at any time. If an End Bracket has not been generated, CICS generates and sends the End Bracket and then frees the session. If there is data in the internal buffer, CICS transmits the data along with the End Bracket.

A transaction receives indication of the need to execute a FREE command in the EIBFREE field. If this field is set on (X'FF'), the transaction *must* issue a FREE command or RETURN to CICS.

12.6.1   The Format of the FREE Command

The format of the FREE command is as follows.

```
EXEC CICS FREE CONVID(field-name)
```

The CONVID option can be omitted if the conversation is the transaction's principal facility.

12.6.2   Unusual Conditions of the FREE Command

The unusual conditions associated with the FREE command are: IN-VREQ, NOTALLOC, and SYSIDERR. These conditions are described above for other commands in this chapter.

12.7   COMMANDS RELATING TO SYNCPOINT EXCHANGES

SYNCPOINT exchanges are engaged in by SYNCLEVEL(2) conversations for the purpose of jointly committing modifications to protected resources. This assumes that the conversation partners are executing in an environment where 1) resources such as files, databases, and data queues can be given protection status and 2) transaction backout facilities are available.

In CICS protected resources can include files defined in the File Control Table as protected, AUX Temporary Storage Queues defined as protected in the Temporary Storage Table, Intrapartition Transient Data Queues defined in the Destination Control Table as protected, Interval Control START requests that specify PROTECT and VTAM messages for transactions defined as requiring message protection. CICS provides backout facilities for transaction failures and system failures. Transactions requiring dynamic backout protection are defined in the Program Control Table as requiring DTB or Dynamic Transaction Backout.

Transactions are normally defined as requiring DTB. When such a transaction modifies its first protected resource, CICS obtains storage for a task unique "log" in which backout information is saved. Subsequent to a successful SYNCPOINT, CICS clears the memory log because modifications are in fact committed. However, prior to a successful SYNCPOINT, a transaction failure results in CICS applying the information contained in the task unique log to effect backout to protected resources.

If a CICS system crashes, an emergency restart is performed. During an emergency restart of CICS, information from the system log, which is kept on tape or disk, is used to back out all uncommitted modifications to protected resources. An emergency restart performs backout on a systemwide basis, meaning that all modifications to protected resources by all inflight logical units of work in the system are backed out. Dynamic Transaction Backout, on the other hand, backs out a single failed transaction while the CICS system itself is up and running.

So for CICS-to-CICS conversations, the required pieces are in place so that distributed modifications to protected resources can be committed or backed out. If the conversation does not involve CICS-to-CICS, it is necessary to know the degree of support provided in the non-CICS LUTYPE 6.2 and plan accordingly.

In an earlier chapter we discussed the INDOUBT period during which a local CICS could not be sure if a failed remote system had indeed committed or backed out. The application designer should not neglect to analyze the potential impact of the INDOUBT period when designing distributed transactions that require protected resource synchronization across systems. If the application requires recovery procedures for dealing with resource inconsistencies arising from INDOUBT processing, it is desirable that they be in place before the application is implemented. In some cases a "recovery procedure" may simply mean that a CICS transaction has to be rerun. In other cases, utility programs may be used to "manually" clean up resources. The recovery procedures don't have to be sophisticated, they just have to work.

In the chapter on Function Shipping we described CICS recovery facilities with regard to Temporary Storage and Intrapartition Transient Data. In that discussion, we pointed out that CICS does not provide forward recovery for the AUX Temporary Storage data set (DFHTEMP) or for the Intrapartition Transient Data data set (DFHINTRA). Backout recovery comes as a standard feature with CICS if these queue resources are defined as protected. However, if physical damage results in the loss of DFHINTRA or DFHTEMP, CICS does not itself provide the mechanisms for forward recovery or rebuilding these data sets.

We should be aware of this limitation in designing applications that use local or remote Temporary Storage or Intrapartition Transient Data queues. We can elect to use these facilities for the storage of information that can be "recreated" by the reexecution of CICS application programs or for non-critical information. If, however, an application designer decides to place critical data in one of these queues, the application must address what happens if one of these data sets is partially or completely destroyed.

If critical data must be recovered, the application must be designed and implemented to do this. For example, programs that write critical data to these queues must save image copies of records. Application programs that alter the contents of critical queues must save information regarding alterations. Finally, application programs that delete critical queues must save an indication of such deletion. CICS automatic journaling (which is provided optionally for files) is not available for TS and TD queues. Application programs that need to save the above-mentioned TS/TD information can, however, perform user journaling via the EXEC CICS JOURNAL command.

Subsequent to DFHTEMP/DFHINTRA damage, application programs would be needed to collect journaled information and rewrite it to Temporary Storage or Transient Data. The likelihood of a head crash occurring or physical destruction of one of these data sets is relatively remote, but, if it occurs and you lose data, what does this mean to your application and the business as a whole? The application designer who elects to use Temporary Storage or Intrapartition Transient Data queues for the storage of critical information must address this issue.

The commands that are used in coordinating commit protocols in a distributed transaction include SYNCPOINT, SYCPOINT ROLLBACK, and ISSUE PREPARE. It should be pointed out that, **unlike other mapped conversation commands, the SYNCPOINT and SYNCPOINT ROLLBACK cannot be directed to a single conversation.** When a distributed transaction takes a SYNCPOINT or SYNCPOINT ROLLBACK, all connected SYNCLEVEL(2) conversations are involved in the commit protocol exchanges. The ISSUE PREPARE, on the other hand, is directed to a single CONVID and can be used in complex SYNCPOINT situations to prepare one or more selected conversation partners for an ensuing SYNCPOINT. Why do we want to prepare a conversation partner? Suppose that a particular conversation partner is not as reliable as our other conversation partners. The ISSUE PREPARE allows a transaction to selectively query one or more individual conversations that may be troublesome, without executing the SYNCPOINT which has global ramifications (within the context of all SYNCLEVEL(2) conversation partners, not worldwide). We will begin our discussion of these commands with SYNCPOINT.

12.7.1   The SYNCPOINT Command

The SYNCPOINT command is used to initiate commit protocols between all SYNCLEVEL(2) conversations in a distributed transaction. When designing an application that involves SYNCPOINTing, it is necessary to identify a single transaction as the INITIATOR of the SYNCPOINT. We have already described the need to design distributed transactions as essentially master/slave processes. If multiple conversations are connected as illustrated in Figure 12-2 then the design should be a master/slave tree.

SYNCPOINTing for a distributed transaction that involves a single conversation between two connected processes is less complex than when multiple conversations are involved. CICS may be involved in numerous data flows to coordinate a successful distributed SYNCPOINT. Figure 12-3 illustrates an example of a distributed SYNCPOINT and specifically the intersystem flows that CICS manages. Look for a moment at the commands that are contained within the connected programs and then at the flows that take place between the connected CICS systems.

Understanding the nature of these exchanges is not necessary for the application developer, because CICS manages the distributed SYNCPOINT. However, it is important for the application desig-

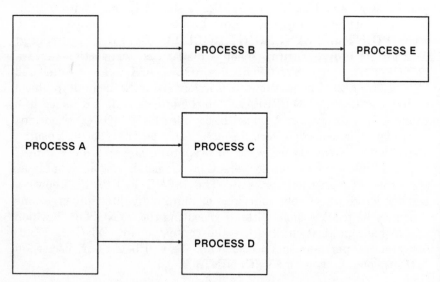

Figure 12-2 Complex transaction involving multiple conversations.

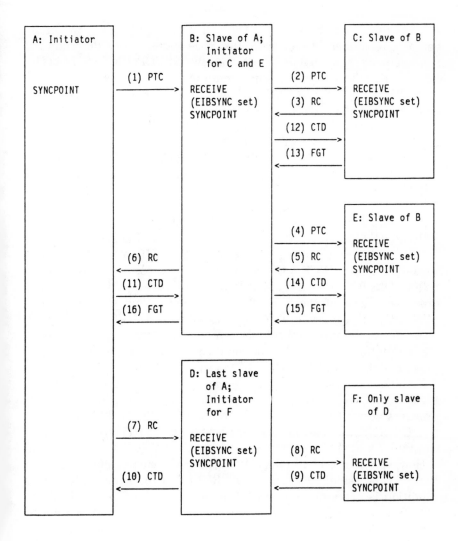

PTC - Prepare to Commit
RC - Request Commit
CTD - Committed
FGT - Forget

Figure 12-3 CICS flows during distributed SYNCPOINT. Reprinted by permission from *CICS/MVS Version 2.1 Intercommunication Guide* © 1987, 1988 by International Business Machines Corporation.

ner/programmer to be aware of the fact that, regardless of the number of interconnected conversations, it is necessary to determine a single one of them that is to serve as the *SYNCPOINT INITIATOR* for the entire unit of work. The remaining transactions are referred to as *SYNCPOINT SLAVES*, although a SYNCPOINT SLAVE may be a SYNCPOINT INITIATOR to its own SYNCPOINT SLAVES. This is illustrated in Figure 12-3. B is a SYNCPOINT SLAVE of A. It is also the SYNCPOINT INITIATOR for C and E.

The SYNCPOINT INITIATOR must be in the SEND STATE on all of its SYNCLEVEL(2) conversations or it cannot initiate a SYNCPOINT. So, in Figure 12-2, if program A is identified as the SYNCPOINT INITIATOR, it must be in the SEND STATE with regard to its conversations with B, C and D. When A executes a SYNCPOINT, its SYNCPOINT SLAVES, B, C and D are informed of the SYNCPOINT request by CICS turning on EIBSYNC (X'FF') subsequent to a RECEIVE command. Thus, our sending of a SYNCPOINT satisfies a RECEIVE in all three of the connected processes. Each of them must test EIBSYNC and respond to the SYNCPOINT request. Failure to respond to a SYNCPOINT request terminates the individual transaction and this termination and ensuing backout is propagated throughout the connected conversations.

After the SYNCPOINT INITIATOR has executed the SYNCPOINT, CICS goes through the sort of processing shown in Figure 12-3. When all of the required flows are complete, CICS prepares to return control to the SYNCPOINT INITIATOR. If the SYNCPOINT was successful, the SYNCPOINT INITIATOR receives control back at the next instruction after the SYNCPOINT command.

However, if a SYNCPOINT ROLLBACK occurred during SYNCPOINT processing, CICS raises the ROLLEDBACK condition. If this condition is not programmatically handled by the SYNCPOINT INITIATOR, the CICS default course of action is to back out and abend the task. Therefore, if the SYNCPOINT is unsuccessful and the ROLLEDBACK condition is not handled, then the SYNCPOINT INITIATOR does not receive control back. If ROLLEDBACK was HANDLEd, IGNOREd, or dealt with through one of the mechanisms for programmatically handling conditions, the SYNCPOINT INITIATOR is backed out and then receives control back from CICS in accordance with condition handling rules.

The SYNCPOINT INITIATOR can then test its EIB in order to determine if the SYNCPOINT was successful. The SYNCPOINT INITIATOR's EIBRLDBK is set on (X'FF') by CICS, indicating that the SYNCPOINT INITIATOR has been ROLLED BACK. This causes any connected transactions that have issued a SYNCPOINT to be

ROLLED BACK as well. As with the SYNCPOINT INITIATOR, they abend or receive control back based upon handling of the ROLLED-BACK condition. For connected transactions that have not issued a SYNCPOINT, a ROLLBACK inidicator EIBSYNRB (X'FF') is set. The presence of EIBSYNRB indicates that the transaction should execute an EXEC CICS SYNCPOINT ROLLBACK. Transactions that can receive ROLLBACK indicators should test EIBSYNRB after every command.

Figure 12-4 illustrates the use of SYNCPOINT ROLLBACK. Transaction A is the SYNCPOINT INITIATOR. It SYNCPOINTS and in flow (1) a Prepare to Commit is sent by CICS. Transaction B receives this (EIBSYNC on) and executes a SYNCPOINT. This drives the exchanges (2) and (3) with Transaction C, as well as flow (4). However, Transaction E responds to EIBSYNC by saying EXEC CICS SYNCPOINT ROLLBACK. That causes the ROLLBACK to be propagated to B, C (flow marked 6), A (flow marked 7), and D (flow marked 8). D has not has not executed a SYNCPOINT. It is aware of the ROLLBACK through EIBSYNRB being set on. It, therefore, executes an EXEC CICS SYNCPOINT ROLLBACK, which propagates to F (flow marked 9), which likewise has not executed a SYNCPOINT and, therefore, receives an indication of the need to ROLLBACK in EIBSYNRB. F executes an EXEC CICS SYNCPOINT ROLLBACK and the entire distributed transaction is rolled back.

Fortunately, much of this happens automatically in CICS. Transactions that are involved in SYNCPOINT exchanges, however, MUST test the appropriate EIB fields and act accordingly. EIBSYNC should be tested after RECEIVE commands. EIBSYNRB should be tested after every command if SYNCPOINT ROLLBACK is used in the distributed transaction. EIBRLDBK indicates that a transaction has been rolled back and therefore can be tested subsequent to a SYNCPOINT to determine if the SYNCPOINT was successful or resulted in a ROLLBACK.

12.7.2   The Format of the SYNCPOINT Command

The format of the SYNCPOINT command is:

```
EXEC CICS SYNCPOINT
          ROLLBACK
```

Note the lack of command options, more specifically, the lack of a CONVID option for qualifying the SYNCPOINT. This means that

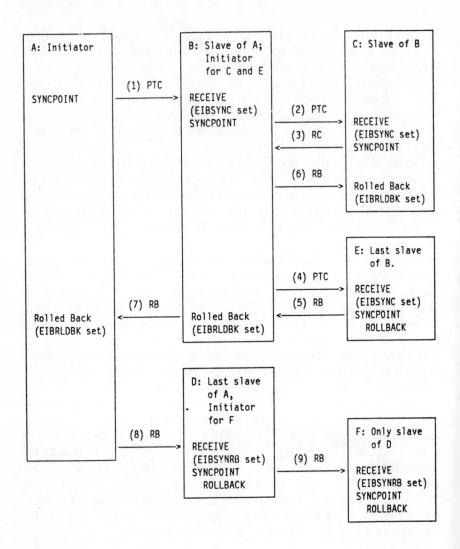

Figure 12-4 CICS flows for unsuccessful SYNCPOINT. Reprinted by permission from *CICS/MVS Version 2.1 Intercommunication Guide* © 1987, 1988 by International Business Machines Corporation.

SYNCPOINT applies to ALL SYNCLEVEL(2) conversations within a distributed transaction.

If the optional ROLLBACK is omitted, a SYNCPOINT operation is initiated. If ROLLBACK is included, a ROLLBACK is initiated.

12.7.3   Unusual Conditions of the SYNCPOINT Command

As described above, the ROLLEDBACK condition is applicable to the SYNCPOINT command. By default CICS terminates a ROLLED-BACK task unless the condition is explicitly handled. If a ROLLED-BACK occurs and the application program has handled the condition, EIBRLDBK can be tested. If EIBRLDBK=X'FF' ROLLBACK has taken place. Otherwise, the SYNCPOINT was successful.

12.7.4   Responding to a SYNCPOINT Request

A RECEIVE STATE SYNCPOINT SLAVE wakes up from a RECEIVE command to discover that EIBSYNC is set on. The trans-action can respond positively by executing a SYNCPOINT command or negatively by executing a: SYNCPOINT ROLLBACK, ISSUE ERROR or ISSUE ABEND. The recommended approach is to SYNCPOINT ROLLBACK, but CICS also supports ISSUE ERROR and ISSUE ABEND. The processing of SYNCPOINT ROLLBACK is described above.

When a SYNCPOINT SLAVE responds to a SYNCPOINT request with an ISSUE ERROR, the SYNCPOINT INITIATOR is abended and backed out by CICS. The abend/backout processing occurs for all of the connected conversations except the transaction that ISSUEd ERROR. The ISSUE ERROR places the transaction into the SEND STATE. Therefore, it is necessary to perform a SEND INVITE WAIT and a subsequent RECEIVE. After the RECEIVE command, EIB-SYNRB should be set on (X'FF'). This indicates that you must ex-ecute a SYNCPOINT ROLLBACK. Therefore, the transaction that is designed to ISSUE ERROR in response to a SYNCPOINT request will contain the following commands in the order illustrated:

```
EXEC CICS RECEIVE CONVID(WS-CONVID) . . .
IF EIBSYNC = HIGH-VALUES and everthing else ok
     EXEC CICS SYNCPOINT END-EXEC
     . . . rest of successful processing
```

```
ELSE
     EXEC CICS ISSUE ERROR CONVID(WS-CONVID) END-EXEC
     EXEC CICS SEND CONVID(WS-CONVID) INVITE WAIT
         END-EXEC
     EXEC CICS RECEIVE CONVID(WS-CONVID) . . . END-EXEC
     IF EIBSYNRB = HIGH-VALUES
         EXEC CICS SYNCPOINT ROLLBACK END-EXEC
         . . . rest of error processing.
```

The use of ISSUE ABEND as a negative response to a SYNCPOINT request results in a conversation abend. This can be intercepted by the SYNCPOINT INITIATOR as a TERMERR. However, ISSUE ABEND should never be used as a negative response to a SYNCPOINT by a transaction that has itself updated protected resources or who has one or more SYNCPOINT slaves who have updated protected resources. Therefore if process B in Figure 12-2 is to use an ISSUE ABEND as a response to a SYNCPOINT request from process A, neither process B nor process E should have modified protected resources.

12.7.5   Using SYNCPOINT ROLLBACK In Splendid Isolation

A transaction can execute a SYNCPOINT ROLLBACK request without having received a SYNCPOINT request (EIBSYNC set on subsequent to a RECEIVE). For example, if a process detects an unrecoverable error that spells doom for the entire distributed unit of work, it might be better to throw in the towel early and EXEC CICS SYNCPOINT ROLLBACK. This can be done when in the SEND or RECEIVE STATE. A successful SYNCPOINT ROLLBACK backs out the current logical unit of work (back to the last SYNCPOINT if one was executed or back to the start of the task). The request for ROLLBACK is sent to all SYNCLEVEL(2) conversation partners (EIBSYNRB set on) who in turn should SYNCPOINT ROLLBACK.

12.7.6   Executing SYNCPOINTs and State Changes

In order to determine what impact the SYNCPOINT or SYNCPOINT ROLLBACK have on a transaction's state, we need to look at the appropriate state diagrams. If we look at the SEND STATE diagram in Figure 10-4, we note that both the SYNCPOINT and the

SYNCPOINT ROLLBACK are listed as valid commands. Let's take the case of SYNCPOINT first. If a SEND STATE transaction issues a SYNCPOINT, it can be in one of two states at the completion of command execution. If the ROLLEDBACK condition has been trapped and EIBRLDBK indicates this, the transaction is now in the RECEIVE STATE. If, on the other hand, the program had not handled the ROLLEDBACK condition and a ROLLBACK occurred, the transaction has been abended. If the SYNCPOINT is successful, the transaction is still in the SEND STATE.

When a SEND STATE transaction issues a SYNCPOINT ROLLBACK, it should remain in the SEND STATE. But it is a good idea to verify this by testing EIBRECV. Why? If both transactions SYNCPOINT ROLLBACK concurrently and the ROLLBACKs cross, we have a *ROLLBACK race*. In that case, CICS places each transaction into the opposite state. Good design should be able to avoid this but if both partners can say ROLLBACK the possibility of a ROLLBACK race cannot be eliminated.

Figure 10-5 is the RECEIVE STATE diagram. You will note that the SYNCPOINT ROLLBACK command is included as a valid RECEIVE STATE command. At the conclusion of command execution the diagram indicates that the new state is 3 or the SEND STATE.

12.7.7   Receiving SYNCPOINTs and State Changes

Figure 10-5 illustrates the RECEIVE STATE diagram. Under the tests required subsequent to the RECEIVE command, EIBSYNC and EIBSYNCRB are listed. If EIBSYNC is set on the transaction's new state is 7. Figure 12-5 illustrates this state diagram. The state name is *RECEIVER TAKE SYNCPOINT*. The valid command responses SYNCPOINT, SYNCPOINT ROLLBACK, ISSUE ERROR, and ISSUE ABEND were discussed above. However, subsequent to these commands you cannot make assumptions about the transaction's state. Based upon the EIBSYNC response you execute, the tests in the state diagram should be coded.

Back in Figure 10-5, you will note that if EIBSYNC, which is tested first (since tests are made in order of listing in state diagram) is not set on, the next test is of EIBSYNRB. If this field is set on, then the transaction's state is 8. Figure 12-6 illustrates the state 8 diagram. This state is called RECEIVER ROLLBACK. Note that the only valid thing you can do is SYNCPOINT ROLLBACK.

STATE 7 MAPPED LUTYPE6.2 CONVERSATIONS		RECEIVER TAKE SYNCPOINT
Commands You Can Issue	What To Test (For EIBERRCD tests see the table on page 199)	New State
SYNCPOINT	EIBFREE (saved value)	10
	EIBRECV (saved value)	5
	Otherwise	3
SYNCPOINT ROLLBACK	-	3
ISSUE ERROR (This will cause the other transaction to abend if it issued SYNCPOINT, but not if it issued ISSUE PREPARE.)	(Now issue SEND INVITE WAIT followed by RECEIVE)	(3) then 5
ISSUE ABEND	-	10

Figure 12-5 State 7 — RECEIVER TAKE SYNCPOINT. Reprinted by permission from *CICS/MVS Version 2.1 Intercommunication Guide* © 1987, 1988 by International Business Machines Corporation.

12.7.8   The ISSUE PREPARE Command

The ISSUE PREPARE command is intended for use only in complex SYNCPOINTing situations. It allows a SEND STATE transaction to specifically query one of its conversation partners regarding its ability to SYNCPOINT.

STATE 8 MAPPED LUTYPE6.2 CONVERSATIONS		RECEIVER TAKE ROLLBACK
Commands You Can Issue	What To Test (For EIBERRCD tests see the table on page 199)	New State
SYNCPOINT ROLLBACK	-	5

Figure 12-6 State 6 — RECEIVER TAKE ROLLBACK. Reprinted by permission from *CICS/MVS Version 2.1 Intercommunication Guide* © 1987, 1988 by International Business Machines Corporation.

12.7.9   The Format of the ISSUE PREPARE Command

The format of the ISSUE PREPARE command is as follows.

```
EXEC CICS ISSUE PREPARE CONVID(field-name)
```

The CONVID option is used to specifically name the conversation to which the ISSUE PREPARE pertains. A transaction ISSUing PREPARE must be in the SEND STATE with regard to the conversation named in the CONVID option.

12.7.10   Receiving the ISSUE PREPARE

A RECEIVE STATE transaction tests EIBSYNC in the same manner as described above for SYNCPOINT. The SYNCPOINT and the ISSUE PREPARE look the same to the remote transaction. The responses to an ISSUE PREPARE request (EIBSYNC set on) are the same as for SYNCPOINT. In other words, the transaction can respond SYNCPOINT, SYNCPOINT ROLLBACK, ISSUE ERROR, or ISSUE ABEND.

12.7.11   Checking the Response Subsequent to ISSUE PREPARE

The EIBERR field is tested subsequent to ISSUE PREPARE. If any error response was executed by the remote process, EIBERR is set on. Therefore, if EIBERR is not set on upon return from ISSUE PREPARE execution, the other process has issued a SYNCPOINT. You are then obliged to SYNCPOINT or SYNCPOINT ROLLBACK so that the remote process either commits or backs out. You do not have to issue the SYNCPOINT or SYNCPOINT ROLLBACK immediately, but one or the other has to be done.

If EIBERR is set on, other fields in the EIB can be tested to determine the type of error response. If EIBERRCD = X'08890000' the remote process performed an ISSUE ERROR. If EIBERRCD = X'08640000' the remote process executed an ISSUE ABEND. If the remote process did a SYNCPOINT ROLLBACK, EIBERRCD = X'08240000' and EIBSYNRB is set on. You should also test EIBFREE and EIBRECV to determine definitively the conversation's state.

12.8　SUMMARY OF EIB FIELDS

The EIB fields that are used during APPC mapped conversations are listed below. Programs that perform distributed transactions must constantly be testing EIB fields subsequent to conversation-related commands. It is recommended that the contents of these fields be saved in a conversation-unique work area in program dynamic storage subsequent to appropriate commands. The status fields are described below as being set on (X'FF') or set off (X'00').

FOR ALL APPC TRANSACTIONS REGARDLESS OF SYNCLEVEL

EIBRSRCE should be saved subsequent to an ALLOCATE command as the field then contains the unique conversation ID assigned by CICS.

EIBTRMID contains the Back-End Transaction's principal resource name. If a Front-End Transaction is initiated via an ATI request that names a remote SYSIDNT, there is no need to perform an ALLOCATE because the transaction is started in STATE 2. The use of CONVID is optional for commands pertaining to a principal facility and the name of the principal facility is contained in EIBTRMID.

EIBCOMPL is tested subsequent to RECEIVE NOTRUNCATE to determine when all data has been RECEIVEd from CICS. CICS sets this field on when all data has been received.

EIBNODAT can be tested to determine if data was RECEIVED. For APPC mapped conversations it is valid to SEND without including FROM and LENGTH options. Therefore, RECEIVE may not yield data. If this field is set on subsequent to a RECEIVE, there is no data.

EIBRECV is used to indicate a transaction's RECEIVE/SEND state. If set on, the transaction is in the RECEIVE state. This field should be tested after every RECEIVE command and in any other context in which a transaction's state may have altered. For example, receipt of ISSUE ERROR places the transaction in the RECEIVE STATE. So if EIBERR is set on, EIBRECV should be tested in most cases.

EIBERR is set on to indicate a conversation-related error such as a remote process ISSUE ABEND, ISSUE ERROR, or SYNCPOINT ROLLBACK. This field should be tested after all conversation-related commands. The exact cause of EIBERR can be ascertained from an examination of EIBERRCD.

EIBERRCD is set with a specific error code which identifies why EIBERR is set on as follows.

> X'08890000' - ISSUE ERROR received
> X'08640000' - ISSUE ABEND received
> X'08240000' - SYNCPOINT ROLLBACK received

EIBSIG is set on to indicate remote process execution of ISSUE SIGNAL. This is normally used by a RECEIVE STATE transaction to request a state change. If used in an application, EIBSIG should be tested after each conversation command.

EIBFREE is set on to indicate that the session must be freed. The remote process has performed a FREE command or a SEND LAST WAIT and the upshot is that the End Bracket has been generated and sent. When End Bracket has been transmitted, the conversation is over. As a great man once said, "It's not over till it's over." When End Bracket has been transmitted, it's over. Therefore, the session must be freed either by executing the FREE command or RETURNing to CICS.

ADDITIONAL EIB FIELDS FOR TRANSACTIONS OPERATING AT SYNCLEVEL 1 OR 2

EIBCONF is set on by a remote process SEND CONFIRM seeking an application dependent confirmation. EIBCONF should be tested after each RECEIVE if this protocol is used in the application.

ADDITIONAL EIB FIELDS FOR TRANSACTIONS OPERATING AT SYNCLEVEL 2

EIBSYNC is set on to indicate a SYNCPOINT/ISSUE PREPARE request. This field should be tested after each RECEIVE command.

EIBSYNRB is set on to indicate the need for a SYNCPOINT ROLLBACK. If this command is used in an application, EIB-

SYNRB should be tested after every command pertaining to the conversation.

EIBRLDBK is set on to indicate the failure of a SYNCPOINT. This indication means that the task has been ROLLED BACK.

12.9 SUMMARY

In this chapter we have completed our examination of the APPC mapped conversation commands for use in CICS application programs performing Distributed Transaction Processing. These commands can be thought of as tools that can be used in the design and implementation of application protocols for distributed applications.

REVIEW EXERCISES

Provide a short answer to each of the following.

1. What does the ISSUE CONFIRMATION mean when used in an application program?
2. How does CICS inform a receiving transaction of a request for confirmation?
3. What does it mean if EIBFREE is set on?
4. When would a transaction test EIBCOMPL?
5. If appropriate to conversation protocols, when should EIB-SYNRB be tested?
6. How does one test a response to a SEND CONFIRM?
7. What is an ISSUE ERROR race?
8. What can be done to detect that a conversation partner has executed an ISSUE ABEND?
9. What is the purpose of the ISSUE SIGNAL command?
10. When is it appropriate to use ISSUE PREPARE?
11. What is a SYNCPOINT INITIATOR?
12. How can a transaction detect that a conversation partner has executed a SYNCPOINT?
13. What is the ROLLEDBACK condition?
14. How can a SYNCPOINT INITIATOR determine if the SYNCPOINT has been successful?
15. What should a transaction do when EIBSYNRB is set on?

16. Which EIB fields should be tested subsequent to a RECEIVE command and in what order should the tests be made?
17. What conditions cause EIBERR to be set on? When should this field be tested?
18. What does it mean if EIBNODAT is set on subsequent to a RECEIVE command?

ANSWERS TO REVIEW EXERCISES

Provide a short answer to each of the following.

1. *What does the ISSUE CONFIRMATION mean when used in an application program?*

   The ISSUE CONFIRMATION means that a conversation partner is responding positively to a request for CONFIRMation. What the confirmation exchange is all about in terms of the conversation is totally dependent upon the conversation.

2. *How does CICS inform a receiving transaction of a request for confirmation?*

   The EIBCONF field is set on to X'FF' subsequent to a RECEIVE command.

3. *What does it mean if EIBFREE is set on?*

   It means that it is necessary to FREE the session. Either the transaction can execute a FREE Command or RETURN immediately to CICS. Essentially, if EIBFREE is set on, the End Bracket Indicator has been received so the conversation is over.

4. *When would a transaction test EIBCOMPL?*

   Subsequent to a RECEIVE NOTRUNCATE.

5. *If appropriate to conversation protocols, when should EIB-SYNRB be tested?*

   EIBSYNRB, which indicates that a conversation partner has issued a SYNCPOINT ROLLBACK, should be tested after every conversation-related command if appropriate to the inter-program protocols.

6. *How does one test a response to a SEND CONFIRM?*

The response to a SEND CONFIRM would involve testing EIBERR. If EIBERR is equal to X'00', then a positive confirmation was issued by the conversation partner. However, if EIBERR is set on to X'FF', then the response was negative. In that case EIBERRCD can be tested to determine the exact response. If EIBERRCD is X'08890000', then ISSUE ERROR was used. If EIBERRCD is X'08640000', then the response was ISSUE ABEND. If EIBERRCD is X'08240000', then SYNCPOINT ROLLBACK was issued.

7. *What is an ISSUE ERROR race?*

An ISSUE ERROR race occurs when two conversation partners both ISSUE ERROR so that their requests cross. It is, therefore, a good policy to test EIBRECV to determine the transaction's state subsequent to the execution of an ISSUE ERROR Command. If EIBRECV is equal to X'00', then the transaction is in the SEND state and its ISSUE ERROR was successful.

8. *What can be done to detect that a conversation partner has executed an ISSUE ABEND?*

If the ISSUE ABEND is requested by a conversation partner, the conversation is abended. Therefore, if an ISSUE ABEND is to be intercepted, the transaction that might receive it must handle the TERMERR condition. When TERMERR occurs, the EIBERR and EIBERRCD can be tested to verify that the ISSUE ABEND was executed. However, the very first thing to do is test EIBFREE and FREE the session.

9. *What is the purpose of the ISSUE SIGNAL command?*

The ISSUE SIGNAL command is used by a RECEIVE STATE transaction to request a flip-flop into the SEND STATE. CICS sets on EIBSIG to the transaction that receives an ISSUE SIGNAL so if the ISSUE SIGNAL is used in a conversation, this field should be tested after all conversation-related commands.

10. *When is it appropriate to use ISSUE PREPARE?*

ISSUE PREPARE is appropriate to complex SYNCPOINTing situations. This command is intended to query conversation partners regarding their ability to SYNCPOINT before the SYNCPOINT is taken by the SYNCPOINT INITIATOR. Once the SYNCPOINT is taken, it is propagated throughout all of the conversations involved in the distributed transaction.

11. *What is a SYNCPOINT INITIATOR?*

The SYNCPOINT INITIATOR is the transaction that initiates SYNCPOINT processing. In any distributed transaction, there should be one SYNCPOINT INITIATOR.

12. *How can a transaction detect that a conversation partner has executed a SYNCPOINT?*

CICS sets on EIBSYNC. This EIB field should be tested after every RECEIVE command because it is necessary to respond appropriately.

13. *What is the ROLLEDBACK condition?*

The ROLLEDBACK condition pertains to the SYNCPOINT command. ROLLEDBACK indicates that a conversation partner has responded to a SYNCPOINT request with a SYNCPOINT ROLLBACK. Unless the ROLLEDBACK condition has been handled, the SYNCPOINTing transaction is abended.

14. *How can a SYNCPOINT INITIATOR determine if the SYNCPOINT has been successful?*

The SYNCPOINT INITIATOR handles the condition ROLLED-BACK and when control is returned subsequent to the SYNCPOINT command the EIBRLDBK field can be tested. If this field is set on, then the SYNCPOINT was unsuccessful and the transaction has been rolled back itself.

15. *What should a transaction do when EIBSYNRB is set on?*

EXEC CICS SYNCPOINT ROLLBACK

16. *Which EIB fields should be tested subsequent to a RECEIVE command, and in what order should the tests be made?*

The following fields should be tested in order: EIBCOMPL, EIBCONF, EIBSYNC, EIBSYNRB, EIBFREE, and EIBRECV. This information is in the RECEIVE STATE diagram. Additionally EIBERR should be tested if appropriate to the conversation.

17. *What conditions cause EIBERR to be set on? When should this field be tested?*

EIBERR is set on when a conversation partner executes any of the following commands. EXEC CICS ISSUE ERROR, EXEC CICS ISSUE ABEND or EXEC CICS SYNCPOINT ROLLBACK. This field should be tested after every conversation-related command when the conversation protocols define the use of any of the three commands named above.

18. *What does it mean if EIBNODAT is set on subsequent to a RECEIVE command?*

EIBNODAT is set on when no data has been RECEIVEd. In this case, the transaction has received only conversation indicators.

13

LUTYPE 6.2 Unmapped Conversations

13.1 INTRODUCTION

The LUTYPE 6.2 is an any-to-any connection. As such, it must provide many application facilities. CICS Function Shipping is an example of a "facility" provided within LUTYPE6 in general. Function Shipping makes the location of resources transparent to application programs. However, particular products need not support all of the functionality that is architected within the LUTYPE 6.2. The LUTYPE 6.2 is intended as an any-to-any connection in the sense that an LUTYPE 6.2 device level product can interface as well. Consequently, there is a minimum support level for product implementations of LUTYPE 6.2, and it is significantly less than the level of support to be found in a host system level product like CICS.

In order to implement LUTYPE 6.2 it is not mandatory to support the "mapped" conversations that we examined in the last three chapters. It is, however, necessary to support the base level conversations that we will be examining in this chapter. Base or unmapped conversations represent the minimum support level for implementation of the LUTYPE 6.2. Therefore, base/unmapped conversations represent a kind of common denominator of any-to-any connections. Using the application programming facilities provided in CICS for LUTYPE 6.2 unmapped conversations, programs may be developed only in assembler language. There is no support for COBOL or PL/I.

13.1.1   The Unmapped Conversation Data Stream

The LUTYPE 6.2 utilizes the *SNA-defined Generalized Data Stream (GDS)*. The Generalized Data Stream contains user data and/or structured fields. A structured field contains information which can be user data in a particular format or information about a control function. In mapped conversations, the data stream consists solely of user data which is transmitted between the logical units. There are no structured fields and, therefore, the characteristics of the SNA Generalized Data Stream are "transparent" to the application program engaged in a mapped conversation. This is not the case in unmapped conversations. The data stream used for unmapped conversations consists of structured fields. Structured fields have a header which provides length and ID information. The structured field header contains an LL field which is 2 bytes in length and a 1- or 2-byte IDentification field.

The LL field is a length indicator that correctly identifies the length of the entire structured field. The ID field uniquely identifies the contents of the field. So, if the field contains data in a particular format or information about a control function, this is identified in the ID field. The data stream used for unmapped conversations thus consists of data and identifiying information contained in GDS headers. Based upon the conversation partner's requirements regarding structured fields, it is up to the CICS LUTYPE 6.2 unmapped application program to correctly format and interpret the GDS headers that precede structured fields. The GDS IDs are documented in the IBM Reference Manual entitled *Format and Protocols Reference Manual: Architecture Logic for LUTYPE 6.2* SC30-3269. Another manual that is handy to have when coding unmapped conversations is *Transaction Programmer's Reference Manual for LU Type 6.2* GC30-3084.

13.1.2   Structured Field Boundary Requirements

For certain commands or command options, it is necessary to ensure that the data stream passed to CICS consists of entire structured fields, i.e., that the data stream is on a structured field boundary.

For example, if a program executes an unmapped SEND LAST, SEND INVITE, or SEND CONFIRM, any data presented to CICS must fall on a structured field boundary. Furthermore, data presented up to a SYNCPOINT command must also be on a structured field boundary. However, for a straight SEND without LAST, INVITE, or CONFIRM, the data presented to CICS need not fall on a structured field boundary. So, in the context of executing certain commands, it is required that the application programmer be aware of exactly what data has been passed to CICS and, if appropriate, what data is contained within an output data area.

13.1.3   Unmapped Conversations and the State Diagrams

Within the context of using unmapped conversation commands, it is absolutely necessary for the application programmer to be aware of and explicitly control the transaction's state with regard to the conversation. CICS does not supply SNA indicators that are implied but not directly created by the application program. For example, in mapped conversations, if a SEND command without either WAIT or INVITE is followed by a RECEIVE, CICS generates the Change-Direction indicator and the implied WAIT. In an unmapped conversation, failure to explicitly code the INVITE and WAIT options would result in a state error. The state error would reflect the fact that no Change-Direction Indicator was sent to the remote process. The state diagrams are important in the coding of mapped conversations but they are absolutely critical in programming unmapped ones. The state diagrams for unmapped conversations are illustrated in Figures 13-1 through 13-10. The state names are the same as for mapped conversations. When we discuss the unmapped conversation commands, we will be referring back to the state diagrams.

13.1.4   Unmapped Conversation Commands and Data Areas

The unmapped conversation is carried on using EXEC CICS GDS commands, which by and large are very similar to the EXEC CICS commands that are used for mapped conversations. Figure 13-11 lists the unmapped EXEC CICS GDS commands. Note that a GDS ASSIGN command is included. This command is used to obtain the CONVersation ID of a transaction's PRINCipal facility. A CONVID is required for all EXEC CICS GDS commands even when the conversation is the transaction's principal facility. Therefore, a Back-

STATE 1 UNMAPPED LUTYPE6.2 CONVERSATIONS		SESSION NOT ALLOCATED
Commands You Can Issue	What To Test (For CDBERRCD tests see the table on page 222)	New State
ALLOCATE [NOQUEUE] *	RETCODE for SYSIDERR (01 .. ..) or SYSBUSY (01 04 04) *	1
	Otherwise (conversation identifier returned in CONVID data area)	2

* If you want your program to wait until a session is available, omit the NOQUEUE option of the ALLOCATE command.

If you want control to be returned to your program if a session is not immediately available, specify NOQUEUE on the ALLOCATE command and test RETCODE for SYSBUSY.

Figure 13-1 State 1 — SESSION NOT ALLOCATED. Reprinted by permission from *CICS/MVS Version 2.1 Intercommunication Guide* © 1987, 1988 by International Business Machines Corporation.

End Transaction coded as an unmapped conversation would use the GDS ASSIGN to obtain its CONVersation ID from CICS. Note, also, that the CONVERSE command is not included in Figure 13-11. There is no unmapped CONVERSE command.

STATE 2 UNMAPPED LUTYPE6.2 CONVERSATIONS		SESSION ALLOCATED
Commands You Can Issue	What To Test (For CDBERRCD tests see the table on page 222)	New State
CONNECT PROCESS	RETCODE for INVREQ, NOTALLOC, or LENGERR	2
	–	3
FREE	RETCODE for INVREQ or NOTALLOC	2
	–	1

Figure 13-2 State 2 — SESSION ALLOCATED. Reprinted by permission from *CICS/MVS Version 2.1 Intercommunication Guide* © 1987, 1988 by International Business Machines Corporation.

STATE 3 UNMAPPED LUTYPE6.2 CONVERSATIONS		SEND STATE
Commands You Can Issue	What To Test (For CDBERRCD tests see the table on page 222)	New State
SEND	–	3
SEND INVITE	–	4
SEND INVITE WAIT	–	5
SEND LAST	–	9
SEND LAST WAIT	–	10
SEND CONFIRM (SYNCLEVEL 1 or 2 only)	–	3
SEND INVITE CONFIRM (SYNCLEVEL 1 or 2 only)	–	5
SEND LAST CONFIRM (SYNCLEVEL 1 or 2 only)	–	10
ISSUE PREPARE (SYNCLEVEL 2 only) Note: If a negative response is received, CDBERR and CDBERRCD will also be set	CDBSYNRB	8
	CDBFREE	10
	Otherwise	3
SYNCPOINT (SYNCLEVEL 2 only) Note: This is not a GDS command.	EIBRLDBK (or ROLLEDBACK condition)	5
	Otherwise (transaction will ABEND if SYNCPOINT fails)	3
SYNCPOINT ROLLBACK (SYNCLEVEL 2 only)	(transaction will ABEND if ROLLBACK fails)	3
WAIT	–	3
ISSUE ERROR	–	3
ISSUE ABEND	–	10

Figure 13-3 State 3 — SEND STATE. Reprinted by permission from *CICS/MVS Version 2.1 Intercommunication Guide* © 1987, 1988 by International Business Machines Corporation.

STATE 4 UNMAPPED LUTYPE6.2 CONVERSATIONS RECEIVE PENDING AFTER INVITE		
Commands You Can Issue	What To Test (For CDBERRCD tests see the table on page 222)	New State
WAIT	–	5
ISSUE ERROR	CDBFREE	10
	Otherwise	3
ISSUE ABEND	–	10
SYNCPOINT (SYNCLEVEL 2 only)	(transaction will ABEND if SYNCPOINT fails)	5
SYNCPOINT ROLLBACK (SYNCLEVEL 2 only)	(transaction will ABEND if ROLLBACK fails)	3

Figure 13-4 State 4 — RECEIVING PENDING AFTER INVITE. Reprinted by permission from *CICS/MVS Version 2.1 Intercommunication Guide* © 1987, 1988 by International Business Machines Corporation.

One major difference between mapped and unmapped commands is that unmapped commands do not cause CICS to place information into the Execute Interface Block. However, the transaction needs conversation status information. It is, therefore, necessary for the application program to contain a 24-byte data area that is explicitly named in appropriate EXEC CICS GDS commands. This data area is called the "CONVDATA" area, and there is a CICS copy statement, DFHCDBLK, that defines the fields in the CONVDATA area. CICS returns status information that would be placed into the EIB for mapped conversations into the CONVDATA area for unmapped commands, but it is necessary for the command to explicitly name the CONVDATA area. The fields within the CICS-supplied copy book are listed in Figure 13-12. As you can see, the field names used are similar to the EIB conversation-related fields except that in the CONVDATA fields, the fields begin a prefix of CDB instead of EIB.

EXEC CICS GDS commands do not raise CICS conditions. **The HANDLE CONDITION or IGNORE CONDITION statements do not have an effect upon EXEC CICS GDS command execution.** Control is always returned to the application program after these commands. That does not mean that errors cannot happen. What it does mean is that the application programmer must explicitly test a

STATE 5 UNMAPPED LUTYPE6.2 CONVERSATIONS		RECEIVE STATE
Commands You Can Issue	What To Test (For CDBERRCD tests see the table on page 222)	New State
RECEIVE	CDBCOMPL *	–
	CDBCONF (SYNCLEVEL 1 or 2 only)	6
	CDBSYNC (SYNCLEVEL 2 only)	7
	CDBSYNRB (SYNCLEVEL 2 only)	8
	CDBFREE	10
	CDBRECV	5
	Otherwise	3
SYNCPOINT ROLLBACK (SYNCLEVEL 2 only)	(transaction will ABEND if ROLLBACK fails)	3
ISSUE ERROR	CDBFREE	10
	Otherwise	3
ISSUE ABEND	–	10

* A zero value in CDBCOMPL indicates incomplete data. CICS saves the
remaining data for retrieval by subsequent RECEIVE commands. CDBCOMPL is
set when the last part of the data is passed back.

Figure 13-5 State 5 — RECEIVE STATE. Reprinted by permission from
CICS/MVS Version 2.1 Intercommunication Guide © 1987, 1988 by International
Business Machines Corporation.

return code subsequent to every EXEC CICS GDS command. To this
end, the application program must contain a 6-byte RETCODE field
into which CICS returns a code. The code *must* be tested if you want
to know if the command worked properly. The RETCODE field is
explicitly named in *all* EXEC CICS GDS commands. Figure 13-13
lists the common return codes placed in the RETCODE field subsequent to EXEC CICS GDS commands. Different "error" codes cor-
responding to mapped conversation condition names are returned
and the error codes are relevant to specific commands, just as condition handling is specific to particular commands.

STATE 6 UNMAPPED LUTYPE6.2 CONVERSATIONS		RECEIVER ISSUE CONFIRMATION
Commands You Can Issue	What To Test (For CDBERRCD tests see the table on page 222)	New State
ISSUE CONFIRMATION	CDBFREE (saved value)	10
	CDBRECV (saved value)	5
	Otherwise	3
ISSUE ERROR	CDBFREE (saved value)	3
	Otherwise	3
ISSUE ABEND	-	10

Figure 13-6 State 6 — RECEIVER ISSUE CONFIRMATION. Reprinted by permission from *CICS/MVS Version 2.1 Intercommunication Guide* © 1987, 1988 by International Business Machines Corporation.

13.1.5   Some Conclusions About Base/Unmapped Conversations

All in all, you should be getting the distinct impression that the unmapped conversation is a rather lower-level conversation than the ones held using mapped commands. And that impression is indeed

STATE 7 UNMAPPED LUTYPE6.2 CONVERSATIONS		RECEIVER TAKE SYNCPOINT
Commands You Can Issue	What To Test (For CDBERRCD tests see the table on page 222)	New State
SYNCPOINT	CDBFREE (saved value)	10
	CDBRECV (saved value)	5
	Otherwise	3
SYNCPOINT ROLLBACK	-	3
ISSUE ERROR	-	3
ISSUE ABEND	-	10

Figure 13-7 State 7 — RECEIVER TAKE SYNCPOINT. Reprinted by permission from *CICS/MVS Version 2.1 Intercommunication Guide* © 1987, 1988 by International Business Machines Corporation.

STATE 8 UNMAPPED LUTYPE6.2 CONVERSATIONS	RECEIVER TAKE ROLLBACK	
Commands You Can Issue	What To Test (For CDBERRCD tests see the table on page 222)	New State
SYNCPOINT ROLLBACK	–	5

Figure 13-8 State 8 — RECEIVER TAKE ROLLBACK. Reprinted by permission from *CICS/MVS Version 2.1 Intercommunication Guide* © 1987, 1988 by International Business Machines Corporation.

correct. Well, why would one want to use unmapped commands rather than mapped ones? For certain device-level products, LUTYPE 6.2 terminals, there is a requirement for the structured fields that are created and passed within the context of unmapped conversations. In other words, not all device-level products support mapped conversations. The program conversing with Displaywriter and the 8815 Scanmaster must use the unmapped interface because with these products there is support only for unmapped conversations. For other device-level products such as the System/38, it is possible to hold a mapped conversation. Obviously, the base conversation interface is used only when required.

STATE 9 UNMAPPED LUTYPE6.2 CONVERSATIONS	FREE PENDING AFTER SEND LAST	
Commands You Can Issue	What To Test (For CDBERRCD tests see the table on page 222)	New State
WAIT	–	10
SEND CONFIRM (no data) (SYNCLEVEL 1 or 2 only)	–	10
SYNCPOINT (SYNCLEVEL 2 only)	–	10
SYNCPOINT ROLLBACK (SYNCLEVEL 2 only)	–	10
ISSUE ABEND	–	10

Figure 13-9 State 9 — FREE PENDING AFTER SEND LAST. Reprinted by permission from *CICS/MVS Version 2.1 Intercommunication Guide* © 1987. 1988 by International Business Machines Corporation.

STATE 10 UNMAPPED LUTYPE6.2 CONVERSATIONS		FREE SESSION
Commands You Can Issue	What To Test (For CDBERRCD tests see the table on page 222)	New State
FREE	–	1

Figure 13-10 State 6 — FREE SESSION. Reprinted by permission from *CICS/MVS Version 2.1 Intercommunication Guide* © 1987, 1988 by International Business Machines Corporation.

13.2 CICS COMMANDS FOR LUTYPE 6.2 UNMAPPED CONVERSATIONS

The LUTYPE 6.2 CICS commands are an implementation of the protocol boundary verbs defined for LUTYPE 6.2 base or unmapped conversations within System Network Architecture. Command options that have been discussed in depth in the prior chapters will be only briefly described here, so it is assumed that the reader has completed the chapters on mapped conversations.

13.3 The GDS ALLOCATE Command

The GDS ALLOCATE command is used by a Front-End Transaction to acquire use of a session to a remote system. The GDS ALLOCATE command requests an alternate facility from CICS. The conversation state for this transaction at this point in processing is state 1 — Session Not Allocated. Figure 13-1 illustrates the state diagram for state 1. According to this state diagram there is only one command that can be used in state 1 and that is the GDS ALLOCATE command to obtain use of a session.

13.3.1 GDS ALLOCATE Command Format

The format of the GDS ALLOCATE command is as follows:

```
EXEC CICS GDS ALLOCATE
          SYSID(sys-name)
          CONVID(data-area-name)
          RETCODE(6-byte-retcode-field)
          MODENAME(name-of-modeset)
          NOQUEUE
```

COMMAND	FUNCTION
EXEC CICS GDS ALLOCATE	Used to request an alternate facility.
EXEC CICS GDS CONNECT PROCESS	Used to initiate a remote process.
EXEC CICS GDS ASSIGN	Used by a Back-End Transaction to obtain its CONVID.
EXEC CICS GDS EXTRACT PROCESS	Used by a Back-End Transaction to obtain information from the ATTACH FMH.
EXEC CICS GDS SEND	Used to SEND data and conversation indicators.
EXEC CICS GDS WAIT	Used to force transmission of buffered data and indicators.
EXEC CICS GDS RECEIVE	Used to RECEIVE data and conversation indicators.
EXEC CICS GDS ISSUE CONFIRMATION	Used as a positive response to a CONFIRMation request.
EXEC CICS GDS ISSUE ERROR	Used to signal an error such as a negative response to a request for CONFIRMation.
EXEC CICS GDS ISSUE ABEND	Used to signal an error such as a negative response to a request for CONFIRMation.
EXEC CICS GDS ISSUE SIGNAL	Used to issue a SIGNAL to request being placed into the SEND State.
EXEC CICS GDS ISSUE PREPARE	Used to prepare a conversation partner for a SYNCPOINT exchange.
EXEC CICS GDS FREE	Used to FREE a session.
EXEC CICS SYNCPOINT	Used to initiate SYNCPOINT or COMMIT protocol exchanges.

Figure 13-11 Summary of unmapped conversation commands.

The SYSID option is used to provide the SYSIDNT of the remote system as it is defined in the local CICS Terminal Control Table.

The CONVID option names a 4-byte data area. Subsequent to allocating the session, CICS returns the CONVersation ID to this field. Since the EIB is not affected by EXEC CICS GDS commands, EIBRSRCE will not contain the name of the conversation. CICS places the name into the program-specified CONVID field.

FIELDS SET ON (X'ff') OR OFF (X'00') AS CONVERSATION INDICATORS

FIELD NAME	FIELD DESCRIPTION	FIELD USE
CDBCOMPL	DS C	Set on to indicate data is complete when NOTRUNCATE is used.
CDBSYNC	DS C	Indicates that a SYNCPOINT must be taken when set on.
CDBFREE	DS C	Indicates that a FREE is mandated when set on.
CDBRECV	DS C	Indicates RECEIVE STATE when set on.
CDBSIG	DS C	Indicates receipt of a SIGNAL when set on.
CDBCONF	DS C	Indicates receipt of a SEND CONFIRM when set on.
CDBERR	DS C	Indicates receipt of conversation error indicator when set on.
CDBERRCD	DS CL4	Contains qualifying information when CDBERR is set on.
CDBSYNRB	DS C	Indicates receipt of a ROLLBACK request when set on.
CDBRSVD	DS CL12	Reserved.

Figure 13-12 Fields contained in CONVDATA DSECT.

The RETCODE option names a 6-byte data field into which CICS places a return code. Since EXEC CICS GDS commands do not raise unusual conditions as do other CICS commands, we must provide a RETCODE field and interrogate the field subsequent to command execution.

The MODENAME option permits the specification of a modename for the GDS ALLOCATE request. The modename relates to a collection of sessions with the remote system. Associated with the modeset name is a VTAM class of service.

The NOQUEUE option indicates that CICS is not to queue your request for a session.

```
00 .. ..    NORMAL RETURN CODE

01 .. ..    SYSIDERR ERROR

01 04 ..    ALLOCATE FAILURE
01 04 04       SYSBUSY (NO BOUND CONTENTION WINNER AVAILABLE)
01 04 08       MODENAME NOT KNOWN ON THIS SYSTEM
01 04 0C       ATTEMPT TO USE RESERVED MODENAME SNASVCMG
01 04 14       AVAILABLE COUNT ZERO FOR THIS MODEGROUP

01 08 ..    SYSID IS OUT OF SERVICE
01 08 00       LOCAL QUEUEING WAS NOT ATTEMPTED
01 08 04       LOCAL QUEUEING DID NOT SUCCEED

01 0C ..    SYSID IS NOT KNOWN IN TCT
01 0C 00       SYSID NAME IS NOT KNOWN
01 0C 04       SYSID NAME IS NOT THAT OF A TCTSE
01 0C 08       SYSID.MODENAME IS NOT KNOWN
01 0C 0C       SYSID.PROFILE IS NOT KNOWN

03 .. ..    INVREQ ERROR
03 00 ..       SESSION IS NOT DEFINED AS LU6.2
03 04 ..       CONVERSATION LEVEL IS WRONG
03 08 ..       STATE ERROR
03 0C ..       SYNCLEVEL CAN NOT BE SUPPORTED
03 10 ..       LLCOUNT ERROR
03 14 ..       INVALID REQUEST
03 18 ..       TPN SEND CHECK FAILED

04 .. ..    NOTALLOC ERROR

05 .. ..    LENGERR ERROR
```

Figure 13-13 Values set in RETCODE field. Reprinted by permission from *CICS/MVS Version 2.1 Intercommunication Guide* © 1987, 1988 by International Business Machines Corporation.

13.3.2   Error Conditions and the GDS ALLOCATE Command

The "error" conditions associated with the GDS ALLOCATE command include SYSBUSY and SYSIDERR.

The SYSBUSY condition indicates that the requested system is busy. Unless the NOQUEUE option has been included in the GDS

ALLOCATE command, the SYSBUSY indication is returned in the RETCODE field. The setting for SYSBUSY is listed in Figure 13-13.

The SYSIDERR indicates an error related to the SYSIDNT named which precludes CICS providing a session to the task. Sessions with the remote system may all be out of service or the SYSIDNT named in the SYSID option may not be defined in the Terminal Control Table. This condition can occasionally happen because an incorrect modename is specified in the MODENAME option of the GDS ALLO-CATE command. Figure 13-13, which lists the RETCODE field contents, illustrates the values that can be used to interrogate the RET-CODE field and determine that SYSIDERR has occurred and the type of SYSIDERR.

13.3.3   Example of GDS ALLOCATE Command Coding

The following code is an example of a GDS ALLOCATE command.

```
DFHEISTG DSECT
      .
CONVID1     DS    CL4
RCODE       DS    CL6
      .
BASESAMP     CSECT
             EXEC CICS GDS ALLOCATE SYSID('CIC1')          X
                  CONVID(CONVID1)                          X
                  RETCODE(RCODE)                           X
                  NOQUEUE
             CLI  RCODE,X'00'
             BNE  ABEND1
* CICS PLACES THE CONVERSATION NAME INTO CONVID1.
```

The state 1 diagram shown in Figure 13-1 indicates that subsequent to execution of a successful GDS ALLOCATE, the new transaction state is state 2. If we look at Figure 13-2, we see that there are two possible commands that can be validly executed when in state 2. The commands are GDS FREE to free or release the session and GDS CONNECT PROCESS to initiate a remote process.

13.4   THE GDS CONNECT PROCESS COMMAND

The GDS CONNECT PROCESS command is used to initiate the Back-End Transaction. Additionally, GDS CONNECT PROCESS can be used to pass initialization parameters to the Back-End Transaction and specify a required synchronization level for the conversation.

13.4.1   GDS CONNECT PROCESS Command Format

The format of the GDS CONNECT PROCESS command is as follows:

```
EXEC CICS GDS CONNECT PROCESS
          PROCNAME(name-of-process)
          PROCLENGTH(length-of-procname)
          CONVID(conversation-name)
          SYNCLEVEL(sync-level)
          PIPLIST(name-of-PIP-data-area)
          PIPLENGTH(total-length-piplist)
          CONVDATA(24-byte-data-area-name)
          RETCODE(6-byte-return-code-field)
```

The PROCNAME option provides the name of the remote process. CICS permits process names to be as long as 32 characters in support of non-CICS products. User process names cannot begin with hex values in the range of X'00' through X'3F' as these are reserved for SNA architected process names.

The PROCLENGTH defines the length of the PROCNAME.

The CONVID option provides the CONVersation ID of the conversation to which this CONNECT PROCESS relates.

The SYNCLEVEL indicates the synchronization level required for this conversation. The valid SYNCLEVEL values are 0, 1, or 2. For a complete explanation of SYNCLEVELs see the discussion of the mapped version of this command in Chapter 10.

The PIPLIST names a data area containing PIP data. For a complete explanation of PIP data see the discussion of PIP data in Chapter 10.

The PIPLENGTH option defines the total length of PIP data.

The CONVDATA option names the 24-byte CONVersation DATA area used by CICS to return conversation-related information subsequent to the EXEC CICS GDS CONNECT PROCESS command.

The RETCODE option names the 6-byte return code field into which CICS places a return code from the command. This field *must* be tested to determine if the GDS CONNECT PROCESS worked correctly.

13.4.2   Errors And The GDS CONNECT PROCESS Command

The error conditions associated with the GDS CONNECT PROCESS command include INVREQ, LENGERR and NOTALLOC. A return code indicating normal processing or an indication of one of the possible errors is placed into the RETCODE field. Figure 13-13 documents the RETCODE values.

The INVREQ indicates that a GDS CONNECT PROCESS command made an invalid requested such as SYNCLEVEL(2) on a session that does not support that level of synchronization.

The LENGERR indicates a problem with either the PROCLENGTH or the PIPLIST/PIPLENGTH specified in the GDS CONNECT PROCESS. The PROCLENGTH value must be greater than 0 or the LENGERR occurs. A PIPLENGTH value must be in the range of 0 to 32,763. CICS checks to ensure that the individual length fields specify a value of at least 4 bytes and that the lengths specified for all PIPs add up to the value defined in PIPLENGTH. The LENGERR occurs if PIPLIST/PIPLENGTH do not conform to the above.

The NOTALLOC indicates that the named facility (CONVID) has not been allocated to the transaction.

13.4.3   Example of the GDS CONNECT PROCESS Command

The following code is an example of the use of the GDS CONNECT PROCESS command.

```
DFHEISTG DSECT
RCODE     DS    CL6
CDATA     DS    0H
          COPY  DFHCDBLK
* EXPANSION OF FIELD NAMES IN DFHCDBLK
CDBCOMPL DS     C
CDBSYNC  DS     C
CDBFREE  DS     C
CDBRECV  DS     C
```

```
CDBSIG    DS    C
CDBCONF   DS    C
CDBERR    DS    C
CDBERRCD  DS    CL4
CDBSYNRB  DS    C
CDBRSVD   DS    CL12
CONVID1   DS    CL4
PROCNM    DS    CL8
*
BASESMP CSECT
        EXEC CICS GDS ALLOCATE SYSID('CIC1')                  *
              CONVID(CONVID1) RETCODE(RCODE) NOQUEUE
        CLI RCODE,X'00'
        BNE ABEND1
              .
              .
              .
        EXEC CICS GDS CONNECT PROCESS                          *
              PROCNAME(PROCNM)                                 *
              PROCLENGTH(8) CONVID(CONVID1)                    *
              SYNCLEVEL(0) CONVDATA(CDATA)                     *
              RETCODE(RCODE)
        CLI   RCODE,X'00'
        BNE   ABEND2
* remainder of conversation code
ABEND1  DS    0H
        EXEC CICS ABEND ABCODE('NSES')
ABEND2  DS    0H
        EXEC CICS ABEND ABCODE('NCNP')
```

13.5   THE NEW STATE — STATE 3

Looking back at Figure 13-2, the state 2 diagram, we can see that as
a result of the successful execution of the GDS CONNECT PRO-
CESS command, a Front-End Transaction enters state 3, the SEND
STATE.

13.6   THE BACK-END TRANSACTION — INITIATED IN
STATE 5

The Back-End Transaction is initiated in state 5, the RECEIVE
STATE. In base conversations all commands must specify a CON-

VID. The Back-End Transaction uses the EXEC CICS GDS ASSIGN command to obtain the CONVID of its principal facility.

13.7   THE GDS ASSIGN COMMAND

The format of the EXEC CICS GDS ASSIGN command is as follows:

```
EXEC CICS GDS ASSIGN
          PRINCONVID(4-byte-data-area-name)
          PRINSYSID(4-byte-data-area-name)
          RETCODE(6-byte-return-code-field)
```

The PRINCONVID option names a 4-byte character field into which CICS places the conversation ID associated with the task's principal facility.

The PRINSYSID option names a 4-byte character field into which CICS places the local SYSIDNT for the remote system.

The RETCODE option names the 6-byte return code field used to test the response to EXEC CICS GDS ASSIGN command.

13.7.1   The Error Condition of the GDS ASSIGN Command

The only error condition that the RETCODE could indicate subsequent to the GDS ASSIGN command is the INVREQ error, which indicates that the request is invalid.

13.7.2   Example of the GDS ASSIGN Command

The following is an example of the GDS ASSIGN command.

```
DFHEISTG DSECT
CONVID1   DS   CL4
SNAME     DS   CL4
RCODE     DS   CL6
.
BASESMP2 CSECT
          EXEC CICS GDS ASSIGN PRINCONVID(CONVID1)          *
              PRINSYSID(SNAME) RETCODE(RCODE)
          CLI RCODE,X'00'
          BNE ABND1
```

```
          .
          .
          .
ABND1     DS   0H
          EXEC CICS ABEND ABCODE('INVR')
```

After acquiring the CONVID of the principal facility, the Back-End Transaction is ready to deal with being in the RECEIVE STATE. Figure 13-5 illustrates the state 5 diagram. Before executing a GDS RECEIVE, however, it may be necessary to execute a GDS EXTRACT PROCESS command which is used to obtain PIP data, the SYNCLEVEL, or other information from the ATTACH Function Management Header.

13.8 THE GDS EXTRACT PROCESS COMMAND

The format of the GDS EXTRACT PROCESS command is:

```
EXEC CICS GDS EXTRACT PROCESS
          PROCNAME(32-byte-field-name)
          PROCLENGTH(2-byte-binary-field-name)
          CONVID(4-byte-field-name)
          SYNCLEVEL(2-byte-binary-field-name)
          PIPLIST(register/register equate)
          PIPLENGTH(2-byte-binary-field-name)
          RETCODE(6-byte-return-code-field)
```

The options of the GDS EXTRACT PROCESS command mirror those of the GDS CONNECT PROCESS command.

The PROCNAME option names a data field to receive the PROCNAME defined in the CONNECT PROCESS. Because CICS supports process names up to 32 bytes in length, the field named by the PROCNAME option must conform to that size. Shorter process names are padded to the right with blanks.

The PROCLENGTH option names a field which receives the length of the process name.

The CONVID option is required in all unmapped conversation commands. This option names the 4-byte field containing the CONVersation ID obtained with the GDS ASSIGN command.

The SYNCLEVEL option names a 2-byte binary field which can be tested to verify the SYNCLEVEL.

The PIPLIST option names a register or register equate used to obtain the address of the PIPLIST.

The PIPLENGTH option names a 2-byte binary field which receives the total length of passed PIP data or 0 if CICS did not receive any PIP data.

13.8.1   Error Condition of the GDS EXTRACT PROCESS Command

The error condition associated with the GDS EXTRACT PROCESS command is INVREQ, and the hex value used to test the RETCODE field is listed in Figure 13-13.

13.8.2   Example of the GDS EXTRACT PROCESS Command

The following code is a sample of the GDS EXTRACT PROCESS command.

```
DFHEISTG DSECT
CDATA      DS OH
     COPY DFHCDBLK
* EXPANSION OF FIELD NAMES IN DFHCDBLK
CDBCOMPL  DS    C
CDBSYNC   DS    C
CDBFREE   DS    C
CDBRECV   DS    C
CDBSIG    DS    C
CDBCONF   DS    C
CDBERR    DS    C
CDBERRCD  DS    CL4
CDBSYNRB  DS    C
CDBRSVD   DS    CL12
RCODE     DS    CL6
PROCNM    DS    CL32
PLEN      DS    H
PIPLEN    DS    H
SYNCL     DS    H
CONVID1   DS    CL4
PIPPTR    EQU   8
BACKEND   CSECT
          EXEC CICS GDS ASSIGN CONVID(CONVID1)         *
               RETCODE(RCODE)
          CLI   RCODE,X'00'
          BE    EXTRCT
```

```
              EXEC CICS ABEND ABCODE('INVR)
EXTRCT        DS   0H
              EXEC CICS EXTRACT PROCESS                      *
                   PROCNAME(PROCNM)                          *
                   PROCLENGTH(PLEN)                          *
                   PIPLIST(PIPPTR)                           *
                   PIPLENGTH(PIPLEN)                         *
                   CONVID(CONVID1)                           *
                   SYNCLEVEL(SYNCL)                          *
                   RETCODE(RCODE)                            *
                   CONVDATA(CDATA)
              CLI  RCODE,X'00'
              BE   CKSYNC
              EXEC CICS ABEND ABCODE('EXTR')
CKSYNC        DS   0H
              CLC  SYNCL,=H'1'
              BE   SYNCOK
              EXEC CICS GDS ISSUE ABEND
              EXEC CICS ABEND ABCODE('SYNC')
SYNCOK        DS   0H
```

13.9 THE GDS SEND COMMAND

The GDS SEND command for use in LUTYPE 6.2 unmapped conversations can be used to send data and/or conversation indicators. The
application programmer must be cautious to include the GDS SEND
command options that generate the appropriate SNA indicators.
CICS will not supply indicators by default — no more Mr. Nice Guy.
You and the SNA indicators are on your own, so stand forewarned!
CICS does, however, buffer output in the same manner as described
for mapped conversations. In the event that the internal buffer becomes full, CICS transmits the data. The accumulated SNA indicators are not, however, transmitted with the data. The SNA indicators and any accumulated data are transmitted when the application program forces a transmission in the same manner as
described for mapped conversations; i.e., the SEND CONFIRM or
WAIT option is included or the WAIT command is executed.

13.9.1   Format of the GDS SEND Command

The format of the GDS SEND command for LUTYPE 6.2 unmapped conversations is as follows.

```
EXEC CICS GDS SEND
          CONVID(field-containing-CONVID)
          FROM(data-area-name)
          LENGTH(value-defining-FROM-area-size)
          INVITE * OR * LAST
          CONFIRM * OR * WAIT
          CONVDATA(24-byte-conversation-data-area)
          RETCODE(6-byte-return-code-field)
```

The CONVID option names the data field which contains the CONVID. Note that CONVID is required for both the Front-End and Back-End Transactions in the GDS SEND command. Principal facilities and alternate facilities must be expressly identified on all GDS commands.

The FROM option names an application data area containing a message to be sent. The inclusion of the FROM area is optional in the SEND command for LUTYPE 6.2 conversations. When CONFIRM, LAST, or WAIT are included in a GDS SEND command, the data presented to CICS up through the current GDS SEND command must be on a structured field boundary. So, when CICS is preparing to transmit or generating the End Bracket indicator, it must have the entire contents of structured fields.

The LENGTH option is used to define the length of the data message contained in the area named with the FROM option.

The INVITE option is used to generate an SNA Change-Direction Indicator. The SEND STATE transaction is now inviting the RECEIVE STATE transaction to start sending. CICS does not generate an implied Change-Direction Indicator so you must code INVITE when a Change-Direction is required.

The transaction receiving a SEND INVITE is informed of its state change, from RECEIVE STATE to SEND STATE via the CDBRECV field in the CONVDATA area. CDBRECV is turned off (X'00') to indicate that the transaction is in the SEND STATE. Conversely, CDBRECV is set on (X'FF') to indicate that the transaction is in the RECEIVE STATE. CICS sets CDBRECV when a GDS RECEIVE command is executed. Therefore, this field should be tested immediately after a GDS RECEIVE command. One last reminder — when the INVITE option is included, data must be on a structured field boundary. The INVITE option and the LAST option which follows are mutually exclusive, just as they are in the mapped version of the SEND command.

The LAST option generates the SNA End Bracket (EB) indicator. SEND LAST can be used with or without data but since no more data can be added to the buffer, the data presented up through a SEND LAST must be on a structured field boundary.

The CONFIRM option is used to requst a private confirmation during LUTYPE 6.2 conversations at SYNCLEVELs 1 or 2. Including CONFIRM in a GDS SEND command causes CICS to transmit the contents of the internal buffer and therefore requires that data be on a structured field boundary.

Including CONFIRM in a GDS SEND command causes the receiver of the GDS SEND CONFIRM, the other transaction, to know that you wish an application dependent confirmation. CICS conveys this information to the receiver of a GDS SEND CONFIRM in the CDBCONF field of the CONVDATA area. The field is set to X'FF' when a CONFIRM has been received. The GDS ISSUE CONFIRMATION is used as a positive response to GDS SEND CONFIRM. The GDS ISSUE ERROR or GDS ISSUE ABEND are used to indicate a negative response. A negative response is indicated in the CDBERR field which is set to X'FF' for ISSUE ERROR or ISSUE ABEND. The CDBERRCD field contains an indication of which command caused the CDBERR field to be set on. CDBERRCD = X'08890000' indicates a GDS ISSUE ERROR. The transaction is now in the RECEIVE STATE and should proceed accordingly. CDBERRCD = X'08640000' indicates a conversation abend precipatated by either a GDS ISSUE ABEND or an abend forced by CICS. If the conversation has abended, it is necessary to GDS FREE the session. These tests and resulting state changes are indicated in the SEND STATE diagram illustrated in Figure 13-3.

The WAIT option is used to force CICS to transmit the data and indicators accumulated within the internal buffer. The transaction receives control back at the next instruction after the GDS SEND command after the data has been transmitted.

The CONFIRM and WAIT options are mutually exclusive as they are for mapped SEND commands because there is no need to have both. CONFIRM flushes the buffer just as well as use of the WAIT option.

13.9.2   Errors and the GDS SEND Command

The possible errors resulting from the GDS SEND command include INVREQ, LENGERR, and NOTALLOC. The contents of the RET-CODE field can be tested according to the hex values illustrated in Figure 13-13.

13.9.3   Summary of the GDS SEND Command

The GDS SEND command can only be used when in the appropriate state. Additionally, the application programmer must ensure that the GDS SEND command is used to generate the appropriate SNA Indicators explicitly. Subsequent to the execution of the GDS SEND command, it is necessary to test the RETCODE field and, potentially, fields in the CONVDATA area. If a conversation partner uses ISSUE ERROR or ISSUE SIGNAL, the CDBERR and CDBSIG fields must be tested in addition to the tests named in the SEND STATE diagram shown in Figure 13-3.

13.10   THE GDS RECEIVE COMMAND

The GDS RECEIVE command is used to receive data and obtain, via the CONVDATA fields, conversation status information. As with mapped conversations that use the EIB, the CONVDATA fields which are important to an application program are to some degree dependent upon the commands and command options that the conversation partner may potentially use. To this extent both conversation partners must be coordinated. Beyond the commands and options that may be coded in a conversing program, there are certain CONVDATA fields that should routinely be tested subsequent to a GDS RECEIVE command.

The CONVDATA fields that may need to be tested subsequent to a GDS RECEIVE are listed in Figure 13-5, the RECEIVE STATE diagram. These fields include CDBCOMPL, CDBCONF, CDBSYNC, CDBSYNCRB, CDBFREE, and CDBRECV.

13.10.1   The Format of the GDS RECEIVE Command

The format of the GDS RECEIVE command for APPC unmapped conversations is as follows.

```
EXEC CICS GDS RECEIVE
          CONVID(field-name)
          INTO(data-area-name)
             * OR *
          SET(register/register-equate)
          MAXFLENGTH(fullword-length-field)
          FLENGTH(fullword-length-field)
          BUFFER * OR * LLID
          CONVDATA(24-byte-convdata-area)
          RETCODE(6-byte-return-code-field)
```

The CONVID option names the data field containing the CONVersation ID.

The mutually exclusive INTO or SET options allow the application to obtain incoming data.

The MAXFLENGTH option names a 4-byte binary field which is used to define maximum length information. When used in a command specifying GDS RECEIVE INTO, this field indicates the maximum size that the program can accommodate in terms of its defined input work area. In a GDS RECEIVE SET command the MAXFLENGTH defines the maximum length of data that the transaction is to receive addressability to. The value contained in the MAXFLENGTH field must not exceed 32,767.

The FLENGTH option names a 4-byte binary field into which CICS places the actual length of data presented to the application program.

The BUFFER or mutually exclusive LLID options define CICS input to the program with regard to received structured fields. If BUFFER is elected, the program receives the MAXFLENGTH amount of information without regard for structured field boundaries. LLID indicates that the program is to receive based upon structured field boundaries.

The CONVDATA option names the program's CONVersation DATA area.

The RETCODE option names the program's return code field.

13.10.2   Errors and the GDS RECEIVE Command

The errors associated with the GDS RECEIVE command include INVREQ, LENGERR, and NOTALLOC. The RETCODE field should be tested accordingly.

13.10.3 An Example of the GDS RECEIVE Command

The following is an example of the GDS RECEIVE command.

```
DFHEISTG DSECT
CDATA      DS   OH
     COPY DFHCDBLK
* EXPANSION OF FIELD NAMES IN DFHCDBLK
CDBCOMPL DS   C
CDBSYNC  DS   C
CDBFREE  DS   C
CDBRECV  DS   C
CDBSIG   DS   C
CDBCONF  DS   C
CDBERR   DS   C
CDBERRCD DS   CL4
CDBSYNRB DS   C
CDBRSVD  DS   CL12
RCODE    DS   CL6
TIAREA   DS   CL250
TLEN     DS   F
MLEN     DS   F
CONVID1  DS   CL4
*
*
BASESMP    CSECT
*   COMMANDS TO GDS ASSIGN TO OBTAIN THE CONVID AND
*     POSSIBLY GDS EXTRACT PROCESS TO OBTAIN
*     INFORMATION FROM THE ATTACH FMH
           MVC  MLEN,=F'250'
           EXEC CICS GDS RECEIVE CONVID(CONVID1)        *
                INTO(TIAREA) FLENGTH(TLEN)              *
                MAXFLENGTH(MLEN) BUFFER                 *
                CONVDATA(CDATA) RETCODE(RCODE)
           CLI  RCODE,X'00'
           BNE  ERR1
* REMAINDER OF TESTS AS INDICATED BY STATE
* DIAGRAM
```

The transaction will receive 250 bytes of data without regard for structured field boundaries because of the inclusion of the BUFFER option.

13.11   THE GDS WAIT COMMAND

The GDS WAIT command can be used to force CICS to transmit the internal buffer with data and control indicators before the task continues its execution.

13.11.1   The Format of the GDS WAIT Command

The format of the GDS WAIT command is as follows.

```
EXEC CICS GDS WAIT CONVID(data-area-name)
               RETCODE(name-of-return-code-field)
               CONVDATA(name-of-convdata-area)
```

The options are used as in all the other APPC unmapped conversation commands.

13.11.2   Errors and the GDS WAIT Command

The errors that can occur for the GDS WAIT command are INVREQ and NOTALLOC. The RETCODE field is tested accordingly.

13.12   THE GDS ISSUE CONFIRMATION COMMAND

The ISSUE CONFIRMATION command is used as in mapped conversations. The format of the GDS ISSUE CONFIRMATION command is as follows.

```
EXEC CICS GDS ISSUE CONFIRMATION
     CONVID(field-name)
     CONVDATA(name-of-convdata-area)
     RETCODE(name-of-return-code-field)
```

Command options are used in accordance with other EXEC CICS GDS commands. To test for receipt of a conversation partner's ISSUE CONFIRMATION, the CDBERR field in the CONVDATA area is tested subsequent to the GDS SEND CONFIRM. If the field contains X'00', then the response to confirmation was positive. The error conditions associated with GDS ISSUE CONFIRMATION are NOTALLOC and INVREQ and the RETCODE field should be tested accordingly. Tests indicated in the state diagram should likewise be performed.

13.13   THE GDS ISSUE ERROR COMMAND

The GDS ISSUE ERROR command can be used as a negative response to a CONFIRMation request or any other purpose devised in the application. The receipt of a GDS ISSUE ERROR causes CICS to set the CDBERR field in the CONVDATA work area. The CDBERRCD field can be interrogated to verify that receipt of the ISSUE ERROR caused CDBERR to be set on. The format of the GDS ISSUE ERROR command is as follows.

```
EXEC CICS GDS ISSUE ERROR
    CONVID(field-containing-conversation-name)
    RETCODE(name-of-return-code-field)
    CONVDATA(name-of-convdata-area)
```

The command options are used in accordance with other EXEC CICS GDS commands. The error conditions associated with GDS ISSUE ERROR are NOTALLOC and INVREQ, and the RETCODE field should be tested accordingly. Tests in accordance with the state diagram should likewise be performed.

13.14   THE GDS ISSUE ABEND COMMAND

The GDS ISSUE ABEND command is used in the same manner as in mapped conversations. The format of this command is as follows.

```
EXEC CICS ISSUE ABEND
    CONVID(field-name)
    RETCODE(name-of-return-code-field)
    CONVDATA(name-of-convdata-area)
```

The command options are used in accordance with the other GDS commands. Receipt of GDS ISSUE ABEND is indicated in the CDBERR and CDBERRCD fields in the CONVDATA area. The error conditions are the same as described above under GDS ISSUE ERROR.

13.15   THE GDS ISSUE SIGNAL COMMAND

The GDS ISSUE SIGNAL command is used by a RECEIVE STATE transaction to indicate its need to have a state change. Execution of this command by a conversation partner causes CICS to set on the CDBSIG indicator in the CONVDATA area. For applications which use the GDS ISSUE SIGNAL, this field should be tested subsequent to every conversation related command. The format of the ISSUE SIGNAL command is as follows.

```
EXEC CICS ISSUE SIGNAL
     CONVID(field-name)
     RETCODE(name-of-return-code-field)
     CONVDATA(name-of-convdata-area)
```

The command options are used in accordance with other GDS commands, and the errors associated with GDS ISSUE SIGNAL are the same as those described for GDS ISSUE ERROR.

13.16   THE GDS FREE COMMAND

The GDS FREE command is used to FREE a session. The format of the FREE command is as follows.

```
EXEC CICS GDS FREE
     CONVID(field-name)
     RETCODE(name-of-return-code-field)
     CONVDATA(name-of-convdata-area)
```

The options of the GDS FREE are used in accordance with other GDS commands. The error conditions are the same as those described for the GDS ISSUE ERROR.

13.17   COMMANDS RELATING TO SYNCPOINT EXCHANGES

The commands and rules for SYNCPOINT exchanges are described in the previous chapters dealing with mapped conversations. There are a couple of factors that are unique to SYNCPOINT exchanges in unmapped conversations.

The GDS ISSUE PREPARE is used in place of the ISSUE PREPARE of mapped conversations. The GDS ISSUE PREPARE includes options for naming the CONVDATA and RETCODE areas defined for GDS commands. The standard SYNCPOINT and SYNCPOINT ROLLBACK commands discussed for mapped conversations are not dependent upon whether the conversation is mapped or unmapped. CICS does, however, use the CONVDATA fields instead of EIB fields to signal the unmapped transaction about SYNCPOINT-related information. The CONVDATA fields of interest are CDBSYNC and CDBSYNRB. The CDBSYNC field when set on (X'FF') indicates a SYNCPOINT request, and the CDBSYNRB when set on indicates the need for a SYNCPOINT ROLLBACK.

The SYNCPOINT command can not be used in an unmapped conversation unless the data presented to CICS up to the execution of the SYNCPOINT is on a structured field boundary.

The valid responses to a SYNCPOINT request are the same as for mapped conversations. Subsequent to a GDS ISSUE ERROR in this context the usual tests indicated in the state diagram should be conducted. The conversation commands subsequent to a successful GDS ISSUE ERROR (as a response to a SYNCPOINT) would be GDS SEND WAIT INVITE followed by a GDS RECEIVE. The CDBSYNRB should be tested and a SYNCPOINT ROLLBACK taken.

REVIEW EXERCISES

Match each of the following CONVDATA fields with a description below.

_____ 1. CDBSYNRB
_____ 2. CDBCOMPL
_____ 3. CDBFREE
_____ 4. CDBSYNC
_____ 5. CDBERRCD
_____ 6. CDBRECV
_____ 7. CDBSIG
_____ 8. CDBERR
_____ 9. CDBCONF

A. Indicates that the transaction is to take a SYNCPOINT.
B. Indicates that CICS has received a SIGNAL request.

C. Indicates the transaction's SEND/RECEIVE state.
D. Indicates that CICS has received a Conversation Error Indicator.
E. Indicates that all data has been RECEIVEd subsequent to a GDS RECEIVE NOTRUNCATE.
F. Indicates that the transaction is to FREE the session.
G. Indicates a confirmation request has been received.
H. Provides a "reason" code for the type of error that caused CDBERR to be set on.
I. Indicates a transaction is to issue a SYNCPOINT ROLLBACK.

Provide a short answer to each of the following.

1. What is a GDS header?
2. Why is it particularly important to be aware of a transaction's state when coding LUTYPE 6.2 unmapped applications?
3. Why is it necessary to define a CONVDATA area in an LUTYPE 6.2 unmapped conversation application program?
4. Why is it necessary to define a RETCODE field in an LUTYPE 6.2 unmapped conversation application program?
5. What is the purpose of the EXEC CICS GDS ASSIGN command?
6. At the point that an unmapped conversation program is about to SYNCPOINT or execute a SEND with CONFIRM, LAST, or WAIT, it is necessary to be conscious of the data that has been sent to CICS. Why is this?

13.18   Answers to Review Exercise

Match each of the following CONVDATA fields with a description below.

I 1. CDBSYNRB
E 2. CDBCOMPL
F 3. CDBFREE
A 4. CDBSYNC
H 5. CDBERRCD
C 6. CDBRECV
B 7. CDBSIG
D 8. CDBERR
G 9. CDBCONF

Provide a short answer to each of the following.

1. *What is a GDS header?*

   The unmapped conversation data stream consists of structured fields which have headers called GDS headers. The GDS header contains two pieces of information about the structured field. First the length of the total field is provided and then an ID indicator defines the kind of data in the structured field.

2. *Why is it particularly important to be aware of a transaction's state when coding LUTYPE 6.2 unmapped applications?*

   CICS does not generate implied SNA indicators. Therefore, the programmer must be aware of the transaction's state so that the correct options can be included in conversation commands.

3. *Why is it necessary to define a CONVDATA area in an LUTYPE 6.2 unmapped conversation application program?*

   EXEC CICS GDS commands do not cause the EIB to be set. The CONVDATA area is used in place of the EIB for unmapped conversations. Therefore, CICS places conversation indicators into the named CONVDATA area and the application program must test fields in this data area.

4. *Why is it necessary to define a RETCODE field in an LUTYPE 6.2 unmapped conversation application program?*

   Unmapped conversation commands do not raise CICS unusual conditions. Therefore, a return code from command execution must be explicitly tested subsequent to every EXEC CICS GDS command. CICS places the return code value into the named RETCODE field.

5. *What is the purpose of the EXEC CICS GDS ASSIGN command?*

   In unmapped conversations both the Front-End and Back-End Transactions must use the CONVID option in EXEC CICS GDS commands. The EXEC CICS GDS ASSIGN command returns the CONVID of the Back-End Transaction.

6. *At the point that an unmapped conversation program is about to SYNCPOINT or execute a SEND with CONFIRM, LAST, or WAIT, it is necessary to be conscious of the data that has been sent to CICS. Why is this?*

The data presented to CICS up to a SYNCPOINT or when one of these SEND command options is included must be on a structured field boundary.

14

LUTYPE 6.1 and MRO Conversations

14.1 INTRODUCTION

Application programming for LUTYPE 6.1 or MRO distributed transaction processing is very similar in conceptual ways to LUTYPE 6.2 mapped conversation programming. There are some different commands that are used and some of the command options vary, but the basic concepts are the same. This chapter assumes that you have read Chapters 10–12 and are familiar with the concepts therein discussed. One immediate difference is that the connection between the conversing programs is called a session in MRO and LUTYPE 6.1. The notion of a "conversation" mapped over a session is particular to the LUTYPE 6.2. But from a programming point of view, this is more a semantic difference than anything else.

Using the application programming facilities provided for LUTYPE 6.1 ISC and Multi-Region Operation Distributed Transaction Processing, application programs may be developed in COBOL, PL/I, or assembler language. As with LUTYPE 6.2, programs that perform distributed transaction processing for LUTYPE 6.1 and MRO must be designed as a matched pair. One program must anticipate what the other does in terms of the interprogram protocols for performing application functionality and managing errors that occur. So, again, coordination is needed in designing the distributed transaction.

Application programmers should also use the appropriate state diagrams when coding application programs. The state diagrams in-

```
STATE 1    LUTYPE6.1 and MRO CONVERSATIONS              SESSION NOT ALLOCATED

Commands You Can Issue       What To Test                    New
                                                             State

ALLOCATE [NOQUEUE] *         SYSIDERR                         1

                             SYSBUSY *                        1

                             Otherwise                        2
                             (obtain session name
                              from EIBRSRCE)

 * If you want your program to wait until a session is available, omit
   the NOQUEUE option of the ALLOCATE command and do not code a HANDLE
   command for the SYSBUSY condition.

   If you want control to be returned to your program if a session is not
   immediately available, either specify NOQUEUE on the ALLOCATE command
   and test EIBRCODE for SYSBUSY (X'D3'), or code a HANDLE CONDITION SYSBUSY
   command.
```

Figure 14-1 State 1 — SESSION NOT ALLOCATED. Reprinted by permission from *CICS/MVS Version 2.1 Intercommunication Guide* © 1987, 1988 by International Business Machines Corporation.

dicate valid commands for particular states, subsequent EIB field tests, and state changes that ensue from command execution.

There are eight states for LUTYPE 6.1 and MRO sessions. The state diagrams are illustrated in Figures 14-1 through 14-8. Figure 14-9 lists the commands for LUTYPE 6.1 and MRO programs. The "new" commands that are unique to LUTYPE 6.1/MRO are 1) BUILD ATTACH to build an attach Function Management Header; and 2) EXTRACT ATTACH to obtain information from the ATTACH Function Management Header. These commands are the LUTYPE 6.1/MRO "equivalent" of CONNECT PROCESS and EXTRACT PROCESS used in LUTYPE 6.2 programs. The LUTYPE 6.2 commands work a bit differently internally, but the same sort of thing is accomplished. Some of the commands listed in Figure 14-9 are appropriate for use on either MRO or LUTYPE 6.1 sessions. Most of the commands are, however, appropriate to both types of sessions.

Basically, LUTYPE 6.1 and MRO programs are quite similar. There are differences, however, and to this end, the state diagrams may indicate that something is permitted for one or the other. The application programmer must be aware of these differences and code accordingly. Before we continue with an examination of the LUTYPE

STATE 2 LUTYPE6.1 and MRO CONVERSATIONS		SEND STATE
Commands You Can Issue *	What To Test	New State
SEND		2
SEND INVITE	–	3
SEND INVITE WAIT	–	4
SEND LAST	–	7
SEND LAST WAIT	–	8

CONVERSE
    Equivalent to:
        SEND INVITE WAIT
        RECEIVE
	Go to the STATE 4 table and make the tests shown for the RECEIVE command	–

RECEIVE (LUTYPE6.1 only)	Go to the STATE 4 table and make the tests shown for the RECEIVE command	–
SYNCPOINT	EIBRLDBK (or ROLLEDBACK condition) (MRO only)	2
	Otherwise (transaction will ABEND if SYNCPOINT fails)	2
SYNCPOINT ROLLBACK (MRO only)	(transaction will ABEND if ROLLBACK fails)	2

FREE
    Equivalent to:
        SEND LAST WAIT
        FREE
	–	1

* For the front-end transaction, the first command used after the session has been allocated must be a SEND command or CONVERSE command that initiates the back-end transaction in one of the ways described under 'Attaching the Remote Transaction' on page 231.

Figure 14-2 State 2 — SEND STATE. Reprinted by permission from *CICS/MVS Version 2.1 Intercommunication Guide* © 1987, 1988 by International Business Machines Corporation.

STATE 3 LUTYPE6.1 and MRO CONVERSATIONS	RECEIVE PENDING AFTER INVITE	
Commands You Can Issue	What To Test	New State
WAIT TERMINAL SESSION	-	4
SYNCPOINT (LUTYPE6.1 only)	(transaction will ABEND if SYNCPOINT fails)	4

Figure 14-3 State 3 — RECEIVE PENDING AFTER INVITE. Reprinted by permission from *CICS/MVS Version 2.1 Intercommunication Guide* © 1987, 1988 by International Business Machines Corporation.

STATE 4 LUTYPE6.1 and MRO CONVERSATIONS	RECEIVE STATE	
Commands You Can Issue	What To Test	New State
RECEIVE [NOTRUNCATE] *	EIBCOMPL *	-
	EIBSYNC	5
	EIBSYNRB (MRO only)	6
	EIBFREE	8
	EIBRECV	4
	Otherwise	2
SYNCPOINT ROLLBACK (MRO only)	(transaction will ABEND if ROLLBACK fails)	2

* If NOTRUNCATE is specified, a zero value in EIBCOMPL indicates that the data passed to the application by CICS is incomplete (because, for example, the data-area specified in the RECEIVE command is too small). CICS will save the remaining data for retrieval by subsequent RECEIVE NOTRUNCATE commands. EIBCOMPL is set when the last part of the data is passed back. If the NOTRUNCATE option is not specified, overlength data is indicated by the LENGERR condition, and the remaining data is discarded by CICS.

Figure 14-4 State 4 — RECEIVE STATE. Reprinted by permission from *CICS/MVS Version 2.1 Intercommunication Guide* © 1987, 1988 by International Business Machines Corporation.

STATE 5 LUTYPE6.1 and MRO CONVERSATIONS	RECEIVER TAKE SYNCPOINT	
Commands You Can Issue	What To Test	New State
SYNCPOINT	EIBFREE (saved value)	8
	EIBRECV (saved value)	4
	Otherwise	2
SYNCPOINT ROLLBACK (MRO Only)	EIBFREE (saved value)	8
	EIBRECV (saved value)	4
	Otherwise	2

Figure 14-5 State 6 — RECEIVER TAKE SYNCPOINT. Reprinted by permission from *CICS/MVS Version 2.1 Intercommunication Guide* © 1987, 1988 by International Business Machines Corporation.

STATE 6 MRO CONVERSATIONS	RECEIVER ROLLBACK OR FREE SESSION	
Commands You Can Issue	What To Test	New State
SYNCPOINT ROLLBACK	EIBFREE (saved value)	8
	EIBRECV (saved value)	4
	Otherwise	2
FREE	—	1

Figure 14-6 State 6 — RECEIVER ROLLBACK OR FREE SESSION. Reprinted by permission from *CICS/MVS Version 2.1 Intercommunication Guide* © 1987, 1988 by International Business Machines Corporation.

350 Distributed Processing in the CICS Environment

STATE 7 LUTYPE6.1 and MRO CONVERSATIONS		FREE PENDING AFTER SEND LAST
Commands You Can Issue	What To Test	New State
WAIT TERMINAL SESSION (do not use for MRO sessions)	–	8
SYNCPOINT	–	8
FREE	–	1

Figure 14-7 State 7 — FREE PENDING AFTER SEND LAST. Reprinted by permission from *CICS/MVS Version 2.1 Intercommunication Guide* © 1987, 1988 by International Business Machines Corporation.

6.1/MRO commands listed in Figure 14-9, we will examine the differences.

14.1.1 Deferred Versus Immediate Transmission

In LUTYPE 6.1 message transmission is deferred. The LUTYPE 6.1 transmission deferral is different from the LUTYPE 6.2 in that CICS does not buffer data to the same extent. For LUTYPE 6.1, CICS defers sending data until the execution of the next session-related command. In this way, CICS is able to potentially "piggyback" SNA indicators with data transmission. For MRO there is no deferral of transmission. When a SEND command is executed, any data and most SNA indicators generated from the command are immediately

STATE 8 LUTYPE6.1 and MRO CONVERSATIONS		FREE SESSION
Commands You Can Issue	What To Test	New State
FREE	–	1

Figure 14-8 State 8 — FREE SESSION. Reprinted by permission from *CICS/MVS Version 2.1 Intercommunication Guide* © 1987, 1988 by International Business Machines Corporation.

COMMAND	FUNCTION
ALLOCATE	Used to request use of a session.
BUILD ATTACH	Used to have CICS build an ATTACH Function Management Header. This header is subsequently named in the first SEND or CONVERSE issued against the session.
EXTRACT ATTACH	Used by a Back-End Transaction to obtain information from an ATTACH FMH.
SEND	Used to SEND data and indicators.
RECEIVE	Used to RECEIVE data and indicators.
CONVERSE	Used to SEND, WAIT, and RECEIVE.
WAIT TERMINAL	For LUTYPE 6.1 sessions forces the transmission of data and indicators.
ISSUE SIGNAL	For LUTYPE 6.1 sessions can be used by a RECEIVE state transaction to request being placed into the SEND state.
FREE	Used to FREE a session.
SYNCPOINT	Used to initiate SYNCPOINT or commit protocols for the session. The ROLLBACK option is not supported for LUTYPE 6.1 links.

Figure 14-9 LUTYPE 6.1/MRO command summary.

sent. In essence, this means that there is an implied WAIT when a SEND command is executed in an MRO program. This means that command sequences that work for LUTYPE 6.1 may cause errors in MRO Distributed Transaction Processing. Consider the following sequence of commands.

```
EXEC CICS SEND FROM(area-name)   INVITE
EXEC CICS SYNCPOINT
```

In LUTYPE 6.1 CICS saves the data and Change-Direction Indicator generated via the SEND command. When the SYNCPOINT is executed, the transaction is still in the SEND state since the Change-Direction Indicator was not transmitted and the SYNCPOINT is valid. For MRO, the SEND INVITE causes the immediate transmission of the data and Change-Direction Indicator. Therefore, the MRO transaction is no longer in the SEND STATE, and the SYNCPOINT is invalid. If you look at Figure 14-3, the RECEIVE PENDING AFTER INVITE state, you will note that SYNCPOINT is a valid option for LUTYPE 6.1 only. Actually, since the SEND IN-VITE is immediately transmitted in MRO, the transaction goes from the SEND STATE directly to the RECEIVE STATE.

14.1.2   RECEIVE Commands While in the SEND STATE

In LUTYPE 6.1 it is possible to perform a SEND and not include the INVITE option, then perform a RECEIVE. CICS generates the implied Change-Direction Indicator and transmits the data. The transaction is thus placed into the RECEIVE STATE. So the following is perfectly valid for LYTYPE 6.1:

```
EXEC CICS SEND FROM(area-name)
EXEC CICS RECEIVE
```

This sequence of commands does not, however, work for MRO, because a RECEIVE is not permitted while the transaction is in the SEND state. Figure 14-2 is the SEND STATE diagram. Note that the RECEIVE command is listed, but only for LUTYPE 6.1 links. For MRO links, CICS does not generate the Change-Direction Indicator implied by a RECEIVE command while in the SEND STATE. Thus, the following would have to be coded explicitly:

```
EXEC CICS SEND FROM(area-name) INVITE
EXEC CICS RECEIVE
```

The best policy to adopt, however, is to not rely upon CICS to generate indicators even where it will. Rather, code commands to contain the options you intend. Programs that explicitly generate SNA indicators are more easily understood by someone performing quick and dirty maintenance (is there another kind?), and they result in the programmer being more aware of the transaction's state because conscious thought is being given to command options.

14.1.3   SEND LAST Option

Another difference between MRO and LUTYPE 6.1 ISC is in the use of the LAST option of the SEND command. In LUTYPE 6.1, the last option causes CICS to generate the End Bracket Indicator, but unless the WAIT option is included, CICS does not transmit the data or End Bracket Indicator.

```
EXEC CICS SEND FROM (area-name) LAST
EXEC CICS RETURN or SYNCPOINT
```

For ISC, the SYNCPOINT or RETURN results in the addition of the SYNCPOINT indicator and a session SYNCPOINT exchange ensues. In MRO, the net result is the same but the internal handling is a little different.

```
EXEC CICS SEND FROM (area-name) LAST
```

For MRO, a WAIT is implied in the sense that CICS transmits for every SEND command. However, for the SEND LAST, CICS anticipates the potential need for a SYNCPOINT exchange and by default "splits" the transmission. **The data from the SEND command is sent immediately but the End Bracket Indicator is not.** CICS can be directed to forward the End Bracket Indicator if the program explicitly includes the WAIT option in the SEND LAST. Therefore, in both MRO and ISC, the WAIT option must be explicitly coded in order to force transmission of the End Bracket and thereby avoid a session SYNCPOINT exchange.

In LUTYPE 6.1 sessions the WAIT TERMINAL command can be used to force a deferred transmission. Thus, the following command sequence could be used to end a session and avoid a session SYNCPOINT flow in an LUTYPE 6.1 session.

```
EXEC CICS SEND FROM(area-name) LAST
EXEC CICS WAIT TERMINAL SESSION(session-name)
EXEC CICS RETURN or SYNCPOINT
```

The SEND LAST generates the End Bracket and the WAIT TERMINAL forces the transmission of the End Bracket Indicator. The session is over when the RETURN or SYNCPOINT is executed.

This WAIT TERMINAL command is not applicable to MRO sessions as it functions as a no operation or null command. If you look at Figure 14-7, the FREE PENDING AFTER SEND LAST state diagram you will note that the WAIT TERMINAL command should not be used for MRO sessions. The only real context in which a programmer would want to use the WAIT TERMINAL for MRO is following a SEND LAST when attempting to avoid a SYNCPOINT as illustrated above for LUTYPE 6.1. There is really no other occasion, because the WAIT option is implied for all SENDs in MRO. The only thing is that, as we also discussed above, the implied WAIT does not force the transmission of an End Bracket Indicator. Since the WAIT

TERMINAL command is not appropriate for MRO sessions, the only way to avoid a session SYNCPOINT exchange in MRO is to include the WAIT option explicitly in the SEND LAST command as illustrated in the following.

```
EXEC CICS SEND FROM (area-name) LAST WAIT
EXEC CICS RETURN or SYNCPOINT
```

So, for both MRO and LUTYPE 6.1 ISC the above commands cause the END Bracket Indicator to be generated (LAST) and sent immediately (WAIT). Thus, the session is terminated before the SYNCPOINT is taken and a SYNCPOINT exchange is avoided in the session.

14.1.4   Use of SYNCPOINT ROLLBACK

The SYNCPOINT ROLLBACK command is not supported on LUTYPE 6.1 ISC sessions. For MRO sessions, the SYNCPOINT ROLLBACK is supported. Figure 14-6 is the RECEIVER ROLLBACK OR FREE SESSION state. Note that this state is indicated for MRO only. Also, if you look at Figures 14-2, 14-4, and 14-5, you will note that the SYNCPOINT ROLLBACK command is listed. However, in all cases it is noted that this command is for MRO only.

14.1.5   Use of ISSUE SIGNAL

The ISSUE SIGNAL command may be used for LUTYPE 6.1 sessions so that a RECEIVE STATE transaction can request a state change as we discussed for LUTYPE 6.2 programming. However, the SIGNAL command is an SNA command and is not supported for MRO sessions. Therefore, this command is not appropriate for MRO. Other commands that may not be used for MRO sessions include EXTRACT TCT and ISSUE DISCONNECT.

14.1.6   Summary of MRO Restrictions

In MRO, CICS transmits for every SEND command. The only partial exception is when SEND LAST is used. In this case, CICS transmits the data, but does not actually forward the End Bracket Indicator unless the SEND LAST command includes the WAIT option. WAIT

TERMINAL and ISSUE SIGNAL are not appropriate for use in programs utilizing an MRO InterRegion Communication Link. Also, CICS does not generate a "default" Change-Direction Indicator, so the INVITE option must be included in the SEND command when it is desired for MRO connections.

14.1.7   Summary of LUTYPE 6.1 Restrictions

CICS does defer sending for LUTYPE 6.1; it waits for the next session-related command before actually performing the transmission. CICS will also generate an implied Change-Direction Indicator if a RECEIVE follows a SEND command without the INVITE option. The SYNCPOINT ROLLBACK is not supported across LUTYPE 6.1 links.

14.2   CICS COMMANDS FOR LUTYPE 6.1 AND MRO SESSIONS

The CICS commands used for LUTYPE 6.1 and MRO distributed transactions are listed in Figure 14-9. We will examine each of the commands. However, command options that were fully explained in Chapters 10–12 will not be discussed in as much detail in this chapter.

14.3   THE ALLOCATE COMMAND

The ALLOCATE command is used by a Front-End Transaction that does not already have use of a session to a remote system. The ALLOCATE command requests an alternate facility from CICS. The session state for this transaction at this point in processing is state 1 — Session Not Allocated. Figure 14-1 illustrates the state diagram for state 1. According to this state diagram there is only one command that can be used in state 1 and that is the ALLOCATE command to obtain use of a session.

14.3.1   ALLOCATE Command Format

The format of the ALLOCATE command is as follows:

```
EXEC CICS ALLOCATE
        SYSID(sys-name)
        * OR *
        SESSION (sess-name)
        PROFILE(profile-name)
        NOQUEUE * OR * NOSUSPEND
```

The SYSID option is used to provide the 1- to 4-character SYSIDNT of the remote system. This is the name defined in the local CICS Terminal Control Table for the remote system. As an alternative, the SESSION option can be used to explicitly name a SESSION. This assumes that the systems programmer has defined sessions with names in the TCT. This option is not recommended because SESSION names are not supported for LUTYPE6.2. In the event that upward compatibility is desired, sessions should be ALLOCATEd using the SYSID option. Also the SESSION option cannot be used for MRO.

The PROFILE option provides the 1- to 8-character name of a communication profile to use for the session. This option is coded only if an installation-specific profile is desired. Otherwise, if omitted, a default CICS Profile, "DFHCICSA," becomes the profile for the session. You will recall that a profile is used to name a collection of terminal control processing options. If the profile specifies that the application program is to receive all INBound Function Management Headers, then such headers are passed along to the LUTYPE 6.1 application program within the RECEIVE data area. "DFHCICSA" does include INBFMH(ALL). The EIBFMH field is set on (X'FF') to indicate the presence of a Function Management Header.

The NOQUEUE or NOSUSPEND option indicates that CICS is not to queue your request for a session. Control is passed back to the application program if a session is not available and the EIBRCODE can be tested to determine if a session has been obtained.

14.3.2   Unusual Conditions and the ALLOCATE Command

The unusual conditions associated with the ALLOCATE command include CBIDERR, EOC, INVREQ, SESSBUSY, SESSIONERR, SYSBUSY, and SYSIDERR.

The CBIDERR indicates that the profile named in the PROFILE option of the ALLOCATE command is not known to CICS. The default action for CICS is to abend the task.

The EOC condition indicates the completion of a chain of input messages (or RUs). CICS sets on EIBEOC and otherwise ignores the condition.

The INVREQ indicates that the request is invalid because the Logical Unit is allocated to the transaction already. The default action is for CICS to abend the task.

The SESSBUSY condition indicates that the named SESSION is busy. This condition is handled in a manner similar to SYSBUSY discussed below.

The SESSIONERR condition occurs when the SESSION option of the ALLOCATE command names a specific session. This condition indicates that the session is unidentified in the TCT or that it is currently out of service. The default action is to abend the task.

The SYSBUSY condition indicates that the requested system is busy. Unless the NOQUEUE/NOSUSPEND option has been included in the ALLOCATE command or the SYSBUSY has been programmatically handled, CICS queues the task until a session becomes available. Handling the condition SYSBUSY takes precedence over the NOQUEUE/NOSUSPEND option.

The SYSIDERR indicates an error related to the SYSIDNT requested, which precludes CICS providing a session to the task. The default action is for CICS to abend the task.

14.3.3   ALLOCATE Command Summary

Subsequent to the ALLOCATE command it is necessary to save the session identifier which is contained in the EIBRSRCE field. The ALLOCATE command, if successful, alters the transactions state with regard to the session. If we look at Figure 14-1, which is the state 1 diagram, we note that if the ALLOCATE command was successful (as indicated by the "Otherwise" entry to the right of the command), the transaction is in a new state, and this is state 2.

14.4   THE NEW STATE — STATE 2

Figure 14-2 is the state diagram for state 2 or the SEND STATE. The Front-End Transaction must, however, do something to initiate the back end. This can be accomplished in one of three ways: 1) the program can use the BUILD ATTACH command to have CICS construct an ATTACH Function Management Header; 2) the program can build its own ATTACH Function Management Header; or 3) for

CICS-to-CICS sessions, the TRANSID of the remote process can be placed in the first 4 bytes of the first message to be sent to the remote system. The third approach is undoubtedly the easiest and it is the recommended approach for CICS-to-CICS. However, if the LUTYPE 6.1 is used to connect with IMS/VS, this cannot be done because IMS does not support the CICS mechanism of examining the first 4 bytes of input for a TRANSID.

14.5   THE BUILD ATTACH COMMAND

The BUILD ATTACH command causes CICS to build an ATTACH Function Management Header. However, the header is not sent to the other system. Rather, it is the programmer's responsibility to ensure that the ATTACH header is named in the first SEND/CONVERSE command issued. This is accomplished by providing CICS with a name for the header when doing the BUILD ATTACH. This ATTACH header name is then specified in the SEND/CONVERSE command.

14.5.1   BUILD ATTACH Command Format

The format of the BUILD ATTACH command is as follows:

```
EXEC CICS BUILD ATTACH
          PROCESS(name-of-process)
          ATTACHID(name-of-attach-header)
          RESOURCE(name-of-resource)
          RPROCESS(name-of-return-process)
          QUEUE(name-of-queue)
          IUTYPE(name-of-Inter-change-Unit)
          DATASTR(name-of-data stream)
          RECFM(name-of-deblocking-algorithm)
```

For CICS-to-CICS connections the only options that are normally used are the PROCESS and ATTACHID options. For non-CICS connections, it is necessary to review the appropriate subsystem documentation and determine the correct values for the Function Managment Header fields which these options correspond to and provide appropriate data values. Figure 14-10 shows the format of the SNA ATTACH Function Management Header which is built in response to the execution of a BUILD ATTACH command.

The ATTACH FMH-5 is sent by either LU_T6 half-session to select a named transaction program. The ATTACH FMH can be followed by other FM headers and FM
data. The ATTACH FMH-5 can optionally be sent with BB, EB, or CD.

Each variable-length field (those fields starting with byte 8) starts with a
1- or 2-byte length field that indicates the number of bytes in the
variable-length field. Field FMH5LNSZ indicates whether the length field is
one or two bytes; the length indicated does not include the length byte(s).

Byte	Bit	Content	Meaning
0		Length	Length of header including length byte
1	0	FMHC	FMH concatenation.
		B'0'	No FMH follows
		B'1'	Another FMH follows
	1-7	B'0000101'	FMH-5 identifier
2-3		FMH5CMD	Command code
		X'0202'	Attach FMH-5
4		FMH5MOD	
	0	FMH5LNSZ	Length of length fields for variable- and fixed-length parameters
		B'0'	Length field is 1 byte long
		B'1'	Length field is 2 bytes long
	1-2		Reserved
	3	FMH5IUE	Interchange unit end indicator
		B'0'	IU not terminated
		B'1'	IU terminated
	4		Reserved
	5	FMH5IUA	Interchange unit queue access
		B'0'	Not session local queue
		B'1'	Session local queue (only session partners can access queue)
	6-7	FMH5IUT	Interchange unit type
		B'00'	IU spans more than one RU chain
		B'01'	IU terminates at end of RU chain
			Others reserved
5		FMH5FXCT	Length of fixed length parameters
		X'02'	Two bytes of parameters follow
6		ATTDSP	Data stream profile used by transaction program
	0-3	DSP	Data stream profile
		X'0'	User defined
			Others reserved
	4-7	DSPMOD	Modifier for user-defined DSP.
7		ATTDBA	Application data handling algorithm
		X'01'	Variable length, variable blocked
		X'04'	A chain of RUs

Figure 14-10 SNA ATTACH function management header. Reprinted by permission from *Systems Network Architecture: Sessions Between Logical Units* ©
1981 by International Business Machines Corporation.

Resource Names:

8-m	ATTDPN	Field length (1 or 2 bytes depending on FMH5LNSZ) plus name of transaction program (DPN) to be initiated. For an IBM service (transaction) program, the DPN starts with a nongraphic; that is, the first byte has a value of X'00' to X'3F'(see list below). For all other programs, the DPN starts with a graphic (X'41' to X'FE').

IBM service program	First byte of name
System message program	X'01'
Scheduler program	X'02'
Queue program	X'03'
DL/1 program	X'05'

m+1-n	ATTPRN	Field length (1 or 2 bytes depending on FMH5LNSZ) plus name of primary resource (PRN) for the transaction program being initiated
n+1-p	ATTRDPN	Field length (1 or 2 bytes depending on FMH5LNSZ) plus name of suggested return program name (RDPN)
p+1-q	ATTRPRN	Field length (1 or 2 bytes depending on FMH5LNSZ) plus name of suggested primary resource for the return program (RPN)
q+1-r	ATTDQN	Field length (1 or 2 bytes depending on FMH5LNSZ) plus name of queue to be associated with the DPN
r+1-s	ATTACC	Field length (1 or 2 bytes depending on FMH5LNSZ) plus access code to be validated before session is attached to transaction program (a symbolic name)

Note: Variable- and fixed-length parameters are positional by command code. A length field, which is 1- or 2-bytes long depending on byte 5, precedes each variable-length positional parameter. If the length field is zero the variable parameter is omitted and the next positional variable-length parameter length field occurs followed by its variable-length parameter field.

Figure 14-10 (continued) SNA ATTACH function management header. Reprinted by permission from *Systems Network Architecture: Sessions Between Logical Units* © 1981 by International Business Machines Corporation.

The PROCESS option provides the name of the remote process. PROCESS corresponds to the ATTDPN field in the LUTYPE 6.1 Function Management Header.

The ATTACHID provides a name for the ATTACH header itself. This name is referenced in the first SEND/CONVERSE issued against the session. The inclusion of ATTACHID in the SEND/CONVERSE causes CICS to concatenate the named ATTACH header to the output data. The name is limited to 8 characters.

The RESOURCE option provides a value for the ATTPRN field in the LUTYPE 6.1 ATTACH Function Management Header.

The RPROCESS option provides a value for the ATTRDPN field in the LUTYPE 6.1 ATTACH Function Management Header.

The RRESOURCE option provides a value for the ATTRPRN field in the LUTYPE 6.1 ATTACH Function Management Header.

The QUEUE option provides a value for the ATTDQN field in the LUTYPE 6.1 ATTACH Function Management Header.

The IUTYPE option provides a value for the ATTIU field in the LUTYPE 6.1 ATTACH Function Management Header.

The DATASTR option provides a value for the ATTDSP field in the LUTYPE 6.1 ATTACH Function Management Header.

The RECFM option provides a value for the ATTDBA field in the LUTYPE 6.1 ATTACH Function Management Header.

For CICS-to-CICS, all of the business with Function Management Headers can be avoided by including the TRANSID in the first 4 bytes of the first output message area. For connections with non-CICS systems (such as IMS), the LUTYPE 6.1 ATTACH Function Management Header must be used. However, the programmer is not required to use the BUILD ATTACH command. The application program can also elect to actually build the Function Management Header in program storage and place this self-constructed header into the first output message area. In this case the FMH option must be included in the SEND/CONVERSE command.

14.5.2   Unusual Conditions and the BUILD ATTACH Command

There are no unusual conditions associated with the BUILD ATTACH. The proof of the pudding is in the correct attachment of the remote process.

14.6   THE BACK-END TRANSACTION — INITIATED IN STATE 4

The Back-End Transaction is initiated in state 4, the receive state. Figure 14-4 illustrates the state 4 diagram. Aside from dealing with session errors the only valid command for a receive state transaction is to RECEIVE. Subsequent to the first receive, the initiated Back-End Transaction can use the EXTRACT ATTACH command to obtain information from the ATTACH Function Management Header. If a Function Management Header is present, the EIBATT field is set on (X'FF'). This indicates that it is valid to perform the EX-

TRACT ATTACH. ATTACH headers are never passed to an application program, whether or not the session profile specifies IN-BFMH(ALL). ATTACH headers are received and processed by CICS, but the application process can obtain information from an ATTACH header with the EXTRACT ATTACH command.

14.7   THE EXTRACT ATTACH COMMAND FORMAT

The format of the EXTRACT ATTACH command is:

```
EXEC CICS EXTRACT ATTACH
     PROCESS(field-name)
     SESSION(field-name)
     RESOURCE(field-name)
     RPROCESS(field-name)
     RRESOURCE(field-name)
     QUEUE(field-name)
     IUTYPE(field-name)
     DATASTR(field-name)
     RECFM(field-name)
```

The EXTRACT ATTACH options correspond to the data specified in the BUILD ATTACH options. The PROCESS option names a field which is used to obtain the process name passed in the ATTACH header in the ATTDPN field. All of the other options work in a similar manner except the SESSION option.

The SESSION option names a data field containing the SESSION ID. For the Back-End Transaction, this ID is contained in EIBTRMID. Specification of the SESSION option is not required, but if used, the SESSION data field must be primed with the value contained in EIBTRMID.

The unusual conditions associated with the EXTRACT PROCESS command are CBIDERR, INVREQ, and NOTALLOC. In all cases, the default action by CICS is to terminate the task.

14.8   THE SEND COMMAND

The format of the SEND command for LUTYPE 6.1 and MRO is as follows.

```
EXEC CICS SEND
          SESSION(field-containing-SESSION-ID)
          ATTACHID(name-of-ATTACH-header)
          FROM(data-area-name)
          LENGTH(value-defining-FROM-area-size)
          INVITE * OR * LAST
          WAIT
          FMH
          DEFRESP
```

The SESSION option names the data field which contains the SESSION-ID obtained by the Front-End Transaction from EIBRSRCE subsequent to the ALLOCATE command. For the Back-End Transaction or a Front-End Transaction that was not required to ALLOCATE a session, the specification of SESSION is optional. In the latter two cases, EIBTRMID contains the value to be specified for SESSION.

The ATTACHID option provides the name of the ATTACH header built by a Front-End Transaction with the BUILD ATTACH command. This option is specified only when an ATTACH header is being used to initiate the remote transaction. In this context the ATTACHID is appropriate only to the first SEND command issued by the Front-End Transaction.

The FROM option names an application data area containing a message to be sent. The inclusion of the FROM area is optional.

The LENGTH option is used to define the length of the data message contained in the area named with the FROM option.

The INVITE option is used to generate an SNA Change-Direction Indicator. The SEND STATE transaction is now inviting the RE-CEIVE STATE transaction to start sending. In MRO sessions the INVITE is transmitted immediately, and the transaction is in the RECEIVE state. For LUTYPE 6.1 the transaction remains in the SEND STATE unless the transmission is forced by other SEND options.

The transaction receiving a SEND INVITE is informed of its state change, from RECEIVE STATE to SEND STATE via the EIBRECV field in the Execute Interface Block. EIBRECV is turned off (X'00') to indicate that the transaction is in the SEND state. Conversely, EIBRECV is set on (X'FF') to indicate that the transaction is in the RECEIVE state. CICS sets EIBRECV when a RECEIVE command is executed. Therefore, this field should be tested immediately after a RECEIVE command when you know it is meaningful. INVITE and the next option, LAST, are mutually exclusive.

The LAST option generates the SNA End Bracket (EB) indicator. SEND LAST can be used with or without data. In MRO, CICS does not defer sending of data. However, in the case of the End Bracket Indicator, CICS does not forward this indicator unless the SEND command explicitly requests this by including the WAIT option.

The WAIT option is used to force CICS to transmit the data and indicators for LUTYPE 6.1 sessions.

The FMH option indicates that the output data contains a Function Management Header.

The DEFRESP option specifies that CICS is to request a "Definite Response" for this output.

The unusual conditions of the SEND command include CBIDERR, NOTALLOC, SIGNAL, and TERMERR. The unusual conditions were discussed in the chapters on LUTYPE 6.2 mapped conversations.

14.9   THE FORMAT OF THE RECEIVE COMMAND

The format of the RECEIVE command for LUTYPE 6.1 and MRO programs is as follows.

```
EXEC CICS RECEIVE
          SESSION(field-name)
          INTO(data-area-name)
             * OR *
          SET(pointer)
          MAXLENGTH(2-byte-binary-field)
          LENGTH(2-byte-binary-field)
          NOTRUNCATE
```

The SESSION option names the data field containing the SESSION ID. The mutually exclusive INTO or SET options allow the application to obtain incoming data. When SET is used, the application program obtains addressability to data that is actually located in a CICS work area. CICS may release this area when the next EXEC CICS command is executed. So you can think of the CICS work area as something that is temporarily loaned to your task and not something that your task owns. INTO copies the data into your dynamic work area (COBOL WORKING-STORAGE or assembler DFHEISTG DSECT). As such, you have your data as long as the task lives.

The MAXLENGTH option names a 2-byte binary field which is used to define maximum length information. When used in a command specifying RECEIVE INTO, this field indicates the maximum size that the program can accommodate in terms of its defined input work area. A RECEIVE SET command that does not include the MAXLENGTH option results in CICS providing addressability to all of the input data. With RECEIVE SET, the MAXLENGTH option defines the maximum amount of data that the program is willing to accept.

If the actual data length exceeds the MAXLENGTH field specification, CICS raises the LENGERR error condition and truncates the remaining data. However, if the RECEIVE command includes the NOTRUNCATE, truncation is not performed and the task may do successive RECEIVEs to obtain the remaining data. If MAXLENGTH is omitted from a RECEIVE command, CICS looks to the LENGTH option to provide any required data length information for RECEIVE INTO.

The LENGTH option names a 2-byte binary field which is used to provide length information when the MAXLENGTH option described above is not included in a RECEIVE command. When LENGTH is used with RECEIVE INTO, the LENGTH field indicates the size of the INTO area. This represents the maximum amount of information that the program can accommodate as a result of a single RECEIVE command. Subsequent to the RECEIVE, CICS updates the length field to indicate the actual size of the data. When used in a RECEIVE SET, CICS returns the actual data length in the LENGTH field. RECEIVE INTO LENGTH can result in a length error if the application program area is not large enough to accommodate all of the input. Again, CICS truncates the data and raises the LENGERR condition unless the NOTRUNCATE option is included in the RECEIVE command.

If NOTRUNCATE is included in a RECEIVE command, CICS does not raise the LENGERR condition and does not truncate data. The application program can then do successive RECEIVE commands and obtain any remaining data. When all data has been passed to the application program, CICS sets on EIBCOMPL (X'FF' is on). Therefore, an application program RECEIVEs NOTRUNCATE until EIBCOMPL is equal to high values. If you omit the NOTRUNCATE option EIBCOMPL is always set on.

The unusual conditions of the RECEIVE command include EOC, INBFMH, LENGERR, NOTALLOC, SIGNAL, and TERMERR.

The only condition not explained in the chapter on LUTYPE 6.2 mapped conversations is the INBFMH condition. This condition indicates that the input message (RU) contains a Function Management Header. It is best to IGNORE this condition and test EIBFMH which is set on (X'FF') when an FMH is received. The default course of action is for CICS to abend the task.

14.10   THE CONVERSE COMMAND

The CONVERSE command functionally combines a SEND INVITE WAIT and RECEIVE. Actually, if this is the function that is desired, one CONVERSE command has a shorter execution path than the processing of the separate commands. CICS generates an SNA Change-Direction Indicator and if you check Figure 14-2, you will note that the transaction enters the RECEIVE STATE subsequent to a CONVERSE command.

The format of the CONVERSE command is as follows.

```
EXEC CICS CONVERSE
          SESSION(field-containing-session-id)
          FROM(data-area-name)
          FROMLENGTH(from-length-info)
          INTO(data-area-name)
                * OR *
          SET(pointer)
          TOLENGTH(input-length-info)
          MAXLENGTH(max-length-info)
          NOTRUNCATE
          ATTACHID(header-name)
          FMH
          DEFRESP
```

The options of the CONVERSE command are a subset of options that can be defined on the SEND and RECEIVE commands. Since we've gone over these options we'll curtail the discussion of them, and merely point you in the direction of the appropriate command if you wish to review these options.

The SESSION option is used as described above for the SEND and RECEIVE commands.

The FROM option names the data area containing the output message to be sent as in the SEND command.

The FROMLENGTH option specifies the length of the FROM data area — the output message length as in the SEND command.

The mutually exclusive INTO or SET options are used as described above in the RECEIVE command.

The MAXLENGTH and TOLENGTH options are used as the MAXLENGTH and LENGTH options of the RECEIVE command.

The NOTRUNCATE option is used as described in the discussion of the RECEIVE command.

The ATTACHID, FMH, and DEFRESP options are explained in the discussion of the SEND command.

The unusual conditions associated with the CONVERSE command are EOC, CBIDERR, INBFMH, LENGERR, NOTALLOC, SIGNAL, and TERMERR. These options excepting INBFMH are explained in the chapter on LUTYPE 6.2 mapped conversations. The INBFMH condition is explained above in the discussion of the RECEIVE command.

14.11   THE WAIT TERMINAL COMMAND

The WAIT TERMINAL command can be used to force CICS to transmit the internal buffer with data and control indicators before the task continues its execution. The WAIT command is not applicable to MRO sessions, wherein it is a null command.

The format of the WAIT TERMINAL command is as follows.

```
EXEC CICS WAIT TERMINAL SESSION(data-area-name)
```

The SESSION option is used as in all the other commands described above.

The unusual conditions that can occur for the WAIT command are NOTALLOC and SIGNAL.

14.12   THE ISSUE SIGNAL COMMAND

The ISSUE SIGNAL command is used by a RECEIVE STATE transaction to indicate its need to have a state change. In other words, a RECEIVE STATE transaction can request being placed into the SEND STATE by executing an ISSUE SIGNAL. CICS turns on EIBSIG (X'FF') to indicate receipt of an ISSUE SIGNAL. As described in the chapter on LUTYPE 6.2 mapped conversations, the transaction receiving the ISSUE SIGNAL is not required by CICS to do anything specific. The ISSUE SIGNAL cannot be used for MRO sessions.

If you can receive an ISSUE SIGNAL because the protocols of your application provide for its use, EIBSIG should be tested after each session-related command.

The format of the ISSUE SIGNAL command is as follows.

```
EXEC CICS ISSUE SIGNAL SESSION(field-name)
```

The SESSION option is not required for a transaction whose principal facility is the conversation over which ISSUE SIGNAL is to flow.

The unusual conditions of the ISSUE SIGNAL are NOTALLOC and TERMERR.

14.13 THE FREE COMMAND

The FREE command is used to FREE a session. This may be used as a normal part of conversation termination.

The format of the FREE command is as follows.

```
EXEC CICS FREE SESSION(field-name)
```

The SESSION option can be omitted if the conversation is the transaction's principal facility.

The unusual conditions associated with the FREE command are INVREQ and NOTALLOC. These conditions are described above for other commands.

14.14 COMMANDS RELATING TO SYNCPOINT EXCHANGES

The SYNCPOINT command is used to initiate commit protocols during LUTYPE 6.1 or MRO sessions. It can be executed only when in the SEND STATE. The ROLLBACK option is not supported for LUTYPE 6.1. Therefore, SYNCPOINT ROLLBACK can only be used for MRO sessions. As with LUTYPE 6.2 conversations, the EIB SYNCPOINT fields are used. These include EIBSYNC, EIBSYNRB, and EIBRLDBK. However, only EIBSYNC is meaningful for LUTYPE 6.1 sessions.

The format of the SYNCPOINT command is:

```
EXEC CICS SYNCPOINT
        ROLLBACK
```

14.15   OTHER LUTYPE 6.1 COMMANDS

There are also some commands that may be used for LUTYPE 6.1 sessions, but which cannot be used for MRO. These include EX-TRACT TCT, WAIT SIGNAL, and ISSUE DISCONNECT. The EX-TRACT TCT permits a transaction to provide a 1- to 8-character NETNAME and obtain in response the local SYSIDNT of the remote system as it is defined in the TCT. The format of this command is as follows:

```
EXEC CICS EXTRACT TCT
        NETNAME(1-8 character netname)
        SYSID(4-byte-data-field)
```

The WAIT SIGNAL allows a task to wait for an incoming SIGNAL from its principal facility. The format of this command is as follows.

```
EXEC CICS WAIT SIGNAL
```

The ISSUE DISCONNECT command is used to end a session. This command is not to be confused with FREE, which frees an allocated session from a transaction that no longer requires the session. The ISSUE DISCONNECT terminates the session from CICS's point of view. The format of this command is as follows.

```
EXEC CICS ISSUE DISCONNECT
        SESSION(name-of-session)
```

The TCT definition of the session must be defined to support dis-connect requests.

14.16   SUMMARY OF EIB FIELDS

The EIB fields that are used during LUTYPE 6.1 and MRO sessions are listed below. Programs that perform distributed transactions must constantly be testing EIB fields subsequent to session-related commands. It is recommended that the contents of these fields be saved in a unique work area in program dynamic storage subsequent to appropriate commands where this is indicated in the appropriate state diagram. The status fields are described below as being set on (X'FF') or set off (X'00').

EIBRSRCE should be saved subsequent to an ALLOCATE command as the field then contains the unique session ID assigned by CICS. EIBTRMID contains the Back-End Transaction's principal resource name. If a Front-End Transaction is initiated via an ATI request that names a remote SYSIDNT, there is no need to perform an ALLOCATE because the transaction is started in STATE 2. The use of SESSION ID is optional for commands pertaining to the principal facility and the name of the principal facility is contained in EIBTRMID.

EIBCOMPL is tested subsequent to RECEIVE NOTRUNCATE to determine when all data has been RECEIVEd from CICS. CICS sets this field on when all data has been received.

EIBRECV is used to indicate a transaction's RECEIVE/SEND state. If set on, the transaction is in the RECEIVE state. This field should be tested after every RECEIVE command and in any other context in which a transaction's state may have altered.

EIBSIG is set on to indicate remote process execution of ISSUE SIGNAL. This is normally used by a RECEIVE STATE transaction to request a state change. If used in an application, EIBSIG should be tested after each conversation command. Since ISSUE SIGNAL is not supported for MRO, this field is not used in programs using MRO links.

EIBFREE is set on to indicate that the session must be freed. The remote process has performed a FREE command or a SEND LAST WAIT, and the upshot is that the End Bracket has been generated and sent. Therefore, when EIBFREE is set on, the only thing that a task can do is FREE the session by executing the FREE command or RETURNing to CICS.

EIBSYNC is set on to indicate a SYNCPOINT request. This field should be tested after each RECEIVE command.

EIBSYNRB is set on to indicate a SYNCPOINT ROLLBACK. If this command is used in an application, EIBSYNRB should be tested after every command pertaining to the session. This field is appropriate only to MRO since SYNCPOINT ROLLBACK is not supported for LUTYPE 6.1.

EIBRLDBK is set on to indicate the failure of a SYNCPOINT. This indication means that the task has been ROLLED BACK. This field is appropriate only to MRO.

15

CICS to IMS ISC

15.1   INTRODUCTION

CICS InterSystem Communication permits Function Shipping requests to be made against an IMS database which is accessible through a remote CICS system. Asynchronous Processing and Distributed Transaction Processing are supported directly between connected CICS and IMS systems. There are, however, limitations in terms of what can be done between CICS and IMS. For example, a CICS application program performing Distributed Transaction Processing does not engage in a dialog with an IMS application program.

Rather, **the CICS program is conversing with the IMS Data Communication component (IMS/DC).** This is because IMS queues application program input/output. Network resources are connected to the IMS control region. Input messages are queued for the appropriate application program. IMS schedules the program's execution and the program reads its queue. The program performs its application functions and passes its "output" to IMS. IMS does not allow an application program to directly "own" a network resource as CICS does. A CICS application transaction temporarily owns a network resource to which it is connected. The CICS application program controls the generation of SNA indicators to a large degree. However, IMS owns all network resources and asynchronously schedules IMS transactions.

Therefore, application protocols relating to SNA flow control and indicators cannot be adjusted between two application programs. The

CICS application program connected to an IMS system is conversing directly with IMS/DC. The CICS application programmer must know and understand the way in which IMS/DC handles SNA protocols. Furthermore, CICS and IMS can be connected only by LUTYPE 6.1 links. Therefore, application programs that engage in distributed transactions with IMS/DC can use only the CICS commands associated with the LUTYPE 6.1 discussed in the previous chapter.

15.2   FUNCTION SHIPPING AND A REMOTE DATABASE

Function Shipping allows a CICS program to access a remote IMS database that is accessible through a remote CICS system. The application program uses either DL/I calls or EXEC DLI commands as if the database were associated with the local CICS system. When the access is made, the local DL/I interface recognizes that the request should be Function Shipped to a remote CICS. The Program Specification Block (PSB) directory list in the local system defines the PSB as being in a remote CICS. In terms of syncpoint processing, the remote Mirror Task's SYNCPOINT results in a DL/I term call to commit database modifications. However, IMS does not permit multiple PSBs to be scheduled within one logical unit of work. This precludes distributed updates in multiple systems.

15.3   ASYNCHRONOUS PROCESSING

As with CICS to CICS there are two means of accomplishing Asynchronous Processing between CICS and IMS. The Interval Control START command or the SEND LAST can both be utilized. Both of these techniques can be used from CICS to IMS.

15.3.1   15.3.1 Interval Control START

Interfacing to IMS through the START command has some limitations in terms of the command options that can be specified. An INTERVAL(0) must always be used either through command coding or by default. It is, therefore, impossible to CANCEL a START sent to an IMS system because only unexpired requests can be cancelled.

The START defines the IMS editor which processes the message and the *IMS transaction (LTERM)* that is to receive the request. The first thing initiated is the *IMS editor* and, therefore, the TRANSID option of the START command names the IMS editor. The IMS transaction or LTERM can be specified in two ways. If the LTERM name is 4 characters, then the TERMID option of the START command can be used to name the LTERM. Otherwise, the LTERM name can be placed in the beginning of the FROM data area. The RTERMID and RTRANSID are used in the normal way to name a CICS terminal and TRANSID for the response back from IMS.

The START command QUEUE option cannot be specified for requests directed to IMS/VS. NOCHECK is required for STARTs sent to IMS, and for IMS-recoverable transactions PROTECT is mandated as well. The START must be followed by either task termination (and its implicit SYNCPOINT) or a SYNCPOINT because no intervening messages between START and SYNCPOINT are permitted on a link to IMS. Therefore, only one START command for IMS is permitted within a logical unit of work.

15.3.2   15.3.2 SEND LAST

SEND LAST is a subject of Distributed Transaction Processing, and both CICS and IMS view it in this manner. There are, however, cases in which SEND LAST (asynchronous processing) can be used but synchronous conversations are not allowed. The converse is true also. For example, if a CICS application program is the front end, then synchronous conversations are permitted with certain kinds of IMS transactions. However, when coming from IMS to CICS Asynchronous Processing is always utilized.

In order to use the SEND LAST interface to IMS, it is necessary to forward an ATTACH Function Management Header according to the requirements of IMS. To this end, the application program can a) dynamically construct the header or b) use the BUILD ATTACH command. The SEND command names the ATTACHID or the header name when BUILD ATTACH is used. When the header is built by the application program, it is the programmer's responsibility to place the header into the output area and include the FMH option of the SEND command. The CICS convention of using the first 4 bytes of input as the transaction name or TRANSID is not supported by IMS — therefore, the requirement for the ATTACH header.

15.4   DISTRIBUTED TRANSACTION PROCESSING — A SYNCHRONIZED CONVERSATION

For a synchronized conversation between a CICS application program and the IMS/DC component, the CICS program is the front end. There are restrictions as to which type of IMS transactions can be initiated in this way. Also, the programmer must understand the IMS/DC use of SNA flow control mechanisms and indicators. IMS/DC is the given and the CICS application program must act/react in accordance with IMS's requirements.

The CICS application programmer would be responsible for building or causing CICS to build an appropriate ATTACH function management header as is the case with the SEND LAST interface described above. The LUTYPE 6.1 commands normally used for CICS to IMS sessions would include ALLOCATE, BUILD ATTACH, EXTRACT ATTACH, SEND, RECEIVE, CONVERSE, WAIT TERMINAL SESSION, ISSUE SIGNAL, and FREE. The EXTRACT ATTACH would only be applicable to the asynchronous SEND LAST because IMS does not initiate synchronous conversations to CICS.

STATE 1 CICS to IMS/VS CONVERSATIONS		SESSION NOT ALLOCATED
Commands You Can Issue	What To Test	New State
ALLOCATE [NOQUEUE] *	SYSIDERR	1
	SYSBUSY *	1
	Otherwise (obtain session name from EIBRSRCE)	2

* If you want your program to wait until a session is available, omit the NOQUEUE option of the ALLOCATE command and do not code a HANDLE command for the SYSBUSY condition.

  If you want control to be returned to your program if a session is not immediately available, either specify NOQUEUE on the ALLOCATE command and test EIBRCODE for SYSBUSY (X'D3'), or code a HANDLE CONDITION SYSBUSY command.

Figure 15-1 State 1 — SESSION NOT ALLOCATED. Reprinted by permission from *CICS/MVS Version 2.1 Intercommunication Guide* © 1987, 1988 by International Business Machines Corporation.

STATE 2 CICS to IMS/VS CONVERSATIONS		SEND STATE
Commands You Can Issue *	What To Test	New State
SEND		2
SEND INVITE	—	3 or 4
SEND LAST	—	6

CONVERSE
Equivalent to:
  SEND INVITE WAIT
  RECEIVE
	Go to the STATE 4 table and make the tests shown for the RECEIVE command	—

RECEIVE	Go to the STATE 4 table and make the tests shown for the RECEIVE command	—
SYNCPOINT	(transaction will ABEND if SYNCPOINT fails)	2

FREE
Equivalent to:
  SEND LAST WAIT
  FREE
	—	1

* For the front-end transaction, the first command used after the session has been allocated must be a SEND command or CONVERSE command that initiates the back-end transaction in one of the ways described under 'Attaching the Remote Transaction' on page 255.

Figure 15-2 State 2 — SEND STATE. Reprinted by permission from *CICS/MVS Version 2.1 Intercommunication Guide* © 1987, 1988 by International Business Machines Corporation.

The commands are used in the context of the transaction's state, and the state diagrams for CICS to IMS conversations are provided in Figures 15-1 through 15-7. The appropriate EIB tests are, as usual, listed in the state diagrams.

STATE 3 CICS to IMS/VS CONVERSATIONS	RECEIVE PENDING AFTER INVITE	
Commands You Can Issue	What To Test	New State
SYNCPOINT	(transaction will ABEND if SYNCPOINT fails)	4

Figure 15-3 State 3 — RECEIVE PENDING AFTER INVITE. Reprinted by permission from *CICS/MVS Version 2.1 Intercommunication Guide* © 1987, 1988 by International Business Machines Corporation.

STATE 4 CICS to IMS/VS CONVERSATIONS		RECEIVE STATE
Commands You Can Issue	What To Test	New State
RECEIVE [NOTRUNCATE] *	EIBCOMPL *	–
	EIBSYNC	5
	EIBFREE	7
	EIBRECV	4
	Otherwise	2

> * If NOTRUNCATE is specified, a zero value in EIBCOMPL indicates that the data passed to the application by CICS is incomplete (because, for example, the data-area specified in the RECEIVE command is too small). CICS will save the remaining data for retrieval by subsequent RECEIVE NOTRUNCATE commands. EIBCOMPL is set when the last part of the data is passed back. If the NOTRUNCATE option is not specified, overlength data is indicated by the LENGERR condition, and the remaining data is discarded by CICS.

Figure 15-4 State 4 — RECEIVE STATE. Reprinted by permission from *CICS/MVS Version 2.1 Intercommunication Guide* © 1987, 1988 by International Business Machines Corporation.

STATE 5 CICS to IMS/VS CONVERSATIONS		RECEIVER TAKE SYNCPOINT
Commands You Can Issue	What To Test	New State
SYNCPOINT	EIBFREE (saved value)	7
	EIBRECV (saved value)	4
	Otherwise	2

Figure 15-5 State 5 — RECEIVER TAKE SYNCPOINT. Reprinted by permission from *CICS/MVS Version 2.1 Intercommunication Guide* © 1987, 1988 by International Business Machines Corporation.

STATE 6 CICS to IMS/VS CONVERSATIONS		FREE PENDING AFTER SEND LAST
Commands You Can Issue	What To Test	New State
SYNCPOINT	-	7
FREE	-	1

Figure 15-6 State 6 — FREE PENDING AFTER SEND LAST. Reprinted by permission from *CICS/MVS Version 2.1 Intercommunication Guide* © 1987, 1988 by International Business Machines Corporation.

STATE 7 CICS to IMS/VS CONVERSATIONS		FREE SESSION
Commands You Can Issue	What To Test	New State
FREE	-	1

Figure 15-7 State 7 — FREE SESSION. Reprinted by permission from *CICS/MVS Version 2.1 Intercommunication Guide* © 1987, 1988 by International Business Machines Corporation.

State Diagrams LUTYPE 6.2 Mapped Conversations

State 1 — SESSION NOT ALLOCATED

STATE 1 MAPPED LUTYPE6.2 CONVERSATIONS		SESSION NOT ALLOCATED
Commands You Can Issue	What To Test (For EIBERRCD tests see the table on page 199)	New State
ALLOCATE [NOQUEUE] *	SYSIDERR	1
	SYSBUSY *	1
	Otherwise (obtain conversation identifier from EIBRSRCE)	2

* If you want your program to wait until a session is available, omit the NOQUEUE option of the ALLOCATE command and do not code a HANDLE command for the SYSBUSY condition.

If you want control to be returned to your program if a session is not immediately available, either specify NOQUEUE on the ALLOCATE command and test EIBRCODE for SYSBUSY (X'D3'), or code a HANDLE CONDITION SYSBUSY command.

State 2 — SESSION ALLOCATED

STATE 2 MAPPED LUTYPE6.2 CONVERSATICNS		SESSION ALLOCATED
Commands You Can Issue	What To Test (For EIBERRCD tests see the table on page 199)	New State
CONNECT PROCESS	TERMERR *	3
FREE	−	1

* The failure of a CONNECT PROCESS command (caused by such things as the unavailability of the remote process or mismatched sync levels) is usually indicated on a later command on the same conversation.

State 3 — SEND STATE

STATE 3 HAPPED LUTYPE6.2 CONVERSATIONS		SEND STATE
Commands You Can Issue	What To Test (For EIBERRCD tests see the table on page 199)	New State
SEND	–	3
SEND INVITE	–	4
SEND INVITE WAIT	–	5
SEND LAST	–	9
SEND LAST WAIT	–	10
SEND CONFIRM (SYNCLEVEL 1 or 2 only)	See "Checking the Response to SEND CONFIRM" earlier in this chapter. New states assume that EIBERR is not set.	3
SEND INVITE CONFIRM (SYNCLEVEL 1 or 2 only)		5
SEND LAST CONFIRM (SYNCLEVEL 1 or 2 only)		10
CONVERSE Equivalent to: SEND INVITE WAIT RECEIVE	Go to the STATE 5 table and make the tests shown for the RECEIVE command	–
RECEIVE (INVITE is sent by CICS)	Go to the STATE 5 table and make the tests shown for the RECEIVE command	–
ISSUE PREPARE (SYNCLEVEL 2 only) Note: If a negative response is received, EIBERR and EIBERRCD will also be set	EIBSYNRB	8
	EIBFREE	10
	Otherwise	3
SYNCPOINT (SYNCLEVEL 2 only)	EIBRLDBK (or ROLLEDBACK condition)	5
	Otherwise (transaction will ABEND if SYNCPOINT fails)	3
SYNCPOINT ROLLBACK (SYNCLEVEL 2 only)	(transaction will ABEND if ROLLBACK fails)	3
WAIT CONVID	–	3
ISSUE ERROR	EIBRECV	5
	Otherwise	3
ISSUE ABEND	–	10
FREE Equivalent to: SEND LAST WAIT FREE	–	1

Reprinted by permission from *CICS/MVS Version 2.1 Intercommunication Guide* © 1987, 1988 by International Business Machines Corporation.

State 4 — RECEIVE PENDING AFTER INVITE

STATE 4 MAPPED LUTYPE6.2 CONVERSATIONS	RECEIVE PENDING AFTER INVITE	
Commands You Can Issue	What To Test (For EIBERRCD tests see the table on page 199)	New State
WAIT	–	5
RECEIVE Equivalent to: WAIT RECEIVE	Go to the STATE 5 table and make the tests shown for the RECEIVE command	–
ISSUE ERROR	EIBFREE	10
	Otherwise	3
ISSUE ABEND	–	10
SYNCPOINT (SYNCLEVEL 2 only)	EIBRLDBK (or ROLLEDBACK condition)	5
	Otherwise (transaction will ABEND if SYNCPOINT fails)	5
SYNCPOINT ROLLBACK (SYNCLEVEL 2 only)	(transaction will ABEND if ROLLBACK fails)	3

State 5 — RECEIVE STATE

STATE 5 MAPPED LUTYPE6.2 CONVERSATIONS		RECEIVE STATE
Commands You Can Issue	What To Test (For EIBERRCD tests see the table on page 199)	New State
RECEIVE [NOTRUNCATE] *	EIBCOMPL *	—
	EIBCONF (SYNCLEVEL 1 or 2 only)	6
	EIBSYNC (SYNCLEVEL 2 only)	7
	EIBSYNRB (SYNCLEVEL 2 only)	8
	EIBFREE	10
	EIBRECV	5
	Otherwise	3
SYNCPOINT ROLLBACK (SYNCLEVEL 2 only)	(transaction will ABEND if ROLLBACK fails)	3
ISSUE ERROR	EIBFREE	10
	Otherwise	3
ISSUE ABEND	—	10

* If NOTRUNCATE is specified, a zero value in EIBCOMPL indicates that the data passed to the application by CICS is incomplete (because, for example, the data-area specified in the RECEIVE command is too small). CICS will save the remaining data for retrieval by subsequent RECEIVE NOTRUNCATE commands. EIBCOMPL is set when the last part of the data is passed back. If the NOTRUNCATE option is not specified, overlength data is indicated by the LENGERR condition, and the remaining data is discarded by CICS.

Reprinted by permission from *CICS/MVS Version 2.1 Intercommunication Guide* © 1987, 1988 by International Business Machines Corporation.

State 6 — RECEIVER ISSUE CONFIRMATION

STATE 6 MAPPED LUTYPE6.2 CONVERSATIONS	RECEIVER ISSUE CONFIRMATION	
Commands You Can Issue	What To Test (For EIBERRCD tests see the table on page 199)	New State
ISSUE CONFIRMATION	EIBFREE (saved value)	10
	EIBRECV (saved value)	5
	Otherwise	3
ISSUE ERROR	EIBFREE (saved value)	3
	Otherwise	3
ISSUE ABEND	-	10

State 7 — RECEIVER TAKE SYNCPOINT

STATE 7 MAPPED LUTYPE6.2 CONVERSATIONS	RECEIVER TAKE SYNCPOINT	
Commands You Can Issue	What To Test (For EIBERRCD tests see the table on page 199)	New State
SYNCPOINT	EIBFREE (saved value)	10
	EIBRECV (saved value)	5
	Otherwise	3
SYNCPOINT ROLLBACK	-	3
ISSUE ERROR (This will cause the other transaction to abend if it issued SYNCPOINT, but not if it issued ISSUE PREPARE.)	(Now issue SEND INVITE WAIT followed by RECEIVE)	(3) then 5
ISSUE ABEND	-	10

Reprinted by permission from *CICS/MVS Version 2.1 Intercommunication Guide* © 1987, 1988 by International Business Machines Corporation.

State 8 — RECEIVER TAKE ROLLBACK

STATE 8 MAPPED LUTYPE6.2 CONVERSATIONS		RECEIVER TAKE ROLLBACK
Commands You Can Issue	What To Test (For EIBERRCD tests see the table on page 199)	New State
SYNCPOINT ROLLBACK	–	5

State 9 — FREE PENDING AFTER SEND LAST

STATE 9 MAPPED LUTYPE6.2 CONVERSATIONS		FREE PENDING AFTER SEND LAST
Commands You Can Issue	What To Test (For EIBERRCD tests see the table on page 199)	New State
WAIT	–	10
FREE	–	1
SEND CONFIRM (no data) (SYNCLEVEL 1 or 2 only)	–	10
SYNCPOINT ROLLBACK (SYNCLEVEL 2 only)	–	10
SYNCPOINT (SYNCLEVEL 2 only)	–	10
ISSUE ABEND	–	10

State 10 — FREE SESSION

STATE 10 MAPPED LUTYPE6.2 CONVERSATIONS		FREE SESSION
Commands You Can Issue	What To Test (For EIBERRCD tests see the table on page 199)	New State
FREE	–	1

B

State Diagrams LUTYPE 6.2
Unmapped Conversations

State 1 — SESSION NOT ALLOCATED

STATE 1 UNMAPPED LUTYPE6.2 CONVERSATIONS		SESSION NOT ALLOCATED
Commands You Can Issue	What To Test (For CDBERRCD tests see the table on page 222)	New State
ALLOCATE [NOQUEUE] *	RETCODE for SYSIDERR (01 .. ..) or SYSBUSY (01 04 04) *	1
	Otherwise (conversation identifier returned in CONVID data area)	2

* If you want your program to wait until a session is available, omit the NOQUEUE option of the ALLOCATE command.

If you want control to be returned to your program if a session is not immediately available, specify NOQUEUE on the ALLOCATE command and test RETCODE for SYSBUSY.

State 2 — SESSION ALLOCATED

STATE 2 UNMAPPED LUTYPE6.2 CONVERSATIONS		SESSION ALLOCATED
Commands You Can Issue	What To Test (For CDBERRCD tests see the table on page 222)	New State
CONNECT PROCESS	RETCODE for INVREQ, NOTALLOC, or LENGERR	2
	–	3
FREE	RETCODE for INVREQ or NOTALLOC	2
	–	1

Reprinted by permission from *CICS/MVS Version 2.1 Intercommunication Guide* © 1987, 1988 by International Business Machines Corporation.

State 3 — SEND STATE

STATE 3 UNMAPPED LUTYPE6.2 CONVERSATIONS		SEND STATE
Commands You Can Issue	What To Test (For CDBERRCD tests see the table on page 222)	New State
SEND	–	3
SEND INVITE	–	4
SEND INVITE WAIT	–	5
SEND LAST	–	9
SEND LAST WAIT	–	10
SEND CONFIRM (SYNCLEVEL 1 or 2 only)	–	3
SEND INVITE CONFIRM (SYNCLEVEL 1 or 2 only)	–	5
SEND LAST CONFIRM (SYNCLEVEL 1 or 2 only)	–	10
ISSUE PREPARE (SYNCLEVEL 2 only) Note: If a negative response is received, CDBERR and CDBERRCD will also be set	CDBSYNRB	8
	CDBFREE	10
	Otherwise	3
SYNCPOINT (SYNCLEVEL 2 only) Note: This is not a GDS command.	EIBRLDBK (or ROLLEDBACK condition)	5
	Otherwise (transaction will ABEND if SYNCPOINT fails)	3
SYNCPOINT ROLLBACK (SYNCLEVEL 2 only)	(transaction will ABEND if ROLLBACK fails)	3
WAIT	–	3
ISSUE ERROR	–	3
ISSUE ABEND	–	10

Reprinted by permission from *CICS/MVS Version 2.1 Intercommunication Guide* © 1987, 1988 by International Business Machines Corporation.

State 4 — RECEIVE PENDING AFTER INVITE

STATE 4 UNMAPPED LUTYPE6.2 CONVERSATIONS	RECEIVE PENDING AFTER INVITE	
Commands You Can Issue	What To Test (For CDBERRCD tests see the table on page 222)	New State
WAIT	–	5
ISSUE ERROR	CDBFREE	10
	Otherwise	3
ISSUE ABEND	–	10
SYNCPOINT (SYNCLEVEL 2 only)	(transaction will ABEND if SYNCPOINT fails)	5
SYNCPOINT ROLLBACK (SYNCLEVEL 2 only)	(transaction will ABEND if ROLLBACK fails)	3

State 5 — RECEIVE STATE

STATE 5 UNMAPPED LUTYPE6.2 CONVERSATIONS	RECEIVE STATE	
Commands You Can Issue	What To Test (For CDBERRCD tests see the table on page 222)	New State
RECEIVE	CDBCOMPL *	–
	CDBCONF (SYNCLEVEL 1 or 2 only)	6
	CDBSYNC (SYNCLEVEL 2 only)	7
	CDBSYNRB (SYNCLEVEL 2 only)	8
	CDBFREE	10
	CDBRECV	5
	Otherwise	3
SYNCPOINT ROLLBACK (SYNCLEVEL 2 only)	(transaction will ABEND if ROLLBACK fails)	3
ISSUE ERROR	CDBFREE	10
	Otherwise	3
ISSUE ABEND	–	10

* A zero value in CDBCOMPL indicates incomplete data. CICS saves the remaining data for retrieval by subsequent RECEIVE commands. CDBCOMPL is set when the last part of the data is passed back.

Reprinted by permission from *CICS/MVS Version 2.1 Intercommunication Guide* © 1987, 1988 by International Business Machines Corporation.

State 6 — RECEIVER ISSUE CONFIRMATION

STATE 6 UNMAPPED LUTYPE6.2 CONVERSATIONS	RECEIVER ISSUE CONFIRMATION	
Commands You Can Issue	What To Test (For CDBERRCD tests see the table on page 222)	New State
ISSUE CONFIRMATION	CDBFREE (saved value)	10
	CDBRECV (saved value)	5
	Otherwise	3
ISSUE ERROR	CDBFREE (saved value)	3
	Otherwise	3
ISSUE ABEND	—	10

State 7 — RECEIVER TAKE SYNCPOINT

STATE 7 UNMAPPED LUTYPE6.2 CONVERSATIONS	RECEIVER TAKE SYNCPOINT	
Commands You Can Issue	What To Test (For CDBERRCD tests see the table on page 222)	New State
SYNCPOINT	CDBFREE (saved value)	10
	CDBRECV (saved value)	5
	Otherwise	3
SYNCPOINT ROLLBACK	—	3
ISSUE ERROR	—	3
ISSUE ABEND	—	10

State 8 — RECEIVER TAKE ROLLBACK

STATE 8 UNMAPPED LUTYPE6.2 CONVERSATIONS	RECEIVER TAKE ROLLBACK	
Commands You Can Issue	What To Test (For CDBERRCD tests see the table on page 222)	New State
SYNCPOINT ROLLBACK	—	5

Reprinted by permission from *CICS/MVS Version 2.1 Intercommunication Guide* © 1987, 1988 by International Business Machines Corporation.

State 9 — FREE PENDING AFTER SEND LAST

STATE 9 UNMAPPED LUTYPE6.2 CONVERSATIONS	FREE PENDING AFTER SEND LAST	
Commands You Can Issue	What To Test (For CDBERRCD tests see the table on page 222)	New State
WAIT	–	10
SEND CONFIRM (no data) (SYNCLEVEL 1 or 2 only)	–	10
SYNCPOINT (SYNCLEVEL 2 only)	–	10
SYNCPOINT ROLLBACK (SYNCLEVEL 2 only)	–	10
ISSUE ABEND	–	10

State 10 — FREE SESSION

STATE 10 UNMAPPED LUTYPE6.2 CONVERSATIONS	FREE SESSION	
Commands You Can Issue	What To Test (For CDBERRCD tests see the table on page 222)	New State
FREE	–	1

Reprinted by permission from *CICS/MVS Version 2.1 Intercommunication Guide* © 1987, 1988 by International Business Machines Corporation.

C

State Diagrams LUTYPE 6.1 and MRO Conversations

State 1 — SESSION NOT ALLOCATED

STATE 1 LUTYPE6.1 and MRO CONVERSATIONS		SESSION NOT ALLOCATED
Commands You Can Issue	What To Test	New State
ALLOCATE [NOQUEUE] *	SYSIDERR	1
	SYSBUSY *	1
	Otherwise (obtain session name from EIBRSRCE)	2

* If you want your program to wait until a session is available, omit the NOQUEUE option of the ALLOCATE command and do not code a HANDLE command for the SYSBUSY condition.

If you want control to be returned to your program if a session is not immediately available, either specify NOQUEUE on the ALLOCATE command and test EIBRCODE for SYSBUSY (X'D3'), or code a HANDLE CONDITION SYSBUSY command.

Reprinted by permission from *CICS/MVS Version 2.1 Intercommunication Guide* © 1987, 1988 by International Business Machines Corporation.

State 2 — SEND STATE

STATE 2 LUTYPE6.1 and MRO CONVERSATIONS		SEND STATE
Commands You Can Issue *	What To Test	New State
SEND		2
SEND INVITE	–	3
SEND INVITE WAIT	–	4
SEND LAST	–	7
SEND LAST WAIT	–	8

CONVERSE
  Equivalent to:
    SEND INVITE WAIT
    RECEIVE
	Go to the STATE 4 table and make the tests shown for the RECEIVE command	–

RECEIVE (LUTYPE6.1 only)	Go to the STATE 4 table and make the tests shown for the RECEIVE command	–
SYNCPOINT	EIBRLDBK (or ROLLEDBACK condition) (MRO only)	2
	Otherwise (transaction will ABEND if SYNCPOINT fails)	2
SYNCPOINT ROLLBACK (MRO only)	(transaction will ABEND if ROLLBACK fails)	2

FREE
  Equivalent to:
    SEND LAST WAIT
    FREE
	–	1

* For the front-end transaction, the first command used after the session has been allocated must be a SEND command or CONVERSE command that initiates the back-end transaction in one of the ways described under 'Attaching the Remote Transaction' on page 231.		

State 3 — RECEIVE PENDING AFTER INVITE

STATE 3 LUTYPE6.1 and MRO CONVERSATIONS	RECEIVE PENDING AFTER INVITE	
Commands You Can Issue	What To Test	New State
WAIT TERMINAL SESSION	–	4
SYNCPOINT (LUTYPE6.1 only)	(transaction will ABEND if SYNCPOINT fails)	4

State 4 — RECEIVE STATE

STATE 4 LUTYPE6.1 and MRO CONVERSATIONS	RECEIVE STATE	
Commands You Can Issue	What To Test	New State
RECEIVE [NOTRUNCATE] *	EIBCOMPL *	–
	EIBSYNC	5
	EIBSYNRB (MRO only)	6
	EIBFREE	8
	EIBRECV	4
	Otherwise	2
SYNCPOINT ROLLBACK (MRO only)	(transaction will ABEND if ROLLBACK fails)	2

* If NOTRUNCATE is specified, a zero value in EIBCOMPL indicates that the data passed to the application by CICS is incomplete (because, for example, the data-area specified in the RECEIVE command is too small). CICS will save the remaining data for retrieval by subsequent RECEIVE NOTRUNCATE commands. EIBCOMPL is set when the last part of the data is passed back. If the NOTRUNCATE option is not specified, overlength data is indicated by the LENGERR condition, and the remaining data is discarded by CICS.

State 5 — RECEIVER TAKE SYNCPOINT

STATE 5 LUTYPE6.1 and MRO CONVERSATIONS		RECEIVER TAKE SYNCPOINT
Commands You Can Issue	What To Test	New State
SYNCPOINT	EIBFREE (saved value)	8
	EIBRECV (saved value)	4
	Otherwise	2
SYNCPOINT ROLLBACK (MRO Only)	EIBFREE (saved value)	8
	EIBRECV (saved value)	4
	Otherwise	2

State 6 — RECEIVER ROLLBACK OR FREE SESSION

STATE 6 MRO CONVERSATIONS		RECEIVER ROLLBACK OR FREE SESSION
Commands You Can Issue	What To Test	New State
SYNCPOINT ROLLBACK	EIBFREE (saved value)	8
	EIBRECV (saved value)	4
	Otherwise	2
FREE	—	1

State 7 — FREE PENDING AFTER SEND LAST

STATE 7 LUTYPE6.1 and MRO CONVERSATIONS	FREE PENDING AFTER SEND LAST	
Commands You Can Issue	What To Test	New State
WAIT TERMINAL SESSION (do not use for MRO sessions)	–	8
SYNCPOINT	–	8
FREE	–	1

State 8 — FREE SESSION

STATE 8 LUTYPE6.1 and MRO CONVERSATIONS	FREE SESSION	
Commands You Can Issue	What To Test	New State
FREE	–	1

Reprinted by permission from *CICS/MVS Version 2.1 Intercommunication Guide* © 1987, 1988 by International Business Machines Corporation.

D

State Diagrams CICS-IMS
Conversations

State 1 — SESSION NOT ALLOCATED

STATE 1 CICS to IMS/VS CONVERSATIONS		SESSION NOT ALLOCATED
Commands You Can Issue	What To Test	New State
ALLOCATE [NOQUEUE] *	SYSIDERR	1
	SYSBUSY *	1
	Otherwise (obtain session name from EIBRSRCE)	2

* If you want your program to wait until a session is available, omit the NOQUEUE option of the ALLOCATE command and do not code a HANDLE command for the SYSBUSY condition.

If you want control to be returned to your program if a session is not immediately available, either specify NOQUEUE on the ALLOCATE command and test EIBRCODE for SYSBUSY (X'D3'), or code a HANDLE CONDITION SYSBUSY command.

State 2 — SEND STATE

STATE 2 CICS to IMS/VS CONVERSATIONS		SEND STATE
Commands You Can Issue *	What To Test	New State
SEND		2
SEND INVITE	–	3 or 4
SEND LAST	–	6
CONVERSE Equivalent to: SEND INVITE WAIT RECEIVE	Go to the STATE 4 table and make the tests shown for the RECEIVE command	–
RECEIVE	Go to the STATE 4 table and make the tests shown for the RECEIVE command	–
SYNCPOINT	(transaction will ABEND if SYNCPOINT fails)	2
FREE Equivalent to: SEND LAST WAIT FREE	–	1

* For the front-end transaction, the first command used after the session has been allocated must be a SEND command or CONVERSE command that initiates the back-end transaction in one of the ways described under 'Attaching the Remote Transaction' on page 255.

Reprinted by permission from *CICS/MVS Version 2.1 Intercommunication Guide* © 1987, 1988 by International Business Machines Corporation.

State 3 — RECEIVE PENDING AFTER INVITE

STATE 3 CICS to IMS/VS CONVERSATIONS	RECEIVE PENDING AFTER INVITE	
Commands You Can Issue	What To Test	New State
SYNCPOINT	(transaction will ABEND if SYNCPOINT fails)	4

State 4 — RECEIVE STATE

STATE 4 CICS to IMS/VS CONVERSATIONS		RECEIVE STATE
Commands You Can Issue	What To Test	New State
RECEIVE [NOTRUNCATE] *	EIBCOMPL *	–
	EIBSYNC	5
	EIBFREE	7
	EIBRECV	4
	Otherwise	2

* If NOTRUNCATE is specified, a zero value in EIBCOMPL indicates that the data passed to the application by CICS is incomplete (because, for example, the data-area specified in the RECEIVE command is too small). CICS will save the remaining data for retrieval by subsequent RECEIVE NOTRUNCATE commands. EIBCOMPL is set when the last part of the data is passed back. If the NOTRUNCATE option is not specified, overlength data is indicated by the LENGERR condition, and the remaining data is discarded by CICS.

Reprinted by permission from *CICS/MVS Version 2.1 Intercommunication Guide* © 1987, 1988 by International Business Machines Corporation.

State 5 — RECEIVER TAKE SYNCPOINT

STATE 5 CICS to IMS/VS CONVERSATIONS	RECEIVER TAKE SYNCPOINT	
Commands You Can Issue	What To Test	New State
SYNCPOINT	EIBFREE (saved value)	7
	EIBRECV (saved value)	4
	Otherwise	2

State 6 — FREE PENDING AFTER SEND LAST

STATE 6 CICS to IMS/VS CONVERSATIONS	FREE PENDING AFTER SEND LAST	
Commands You Can Issue	What To Test	New State
SYNCPOINT	-	7
FREE	-	1

State 7 — FREE SESSION

STATE 7 CICS to IMS/VS CONVERSATIONS	FREE SESSION	
Commands You Can Issue	What To Test	New State
FREE	-	1

Reprinted by permission from *CICS/MVS Version 2.1 Intercommunication Guide* © 1987, 1988 by International Business Machines Corporation.

Command Summary for LUTYPE 6.2 Mapped Conversations

The ALLOCATE command requests an alternate facility from CICS.

```
EXEC CICS ALLOCATE
         SYSID(sys-name)
         PROFILE(profile-name)
         NOQUEUE
         NOSUSPEND
```

The unusual conditions associated with the ALLOCATE command include CBIDERR, INVREQ, SYSBUSY, SESSBUSY, and SYS-IDERR.

The CONNECT PROCESS command is used to initiate the Back-End Transaction.

```
EXEC CICS CONNECT PROCESS
         PROCNAME(name-of-process)
         PROCLENGTH(length-of-procname)
         CONVID(conversation-name)
         SYNCLEVEL(sync-level)
         PIPLIST(name-of-PIP-data-area)
         PIPLENGTH(total-length-piplist)
```

The unusual conditions associated with the CONNECT PROCESS command include INVREQ, LENGERR, and NOTALLOC.

The EXTRACT PROCESS command allows a newly initiated Back-End Transaction to obtain conversation-related information.

```
EXEC CICS EXTRACT PROCESS
          PROCNAME(32-byte-field-name)
          PROCLENGTH(2-byte-binary-field-name)
          CONVID(4-byte-field-name)
          SYNCLEVEL(2-byte-binary-field-name)
          PIPLIST(pointer)
          PIPLENGTH(2-byte-binary-field-name)
```

The unusual conditions associated with the EXTRACT PROCESS command are INVREQ and NOTALLOC.

The SEND command for use in LUTYPE 6.2 mapped conversations can be used to send data and/or conversation indicators.

```
EXEC CICS SEND
          CONVID(field-containing-CONVID)
          FROM(data-area-name)
          LENGTH(value-defining-FROM-area-size)
          INVITE   * OR *   LAST
          CONFIRM  * OR *   WAIT
```

The unusual conditions of the SEND command include EOC, IN-VREQ, LENGERR, NOTALLOC, SIGNAL, and TERMERR.

The RECEIVE command is used to receive data and obtain, via Execute Interface Block Fields, conversation status information.

```
EXEC CICS RECEIVE
          CONVID(field-name)
          INTO(data-area-name)
              * OR *
          SET(pointer)
          MAXLENGTH(2-byte-binary-field)
          LENGTH(2-byte-binary-field)
          NOTRUNCATE
```

The unusual conditions of the RECEIVE command inclu
LENGERR, NOTALLOC, SIGNAL, and TERMERR.

The CONVERSE command functionally combines a SEND INVI
WAIT and RECEIVE.

```
EXEC CICS CONVERSE
          CONVID(field-containing-convid)
          FROM(data-area-name)
          FROMLENGTH(from-length-info)
          INTO(data-area-name)
              *  OR  *
          SET(pointer)
          TOLENGTH(input-length-info)
          MAXLENGTH(max-length-info)
          NOTRUNCATE
```

The unusual conditions associated with the CONVERSE command
are EOC, LENGERR, NOTALLOC, SIGNAL, and TERMERR.

The WAIT command can be used to force CICS to transmit the
internal buffer with data and control indicators.

```
EXEC CICS WAIT CONVID(data-area-name)
```

The only unusual condition that can occur for the WAIT command is
the NOTALLOC condition.

The ISSUE CONFIRMATION command is used to provide a positive response to a request for CONFIRMation.

```
EXEC CICS ISSUE CONFIRMATION CONVID(field-name)
```

The unusual conditions associated with the ISSUE CONFIRMA-
TION command are NOTALLOC, TERMERR, and INVREQ.

The ISSUE ERROR command can be used as a negative response
to a CONFIRMation request or to signal an application-defined
error.

```
EXEC CICS ISSUE ERROR CONVID(field-name)
```

unusual conditions associated with the ISSUE ERROR command are NOTALLOC and INVREQ.

The ISSUE ABEND command can be used to abend a conversation as an indication of an application-defined error.

```
EXEC CICS ISSUE ABEND CONVID(field-name)
```

The unusual conditions of the ISSUE ABEND command are NOTALLOC and INVREQ.

The ISSUE SIGNAL command is used by a RECEIVE STATE transaction to indicate its need to have a state change.

```
EXEC CICS ISSUE SIGNAL CONVID(field-name)
```

The unusual conditions of the ISSUE SIGNAL are NOTALLOC and TERMERR.

The FREE command is used to FREE a session.

```
EXEC CICS FREE CONVID(field-name)
```

The unusual conditions associated with the FREE command are INVREQ and NOTAUTH.

The SYNCPOINT command is used to initiate commit protocols between all SYNCLEVEL(2) conversations in a distributed transaction.

```
EXEC CICS SYNCPOINT
       ROLLBACK
```

The ROLLEDBACK condition is applicable to the SYNCPOINT command.

The ISSUE PREPARE command is intended for use only in complex SYNCPOINTing situations. It allows a SEND STATE transaction to specifically query one of its conversation partners regarding its ability to SYNCPOINT.

```
EXEC CICS ISSUE PREPARE CONVID(field-name)
```

Command Summary for LUTYPE 6.2 Unmapped Conversations

The GDS ALLOCATE command is used by a Front-End Transaction to acquire use of a session to a remote system.

```
EXEC CICS GDS ALLOCATE
          SYSID(sys-name)
          CONVID(data-area-name)
          RETCODE(6-byte-retcode-field)
          MODENAME(name-of-modeset)
          NOQUEUE
```

The error conditions associated with the GDS ALLOCATE command include SYSBUSY and SYSIDERR.

The GDS CONNECT PROCESS command is used to initiate the Back-End Transaction.

```
EXEC CICS GDS CONNECT PROCESS
          PROCNAME(name-of-process)
          PROCLENGTH(length-of-procname)
          CONVID(conversation-name)
          SYNCLEVEL(sync-level)
          PIPLIST(name-of-PIP-data-area)
          PIPLENGTH(total-length-piplist)
```

```
                    CONVDATA(24-byte-data-area-name)
                    RETCODE(6-byte-return-code-field)
```

The error conditions associated with the GDS CONNECT PROCESS command include INVREQ, LENGERR and NOTALLOC.

The Back-End Transaction uses the EXEC CICS GDS ASSIGN command to obtain the CONVID of its principal facility.

```
          EXEC CICS GDS ASSIGN
                 PRINCONVID(4-byte-data-area-name)
                 PRINSYSID(4-byte-data-area-name)
                 RETCODE(6-byte-return-code-field)
```

The only error condition subsequent to the GDS ASSIGN command is the INVREQ.

The GDS EXTRACT PROCESS command is used to obtain PIP data, the SYNCLEVEL or other information from the ATTACH Function Management Header.

```
          EXEC CICS GDS EXTRACT PROCESS
                 PROCNAME(32-byte-field-name)
                 PROCLENGTH(2-byte-binary-field-name)
                 CONVID(4-byte-field-name)
                 SYNCLEVEL(2-byte-binary-field-name)
                 PIPLIST(register/register equate)
                 PIPLENGTH(2-byte-binary-field-name)
                 RETCODE(6-byte-return-code-field)
```

The error condition associated with the GDS EXTRACT PROCESS command is INVREQ.

The GDS SEND command can be used to send data and/or conversation indicators. The application programmer must be cautious to include the GDS SEND command options that generate the appropriate SNA indicators. *CICS will not supply indicators by default.*

```
          EXEC CICS GDS SEND
                 CONVID(field-containing-CONVID)
                 FROM(data-area-name)
                 LENGTH(value-defining-FROM-area-size)
                 INVITE   * OR *   LAST
```

```
CONFIRM  * OR *  WAIT
CONVDATA(24-byte-conversation-data-area)
RETCODE(6-byte-return-code-field)
```

The possible error resulting from the **GDS SEND** command include INVREQ, LENGERR, and NOTALLOC.

The **GDS RECEIVE** command is used to receive data and obtain, via the CONVDATA fields, conversation status information.

```
EXEC CICS GDS RECEIVE
        CONVID(field-name)
        INTO(data-area-name)
            *  OR  *
        SET(register/register-equate)
        MAXFLENGTH(fullword-length-field)
        FLENGTH(fullword-length-field)
        BUFFER  * OR *   LLID
        CONVDATA(24-byte-convdata-area)
        RETCODE(6-byte-return-code-field)
```

The errors associated with the **RECEIVE** command include IN-VREQ, LENGERR, and NOTALLOC.

The **GDS WAIT** command can be used to force CICS to transmit the internal buffer with data and control indicators before the task continues its execution.

```
EXEC CICS GDS WAIT CONVID(data-area-name)
        RETCODE(name-of-return-code-field)
        CONVDATA(name-of-convdata-area)
```

The errors that can occur are INVREQ and NOTALLOC.

The **GDS ISSUE CONFIRMATION** command is used to request an application-specific confirmation.

```
EXEC CICS GDS ISSUE CONFIRMATION
        CONVID(field-name)
        CONVDATA(name-of-convdata-area)
        RETCODE(name-of-return-code-field)
```

The errors that can occur are INVREQ and NOTALLOC.

The GDS ISSUE ERROR command can be used as a negative response to a CONFIRMation request or any other purpose devised in the application.

```
EXEC CICS GDS ISSUE ERROR
        CONVID(field-containing-conversation-name)
        RETCODE(name-of-return-code-field)
        CONVDATA(name-of-convdata-area)
```

The errors that can occur are INVREQ and NOTALLOC.

The GDS ISSUE ABEND command is used as a response to an application error.

```
EXEC CICS ISSUE ABEND
        CONVID(field-name)
        RETCODE(name-of-return-code-field)
        CONVDATA(name-of-convdata-area)
```

The errors that can occur are INVREQ and NOTALLOC.

The GDS ISSUE SIGNAL command is used by a RECEIVE STATE transaction to indicate its need to have a state change.

```
EXEC CICS ISSUE SIGNAL
        CONVID(field-name)
        RETCODE(name-of-return-code-field)
        CONVDATA(name-of-convdata-area)
```

The errors that can occur are INVREQ and NOTALLOC.

The GDS FREE command is used to FREE a session.

```
EXEC CICS GDS FREE
        CONVID(field-name)
        RETCODE(name-of-return-code-field)
        CONVDATA(name-of-convdata-area)
```

The errors that can occur are INVREQ and NOTALLOC.

The GDS ISSUE PREPARE is used in complex syncpointing situations to prepare a conversation partner for a SYNCPOINT.

```
EXEC CICS GDS ISSUE PREPARE
    CONVID(field-name)
    RETCODE(name-of-return-code-field)
    CONVDATA(name-of-convdata-area)
```

The errors that can occur are **INVREQ** and **NOTALLOC**.

The **SYNCPOINT** command may also be used if appropriate to the **SYNCLEVEL**.

G

Command Summary for LUTYPE 6.1 ISC and MRO

The ALLOCATE command is used by a Front-End Transaction that does not already have use of a session to a remote system.

```
EXEC CICS ALLOCATE
          SYSID(sys-name)
            *  OR  *
          SESSION (sess-name)
          PROFILE(profile-name)
          NOQUEUE  *  OR  *  NOSUSPEND
```

The unusual conditions associated with the ALLOCATE command include CBIDERR, EOC, INVREQ, SESSBUSY, SESSIONERR, SYS-BUSY, and SYSIDERR.

The BUILD ATTACH command causes CICS to build an ATTACH Function Management Header.

```
EXEC CICS BUILD ATTACH
          PROCESS(name-of-process)
          ATTACHID(name-of-attach-header)
          RESOURCE(name-of-resource)
          RPROCESS(name-of-return-process)
          QUEUE(name-of-queue)
          IUTYPE(name-of-Inter-change-Unit)
```

```
                    DATASTR(name-of-data stream)
                    RECFM(name-of-deblocking-algorithm)
```

There are no unusual conditions associated with the BUILD AT-
TACH.

A Back-End Transaction can use the EXTRACT ATTACH command to obtain information from the ATTACH Function Management Header.

```
         EXEC CICS EXTRACT ATTACH
              PROCESS(field-name)
              SESSION(field-name)
              RESOURCE(field-name)
              RPROCESS(field-name)
              RRESOURCE(field-name)
              QUEUE(field-name)
              IUTYPE(field-name)
              DATASTR(field-name)
              RECFM(field-name)
```

The unusual conditions associated with the EXTRACT PROCESS
command are CBIDERR, INVREQ, and NOTALLOC.

The SEND command is used to SEND data and indicators.

```
         EXEC CICS SEND
              SESSION(field-containing-SESSION-ID)
              ATTACHID(name-of-ATTACH-header)
              FROM(data-area-name)
              LENGTH(value-defining-FROM-area-size)
              INVITE   * OR *   LAST
              WAIT
              FMH
              DEFRESP
```

The unusual conditions of the SEND command include CBIDERR,
NOTALLOC, SIGNAL, and TERMERR.

The RECEIVE command is used to RECEIVE data and indicators.

```
         EXEC CICS RECEIVE
              SESSION(field-name)
```

```
INTO(data-area-name)
     *   OR   *
SET(pointer)
MAXLENGTH(2-byte-binary-field)
LENGTH(2-byte-binary-field)
NOTRUNCATE
```

The unusual conditions of the RECEIVE command include EOC, IN-BFMH, LENGERR, NOTALLOC, SIGNAL, and TERMERR.

The CONVERSE command functionally combines a SEND INVITE WAIT and RECEIVE.

```
EXEC CICS CONVERSE
     SESSION(field-containing-session-id)
     FROM(data-area-name)
     FROMLENGTH(from-length-info)
     INTO(data-area-name)
        *   OR   *
     SET(pointer)
     TOLENGTH(input-length-info)
     MAXLENGTH(max-length-info)
     NOTRUNCATE
     ATTACHID(header-name)
     FMH
     DEFRESP
```

The unusual conditions associated with the CONVERSE command are EOC, CBIDERR, INBFMH, LENGERR, NOTALLOC, SIGNAL, and TERMERR.

The WAIT TERMINAL command can be used to force CICS to transmit the internal buffer with data and control indicators before the task continues its execution. The WAIT command is not applicable to MRO sessions, wherein it is a null command.

```
EXEC CICS WAIT TERMINAL SESSION(data-area-name)
```

The unusual conditions that can occur for the WAIT command are NOTALLOC and SIGNAL.

The ISSUE SIGNAL command is used by a RECEIVE STATE transaction to indicate its need to have a state change.

```
EXEC CICS ISSUE SIGNAL SESSION(field-name)
```

The unusual conditions of the ISSUE SIGNAL are NOTALLOC and TERMERR.

The FREE command is used to FREE a session.

```
EXEC CICS FREE SESSION(field-name)
```

The unusual conditions associated with the FREE command are INVREQ and NOTALLOC.

The SYNCPOINT command is used to initiate commit protocols during LUTYPE 6.1 or MRO Sessions. *The ROLLBACK option is not supported for LUTYPE 6.1.*

```
EXEC CICS SYNCPOINT
```

The EXTRACT TCT permits a transaction to provide a 1- to 8-character NETNAME and obtain a local SYSIDNT for the named system. This command is not applicable to MRO.

```
EXEC CICS EXTRACT TCT
        NETNAME(1-8 character netname)
        SYSID(4-byte-data-field)
```

The WAIT SIGNAL allows a task to wait for an incoming SIGNAL from its principal facility. This command is not applicable to MRO.

```
EXEC CICS WAIT SIGNAL
```

The ISSUE DISCONNECT command is used to end a session. This command is not applicable to MRO.

```
EXEC CICS ISSUE DISCONNECT
        SESSION(name-of-session)
```

EIB Fields for LUTYPE 6.2 Mapped Conversations

The status fields are described below as being set on (X'FF') or set off (X'00').

FOR ALL APPC TRANSACTIONS REGARDLESS OF SYNCLEVEL

EIBRSRCE should be saved subsequent to an ALLOCATE command as the field then contains the unique conversation ID assigned by CICS.

EIBTRMID contains the Back-End Transaction's principal resource name. If a Front-End Transaction is initiated via an ATI request that names a remote SYSIDNT, there is no need to perform an ALLOCATE because the transaction is started in STATE 2. The use of CONVID is optional for commands pertaining to a principal facility and the name of the principal facility is contained in EIBTRMID.

EIBCOMPL is tested subsequent to RECEIVE NOTRUNCATE to determine when all data has been RECEIVEd from CICS. CICS sets this field on when all data has been received.

EIBNODAT can be tested to determine if data was RECEIVED. For APPC mapped conversations it is valid to SEND without including FROM and LENGTH options. Therefore, RECEIVE may not yield data. If this field is set on subsequent to a RECEIVE, there is no data.

EIBRECV is used to indicate a transaction's RECEIVE/SEND state. If set on the transaction is in the RECEIVE state. This field should be tested after every RECEIVE command and in any other context in which a transaction's state may have altered. For example, receipt of ISSUE ERROR places the transaction in the RECEIVE STATE. So if EIBERR is set on, EIBRECV should be tested in most cases.

EIBERR is set on to indicate a conversation-related error such as a remote process ISSUE ABEND, ISSUE ERROR or SYNCPOINT ROLLBACK. This field should be tested after all conversation-related commands. The exact cause of EIBERR can be ascertained from an examination of EIBERRCD.

EIBERRCD is set with a specific error code which identifies why EIBERR is set on as follows.

X'08890000' — ISSUE ERROR received
X'08640000' — ISSUE ABEND received
X'08240000' — SYNCPOINT ROLLBACK received

EIBSIG set on to indicate remote process execution of ISSUE SIGNAL. This is normally used by a RECEIVE STATE transaction to request a state change. If used in an application, EIBSIG should be tested after each conversation command.

EIBFREE set on to indicate that the session must be freed. The remote process has performed a FREE command or a SEND LAST WAIT and the upshot is that the End Bracket has been generated and sent. When End Bracket has been transmitted, the conversation is over. Therefore, the session must be freed either by executing the FREE command or RETURNing to CICS.

ADDITIONAL EIB FIELDS FOR TRANSACTIONS OPERATING AT SYNCLEVEL 1 OR 2

EIBCONF is set on by a remote process SEND CONFIRM seeking an application-dependent confirmation. EIBCONF should be tested after each RECEIVE if this protocol is used in the application.

ADDITIONAL EIB FIELDS FOR TRANSACTIONS OPERATING AT SYNCLEVEL 2

EIBSYNC is set on to indicate a SYNCPOINT/ISSUE PREPARE request. This field should be tested after each RECEIVE command.

EIBSYNRB is set on to indicate a SYNCPOINT ROLLBACK. If this command is used in an application, EIBSYNRB should be tested after every command pertaining to the conversation.

EIBRLDBK is set on to indicate the failure of a SYNCPOINT. This indication means that the task has been ROLLED BACK.

CONVDATA Summary for LUTYPE 6.2 Unmapped Conversations

FIELDS SET ON (X'FF') OR OFF (X'00') AS CONVERSATION INDICATORS

FIELD NAME	FIELD DESCRIPTION	FIELD USE
CDBCOMPL	DS C	Set on to indicate data is complete when NOTRUNCATE is used.
CDBSYNC	DS C	Indicates that a SYNCPOINT must be taken when set on.
CDBFREE	DS C	Indicates that a FREE is mandated when set on.
CDBRECV	DS C	Indicates RECEIVE STATE when set on.
CDBSIG	DS C	Indicates receipt of a SIGNAL when set on.
CDBCONF	DS C	Indicates receipt of a SEND CONFIRM when set on.
CDBERR	DS C	Indicates receipt of conversation error indicator when set on.
CDBERRCD	DS CL 4	Contains qualifying information when CDBERR is set on.
CDBSYNRB	DS C	Indicates receipt of a ROLLBACK request when set on.
CDBRSVD	DS CL 12	Reserved

J

RETCODE Summary for LUTYPE 6.2 Unmapped Conversations

RETCODE Settings:

```
00 .. ..    NORMAL RETURN CODE

01 .. ..    SYSIDERR ERROR

01 04 ..    ALLOCATE FAILURE
01 04 04       SYSBUSY (NO BOUND CONTENTION WINNER AVAILABLE)
01 04 08       MODENAME NOT KNOWN ON THIS SYSTEM
01 04 0C       ATTEMPT TO USE RESERVED MODENAME SNASVCMG
01 04 14       AVAILABLE COUNT ZERO FOR THIS MODEGROUP

01 08 ..    SYSID IS OUT OF SERVICE
01 08 00       LOCAL QUEUEING WAS NOT ATTEMPTED
01 08 04       LOCAL QUEUEING DID NOT SUCCEED

01 0C ..    SYSID IS NOT KNOWN IN TCT
01 0C 00       SYSID NAME IS NOT KNOWN
01 0C 04       SYSID NAME IS NOT THAT OF A TCTSE
01 0C 08       SYSID.MODENAME IS NOT KNOWN
01 0C 0C       SYSID.PROFILE IS NOT KNOWN

03 .. ..    INVREQ ERROR
03 00 ..       SESSION IS NOT DEFINED AS LU6.2
03 04 ..       CONVERSATION LEVEL IS WRONG
03 08 ..       STATE ERROR
03 0C ..       SYNCLEVEL CAN NOT BE SUPPORTED
03 10 ..       LLCOUNT ERROR
03 14 ..       INVALID REQUEST
03 18 ..       TPN SEND CHECK FAILED

04 .. ..    NOTALLOC ERROR

05 .. ..    LENGERR ERROR
```

Reprinted by permission from *CICS/MVS Version 2.1 Intercommunication Guide* © 1987, 1988 by International Business Machines Corporation.

EIB Summary for LUTYPE 6.1 ISC and MRO

The status fields are described below as being set on (X'FF') or set off (X'00').

EIBRSRCE should be saved subsequent to an ALLOCATE command as the field then contains the unique session ID assigned by CICS.

EIBTRMID contains the Back-End Transaction's principal resource name. If a Front-End Transaction is initiated via an ATI request that names a remote SYSIDNT, there is no need to perform an ALLOCATE because the transaction is started in STATE 2. The use of SESSION ID is optional for commands pertaining to the principal facility and the name of the principal facility is contained in EIBTRMID.

EIBCOMPL is tested subsequent to RECEIVE NOTRUNCATE to determine when all data has been RECEIVEd from CICS. CICS sets this field on when all data has been received.

EIBRECV is used to indicate a transaction's RECEIVE/SEND state. If set on the transaction is in the RECEIVE state. This field should be tested after every RECEIVE command and in any other context in which a transaction's state may have altered.

EIBSIG is set on to indicate remote process execution of ISSUE SIGNAL. This is normally used by a RECEIVE STATE transaction to request a state change. If used in an application, EIBSIG should be tested after each conversation command. Since ISSUE SIGNAL is not supported for MRO, this field is not used in programs using MRO links.

EIBFREE set on to indicate that the session must be freed. The remote process has performed a FREE command or a SEND LAST WAIT and the upshot is that the End Bracket has been generated and sent. Therefore, when EIBFREE is set on the only thing that a task can do is FREE the session by executing the FREE command or RETURNing to CICS.

EIBSYNC set on to indicate a SYNCPOINT request. This field should be tested after each RECEIVE command.

EIBSYNRB set on to indicate a SYNCPOINT ROLLBACK. If this command is used in an application EIBSYNRB should be tested after every command pertaining to the conversation. This field is appropriate only to MRO since SYNCPOINT ROLLBACK is not supported for LUTYPE 6.1.

EIBRLDBK set on to indicate the failure of a SYNCPOINT. This indication means that the task has been ROLLED BACK. This field is appropriate only to MRO.

Glossary

ACF/VTAM — A Telecommunication Access Method which provides access to an SNA network. CICS uses the services of ACF/VTAM to BIND sessions with other Logical Units and to send and receive data to/from its session partners.

Application-to-Application Services — A collection of Function Management Services provided to application programs utilizing the LUTYPE 6. One of these services is the ability to access resources without regard for the location of the resource in the SNA network. Another service is the support for distributed and coordinated synchronization of updates to protected resources. The third application-to-application service is the support for program-to-program communication. The application-to-application services are architected within SNA InterSystem Communication. These services are implemented within Transaction Processing Systems such as CICS or IMS.

Architected Process — A process defined in SNA to perform application-to-application services. The CICS Mirror Program, DFHMIR is an example of an implementation of SNA architected processes. The formats and protocols of architected processes are defined so that there is compatibility between different product implementations of an architected process.

Architected Process Name — The identifier or name by which an architected process is known and thereby invoked. In CICS, the mirror TRANSIDs are architected process names.

Advanced Program-to-Program Communication — The type of communication that takes place between two processing programs using the LUTYPE 6.2. In advanced program-to-program communication, application programs are able to communicate with each other without regard for communication network protocols. APPC is considered to be an any-to-any connection because of its support for non-system level products. The LUTYPE 6.2, which is synonomous with APPC, provides flexibility with regard to synchronization level and support for device-level products.

ALLOCATE Command — A command used in Distributed Transaction Processing to acquire use of a session. The ALLOCATE command is used by the task that initiates the distributed transaction. The allocated session becomes an additional network facility or alternate facility of the task issuing the ALLOCATE command. The allocated session is used to hold a distributed conversation.

Alternate Facility — A network resource allocated to a task that is in addition to the task's principal facility or the facility which caused the task to be initiated. An alternate facility is obtained via the ALLOCATE command, and the purpose of requesting the alternate facility is to perform distributed transaction processing.

APPLID — The logical name by which a system such as CICS is known to ACF/VTAM. CICS is defined as an APPLication to VTAM with an APPL statement. The characteristics of an application region are defined in the APPL statement. The APPLID associates a system such as CICS with the definition provided to ACF/VTAM in the APPL statement.

APPC — See Advanced Program-to-Program Communication.

Asynchronous Processing — A type of CICS Intercommunication in which a task can initiate a remote asynchronous process and pass the process data. The tasks are asynchronous in the sense that CICS sees no relationship between them.

ATI — See Automatic Transaction Initiation.

Attach Function Management Header — A type of Function Management Header which defines a process to be initiated. The attach header can also contain additional information which may be relevant to the process being initiated.

Automatic Transaction Initiation — In CICS, the automatic initiation of a task. CICS itself, as opposed to a terminal user, initiates the task. This can be accomplished by using Interval Control to START a task or because a trigger level or record count is reached for an Intrapartition Transient Data Queue.

Back-End Transaction — In distributed transaction processing, the task initiated in the remote system. The Back-End Transaction is initiated because the Front-End Transaction builds or causes CICS to build an ATTACH Function Management Header. When the attach header is sent to the remote system, a remote task is attached. The Back-End and Front-End Transactions can then engage in a distributed conversation.

Base Conversation — A low-level type of LUTYPE 6.2 conversation. In this type of conversation in CICS, for example, EXEC CICS GDS commands are used by assembler language programs. The EIB is unaffected by GDS commands, and unusual conditions are not raised. The application programmer is responsible for building and interpreting the SNA GDS headers. Unmapped conversation is a synonym for base conversation.

Begin Bracket — An SNA indicator which signifies the beginning of a unit of work or transaction. The LUTYPE 6 requires the use of bracket protocol which delineates the beginning and ending of a transaction with bracket indicators. CICS automatically generates and sends the Begin Bracket Indicator.

BIND — The SNA Request Unit (RU) which initiates an LU-LU session. CICS can send or receive BIND requests, and it is through the BIND that CICS or any SNA network user establishes sessions or connections.

BID — An SNA Request Unit which is used to request permission to initiate a transaction or bracket. A BID is sent by a contention loser if it wishes to initiate a unit of work on a contention losing session.

Bracket Protocol — An SNA protocol for marking off the separate bidirectional data flows that constitute a unit of work or transaction. Bracket protocol is architected or defined for LUTYPE 6 sessions.

BUILD ATTACH Command — A command used in MRO/LUTYPE 6.1 sessions to cause CICS to build an ATTACH Function Management Header. When the attach header is sent to a remote system, the named process is initiated. Attach headers are not required for CICS-CICS connections, as the typical way of initiating a remote unit of work for these types of connections is to include a 1- to 4-character TRANSID in the first 4 bytes of the first message sent to the remote CICS. However, for CICS-IMS connections, the ATTACH header must be used because IMS does not support the CICS convention of scanning the input for a TRANSID in the first 4 bytes.

CDBCOMPL — An indicator in the CONVDATA area used in unmapped LUTYPE 6.2 conversations. The CDBCOMPL flag is set to X'FF' when all data have been received subsequent to a GDS RECEIVE NOTRUNCATE.

CDBCONF — An indicator in the CONVDATA area used in unmapped LUTYPE 6.2 conversations. The CDBCONF flag is set to X'FF' when a CONFIRMation request is received from a remote conversation partner.

CDBERR — An indicator in the CONVDATA area used in unmapped LUTYPE 6.2 conversations. The CDBERR flag is set to X'FF' when CICS receives an error indicator from the remote conversation partner. The error indicator can be caused by the execution of a GDS ISSUE ERROR, GDS ISSUE ABEND, or SYNCPOINT ROLLBACK.

CDBERRCD — A data field in the CONVDATA area used in unmapped LUTYPE 6.2 conversations. The CDBERRCD contains a definitive reason code for why CDBERR is set on. By interrogating the contents of CDBERRCD, the application programmer is able to distinguish between the possible causes of CDBERR being set on.

CDBFREE — An indicator in the CONVDATA area used in unmapped LUTYPE 6.2 conversations. This flag is set on to inform a task that it must FREE the session.

CDBRECV — An indicator in the CONVDATA area used in unmapped LUTYPE 6.2 conversations. This flag is set on or set off to indicate the task's SEND/RECEIVE state. When CDBRECV is set to X'00' subsequent to a GDS RECEIVE command, the task is in the SEND state. When CDBRECV is set to X'FF' subsequent to a receive, the task is in the RECEIVE state.

CDBSIG — An indicator in the CONVDATA area used in unmapped LUTYPE 6.2 conversations. This flag is set on (X'FF') when CICS receives a SIGNAL from the remote conversation partner. The SIGNAL is caused by the execution of the GDS ISSUE SIGNAL command which is typically used by a RECEIVE state transaction to request being placed into the SEND state.

CDBSYNC — An indicator in the CONVDATA area used in unmapped LUTYPE 6.2 conversations. This flag is set on (X'FF') to indicate that a SYNCPOINT request has been received. The transaction can then respond positively by issuing a SYNCPOINT or issue a negative response to the SYNCPOINT request.

CDBSYNRB — An indicator in the CONVDATA area used in unmapped LUTYPE 6.2 conversations. This flag is set on (X'FF') to indicate that the transaction must execute a SYNCPOINT ROLL-BACK.

Chain — A collection of related message units that are "chained" together for recovery purpose. The message units in a chain are traveling in one direction so all of the chained message units constitute a single message.

Chained Mirror — A type of Function Shipping in which a resource access request is forwarded to a remote CICS system. In the remote system, the resource is again defined as remote and the request is shipped off yet again to another CICS system. In other words, a remote CICS is used as a pass through to access a resource in another system. Chained mirrors should be used for inquiry access only.

Change-Direction Indicator — In Distributed Transaction Processing, an SNA indicator which signals a SEND/RECEIVE state change. The Change-Direction is generated by including the INVITE option in a SEND command (or GDS SEND). In some cases CICS generates the Change-Direction Indicator because it is implied in the series of commands executed in a transaction. However, it is a better programming practice to explicitly code options that generate the desired SNA indicators.

Class Of Service — A prioritization mechanism that can be used in SNA networks. A class of service maps to a specific virtual route between two connected SNA nodes. Priority is associated with a virtual route and a virtual route is assigned when a session is bound. ACF/VTAM maintains a Class of Service Table which is referenced via a VTAM logon mode table entry associated with a mode name defined for a group of sessions in the Terminal Control Table.

CONFIRM Option — See SEND CONFIRM.

CONNECT PROCESS Command — In Distributed Transaction Processing, a command used by a front end transaction to initiate a remote process — the Back-End Transaction. This command is applicable to LUTYPE 6.2 mapped conversations.

Contention Loser — In an LU-LU session, one of the session partners has the authority to begin a transaction (i.e., begin a bracket) at will; the other, the contention loser, must gain its session partner's approval in order to initiate a transaction. A contention loser BIDs for this permission.

Contention Winner — In an LU-LU session, the session partner that can initiate a transaction, i.e., begin a bracket at will.

CONVDATA Area — A work area used in LUTYPE 6.2 unmapped or base conversations. The EXEC CICS GDS commands used in base conversations do not cause EIB indicators to be set on so the CONVDATA area is used as a place where CICS can pass conversation-related information to the application transaction.

Conversation — In Distributed Transaction Processing, a dialog takes place between distributed transactions. This dialog is termed a conversation in relation to a CICS session. The session is a CICS system resource, but is temporarily given over to a transaction so that it can engage in a dialog or conversation with a remote process.

CONVERSE Command — A command that combines a SEND, WAIT, and RECEIVE. This command can be used in LUTYPE 6.2 mapped, LUTYPE 6.1, or MRO conversation.

CONVID Option — IN LUTYPE 6.2 application programming the CONVID is used to direct terminal control commands to the appropriate facility. In mapped conversations the CONVID is required only when a Front-End Transaction is directing terminal control output to an alternate facility. In unmapped or base conversations, the CONVID is always required.

COS — See Class Of Service.

CRTE — The CICS-supplied routing TRANSID. CRTE enables a terminal user in one CICS system to temporarily obtain a connection with another CICS system. During this connection, TRANSIDs entered from the terminal are directed to the other CICS system for processing. This transaction enables an application programmer to use EDF to test remote transactions.

Data Flow Control — A layer of SNA that is concerned with logically controlling the flow of data to end users. This layer controls the SEND/RECEIVE correlation during a session and the use of bracket protocol.

Data Link Control — A layer of SNA that is concerned with physically managing data transmission between SNA nodes or machines. Data Link Control is the lowest layer architected within SNA.

DCT — See Destination Control Table.

Deferred Transmission — A technique used by CICS in LUTYPE 6 conversations to minimize data flows between conversing transactions. When a SEND or GDS SEND command is issued, CICS does not immediately transmit the data and SNA indicators, rather data and indicators are accumulated. In LUTYPE 6.2 conversations, CICS places data and SNA indicators into an internal buffer. In LUTYPE 6.1 CICS holds output until the next session-related command. The application programmer can force the transmission via the appropriate SEND command options or via the WAIT command. MRO connections do *not* use deferred transmission.

Destination Control Table — A CICS Control Table that defines transient data queues. The Destination Control Table can be used to define local or remote transient data destinations. Both types of transient data queues, intrapartition and extrapartition, are defined in the DCT. An intrapartition destination can be defined as a protected resource in its local DCT definition.

DFHCRP — The CICS relay program. This program is used during transaction routing. In the terminal-owning region, a relay task is initiated to provide the communication mechanism between the terminal and the remote task in the Transaction-Owning Region. The relay task executes in DFHCRP.

DFHIRP — The CICS InterRegion Program. DFHIRP is used during MRO. This program is responsible for "opening" IRC links and may be utilized for actual cross-region exchanges. As an alternative, MVS cross memory services can be used for actual cross region communication. However, even if cross-memory services are used for communication between regions, DFHIRP is required to open the IRC link.

DFHMIR — The CICS MIRror Program. The mirror program is used during CICS Function Shipping. When a request is Function Shipped to a remote CICS, a task is initiated in the remote system to actually execute the request and this task executes in the mirror program.

DFHXFP — For InterSystem Communication Function Shipping, requests and responses between CICS systems must correspond to the architected formats and protocols of SNA. The transformer program, DFHXFP, transforms Function Shipping requests/responses into a format suitable for transmission in an SNA network. In the receiving CICS system, the Transformer Program is again used to decode the request/response.

DFHXFX — For MRO Function Shipping subsequent to CICS release 1.6, a short path transformer program, DFHXFX, is used to encode and decode function shipping requests sent between CICS systems. The short path transformer program uses a private CICS protocol as opposed to the SNA format utilized by DFHXFP. This results in a shorter execution path for transforming Function Shipping requests. For MRO, CICS need not be compatible with SNA because the connection is directly CICS-to-CICS without an intervening SNA network.

Distributed Transaction Processing — In CICS Intercommunication a facility which permits transactions executing in different CICS regions/systems to engage in a synchronized conversation. The conversation is synchronized in that CICS sees the conversation partners as parts of a larger whole, the distributed transaction.

DTB — See Dynamic Transaction Backout.

DTIMOUT — A deadlock timeout which can be defined for TRANSIDs in the Program Control Table. This timeout is recommended for TRANSIDs used in CICS intercommunication so that there will not be indefinite waits for use of sessions to remote systems.

DTP — See Distributed Transaction Processing.

Dynamic Transaction Backout — A CICS facility which dynamically reverses modifications to protected resources done within an abended Logical Unit of work.

EDF — The CICS Execute Diagnostic Facility which enables an application programmer to interactively test a program. EDF is invoked by entering the CICS-supplied TRANSID of "CEDF."

EIB — See Execute Interface Block.

EIBATT — An EIB flag which is set on to indicate the presence of an attach header. This flag is used to signal the LUTYPE 6.1 or MRO application transaction that it is valid to perform an EX-TRACT ATTACH command.

EIBCOMPL — An EIB flag which is used during Distributed Transaction Processing. This flag is set during LUTYPE 6.2 mapped, LUTYPE 6.1, and MRO conversations. EIBCOMPL indicates (X'FF') that all data have been received subsequent to a RECEIVE NOTRUNCATE command.

EIBCONF — An EIB flag which is used during Distributed Transaction Processing. This flag is set during LUTYPE 6.2 mapped conversations. EIBCONF is set on (X'FF') to indicate the receipt of a request for confirmation.

EIBERR — An EIB flag which is used during Distributed Transaction Processing. This flag is set during LUTYPE 6.2 mapped conversations. EIBERR is set on (X'FF') to indicate receipt of an error indicator.

EIBERRCD — An EIB field which contains a reason code for the setting of EIBERR. Using the information contained in EIBERRCD, it is possible to distinguish between the causes of a received error indication.

EIBEOC — An EIB flag which is set on to indicate the end of chain.

EIBFREE — An EIB flag which is used during Distributed Transaction Processing. This flag is set during LUTYPE 6.2 mapped, LUTYPE 6.1 and MRO conversations. When set on (X'FF'), EIBFREE indicates that the transaction *must* free the session.

EIBFMH — An EIB flag which is set on to indicate the presence of a Function Management Header in received terminal control input.

EIBNODAT — An EIB flag which is set on to indicate that no data, only SNA indicators have been received.

EIBRECV — An EIB flag which is used during Distributed Transaction Processing. This flag is set during LUTYPE 6.2 mapped, LUTYPE 6.1, and MRO conversations. EIBRECV indicates the SEND/RECEIVE state of the transaction. This field should be tested immediately after a RECEIVE command because it is when processing a RECEIVE that CICS sets the flag.

EIBRLDBK — An EIB flag which is set on to indicate the failure of a distributed SYNCPOINT. The EIBRLDBK flag when set on indicates that a ROLLBACK has occurred and that the task has indeed been rolled back.

EIBRSRCE — An EIB field that contains a resource name. Subsequent to an ALLOCATE command, the Front End Transaction must save the contents of EIBRSRCE because this field returns the CONVID assigned by CICS during the processing of the ALLOCATE command.

EIBSIG — An EIB flag which is set on to indicate the receipt of an ISSUE SIGNAL request from a remote conversation partner. This field is not applicable to MRO connections because the ISSUE SIGNAL command is not applicable to MRO.

EIBSYNC — An EIB flag which is used during Distributed Transaction Processing. This flag is set during LUTYPE 6.2 mapped, LUTYPE 6.1, and MRO conversations. EIBSYNC, when set on (X'FF'), indicates receipt of a SYNCPOINT request.

EIBSYNRB — An EIB flag which is used during Distributed Transaction Processing. This flag is set during LUTYPE 6.2 mapped and MRO conversations. When set on (X'FF'), EIBSYNRB indicates receipt of a ROLLBACK request. This flag is not appropriate for LUTYPE 6.1 because the SYNCPOINT ROLLBACK is not supported for LUTYPE 6.1.

EIBTRMID — An EIB field which contains the name of a transaction's principal facility.

Emergency Restart — A type of CICS startup which is used subsequent to a system crash. During an emergency restart, CICS reverses modifications to protected resources done by *all* logical units of work that were inflight (i.e., incomplete) at the time of the crash.

Emergency Restart Subsystem — The component of CICS that is responsible for performing an emergency restart.

End Bracket Indicator — An SNA Indicator which marks the end of a transaction or bracket. The End Bracket Indicator is generated by including the LAST option of the SEND command and when this indicator is transmitted, the conversation is *over*. The only valid conversation-related action once the End Bracket has been sent/received is to free the session.

EXtended Recovery Facility — XRF is a facility of CICS whereby there are actually a pair of CICS systems. One of the systems is fully up and running, handling the realtime workload. The other, an alternate CICS, is partially initialized and waiting to take over in the event that the executing CICS fails.

EXTRACT ATTACH Command — A command used to obtain information from an attach Function Management Header. This command is applicable to LUTYPE 6.1 or MRO.

EXTRACT PROCESS Command — A command used to obtain conversation-related information from CICS. This command is used by a Back-End Transaction during LUTYPE 6.2 mapped conversations.

FCT — See File Control Table.

File Control Table — The CICS table in which local and remote files are defined. Local files can be defined as protected resources of CICS.

FMH — See Function Management Header.

Function Management — A layer of SNA which provides, among other things, application-to-application services.

Function Management Header — An SNA-defined header used to coordinate Function Management Services. An attach header is used to name a remote process to be initiated. Another type of FMH is used during SYNCPOINT flows between Transaction Processing Systems such as CICS or IMS.

FREE Command — A command used in Distributed Transaction Processing to FREE a session once a conversation has ended.

Front-End Transaction — In Distributed Transaction Processing, a transaction which obtains use of a session with another system and initiates a remote process so that a distributed transaction or conversation can take place.

Function Shipping — A type of CICS Intercommunication which enables a transaction to access remote resources.

GDS — See Generalized Data Stream.

GDS ALLOCATE Command — A command used during LUTYPE 6.2 base/unmapped conversations. Functionally, it is the equivalent of the ALLOCATE command used in LUTYPE 6.2 mapped conversations.

GDS ASSIGN Command — A command used during LUTYPE 6.2 base/unmapped conversations. This command enables a Back-End Transaction to obtain its CONVID.

GDS CONNECT PROCESS Command — A command used during LUTYPE 6.2 base/unmapped conversations. Functionally, it is the equivalent of the CONNECT PROCESS command used in LU-TYPE 6.2 mapped conversations.

GDS EXTRACT PROCESS Command — A command used during LUTYPE 6.2 base/unmapped conversations. Functionally, it is the equivalent of the EXTRACT PROCESS command used in LU-TYPE 6.2 mapped conversations.

GDS FREE Command — A command used during LUTYPE 6.2 base/unmapped conversations. Functionally, it is the equivalent of the FREE command used in LUTYPE 6.2 mapped conversations.

GDS Header — The SNA generalized data stream may contain structured fields. Structured fields have a self-defining header called a GDS header. The header indicates the length of the structured field and identifies the type of information contained within the field.

GDS ISSUE ABEND Command — A command used during LU-TYPE 6.2 base/unmapped conversations. Functionally, it is the equivalent of the ISSUE ABEND command used in LUTYPE 6.2 mapped conversations.

GDS ISSUE CONFIRMATION Command — A command used during LUTYPE 6.2 base/unmapped conversations. Functionally, it is the equivalent of the ISSUE CONFIRMATION command used in LUTYPE 6.2 mapped conversations.

GDS ISSUE ERROR Command — A command used during LU-TYPE 6.2 base/unmapped conversations. Functionally, it is the equivalent of the ISSUE ERROR command used in LUTYPE 6.2 mapped conversations.

GDS ISSUE PREPARE Command — A command used during LUTYPE 6.2 base/unmapped conversations. Functionally, it is the equivalent of the ISSUE PREPARE command used in LUTYPE 6.2 mapped conversations.

GDS ISSUE SIGNAL Command — A command used during LU-TYPE 6.2 base/unmapped conversations. Functionally, it is the equivalent of the ISSUE SIGNAL command used in LUTYPE 6.2 mapped conversations.

GDS RECEIVE Command — A command used during LUTYPE 6.2 base/unmapped conversations. Functionally, it is the equivalent of the RECEIVE command used in LUTYPE 6.2 mapped conversations.

GDS SEND Command — A command used during LUTYPE 6.2 base/unmapped conversations. Functionally, it is the equivalent of the SEND command used in LUTYPE 6.2 mapped conversations.

GDS WAIT Command — A command used during LUTYPE 6.2 base/unmapped conversations. Functionally, it is the equivalent of the WAIT command used in LUTYPE 6.2 mapped conversations.

Generalized Data Stream — A type of SNA data stream. User data and possibly structured fields are contained in the generalized data stream.

Generic APPLID — An APPLID assigned to an XRF pair of CICS systems. This APPLID relates to a VTAM USERVAR which can be set equal to the specific APPLID of either system in the XRF pair. The CICS systems take care of setting the appropriate APPLID in the USERVAR so that everyone outside of the XRF pair can use a single APPLID to log on and establish sessions with whichever system happens to be active.

Half-Duplex Flip-Flop — An SNA-defined SEND/RECEIVE protocol used during LUTYPE 6 sessions. In half-duplex flip-flop, the session partners take turns in sending. One is in the send state and the other is in the receive state. A Change-Direction Indicator generated by the send state transaction causes the flip-flop or switch in send/receive states.

Indirect Links — Links used through other CICS systems for the purpose of permitting transaction routing to take place between two CICS systems that are not directly connected.

INDOUBT Period — The period of time between CICS sending a SYNCPOINT request to a connected system and the receipt of the response. If the remote system fails and does not return either a positive or negative response, CICS is INDOUBT about whether the SYNCPOINT was received and processed.

Intercommunication — A component in CICS which permits CICS to be connected to other transaction processing systems in support of application-to-application services. There are two types of Intercommunication: MRO and ISC.

InterRegion Communication — The type of Intercommunication that takes place during MRO. In this type of communication, CICS communicates directly with another CICS system via Inter-Region SVCs or MVS Cross Memory Services.

InterSystem Communication — The type of Intercommunication that takes place between CICS and another Transaction Processing System which may or may not be a CICS system. During InterSystem Communication, an SNA network provides the communication path between the connected systems. InterSystem Communication can also take place between CICS and an LU-TYPE 6.2 terminal.

Interval Control — The component of CICS that provides time services such as STARTing of tasks.

INVITE Option — see SEND INVITE.

IRC — See InterRegion Communication.

IRCSTRT — A parameter in the System Initialization Table which can be used to start InterRegion Communication during CICS system initialization.

ISC — See InterSystem Communication.

ISSUE ABEND Command — A command used during LUTYPE 6.2 mapped conversations to ABEND a conversation.

ISSUE CONFIRMATION Command — A command used during LUTYPE 6.2 mapped conversations to send a positive response to a request for confirmation. This command can only be used for conversations at SYNCLEVEL 1 or 2.

ISSUE ERROR Command — A command used during LUTYPE 6.2 mapped conversations to send a negataive response to a request for confirmation or signal any other application-dependent error.

ISSUE PREPARE Command — A command used during LUTYPE 6.2 mapped conversations to prepare a single conversation partner for a SYNCPOINT. This command is used only in complex transactions involving multiple conversations.

ISSUE SIGNAL Command — A command used during LUTYPE 6.2 mapped or LUTYPE 6.1 conversations to request a change of direction from the RECEIVE state to the SEND state.

LAST Option — See SEND LAST.

Layered Architecture — An architecture such as SNA which is composed of a clearly defined and functionalized set of layers. Each layer provides a service to the layers above it and as a result of the services of all layers, the communication network is managed in a cohesive and functionalized manner.

Local Resource — In CICS Intercommunication a resource which is owned and managed by the local CICS system.

Local System — In CICS Intercommunication the region that owns and manages a resource. From the perspective of a task using CICS Intercommunication services, the local system is the system in which the task is executing.

Logical Unit — In SNA, the port provided to end users.

Logical Unit of Work — A logical unit of work is all or a portion of a task's processing that is logically complete for recovery purposes. Once a task has completed an LUW, CICS backout is no longer required. A logical unit of work is denoted by a task SYNCPOINT. If a task does not explicitly execute a SYNCPOINT, then one is taken when the task RETURNs to CICS normally.

LU — See Logical Unit.

LUTYPE6.1 — A type of LUTYPE 6 which supports communication between System Level products such as CICS and IMS.

LUTYPE6.2 — A type of LUTYPE 6 which has more functionality than the LUTYPE 6.1. The LUTYPE 6.2 has enhanced support for system level products and it also supports device level products.

LUW — See Logical Unit of Work.

MAPPED Conversation — A type of LUTYPE 6.2 application programming which operates at a higher level than base or unmapped conversations. The mapped conversation program can be written in COBOL, PL/I, or assembler language. Regular EXEC CICS Commands are used and CICS returns conversation status information in the EIB. Additionally, the SNA generalized data stream is transparent to the application programmer in that there is no need to build or interpret GDS headers.

MAXMIR — A value that limits the number of suspended mirror tasks in a CICS MRO region. MAXMIR is a parameter of the System Initialization Table (SIT).

Mirror Program — See DFHMIR.

Mirror Task — A task executing in DFHMIR to execute function shipping requests.

Modename — A name associated with a VTAM logon mode table entry. The logon mode table entry defines such things as a class of service for session traffic. The modename can be assigned to LU-TYPE 6.2 sessions defined in the Terminal Control Table.

MRO — See Multi-Region Operation.

MROBTCH — A System Initialization Table value which can be used to batch up MRO requests prior to activating a CICS region to perform MRO services.

MROLRM — A System Initialization Table value which can be used to define long-running Mirror Tasks. In a system where remote tasks make numerous read-only Function Shipping requests against a region, long-running Mirror Tasks may optimize performance. Once activated, long-running mirrors remain in place to service further task requests until the requesting task takes a SYNCPOINT.

Multiple Mirror Situation — A situation in which a task is connected to multiple remote Mirror Tasks. This occurs because of multiple Function Shipped updates against two or more remote CICS regions.

Multi-Region Operation — A type of Intercommunication where two CICS regions in the same machine communicate.

NETNAME — A name which uniquely identifies a user in an SNA network. CICS systems, for example, are assigned netnames, as are terminals. Session initiation requests are made based upon NETNAMEs as opposed to network addresses. ACF/VTAM translates NETNAMEs into actual network addresses. This insulates SNA users from having to know network addresses for connection purposes.

Path Control — The layer of SNA that is concerned with source-to-destination routing of messages through the network.

PCT — See Program Control Table.

Physical Unit — In SNA a type of Network Addressable Unit that manages a node and its resources in a network sense.

Piggy Backing — CICS defers message transmissions for LUTYPE 6 sessions so that such messages can include SNA indicators. The SNA indicators are said to be piggybacked when transmitted with buffered messages.

PIP Data — see Process Initialization Parameters.

Process Initialization Paramenters — Parameters that can be included when an LUTYPE 6.2 transaction initiates a remote process. CICS does not use such information; it is merely passed along to the receiving application process. However, other implementations of LUTYPE 6.2 may, in fact, use PIP data for some particular purpose.

Process Name — A way of naming or identifying a process. In CICS, a process name is a TRANSID.

Profile — A profile is a named collection of terminal control processing options. A profile determines such things as message journaling and whether or not an application task is passed inbound Function Management Headers.

Program Control Table — The CICS table in which local and remote TRANSIDs are defined.

Protected Resource — A protected resource is one which is defined as requiring CICS backout protection. Protected resources can include files, intrapartition transient data queues, temporary storage AUX queues, Interval Control START requests, and VTAM messages.

PU — See Physical Unit.

RDO — See Resource Definition Online.

RECEIVE Command — A command used to obtain terminal input. For LUTYPE 6.2 mapped, LUTYPE 6.1, and MRO conversations, the RECEIVE command also enables a transaction to obtain conversation status indicators which are posted to the EIB by CICS.

Receive Sessions — In MRO and LUTYPE 6.1 sessions are defined as either RECEIVE or SEND sessions. RECEIVE sessions are used to receive incoming requests from a remote system, and SEND sessions are used to send requests to a remote system. The receive session is thus like a contention loser and the send session corresponds to a contention winner. For MRO, CICS does not BID to use a receive session.

RECEIVE State — A transaction state with regard to a distributed conversation. When in the RECEIVE State, a transaction cannot do much else except RECEIVE input and signal conversation-related errors.

Remote Resource — A resource which is owned and managed by a remote system.

Remote System — A remote system is any connected system beyond the region in which a transaction executes.

Request/Response Unit — The name given in Systems Network Architecture to a message unit.

Resource Definition Online — A CICS facility which permits a systems programmer to define certain resources interactively using a CICS-supplied transaction. Resource definitions created online are saved in a VSAM file known as the CICS system definition file, and defined resources can be installed dynamically while CICS is up and running. Resources that are candidates for RDO definition include TRANSIDs, PROGRAMs, and VTAM network resources.

RETRIEVE Command — An Interval Control command which permits a STARTed task to obtain data passed to it by the originating task which issued the START request.

RETCODE — A field used in base or unmapped LUTYPE 6.2 conversations. The execution of EXEC CICS GDS commands used for base conversations do not cause unusual conditions to occur. Therefore, EXEC CICS GDS commands provide a RETCODE option which names a return code field. CICS places the command response into the named RETCODE field and the application programmer tests the RETCODE to determine whether command execution proceeded normally.

ROLLBACK — An option of the SYNCPOINT command which requests that CICS back out modifications to protected resources up to the start of the last logical unit of work. This option is not supported for LUTYPE 6.1 links.

Routing Transaction — See CRTE.

RU — See Request/Response Unit.

SEND Command — A Terminal Control command which is used to send data. In LUTYPE 6.2 mapped, LUTYPE 6.1, and MRO conversations, the SEND command can also be used to generate SNA and conversation state indicators.

SEND CONFIRM — A SEND CONFIRM request is used to initiate a CONFIRMation exchange for LUTYPE 6.2 mapped conversations. A confirmation exchange can only take place for conversations operating at a SYNCLEVEL greater than 0.

SEND INVITE — A SEND INVITE generates the Change Direction Indicator which flip-flops transaction SEND/RECEIVE states. The

SEND INVITE thus is used to place a conversation partner into the SEND state. In MRO, CICS does not defer sending data and indicators and, therefore, as soon as the SEND INVITE is executed, the issuing transaction enters the RECEIVE state. In LU-TYPE 6 conversations, CICS defers transmission and therefore, the issuing transaction enters a state in which receive state is pending.

SEND LAST — A SEND LAST causes CICS to generate the End Bracket Indicator. Unless the WAIT option is included in the SEND LAST command, however, the End Bracket indicator is not transmitted. Once the End Bracket Indicator is actually sent, the conversation is over.

SEND WAIT — A SEND WAIT forces CICS to transmit deferred data and indicators.

Send Sessions — In MRO and LUTYPE 6.1 sessions are defined as either RECEIVE or SEND sessions. RECEIVE sessions are used to receive incoming requests from a remote system, and SEND sessions are used to send requests to a remote system. The receive session is thus like a contention loser, and the send session corresponds to a contention winner.

SEND State — A transaction state with regard to a distributed conversation. When a transaction is in the SEND state, it can SEND data and indicators to its remote conversation partner. A SEND state transaction can also initiate a SYNCPOINT.

Session — A logical connection between two SNA Network Addressable Units. An LU-LU session is an example of an SNA session. The LU-LU sessions are between end users of the SNA network and represent a pairing of matched logical units for communication purposes.

SNA — See Systems Network Architecture.

SSCP — See System Service Control Point.

START Command — An Interval Control command which can be used to initate tasks in a local or remote system. When used to initiate a remote task, the START request is function shipped to the remote system. However, this is considered a special case of function shipping and is termed Asynchronous Processing.

Surrogate TCTTE — In Transaction Routing a remote TRANSID is sent to another CICS region/system for processing. In the remote region/system, an application task is initiated to service the request. This task is given a surrogate TCTTE as its principal network facility. To all extents and purposes, the surrogate looks just like a real TCTTE except that operator security information is not available.

SYNCLEVEL — A variable level of conversation synchronization is possible for conversations taking place over LUTYPE 6.2 sessions. The synchronization level can be specified in the CONNECT PROCESS command via the SYNCLEVEL option. The SYNCLEVEL for a conversation cannot exceed the SYNCLEVEL agreed upon when the session was bound. SYNCLEVELs can be 0 (no synchronization supported) 1 (private synchronization supported) or 2 (full CICS syncpointing and private synchronization supported).

SYNCPOINT — A command which commits modifications to protected resources. As such, the SYNCPOINT command terminates a Logical Unit of Work. When a task RETURNs normally to CICS, an implicit SYNCPOINT is taken.

SYNCPOINT Initiator — In distributed transaction processing, the transaction that is defined as the initiator of a distributed SYNCPOINT between conversation partners.

SYNCPOINT Slave — In distributed transaction processing, a transaction that receives a SYNCPOINT request.

SYSID Option — A command option that can be included in File, Transient Data and Temporary Storage commands which names a CICS system which is to provide resource access. If a remote system is named in the SYSID option, then CICS Function Ships the command request to the named system. The SYSID option is also possible for START commands.

SYSIDNT — A symbolic name assigned to a connected system. In the terminal control table system definition, the SYSIDNT is paired to the NETNAME of system. In all subsequent references to that system, including resource definitions, the SYSIDNT is used. The SYSIDNT is significant only within the context of a CICS region.

System Service Control Point — A type of SNA Network Addressable Unit which is responsible for a network domain. The SSCP provides activation, deactivation and connection services for all PUs and LUs within its domain.

Systems Network Architecture — IBM's master plan for building communication-related products. The purpose of having SNA is so that product developers build compatible network-oriented products. SNA defines the formats and protocols for interproduct communication.

TCT — See Terminal Control Table.

Temporary Storage Table — A table used to define Temporary Storage Queues with special processing requirements. A local TS queue can be made a protected resource by naming it as requiring recovery in the TST, or a remote queue can be defined in the TST. Additionally, a resource security level can be defined for local TS queues.

Terminal Control Table — A CICS table in which network resources are defined.

Transformer Program — See DFHXFP.

Transaction Backout — Transaction backout is when CICS reverses modifications to protected resources done by incomplete logical units of work. Transaction backout can take place dynamically after a transaction abend, in which case it is referred to as dynamic transaction backout. The emergency restart subsystem of CICS performs transaction backout for all incomplete logical units of work that were pending when the system crashed.

Transaction Routing — A type of Intercommunication in which a Terminal-Owning CICS can route a remote TRANSID to another CICS system for processing. This is supported over MRO or LU-TYPE 6.2 links.

Transmission Control — A layer of SNA that controls data flow during sessions. This layer is concerned with pacing data flow and ensuring that data messages are correctly sized.

TST — See Temporary Storage Table.

UNMAPPED Conversation — See Base Conversation.

WAIT Command — A command applicable to LUTYPE 6.2 mapped conversations which forces CICS to transmit accumulated data and conversation indicators.

WAIT TERMINAL Command — A command applicable to LU-TYPE 6.1 conversations which forces CICS to transmit accumulated data and indicators.

WAIT Option — See SEND WAIT.

XRF — See eXtended Recovery Facility.

Index

456 Distributed Processing in the CICS Environment